MESSAGES
TO
OUR
FAMILY

MESSAGES
TO OUR
FAMILY

FROM THE BROTHERHOOD,
MOTHER MARY AND JESUS

ANNIE AND BYRON KIRKWOOD

BLUE DOLPHIN PUBLISHING
1994

For further information, and
for correspondence to the authors, write to:
Blue Dolphin Publishing, Inc.
P.O. Box 1920, Nevada City, CA 95959
Orders: 1-800-643-0765

ISBN: 0-931892-81-3

Library of Congress Cataloging-in-Publication Data

Kirkwood, Annie, 1937–
    Messages to our family / by Annie and Byron Kirkwood
      p. cm.
    ISBN 0-931892-81-3 : $17.95
    1. Spirit writings. 2. Spiritual life. 3. Brotherhood of God
(Spirit) 4. Kirkwood, Annie, 1937– . 5. Kirkwood, Byron.
I. Kirkwood, Byron. II. Title.
BF1301.K56 1994
133.9'3—dc20   94-3988
                                               CIP

Cover illustration: Stan Padilla

First printing, May 1994

Printed in the United States of America by
Blue Dolphin Press, Grass Valley, California

9   8   7   6   5   4   3   2   1

Acknowledgments

We want to thank the following people for their help and encouragement in making this book happen.

First, I (Byron) want to thank my wonderful wife, Annie, for having the foresight to get interested in what was going to happen and starting us on our path of this work.

I (Annie) thank my husband, Byron, for all his work of getting the lessons into book form. He did what appeared to be impossible to me. I thank him for being a true helpmate.

We want to thank the members of our family for their support and participation in these family group meetings, including the many people who have attended our family prayer and meditation meetings in the past and whom we consider part of our extended family. We thank Jean and Carl Foster of TeamUp for their original encouragement and continuing support.

We really appreciate our publisher, Paul Clemens, and the staff of Blue Dolphin Publishing. Without Paul, the series of events that led to this book would never have happened.

We appreciate the help in proofreading the manuscript and the support provided by Joseph and Nancy Kopf and Mary Burke.

We want to thank Corinn Codye for the excellent job of editing the manuscript to make it easier to read and understand, and for her insight in selecting the titles for the individual lessons, chapters and sections.

We are especially thankful to everyone who offered to help financially with the book. To the two wonderful people who did help, we are sincerely grateful. One coincidence is that their first names are Mary and Joseph, something we didn't realize until after the agreement was completed. They live in different parts of the country and have never met.

And finally we want to thank Father God, the Brotherhood, Jesus, Mother Mary, and Love Being, for their patience and understanding in working with us, first for their individual messages, and then in helping to bring those messages together into this book.

Table of Contents

PART 3   1990   YOUR GOD-MIND CONNECTION

Introduction

ANNIE KIRKWOOD is the author of *Mary's Message to the World*, a message sent by Mary, Mother of Jesus to Annie through her mind. *Mary's Message to the World* was received as "daily lessons" of two to three pages each, from 1987 to 1990, was published and released in 1991, and has since become a bestseller. It has been translated into several foreign languages, including German, French and Spanish.

Annie had read predictions from Ruth Montgomery and others who told of the upcoming earth changes. Her concern for her family and how to handle these events started her on a search for additional information. She visited bookstores, looking for one book that had "all the answers" in it, never dreaming such a book would eventually come through her.

While visiting a local bookstore, a book fell off the shelf near her. She glanced at it and put it back on the shelf. She continued to look in the bookstore for the book with "all the answers." Finally, when the same book fell off the shelf for the third time, the store clerk said, "I think that book is trying to get your attention."

Annie bought the book, *The God-Mind Connection* by Jean Foster, and took it home. When she started reading it, she couldn't figure out why she had bought it—it didn't have all the answers. In fact, it raised even more questions. Finally

Annie read the chapter that told how Jean communicated with the spiritual entities called the "Brotherhood." In that book are instructions on how to receive your own messages from the Brotherhood. Annie sensed that she too could communicate with the Brotherhood, through what Jean at that time called "automatic writing." Annie now calls it "cosmic dictation," after a friend of hers came up with that description.

After several false starts, Annie was able to contact the Brotherhood. They are a group of highly advanced spiritual entities who aid people in their spiritual advancement. They are also known as the Holy Ghost and are the counselors whom Jesus appointed.

The Brotherhood have taken an oath to shed their personal identities and not to use names from previous lifetimes. One day, after Annie had been communicating with the Brotherhood for several months, an entity named "Mary" came through. This seemed strange, since the Brotherhood didn't use names. Annie wanted to know who this was. The entity responded with, "Mary, Mother of Jesus." Annie, not being Catholic, argued with the entity that she (Mary) had made a mistake. Annie said, "I'm not Catholic." Mary finally responded with, "Nor am I." Previously Annie had assumed that Mary, the mother of Jesus, was Catholic. Mary said to Annie that she had a message that she wanted to send through Annie to the world. The message eventually became the book, *Mary's Message to the World.*

Mary's Message to the World was compiled from daily messages, or lessons, given over a four-year period. These lessons filled a large, four-inch, three-ring binder, which was then compiled into the present book form. During this period Annie was still communicating with the Brotherhood. Their communications filled several four-inch, three-ring binders.

Through one of the writings (August 14, 1988) the Brotherhood requested, "Gather your children together and pray, and teach them to meditate. Teach them how you meditate and how you pray. They in turn will revise this method to suit themselves. Come together once a week to pray and learn to meditate. Together and united you will survive and become great leaders in the new time. This we request and have been commissioned by the One God to commence. In this once-a-week meeting you are to discuss and question those topics which bewilder you. We will give the group special messages to read at this time. Only united will you stand. And if there are others who wish to join this family group, welcome them and urge them to pray for guidance."

This became what we later called our "family meeting." Another way of explaining this is that it is simply a "prayer and meditation" gathering, originally just for our immediate family. Through the lessons the Brotherhood provided, we learned many spiritual concepts. This book contains most of those lessons. Some of the lessons were also given by Jesus and by Mother Mary. A few of the lessons were of too personal a nature to be included, and a few of the lessons may have been lost because of a computer hard disk failure.

How to Use These Messages

If you choose to start your own family meeting or prayer and meditation group based on these lessons, here is a suggested format.[1]

First, appoint a person to lead this group, either for this one particular session or for all sessions.

Have the leader read the lesson before the meeting and understand the basis of the lesson. At the beginning of the meeting, the leader gives a short overview of the lesson. Next, the leader, or an appointed person, leads the group in a meditation. This can be a personalized, guided meditation, if this skill exists in the group. A meditation tape may be used, or it can be as simple as a "silent moment." If you choose to have a

---

[1] Additional suggestions can be found in a lesson given on August 2, 1992 (see page 456).

silent moment meditation, meditate on being able to understand and accept the message.

After meditating, pray. We use a group prayer, where one person starts the prayer, then the next person prays, each in his or her own way. If anyone in the group feels uncomfortable, he or she can simply say "pass," and the next person will continue. We usually end our prayer time with everyone joining in to say The Lord's Prayer. We form a circle to pray, but not to meditate.

Next read the lesson. We prefer to have everyone participate by having each read a short paragraph, with the next person reading the following paragraph, until the entire lesson has been read. Again, anyone in the group who is uncomfortable reading out loud can simply say "pass." At this time, someone may read a scripture from the Bible, especially if it is pertinent to the lesson.

Then follows a discussion of the lesson. What did you feel? Were there any questions or was anything unclear? If so, get opinions and thoughts from the others in the group.

After the discussion on the lesson, open the meeting up to any topic that is important to anyone in the group. Consider this a "question and answer" time. If one person has a question, someone else may have an answer or can at least express a view or feeling about the subject. Individuals may just want to share what they are feeling or their concerns with the group. Please keep criticism and/or judgments out of the discussion.

This is just one format for a meeting and reading of the lesson, fashioned after our original family meetings. Please change or revise this plan as it suits your group. There are no set formats. Mother Mary and the Brotherhood have emphasized that this is not to become a "religion." They emphasize that there are enough religions in the world, so no rituals are necessary or formats absolute. To paraphrase what Mary has taught us, "If these things help you find God, use them. If they detract, forsake them."

God Bless You,
Byron and Annie

PART 1

1988
Prayer and Meditation

1

Learning to Pray and Meditate

I N LATE 1986 *Annie Kirkwood, author of* Mary's Message to the World, *started receiving messages from the spiritual entities known as the Brotherhood of God. It started in a simple manner, with Annie handwriting the messages using pencil and paper. However, with my (Byron's) background in microcomputers, I soon had Annie set up on the computer using WordPerfect,[1] complete with the internal "speller" program for correcting spelling errors. Now all she had to do was key in the program name "ANNIE," and the computer would be ready to enter the messages, complete with a heading and the date the message was being received.*

After receiving messages from the Brotherhood and Mother Mary for two years, they requested that we share what we were learning with our family. The following is a portion of the message Annie received on August 14, 1988, which explained how this was to be accomplished.

---

[1] A popular computer word processing program.

Gather Your Family Together
(August 14, 1988)

... Now then, prepare your children and your friends by publishing the words which you will receive from Mary.[2] Gather your children together, and teach them to pray and meditate. Teach them how to meditate and how to pray. They in turn will revise this method to suit themselves. But at this time they are not meditating. Some are trying, and we regard these efforts well worthwhile. It is not to these few, but to the others who are not even trying, that we wish to speak.

Children of Annie and Byron, listen to these writings that your mother is receiving. These writings are all truth. The events that are predicted will occur.[3] There is no way to avoid them now. The planet Earth needs this turning over in order to heal and survive. Learn from these parents, who so love each of you. Come together once a week and pray and learn to meditate. This we request and have been commissioned by the One God to commence. In this once-a-week meeting you are to discuss and question those topics that bewilder you. We will give the group special messages to read at this time. Only united will you stand. And, if there are others who wish to join this family group, welcome them and urge them to pray for guidance.

Your first task as a group is to discuss the imaging of your individual temples. Each of you will build a temple in your mind to suit yourself. Do not tell anyone what your temple is like. This will be your special place to meet with us and with the One God. This is imperative. During the first week, work to build your temple elegantly. It should be so detailed and complete that you could build it on earth out of three-dimensional materials. Read excerpts from Jean's book[4] that give the instructions on building your temple. We will be with this

---

[2] This became the book, *Mary's Message to the World*.
[3] This refers to the earth changes predictions as foretold in Chapter 2 of *Mary's Message to the World*.
[4] *The God-Mind Connection*, by Jean Foster.

family gathering and will be teaching each person to open their mind to receive all the material we will be giving you. We once again urge each of you to comply with this request. We are always available to you for anything and at any time.

This next message shows the complete format in which each message was received, including the heading with Annie's name, the date the message was received and from whom she received that message (the Brotherhood, Mary, Jesus, etc.). This message also contains the typical introduction and closing of the message. We have removed these elements from succeeding messages, along with personal information and references, to minimize repetition.

The titles for the lessons and chapters were added later as this became the book, Messages to Our Family. *At the time we were receiving each lesson, we had no idea that there was any continuity between lessons or even a consistent "theme" to what we were being given. As the old saying goes, "We couldn't see the forest for the trees." We didn't realize that there was a grander scheme of things and did not anticipate the lessons forming a book. But this is often the way we are taught to be of service.*

Annie Kirkwood   August 21, 1988   Brotherhood

I call on the Brotherhood. Today my children will come to pray and meditate; can you give them some words of encouragement or any message?

Good morning, little one. Yes, we know your children will be meeting with you to learn more about us, God and themselves. First, you should have a discussion on what they know, believe and wish to have happen during these sessions. Then you will know how to start and how to proceed. We will of course have a message for them.

We think that your children should be led into a discussion of building their inner temples, as this is most important.

It is this inner temple where each will come to meet and to meditate and seek answers from the One God of the Universe. Since some of them have read Jean's book, which gives directions in this procedure, this will be a review, and for the others it will be instructional. Even the little children will benefit from these discussions. Do not make them listen, but at the same time include them in the prayer and meditation part. Small children are not able to pay attention for long periods of time, and they will be in and out while you are discussing, but make sure they are included in the part where you pray and meditate. Tell these small ones the importance of seeking God, who made them, in their hearts and in their minds. In a few weeks, they will be instructed in the care of their thinking and how these thoughts are sometimes heard as prayers. Take these children slowly and, in time, as they become comfortable with these sessions, they themselves will take a bigger part in the discussions.

As you proceed in these weekly sessions, an agenda will come forth through your questions, and discussions will take place naturally. Here is how to proceed. First, instruct in the importance of having an inner temple. Second, instruct in the use of the Light, which they will see in their imaginations. This light brings knowledge and wisdom, and it sparks the intuition. Third, through reading of the writings which we give, new questions will arise. We will answer their questions. It is quite simple. As you pray, always include a special prayer for the planet and for all the people of the world.

We will be with you, with each group and with their families, as will Mary. We are happy that your children are in agreement with this request. They truly have been thinking rightly and are being prepared to take their part in the events of the future.

Children of Byron and Annie, listen to your inner self as it speaks and leads you in the search for truth. Today will simply be a preparation for what you can hope and expect to accomplish with these weekly meetings. One important thing you need to do is pray for the planet and for all the people of the world. This is your mission now. The hope of the future is in your hands. The purpose of life will be revealed to you in the near future. The peace which will envelope the world in the aftertime will begin in your hearts, family, and in your part of the world. This is always how it comes about. God is your origin point. Each of you began as a spark of Divinity, and each of you carries this spark inside your mind, body and soul. Allow this spark of Divinity to connect to the Source of all Divinity, which is the one God of the Universe. This is your inner desire and your inner hope. It carried you through many lifetimes to this point.

The most important thing to guard and tend is your thinking pattern and your thoughts, because as you think, so you will become. Each person is made in the image of God. Understand that you are of much value. You search for this value. It is in your heart and mind. During the week, remind yourself of the spark of Divinity which is in all men. Keep this thought in the forefront of your mind. Think it through. You are Divine because you came from God. You are, and can be, as wonderful and marvelous as God, because in you are all His attributes. Keep this thought present daily. Tell God how grateful you are for placing His attributes inside of you. With gratitude and sincere searching, you will find these attributes. They will spring forth to enhance your world and your life in this lifetime. Prepare for the coming times through these weekly meetings. These meetings will be an answer to all your prayers. We will consider each question and discussion, and give you the benefit of our knowledge and wisdom. Meet in peace and forgive all people, even those whom you think have wronged you. Forgiveness not only benefits the other person, but, more important, it benefits you. Forgiveness cleans your heart of hurt and anger. Look deeply into the anger, envy, jealousy, hurt feelings and fear. See where they come from. Forgive everyone and change your attitude toward these feelings. These are emotions that distract from your good.

Forgive your family members who don't agree with you or who have angered or harmed you. Pray for them to open their hearts and minds to the truth that is in their own being. Let us take this issue for consideration. Sometimes families can be closed-minded and think they have all the answers for your life. They think that they know truth, God and all religious matters. Those who set themselves up as authorities are in truth far from it, and in truth they will still be in the darkness of their own minds, until they open their heart. Pray for these family members and for all members of your families. Soon many will see the difference in you, and others will not. You can only help each other by praying. The only hope those who are closed-minded have is in the prayers which are said for them. Do not talk badly about anyone, for "there but for the grace of God go you." This is true. **Be grateful for your open mind and listen to your open heart.** This openness will give each of you instruction in all areas of your lives.

First, the changes will be inside you, in the way you feel toward yourself and others. Then the changes will come about in your relationship with others. The changes will continue to expand out to the whole world. Later you will think all people think as you do. You will wonder at the unhappiness and unpleasantness of others. This is our goal with you and with your lives. We wish only to instruct you in how to be happy, peaceful, prosperous, and healthy. Our aim is to connect you to God-Mind, which has all the answers and gives all good gifts. We are very proud of you, and your efforts are now being rewarded with our prayers and all we have to give.

Now, little one, continue to seek and instruct your family, for many will be coming to your door for instruction and help. The instruction you will give each person is to seek God in their heart and mind, as you have. You will know what to say at the time. Do not allow anything to keep you from this all-important mission, for this is what you came to earth to do.

We are surrounding you and your loved ones in Divine Love.

                                                    The Brotherhood

The date the message was received and who the communication was from (normally the Brotherhood) are shown for reference only. In a few cases, the date has significance to the message, for example on Christmas, Thanksgiving, Easter and at the beginning or ending of the year.

How to Begin: Enlarge Your Idea of God
(Brotherhood, August 28, 1988)

We commend each person who has gained the new attitude of prayer and is seeking to find the Truth. We are with each of you during the week. Every person who asked has their own Brother,[5] who is always available. Talk to us in your mind, and get comfortable with this conversation that is in your mind. You will find that at the appropriate time you will simply know what you need to know in any particular situation. This is how we aid you. We are with you in the workplace and as you are commuting between the workplace and your home. We are with you in your respective homes, for any need. We will not, however, do what is your duty to do. We will not live your life for you. Nor will we make any of your decisions. We will help you in any decision and will be available to you as a guide and counselor. This is our promise to you. You will have the energy you need to complete all your tasks. You are never alone.

Our message today will tell you how to start. **Begin with the concept of God that is in your mind. God is so much Greater, Grander and more Magnificent than you can imagine.** He is more Powerful, Tender and Loving than you have imagination to use. Understand that you are like God, because you were made by Him in His Image and Likeness. The part of you that is like God is your Spiritual self. It is inside your soul

---

[5] The Brotherhood has told us that we can request a member of the Brotherhood be assigned to work with each person, if we so desire. Their task is to help us with our spiritual advancement and understanding of Spirit. If you so desire, you can request that a Brother work with you.

that you look like God and where all of God's attributes are found.

Enlarge your idea of God and the spirit world. Enlarge your basic concepts of Love and Tenderness. Feel the larger idea of God's Love as it surrounds you. Be forgiving and kind, as God is. Bring quietness and calmness to your inner self. In quietness and in this inner temple, you can commune with God. Ask God to give you a glimpse of His Grandeur and Greatness. **Ask God to enlarge in you and allow you to understand how to approach Him.** We come to aid you in connecting to the real Truth, which is found only in the God-Mind. We help you discern what is real and true in the earth-mind. This is our promise to you.

Take with you the idea that God is gentle and can love you in ways which you know not. Allow these ideas to permeate your mind. Think on these words to aid you to find your own God-connection.

Meditate daily. Use a guided meditation or create one. Study how others meditate. Then use those as examples, and modify them to accommodate and satisfy your own needs. At first it is important to quiet the body and relax each part of the physical body. Then cleanse and rejuvenate each area in your body. Simply know that your body is comprised of many areas of which no one is aware. There are cells in your bodies and places in your heart and mind that even your learned ones are ignorant of. Use the idea of a cleansing Light of God to heal all areas. Take these steps and refine them to fit your needs. In the beginning it may be wise to follow the steps closely, but in time you will be able to quiet and still the physical body. Then you will perfect and add steps as you are guided from your own higher self. Don't be in a hurry to redefine the procedure. Practice your meditations and continue to build your temple in your heart and mind. **All prayers are individualized; you are praying correctly, however you pray.** Remember one thing: there is no need to beg God for your Good; it is waiting for you. What you do need to ask for is to be prepared to receive all your good.

Let us use an analogy—how you would treat a little child. You have his college fund all ready for him by age twelve, but he is not prepared to enter college, nor is he capable of managing these monies. Would it be wise to give him access to a large sum of money? Would you be doing him a good or would you be harming him, if he is not prepared to make intelligent decisions? So, you also are to ask God to prepare you to receive. Ask Him to cleanse anything from your mind and heart that prevents you from receiving your good. Is this clear? You, in your own way, are preventing yourself from growing and having all manner of good. **Seek first to have spiritual growth, healing and good.** Then the rest will be added. Remember Jesus' words, "Seek ye first the kingdom of God and all things will be added unto you." (Mt 6:33)

First comes the spiritual healing of all ignorance and ideas that inhibit your good. Then comes the physical good that you desire. In everything include God. Bring all your thoughts to God to be corrected and healed in spirit. Bring your attitudes and give them up to be changed into that which is Godlike. This is the true way to pray and seek God.

Our aim is to assist you in this method. We are with you as you pray and as you meditate. It all takes practice and will become easier as time goes by. Allow us to continue to inform and guide your efforts. We are proud of each of you. Your efforts are being sustained in spirit. Ask God to fill your heart and mind with understanding and intelligence. Our love and our help is with you.

The Brotherhood

Trust Yourself and God
(Brotherhood, September 5, 1988)

We come to impart Truth and Truth as it comes directly from God, the Father of the Universe. Some people think of God as Father-Mother God. This is an interesting idea. On earth it takes both father and mother to create life. Perhaps this is a good idea, to remind yourself that God is the Creator of all life. We wish to encourage you to pray. Every person who requests it has their own special Brother (of the Brotherhood) to be with them as they go through their activities. We are available to help and assist in every way. If you have a question, even if it seems to be mundane, ask us and let us talk it over. By the time you know it, there will be an idea on how to solve this problem. We will simply input a thought or idea, and it will be resolved easily. This is our promise to each person. Do not become frightened; we are not in the least bit a ghost as you consider "ghosts" on earth. Jesus referred to us as the Holy Ghost (as in Mk 13:11 or Lk 12:12), but that was because he wished to imply that we are spiritual beings. The ghosts that you consider as "ghosts" are also spiritual beings, who have lived recently on earth and are more into mischievousness. We do not play games on anyone, nor do we scare people who are vulnerable. We come to impart the Truth of the One God of the Universe. We are commissioned to give Truth to all people.

Our message for today is trust. **Trust in yourself. Trust in God.** Trust in your prayers to God, and see the wondrous happenings as your prayers are answered. This is how to prove to yourself and to each other the Truth. The lessons you are learning are for your benefit and for you to teach your loved ones. These lessons will guide you safely into the coming era. Bring trust into your lives by trusting your friends and your spouses. But first, we warn, try your friends and see if they can be trusted. Prove everyone, and then prove to yourself that you can be trusted. Prove our trust and God's trust. We are sure of ourselves and of God. We have known for many centuries the Power and Wonder of God. You are just beginning to learn this. Allow us to help you find the way to God-Mind and His Power to convert all your problems to answers, to smooth your way daily, to bring into your paths the easiest way to learn and to see. Allow us to help you in every way. Try us; allow us into your life and your home. Ask what you will of us. Ask for all things to work out for good. Ask for our help in your work and as you relate one to the other. Ask for our help as you drive your cars through the traffic, and allow us to bring Divine protection to you daily. We are here only to help.

But most of all we ask you to allow us to help you spiritually. If you do not know how to ask for this, simply say so. Say, "I don't know how or what to ask for, but I would like to be _____, have _____ or understand _____." You fill in the blanks. Ask for God's Truth to infuse your mind. Our true purpose and mission is to help you connect to God-Mind, from which all good things flow.

As you join together to pray and to learn, and to plan for the intervening years, allow us to help in these plans. Bring all your questions to us in your mind. We will answer in many ways—by an idea that pops into your mind, a dream, or in something you read or hear. There are many ways for us to answer you. Your answers will come from the most unlikely places at times. We can use this means of writing[6] with each of you. These thoughts are placed in Annie's mind one at a time. She has no way of knowing what the end results will be. She is not formulating these messages, but is only writing them down as we give them. Never, ever think these are her words. These are our words. We give Truth as it comes to us from God, Creator of All.

There is more to God and to you than you know. There is more to God's creation than you are aware of. By now you have an inkling of the wonders of God's worlds and yes, these are plural, for God has not only created one world and one solar system, but many. He also has created many ways to live. Life is eternal, of this Jesus was sent to tell. Life is ongoing and ever-expanding into the Universe. As one solar system fails, many more are born. As one civilization is gone, many more come into being. There is always life and there is always increase. Allow these ideas to enter your mind and expand your thinking. Fill your mind with the wonder and greatness of life.

---

[6] Automatic writing.

↓

Expand your thinking and put fear outside of yourself. Do not allow fear to enter your mind. This is how to get rid of it: when you feel fear entering your mind, simply say the words, "Cancel, cancel; I do not wish to fear anything anymore." This is all it takes for those fears that are not of the long-lingering type. Is this not simple? Try this method for one week. You will see amazing results.

We know those who are working with us by name, and we love you. We are aware of who is who, and who thinks which way, and who is afraid and who is not. We also know which ones believe and which are still doubting. But do not take this as an admonition, for we are working with your doubts, and soon you will see the Truth and know the Truth.

The Brotherhood

How to Use Divine Love Daily
(Mary, September 5, 1988)

Dear ones, children of God, you are special because of your desire to know the Truth. You will have an easier time of the coming events because you seek. I have great concern for all of you. All people are God's children and as such are mine. I have learned to love unconditionally, as does God.

This is my message today. Unconditional Love is Divine. This love does not say, do this or do that, and then I will love you. It says, "I love you, no matter what you do or say." This is God's Love. **You cannot be outside of God's love for any reason, except that you choose to be.**

This is the Love that heals, because it is Divine. It heals bodies and minds. It heals family relationships and cities of fear and greed. Divine Love, when sent from your mind, will return to you bearing many rewards. These rewards will be small things that enter so smoothly that it will seem that unconditional Love was always present. And it has been! This world was made out of Divine Love. You each were born and created in the beginning out of Divine Love. This world and all planets were created out of Divine Love. We could go on and on throughout the Universe, for all creation was made out of Divine Love and in Divine Love.

Take this thought with you into the marketplace, into your home and into your family: **"Divine Love created me and all that I encounter. Divine Love soothes my life and brings rich rewards to me and my family."** Repeat this affirmation over and over as you travel and before you sleep. In one week, this thought will be imbedded in your mind and will have become a part of your belief system. This is Truth. This is God's Truth. When you get the idea of how much you are loved and how you can live life so easily in Divine Love, you will be grateful to God for all you are today. This is how to live life in spirit. Send the thought of Divine Love to anyone who frustrates you. Send it into your workplace and see the days progress smoothly. Whenever you become upset and angry, think, **"Divine love is now flowing through me instantly."** These kinds of Truth thoughts will help you as you go about your daily activities. They will also remind you that you believe in the spiritual realm. You live in the spirit realm simultaneously while you live on earth. You grow in spirit, but it is easier to do so on earth. Take this advice: continue to pray and prepare for your survival in the coming years. These thoughts will not only help you today, but as you approach the earth changes.

Bring the Love of God into your home. This will help you by replacing fear with Divine Love. Take Divine Love with you daily as you go about your activities. Send Divine Love as a thought to your loved ones. As you work with Divine Love, God will work with your loved ones to prepare them for events. This preparation will take place behind the scenes, so to speak. Fill your body with Divine Love and use Divine Love to correct any habits or behaviors that harm you. Lead your children with Divine Love, and not just earth-mind love, which is changeable. Walk through your home and workplace and repeat the thought, Divine Love. See changes as they take place before your eyes.

Use Divine Love in all your dealings with others. Send the thought of Divine Love into every area of all hospitals. This gives you the opportunity to send the Healing of Divine Love to many whom you will never know. God will see your efforts and will reward you. Enter your home with the thought of Divine Love. As you go into any educational phase, prepare by relying on Divine Love. God's Love, which is Divine, will help you understand your lessons, your work and your loved ones. Send Divine Love to all students and teachers with a thought. Allow Divine Love to instruct the coming generations.

Each person can use God's Love to enhance their home, car, clothes, money, and family. Send the thought, Divine Love, to everyone in the world, and ask God to allow people to feel His peace for one moment. As you pray for others, you are also praying for yourself. Take these messages seriously. My wish is for you to use these lessons daily and count on the Brotherhood to help you in every situation. Each of you has your own Brother, and he is with you to aid you in every endeavor, not just in your spiritual problems, but also with your problems in all parts of your life.

Continue the good work in your prayers and feel the Love of God as we surround each of you daily.

Mary, Mother of Jesus

Build a Temple in Your Mind
(Brotherhood, September 11, 1988)

There is more to life than what is seen, heard and felt. Meditate daily and give yourself time to consider your individual goals. It is important to build a temple in your mind. This temple will be a haven where you will find rest, comfort and tenderness. The ability to enter your temple during times of pain and weariness is very beneficial to you. *(On this day, during her morning meditation, Annie heard the words that are transcribed below.)* These are the words you heard as you were in your temple:

> When the storms of life are gathering around you and frighten and scare you, there is a haven in your mind, one that you've erected with your thoughts. This beautiful temple, which no one can see or enter, is for you alone. In the peace and love that warms you as you enter, you are ageless and weightless. You are all you desire to be. In this inner temple of your mind is a connection to all energy, love, peace, health, wealth and happiness. Herein lies the answer to all your prayers. In your beautiful temple is the door to God and everything.[7]

Our advice is to concentrate on building the most beautiful and fabulous temple you can envision. Enter your temple to give all problems, questions and requests to God. Give all fear, worry or thought to God. In your temple, place concerns in a fire to be consumed by the pure energy of God. Other suggestions are to leave them in a trash receptacle outside, or throw your worries out a temple window to return to God's pure converting Energy. It is the act of releasing that places in your mind the idea that God is taking care of this, that it no longer is your concern. Afterwards, until the answer is evident, you are to be grateful to God for the perfect outcome.

The Brotherhood

---

[7] This is an example of the beautiful poetry you may at times receive in your meditations.

CHAPTER

2

Talking to God

The Key to the Riddle
(Byron)

In Mary's message given to Annie on September 9, 1988, I found "the key to the riddle." In one paragraph, I found the following:

. . . But you as humans have always had the power of choice. This power is one you have not learned to use. When you wish to learn to use it, all you have to do is ask God to teach you how to choose rightly. In giving up this power of choice to God, you come out the winner, for there is so much that is awaiting you. But God will not deter you from your path of birth and rebirth on earth. This is not sacrilege or blasphemy, as some would tell you. For you do not have to do anything you do not want to do, not even die for real. The dying is for your benefit, for in death are lessons that you learn and cannot learn in any other way.

When I reread it and was highlighting key phrases, I noticed that this was something really significant. I interpreted it to mean:

1. *That we have been given the power of choice, but we haven't yet learned how to use it properly.*
2. *Our next step is to ask God to teach us to use it properly.*
3. *We really win when we give up our freedom of choice to God. This is the next giant step in our spiritual evolution.*

I was later told, "There is more after this, but it is all easier once you've learned to give up yourself to God. There is still more life and wonderful things in store for you. This is a form of graduation to a higher level."

I perceived that the alternative to this is having to reincarnate over and over, until one gets it right, or until one finds the "key to the riddle."

Give Everything Up to God
(Mary, September 11, 1988)

Tell Byron he has indeed found the key.[8] He will find that this key fits many other riddles. It is in the faith of things to come: **In giving up your problems, your worries, your freedom of choice and your whole self to God's wonderful Essence, you come out a winner.** At last someone understands! This is not a sacrilege, blasphemy or giving up anything to an "evil spirit called Satan." As we have told you repeatedly, there is either God and All His Power, or there is nothing. The evil spirits, devils and the satans of this world are all in your mind and your incorrect concepts.

Prayers, meditations and statements of Faith are all for your benefit. God Is! He has no need for statements of faith to increase His Power, Life or Energy. Do not think for one minute

---

[8] See "The Key to the Riddle" given on Sept. 9, 1988 (pages 18-19)

that these prayers add anything to God. God is Life. God is Pure Love. God is Pure Energy. God is Pure Power. **GOD IS WHOLE AND COMPLETE.** Now do you begin to understand? All these lessons about how to pray and meditate and my calls for conversion are for mankind's benefit. God does not need anything of you, but you who are His creation have much need of Him. God created us all and from the beginning has had all the necessary elements and capability to continue to create.

It is mankind that has a need for super-beings to help and give counsel. All people on earth, even the most ignorant, call on some kind of Higher Power. They may think of Him as the Sun, or in the trees, or as a spirit who is as capricious and ignorant as they are, but they recognize the need to have help.

The need is yours and everyone's who is on earth. This is the message I bring today. This is the way to help yourselves to the total enjoyment of being united with God in everything. It is blessed and wonderful. Your language lacks words to describe the magnificence and brilliance of living in total unity with God. It is so marvelous that I wish everyone would recognize that what is lived on earth is but a shadow of reality. Imagine your most wonderful moments. This is life in God all the time. Think back to the realization of your true love. This is an inkling of God's love. It is still a pale comparison of God's life and love.

The key is to give up everything to God. This is what Jesus meant, not that you on earth should have more religions. Today there are already so many religions and churches, and still people are ignorant of where to seek God. It is not in a building, Mass, or religious service. It is not through your repeating of prayers in rote. **The only place to find God is in your heart, and in every mind is the door.** Another mistaken idea is that there is only one door to God. There are as many doors as there are people, for each has in their own mind the door to God.

All of the religions are for people's benefit. The inner service of each religion gives you the feeling of Holiness. Each religion has some Truth, but the most crucial issue in all religions is the instruction in how to commune with God. The services are outer manifestations of what should be happening in your heart. **With your thoughts, attitudes and longings, worship God.** It is not by kneeling and praying in rote, without truly meaning the words you are repeating, that you worship. I have not come to give this message to cause anyone pain. It has been in ignorance of spiritual matters that all these religions continued. They merely provided each person a sense of spirituality. This is a basic need, as are food, air and water. You are spirit and you need to return to commune with the Spirit which created you, but over the centuries mankind has made this difficult and complicated. However, it is simple and not at all frightening. When you see a demonstration of God's Power, you are frightened, but consider that there is also Love in His Power. You on earth have found some of the power of the universe, but you have used it only for destruction of life. This is the blasphemy and the satanic reality, the use of your wonderful minds to devise ways to destroy life and God's creation. The total ignorance of what you are doing to yourselves is amazing. In total ignorance you live, and you do not see that as you destroy, it is yourselves whom you destroy.

Let's continue with how to do, and not with what is wrong, for many things are wrong in your approach to your own spirituality. **Talk to God in your heart and mind.** Tell the Creator your problems, and then give them up to God. Allow Him the time and the use of your problems to bless you. When you worry and continue to think of these same problems, this is where your mind is. Your mind should be in worshipping God, in strengthening your faith through prayer, and in making statements of faith. That is, make up your own statements of faith in God, Creator of All. When you are using your mind to worry, you are too busy with yourself and your problems to

consider God and His Goodness. If all you think of is you and
your problems, you have not given up anything to God to help
you. When you pray and talk to God, tell Him your problems,
then make a statement releasing these problems to God. The
mind is also a way to deter your answers, for every time you
worry about what you have already given up to God, you are
taking away from your faith and hope. **The key is giving up,
giving your problems in payment for answers.** Give your faith
for an increase of all good things. Give your belief in sickness
and evil, for total health. Give your heart and mind to be filled
with the very Spirit of God. This is the key, to give up, to release,
to choose God in all things.

Begin to comprehend that the choice is always yours. It is
in giving up your choice to God that you win. All the worrying
and fretting serve only to delay your good. Ask God to increase
your faith and ability to understand the true meaning of life.
Ask God for all the help you need. This is Truth.

Mary, Mother of Jesus

Contact God Within
(Mary, September 17, 1988)

We will give you some suggestions on how to contact us
by your mind. As you see, we all have the same theme. We are
all giving everyone knowledge of where to find God. Jesus, my
son, came to earth two thousand years ago to bring this same
message. **The kingdom is within you!** (Lk 17:21) **He also told
you that as you think so shall you be.** If you are meek of heart,
you will be rewarded. When you find love in your heart,
understand it was placed there by God. Jesus also brought
many new ideas and concepts that were not well received in his
day. These are the same messages I bring today.

As you read the Bible, know in your heart that not everything is included in the Bible. The stories that were told concerning Jesus were placed there for the reason of showing you

how He thought and what He stood for. There was much in Jesus' life that was not included in the Bible. But what was important for the ages was included, because God directed the writing and compiling of the Bible.

Too many religions rely too heavily on the Bible as the last authority, and neglect the truth that comes into people's minds in prayer and meditation. Too many preachers and priests are good at preaching the word but not in living the word. That is why you should not look to any man, woman, or child to guide you to God, or to give the last word on how you are to worship God. This is what is between you and God Himself—how you think, your attitudes, your beliefs, your way of facing life in general and your internal worship of God. Have you not thought that God is in your mind and your heart? He knows every thought, every hurt, every breath, every lingering feeling that is inside you. There is nothing hidden from God. Do you not see how useless it is to try to hide from God? He is in you and all around you. He sees your coming and He also sees you as you go. I do not wish to criticize the religions of the world, but they have not done their job of leading people to a close union with God. Too much emphasis is placed on money, testimony, numbers of people who attend the churches; these are simply vanities. Vanities in the churches keep people from truly seeking God. No one is to judge your efforts; no one knows your heart or your sincerity. Only God knows!

I will give you the benefits that you receive as you pray. When you enter into prayer, fill your mind totally with the solution to your problems and with the outcome you desire. If you pray for someone who is sick, pray for that person's total health. Give God the pattern of what you wish. He will have an idea of what you want. **Always ask God to give you "this or something better," as this opens the door for all of God's Goodness to enter into the flow.**

To meditate, this is what you must do. Find a moment that will allow you to quiet your mind. Become dreamy, in a half-awake and half-asleep mood. This is the meditative mood you are looking for. Picture in your mind a most peaceful place. Perhaps it's the seaside, or mountains or your backyard. It does not matter where this place is; it is the mood of the place that is important. Continue to feel this half-asleep mood. Picture your dreams about the life that would be your ideal. Then stop all thoughts and simply feel Light as it pours into your head. Stay as quiet in your mind as you can, for as long as you can. **Allow God one split second to pour knowledge and understanding into your mind. You can help Him do this by thinking, "As I blank my mind, God is pouring in knowledge, understanding and wisdom."** Then blank your mind as best you can. Try this for one week.

Prayer is one part—it is the talking and asking part. Meditation is the picturing and quieting part, your ideal picture of yourself and your life, and your picture of yourself receiving knowledge, understanding and wisdom. Allow us to say it this way: **Prayer is the thought and the words going up out of your mind. Meditation is the coming into your mind of all of God's Goodness.**

Ask for God's Goodness. It is knowledge, understanding, wisdom, love, peace, intelligence, energy, light of illumination, wealth and goods, health, beauty, strength, order, enthusiasm, life, power and many more attributes of which you are not aware. With all of this at your beck and call, why do you continue to turn away from God? Why do you not want to be close to God? You cannot bring all these attributes to yourself without His help. Yet you on earth today are puffed up and engrossed in your power plays and games. You are so intrigued with yourself, you do not have time to think of eternity. This is all the good God has prepared for you. There is so much more, but you have not accepted these gifts yet. You have not accepted the gift of God's total and complete Love.

Put your fears behind you and allow the total goodness of God to enter your mind. Fear and anger are your destruction. Hostility, envy, jealousy, avarice and possessiveness are your undoing. These are emotions that you must set behind you.

These you are not to look to. As Lot's wife, d
them, for you could also turn to salt, which s'
heart could turn to stone and feel nothing. T
the ones that God has come to help you elim....
and fears that cause you so much harm are all of your min... .
making. The fear of the unknown was instilled in you to make
you wary and careful, but not to immobilize you or lead you
into wars and fights with your fellow man. These are the
"things" that keep you enslaved to the wheel of karma. Be
healed and become blessed with God's Almighty Love. If you
find it too hard to put these emotions behind you, ask God for
help. Ask God to send the Holy Spirit, which is the Brotherhood. Ask me; I will be happy to teach you, with the help of a
host of angels. Only through your own decision do you open
your mind and heart for our help. Ask God for help; He will
know how to help you overcome your fears and angers.

There is nothing that you cannot ask God. He is Pure
Energy, Love and Wholeness. He wants you to talk to Him and
to ask for His help.

Do you not realize that the best gift you can give someone
is to ask for their help? Everyone loves to give advice; everyone
loves to be thought of as wise. Ask for advice from someone
and see the light in their eyes turn on. This is a great compli-
ment. Now how much more could you receive if you ask God
not only for advice, but for the solutions to all your problems?
Then, you say, what would I do? Can you imagine a life
without problems? Can you believe that you could live in peace
and happiness? What would you have to do? Well dear ones,
you would have plenty to do and plenty to enjoy. This life does
not need to be lived from the angle of problems. It can be lived
from the angle of **trust in God for everything.**

For one week, meditate on seeing only good in your life.
Daydream or night dream about your life as you would like it
to be. See the ideal. Set the best as your goal. Dream while you
work and talk to God; He is always listening. Learn now to rely
on God for everything, and in the future all things will come

easily to you. **Now is the time to practice relying on God. Seek God in your heart and mind.** We will repeat this over and over until you are relying on God for every need and every desire.

Pray in your own way. Talk to God as you would a friend. You do not need to yell or holler; God is in your mind. There is no need for fancy words or for long pleas; God is in your heart and already knows what you have need of. There is no need to tell anyone else about your prayers. These prayers are what Jesus made reference to when he said to go into the closet to pray. The closet is your mind. The closet is your thoughts. In a crowded room you can pray, in an instant you can pray, or for long periods of time you can pray, and no one need know. All prayers are good. All prayers are heard. But remember that when you worry, you interfere in the arrival of your answers. So, place worry in God's hands.

I ask, for a period of one week, for you to increase your prayers and meditations. In this way, your prayers for the world and the people of this planet are increased too. I want everyone to have a close union with our Father God. In Divine Love and Divine Peace I leave you.

Mary, Mother of Jesus

Go to the Source with Your Problems
(Mary, September 25, 1988)

It is another worship and training day. This is good; learn how to follow your own path and find a God-connection within. This is what Jesus came to teach, but still not enough people are looking in the right place. Understand with certainty that you are finding the right place to look for your connection to God. **In His Great Wisdom, God placed everyone's connection inside their own spirit.** This God-Mind Connection is real. It is the way to find your truth. Remember not to be upset with any of your families or friends, even when at times they tell you you are losing your mind or that you have gone crazy. This is the Truth of the Ages, and you have not lost your mind. But your Truth is individualized and will not be for anyone else. What you sense and what comes to you in your mind is your truth and guidance. It probably will not be right for anyone else. So how do you help your loved ones?

First—through prayer for their spiritual good.

Second—for the opportunity to give them joy and comfort.

Third—pray to know the correct time and method to approach them with your truth.

Fourth—pray to use the correct words to tell them what you are feeling.

Continue to modify your temple and to enter it on every opportunity to be relieved of worry and to be instructed. Talk to us in the Spirit world; we hear your thoughts when they are directed to us. But most important is to speak to God, who is in every cell in your body and already knows your thoughts and feelings. It is all right to verbalize what you are thinking and feeling. God is very patient and will be happy to listen to you explain what He already knows. It is the turning to God that He looks for. When you change your thought direction toward God, it is like setting the direction of your automatic pilot toward the supreme Good and your final destination. Perhaps you will delay to view and learn, but once you have set your sights on God as your destination and purpose in life, you will be Divinely guided into those situations that will give you the most learning in the least amount of time.

Talk to God as you do yourself, but remember that you are speaking to God, who Created you. This is the way Annie speaks to God. She always starts off directing her conversation to God by calling His name, "God, I am feeling low and I don't know why. Will you point out to me the way to get out of this terrible mood?" Or "God, Byron and I had a disagreement. Please pour your Divine Love and Peace into our hearts and help us to solve this problem in a way that will be agreeable to both of us." Or, "God, I want a parking place up by the front door." Or now, "God, please bring the right renters to see the rental house and allow them to be able to rent it and love it and live in it for a year." Talk to God about your need for money. He knows that each of you have a need for money and to be taught to manage your money in a way that will be beneficial to each one in the home. Talk to God and ask for all your needs. Bring Him the entire problem and always ask for the best solution possible, where everyone comes out the winner and feels good.

You may of course talk to me or the Brotherhood, but know that in time you will want to go to the Source Himself for all your problems to be solved. Ask God to help you put the fear you have of Him away. Understand that this fear is what keeps you from having a close relationship with God. It is this fear that needs to be released, for your prayers to be answered directly and without delay. When you ask someone else to ask for you, there may be something lost in the conveying of the message. **So, it is better for each of you to go directly to God with everything.** He knows when you are depressed and angry, so don't wait to approach Him only at certain times. Simply ask Him to help you get out of the mood you are in and to teach you how to handle the situation.

Never, ever, pay attention to anyone who tells you that you are to do anything other than this—to contact God. It is God's life force that animates and gives you breath and heartbeat. Seek to find your connection to God. Enter the door that was placed in your spirit and mind. Know God in your heart, and feel the Love used to create you in the very beginning. God is Pure Love. He corrects and counsels you always in Love and Understanding of all your ways. Nothing is hidden from God, not one thought or feeling. Humans have always tried to hide themselves from God; thus the story of the Garden of Eden. When Adam and Eve had eaten of the fruit of the tree of knowledge, they approached God, trying to hide their nudity. Each of you try to hide your nudity from God. When you

become aware and judge some act, condition or situation to be
wrong, then you have eaten of the tree of knowledge. Then, you
try to hide your nudity from God, which is a farce. God is in
every cell and not only hears, feels, sees and smells all you're
sensing, He is in every thought. God is not the one who
punishes you. It is your higher self who is the punisher and
corrector. It is this higher self who knows right from wrong for
you and makes this decision. **God is and always will remain
total and complete, Pure Love and Understanding.** It is His
Will that you turn over your whole self to Him, all of your
faults, which He loves as much as He loves your talents.

Always remember that God Loves unconditionally and
without any reservations. He loves every part of you. Ask God
to help you correct those areas that you would like to correct.
He will be more than happy to help. God is always loving you
and understands better than you why you are as you are. God
sees the entire picture, not only this lifetime. He knows your
goals in this life. Ask for His help in achieving these goals. It is
His pleasure to help you. Did not Jesus say, "It is the Father's
pleasure to give you the kingdom?" (Lk 12:32) With this insight,
return and read these passages in the Bible. Seek and ask God
to open you to the Truth behind what you read. Remember that
Spiritual matters are hard to explain in earthly language and
terms.

Another reason for meditation is to receive knowledge in
a nonverbal way. True knowledge can be given to you non-
verbally. It is mankind who needs words to describe everything. In spirit we have methods that are as elementary in
nature as the amoeba. These are pure communication, in which
words or terms are not needed. That is why Jesus taught in
stories and parables. He always started off by saying, "The
kingdom of heaven is likened unto this." God in His Infinite
Intelligence has many ways to give knowledge and understanding that do not require words. When you are able to quiet
your mind, you can receive knowledge, wisdom, know-how,

practicality and many more things in total that will help you
with your life goals. At first you may envision knowledge,
understanding, all the good God has to give, as a stream of
Light that enters the head. Be aware that something is transpiring in and around your body.

Set up, as a goal in meditation, the ability to communicate
with God in nonverbal terms, simply to sense the Love and
Understanding which God gives happily. As you persist, God
is more and more joyful, and so are we. As each of you seeks
God in your heart and mind, we in spirit are joyful, for we have
the assurance that you will get the results you desire—that is,
if your desires do not in any way harm anyone. At times you
can simply sit and tell your mind and heart to communicate
with God in nonverbal terms. Then bask in the Love that is
yours and everyone's.

Now I commend your efforts in living these concepts. We
will enhance every effort to understand and to achieve.

Mary, Mother of Jesus

Call On Us for Help
(Brotherhood, September 25, 1988)

The stories in the Bible are to be used for any time period.
These stories and parables have some message that is applicable to everyday life. Pray to understand the truths contained
in these stories and parables. The story of the tree of knowledge
in the Garden of Eden was not a one-time event. It happens
each time you think that something you are doing is wrong for
you or someone else, or that some thought is not beneficial to
you. Nothing in the Bible is a one-time event. Everything is, and
can be, used to benefit your daily life. The nakedness that
Adam and Eve felt, you feel each time you realize the error of
your ways. As they could not hide from God in their day,
neither can you. It is useless and futile to try to hide from God.

As you become more open to the spiritual realm, you will receive knowledge non-verbally. You will simply know things or be able to figure them out easily. This is the kind of knowledge that will help you in your daily life. Parents will know when to correct the children and how, so as not to frighten them into being afraid to live or die.

We are available anytime. We are here to help as you release the fear of God and make the connection to the God-Mind. When you no longer need us in this, we will simply back away until you call upon us again. At that time you will talk directly to God without any fear. In that day you will be able to listen and communicate with Him. Many people can talk to Him, but if He were to answer, they would be overcome in fear. It is our duty to help you, who have requested our help, to understand that God is not to be feared in any way. We will remain close to you. Ask us to be with you as you begin to communicate with God. The open, two-way communication with God gives knowledge and understanding. When you begin to communicate with God, you could say you have begun to get a root system, this being an analogy to a plant. In the growth of a plant, the root system grows in place first. As the root system grows stronger, the seedlings are better able to break out of the ground and grow. Until such time as you are able to have a strong root system in God, you need to be propped up in order to survive. We are the props that help you reach spiritual maturity. We are happy to be used as props, in order to have you turn to the Source.

Our duty is as a counselor, guide and helper. This is what Jesus asked us to do with each of you. We were sent out by the Christ, Son of God, and we take our work very seriously. Jesus was Christed on earth, and He remains the only one who has attained the Christdom while on earth. He is the True Spiritual Son of God. Jesus was the person who attained the Christing, so thus he is called Jesus Christ. You may at any time call on Jesus the Christ to help you, and bypass our aid. He is always

available to each of you. Call on whomever you are comfortable with in the Spirit world. Ask for our help to connect you to
the God-Source and Creator.

Now, as you go about your daily lives, we ask that you
speak to us in your mind. If there is something happening to or
around you, ask us to intervene on your behalf. We will do it
non-verbally and it will simply work out. Take us with you into
every situation—as you correct your children or speak to your
spouse, as you relate to parents or co-workers. As you go to
sleep, ask us to enter and heal you spiritually while you sleep.
It is your conscious mind that sleeps, but during sleep your
subconscious mind is at work, ever alert and working on the
last thought you gave it. So as you go to sleep, ask your higher
self to bring your spirit healing, understanding and knowledge. This will occur in a nonverbal method. Your sleep will
not be disturbed. Ask God to open your mind with understanding so you can see the Truth of your being. Do not waste one
minute, not while you are awake or while you sleep. Your
learning can continue at all times.

Feel the Love of God as it gives you knowledge, understanding, intelligence, wisdom, patience, know-how and self-
confidence. In Love, God is willing to enhance all these talents
in you. These things you already have, but you know not that
you have them. Children also have these abilities. Use these
abilities to help you make every decision. We ask to be included
in your daily life. Rely on us daily and in all situations. This will
help you begin to rely on and trust in God, all Good.

Whenever you think of God, think in terms of All Good,
Pure Love, Complete and Total Acceptance and Total Understanding. These are the terms to associate with God. Yet He is
all this and more. **Become comfortable with a God who Loves
you very much and is not at all critical of your actions.** It is
your higher self who is keeping you in line. It is your higher self
who corrects from time to time. Your higher self acts as an
automatic pilot to keep you on the path. Your higher self will
take each choice and use it for your highest good. At times this

is not apparent, because you see many people who look like they are off a spiritual path. But do not judge, because this may be the way they are learning. **God's Love is unconditional. You are completely accepted by God, just as you are this very moment.** Remember this always.

Now in this Great Love we are all surrounded and cared for. In this Great Understanding we all live. We remain your friends.

The Brotherhood

3

Growing in Spirit

All Life Is Eternal
(Mary, October 2, 1988)

T
HIS IS A DAY OF JOY for today you come with a purpose. **The purpose is the most beneficial purpose there is, and that is learning more about God, the Father of All Creation.** Bring your enthusiasm, earnestness and sincerity of heart and minds, and grow. Use the events of your daily life to learn. Expand your thinking to include all the good God has in store for you.

I will continue with the story of creation. This is the beginning and is the first place you make your mistakes in beliefs.

The story of creation is too long to go over in detail now, but in a nutshell, I said that here in spirit we do not have days as you do on earth. Our days and nights are as we desire them to be. All is lived mentally. We think a thing and it appears, but it is not solid in form as on earth. It is as when you use your imagination.

In the beginning of our awareness, we were with God as rays of light. There was God the Father and there were the rays of light which He emitted. We are filled in this manner with all the essence and attributes of God. In the core of ourselves, we still exist as these same rays of light. This is our spirit self, which is and always has been one with God the Creator. This is an analogy, as there are no words in any earth language that can be used to describe the spirit world. As small God-rays, we asked the Father, or huge Light Source, will we ever become as big as you and be able to know, discern and understand how to create? This set the Father God to thinking, and He thought this was a good idea, to create not only worlds, but to create God-beings to inhabit these worlds, to play and to learn to become one large source of All. This was the primary purpose of you becoming humans. We were given this beautiful world to work and play in. God created all His worlds with the same, self-sustaining qualities as are found on earth. In the universe, all worlds can and are rejuvenated through natural laws. Today it's called ecology, but whatever the name, it is all the same, self-renewing quality.

In the beginning, God allowed you to live in the Garden of Eden, which I explained to be a state of mind, a state of mind wherein you are totally connected to God. He provided for all your needs, and you were fully trusting that all would be given in love. This was your infancy as spirits. In infancy you played, frolicked and generally had a wonderful time in the Garden of Eden. It was a joyous time for you as spirits, for all you needed to do was think of something, and there it was. There was nothing to fear or to become angry about. Then you began to grow as spirits, and you wanted to do things yourselves. You wanted to know what, where and how things were created. You were learning at a good rate, when the snake of your dark side reared its ugly head and began to question you about what you had learned and not learned. This was the opposite side from the side that sees all things and is able to discern the best possible answer for all concerned. **The snake is all those small, little thoughts that creep into your mind with doubts, skepticism, fear, anger and such. These are the satans of your mind.** There is not a spirit of evil, or one great evil spirit, who can cast spells or cause harm. **The satans of this or any other world are your own negative thoughts, attitudes and beliefs, which cause you or anyone else pain of any kind.** Allow us to return to our analogy. The Father God came and gave you the lessons on becoming self-sustaining spirits, who are mature and able to make clear decisions without causing harm to anything or any other being or world. But mankind wanted to do it himself. God in essence told you (humanity) that you were not ready to care for yourself as a separate and responsible spiritual being. But in your immaturity, man became upset and had a temper tantrum. With this act, mankind ate of the tree of knowledge of good and evil. Through the tantrum-throwing, mankind became enmeshed in the evilness of all time, which is selfishness and self-serving ways. So God banned you from the Garden of Eden as long as you were in this kind of temperament or conduct. He will not allow you to stay in the Garden of Eden when you become selfish or self-serving. These attributes are not Godlike and, as such, are not pleasing to God.

As the spirit of humanity was banished from the garden state of mind, God said to man, "From now on, you must work to produce and provide food and shelter for yourselves, and woman will bear her young with pain, in order that these young will be appreciated and cared for." You will not enter the Garden of Eden to partake of the tree of life until you have proven to be a mature, responsible spirit being.

At this time God set up the laws of reincarnation in order to give more opportunities to learn anew the lessons that life can and does teach. The lessons of life are the lessons that you did not have to learn in this manner, but it was your choice to be allowed to act independently of God the Father. Mankind began a series of lives on earth, first to learn one lesson and then another. But the part of yourself that is now called the higher self is the spirit being in charge of your life and lessons. This is the spirit who returned one day to God the Father (in the analogy) and asked, how do I return to the former life of leisure in the garden? What can I do to quickly be able to attain the knowledge of life? The Father God gave you this method of learning to be Godlike and to grow in spiritual values. Father God said (in the analogy), "You will return to earth and be born time and again to live life over and over, until such a time as you have learned to be the spiritual being whom I know you can be." This is the reason for becoming different personalities and having many lives on earth.

Now there were those spirit souls who did not rebel against God the Father and are still at His side. At times, some have volunteered to become Angels and bring words of warning and words of caution from God the Father. Some of these souls, from time to time, walked on earth to teach you how to rely on God and where to find God. There have also been those souls who have learned quickly and have returned, as did Jesus. **It is in the innermost parts of your hearts that these lessons on spiritual values are stored. In the inner recesses of your mind is the door to all knowledge and all that is needed in order to return to the Garden of Eden.** You can become reliant and totally dependent on God for everything.

Life then, it appears to you on earth, is short and only for one brief span of time. Consider how long the rocks, mountains and oceans have been on earth. Do you not think for one minute that as God's living children you would not have the same life span? Are you not, as spirits, of more value? These mountains, rocks and oceans have been here for millions of years. This has been proven to you through scientific methods. Can you honestly believe that God, who is All and Total Love, would only give you a span of life shorter than one hundred years, as compared to the millions of years that the mountains have? This wrong concept has been your undoing. For how many believe, "I will only come around once, so I want to do all the

naughty things I can?" These are the satanic thoughts of your
own mind. You are always alive, as is God. You have been
coming to earth to live and to learn to be spiritual, to learn that
as you think, so you will be—that to think only of yourself is
wrong, spiritually. To become self-centered is not spiritually
good. How easy it is for you today to think, I will sow my wild
oats and then, when I am old, I will settle down and go to
church, as if this were all that is required of your spirit. These
wild oats you are sowing in this life, you will need to reap in
another life. Be careful of your thoughts, deeds, attitudes and
beliefs. These are your undoing, not only for this lifetime, but
for your real life, which is your spiritual life.

Start to see life as it truly is, eternal. **Your true essence is
spirit and not flesh. The life force which animates you is
spirit.** The flesh part of you is what is buried and returned to
earth. The spirit part of you keeps on living and living. Can you
not see the fallacy of some of your religions, which say you
must do this ceremony or that sacrament, or confess publicly
your sins in order to go to heaven? What of all the ones who
lived before these religions came into existence and set down
their laws? Do they not enter "heaven?"

The Truth is that everyone has been alive for millions and
millions of earth years. You are born, live in certain circumstances and die. Upon death you return to the spirit "world" (I
enclosed this word in quotation marks to denote that this is
your term and does not in actuality exist as you think). Here
your spirit soul does a review of your life, as you lived it daily.
You see through your true spiritual eyes, which also understand all things. This is the time of judgment, when your
spiritual soul decides how it did. If there is a question, you
consult with God, and He helps you review your life and gives
you hints on how best to correct the error of your ways. That is,
if you ask God for help, He will tell you in which circumstances
and under what earthly conditions you can progress rapidly in
spirit. But you must invite God to enter your judgment and
learning process. This is the time when you review your book

of life. You on earth at times keep diaries of your daily activities. Your book of life is your spiritual diary. In this diary is recorded all your thoughts, actions, attitudes, words and beliefs. As you review the life you have just left, you give yourself a score on how well you learned whatever your lessons were at the beginning of this life. You do not come randomly to life, to act and to be without a plan. While you are in spirit, you are able to observe some of the ways other spirit beings live on earth. You can see what is inherent in different cultures, sexes and conditions of life. You are the one who sets up your goals for the next life. You are the one who is in charge of where you will be born and under what circumstances. Now this does not mean you cannot better yourself on earth. You can better yourself both spiritually and in earthly conditions. Have you not known of men or women who have been born poor and as young men built a fortune? These men had learned in former lives to think in spiritually correct ways. It was not hard for some. But then there are those men who have been born into a fortune and lost it in living the "good" life, that is, in parties, liquor and drugs.

Some of the Eastern cultures and religions have been teaching reincarnation, as it is called today, for centuries. Some of these people have simply given up and said: it is destiny, or fate, or this is why I came to this lifetime. Perhaps the next time I will be born rich and healthy. This way of thinking is also a fallacy. You always have the power to choose and to decide to improve your status. On earth, as in spirit, you are always alive and deciding how, with what and when to improve yourself. Do not sit with your hands across your chest and say, "It is no use to fight destiny; this is how God ordained it." These words are false, and God does not ordain anyone to a life in poverty, illness or any condition that is unpleasing to the individual. This is and always has been your choice. Live each day as if you had to make all your life decisions in that one day, for all you have on earth is the present moment in time. You cannot relive yesterday, and tomorrow has not arrived. Now, this very moment, is the time to decide to improve your life, to ask God for help. Now, in this instant, is the time to return to trusting, relying and becoming totally dependent on God the Father. You can return to the Garden of Eden and live life easily and happily.

Now take this lesson and see the truth of the lesson. You are alive and have been for centuries and for millions of years. You will continue to live forever. **This moment is all you have to work with. This moment is all that is with you.** Do not live in tomorrow or in yesterday. Live constantly in the present or in the presence of God.

Pray and ask God the Father to help you with your life goals, those you have set up for this week, this year, this lifetime. Rely and trust God to help with all your goals. Talk to Him and tell Him, perhaps, "This is new and I do not know how to think of this. Help me learn the lessons I came into this lifetime to learn. Help me with my goals for this year, this week and today." You are alive forever. But **forever is lived one moment at a time, one minute and one thought at a time.** Watch your thoughts and your time. Time was put into place to aid you, to give you notice of what is going on around you. In the spirit world we do not have time as you do on earth. Take time and use it wisely.

Mary, Mother of Jesus

Appreciate All Your Circumstances
(Brotherhood, October 2, 1988)

First read and learn your (previous) lessons, and allow your mind to contemplate and think on these new thoughts. Discuss them during the week and reread the lessons given to you. It is best if you will try out some of the ideas that these lessons spark in your mind. In this manner you will be practicing for the coming time. This will be the lesson for today—how to use what is given to you by all of us. It will do no good if you take these pages and keep them hidden away in a drawer. This is not where to lay up your treasure. Remember Jesus' words to this effect, "Lay not your treasure on earth where it can rot away, but lay up your treasure in heaven where neither corruption nor thieves can take your treasure." (See Mt 6:19-21, Lk 2:32-34) These lessons and words are your treasure. The heaven in which you should hide them is your mind. The way to keep your treasure in place and beautiful is by using what you learn, to better your life on earth and to better your life in heaven, which is in your mind. See, "heaven" is a state of mind. We are repeating to you that all is lived mentally. Your treasure is the spiritual way to ease your life and your learning. This is the treasure we are giving you each week: to learn Truth and to be able to use the ways of spirit to ease your lifetime goals and heal you spiritually.

Take the words of Mother Mary and summarize them into short sentences or words to remind you of your lesson for that particular week. This week it could be something like this, **"I am alive forever and ever,"** or **"All Life is eternal."** Another thought to keep with you is, **"God is always available to help, and He is happy to answer me."** Perhaps you need to remind yourself that you are loved. Then you would say to yourself, **"I am Divinely Loved by God Himself, and I do not have to do anything to receive this love."** See, this is the way to bring a few words to mind to remember the lesson. These words, stated positively and without doubt, enter the furthest recess of your mind, and it will recognize the Truth. The earth-mind part of your mentality will not argue with the Truth of the Ages. It also recognizes the Truth. So tell yourself always the truth of how wonderfully made you are. Appreciate the body and the mind, which holds the memories, thoughts, attitudes and beliefs. In this manner, you begin to change earth-mind concepts to God-Mind concepts, which will help you grow spiritually.

Learn to appreciate life and all your circumstances. In this manner, you will arrive at the best of these circumstances quickly and then be able to move on. State your appreciation in your mind. People may judge you if they hear you. The earth-mind mentality of the world does not understand how to live this way. This is for your understanding only. These are the prayers and meditations of your heart, which will be said in secret and rewarded openly. These words will help to increase your faith and hope in the Truth of God. Start out your work week by saying to yourself and God, **"Thank you Father God for this job, the people and the method in which I earn my living."** Thank God for your possessions, such as your car, and tell your car that you love it as a gift from God. Appreciate your home by walking through it, stating your appreciation for the shelter, comfort and ease that it provides. Oh, you say, I am not satisfied with this old house. Well, look around and see those poor souls who do not have a home, a bed or food to eat. You are truly blessed and have much to appreciate. In life there will always be those who have more than you and those who have less. You can look at it from both angles. But be smart and look both ways. See that you could improve in many ways and vow to improve spiritually with God's help, and materially too, if possible. "But seek first the kingdom of Heaven, and the rest will be added unto you." These are the very words of Jesus and they are true two thousand years later. First ask for a spiritual healing, and at the same time you will receive a physical, mental, emotional, psychic, ethereal, and many other healings. It is like going to the store and asking for a loaf of bread, instead of asking for just a slice. Find your God-connection, and all things will be enhanced. Ideas on how to progress spiritually and physically will be revealed to your mind and heart for contemplation.

In learning to appreciate the very life you are living, you receive the benefits that are inherent. This means you will have physical, spiritual, emotional, psychic and mental advantages, which will set you ahead. Perhaps you will not see physical evidence of this right away, but know that it is happening first spiritually, and then it will seep down into your life on earth. Do not give up or lose faith, for that is where it will stop. Your loss of faith is like a dam that stops the flow of spiritual good. Your appreciation is like the opening of this dam. The floodgates are opened wide with appreciation, and good things flow to you in all planes, all dimensions and through every area.

Most of all, appreciate your partner in life. Understand that you can improve your marriage and life together, as you appreciate your mate and his or her work. As you see the good in your mate's eyes, you will see the love grow. For those of you who are not married, appreciate your parents and see the love that is in their eyes. Appreciate your schooling and your friends. Appreciation is like having your possessions, life and loved ones dipped in gold. All will shine with new vigor. New energy will enter your life in all areas. Your home will take on a new look and a new feeling. It will be a pleasure to return to this haven of rest. Your possessions, such as your car, will return the love and appreciation by performing well. Even inanimate objects sense the love with which they are cared. Appreciate your children. Appreciate the lessons these young ones are bringing to you as parents. You are learning patience, understanding, comprehension, and you have the opportunity to see the world through their eyes.

Get involved in your children's lives and get them involved in activities that will make good use of their energy. One young child asked God how to stop wiggling. It is this unused energy that causes him to feel restless. Allow the child to engage in activities to use his energy, being careful not to place a child in situations where he is pressured to compete or perform beyond his abilities. This will only discourage the child. Let the child compete only with himself. Encourage the children to use their energy productively, and allow them to increase their self-confidence. **Spend more time appreciating the little children.** As you rear children through the stages of life, you will learn many lessons too. Rear children gladly, and consider the honor it is to be a parent.

Now I speak to the children: as you are learning your school lessons, appreciate your whole day. Appreciate the lessons, homework, teachers, fellow students and all school activities. Appreciate your homes and possessions. Appreciate your parents. They may have their faults, but they also have their strengths. Like you, they are on this earth to learn life's lessons.

To the adult, married children, also appreciate your home and notice not what is lacking, but what you have attained. Appreciate your lives together and your work. Continue to pray for your loved ones. Forgive your parents for being human, and understand that they did the best they could at the time. You too may soon become parents, and it is always good to treat others as you would like to be treated. How you treat your parents is how your children will treat you.

This is your lesson for this week. In keeping with this lesson, allow us to express our appreciation to each of you. We see the real you, your spirit. Each one is a beautiful and rich child of God. Truly you have been looking for answers where they can be found. The place is not in buildings, but in your heart. Our words of appreciation include the calls from you. We are privileged to be able to help you and be with you through your week. You are special to us and to God.

The Brotherhood

Bypassing Earth-Mind to God-Mind
(Brotherhood, October 9, 1988)

Welcome to our communication for this day. We will tell you how we are working through you to support your connection to God, Creator. Our aim and task is to help make this connection to God-Mind strong. We are to help you as you try to make this all-important connection. Our purpose is to be your counselor and not your fairy godmother. Our only purpose is to have you grow in spirit, not in worldly goods.

When you open your mind and ask God to enter, it is not difficult for Him to enter your mind and heart, but it is difficult for you to ask. The earth-mind that covers your thinking is inundated in false concepts of God. Earth-mind, remember, is made up of all the concepts, thoughts, attitudes and beliefs mankind has held since the beginning of man on earth. Earth-mind tells you that God is an old, grey-haired man, who sits on a cloud up in the sky somewhere. He is seen as angry, capricious and judging. You are not sure where He is, but you are terrified of Him. This is an error in thinking, and it is one of the falsehoods we wish to correct. **God is a loving Being, and His Love is what created this world and you.** God is Spirit and is unseen, but not unfelt. You may not be able to see God, but you can feel His presence in your midst. **Our purpose is to take you past your fears of God, to see the Truth of God, to see that God is Love, total unconditional Love.** It is the earth-mind that conjectures up the devils and evil spirits. It is the earth-mind that tells you to fear. God only wants you to love as He does.

Because God has given each individual freedom of choice, it is up to you to ask God to come into your mind and heart. It is up to you to ask for God's help. While you are still in the earth-mind concepts, we have been sent to aid you to get past your fears and wrong concepts of spirit. Our duty is as a helper in guiding your thoughts past the earth-mind consciousness to find God-Mind and Truth.

At times, perhaps God's way seems magical and mystifying, because He is above natural laws. He can make the impossible happen. God would rather work through you and teach, while you rely on Him to work your own problems out. He gives wisdom and understanding to avoid problems. This is the root of true knowledge. God's knowledge is above earth-mind knowledge and lore.

Please see God as He is—Love, Intelligence, Energy, Knowledge, Wisdom and All Good. Know in your hearts and minds that when you ask us, we will be with you as you begin to connect to this Great Spirit. But see that God is not magical, or a fairy godmother, or a genie who will grant your every desire. God will not harm another, nor will He do anything for you. He will do everything through you. The only way He works is through you to teach.

Perhaps you see the miracles that Jesus performed while he was on earth as magical. Remember that Jesus knew God personally and knew the workings of Spirit. Jesus knew in His heart that with God all things are possible, and His faith was great. He trusted God the Father and loved God the Father. It was through Jesus that God healed the sick and made the blind to see. It was through Jesus that the lame walked and the deaf could hear. There was no magic working in these cases, nor in the cases of healing today. God's laws are many and there are many that you are not aware of. You have no need to know the workings of these natural laws, because you can bypass them with faith and prayer.

You too can ask God to calm the storms. There are all kinds of storms—physical, mental, emotional and spiritual storms. The storms of anger, fear and hatred in your heart can be calmed with God's love. Perhaps you have money problems or personality problems; these can be healed, as can the blind or lame. **You must take responsibility and ask God to work through you to bring relief and comfort. The point is that God can work only through your heart and mind.** It is up to each of you to find the ability to allow God to work through you.

God is in the hearts and minds of those who do not fear Him and who welcome Him. Bring this Great Creative Spirit into your heart to fill your heart with all manner of good emotions—love, respect, honor, caring, kindness, compassion, peace, plenty, hope and so much more. Bring God into your mind to help you discern the truth of all things. God is willing and able to show you the way to think correctly, but only if you invite His help. God is desiring to become alive in your being and in your homes. Consider that God is respectful of you and honors His pact with mankind and will not enter unless asked to. Consider the great restraint it takes to see His creations falter and fail and be unhappy and fearful. His Spirit desires to work through you and make the rough places smooth. God's Love desires to bring you all the serenity and happiness that can be yours.

Ask daily to have God work through you to live in peace, love and total happiness, to see clearly the error of old thinking patterns, to clear out of your mind old and harmful concepts and ideas. Ask daily for God to teach you how to enjoy His great abundance and to have all your needs met. It is all up to you individually to invite God in. It is up to you to learn the lessons, to ask for our help and God's help. This is not a onetime offer for your entire life. It is a daily and hourly event, this living in spirit. It is a daily invitation that needs to be made to God.

This is how to live spiritually. This is how to live in God-Mind and have all knowledge and wisdom lead you in the right paths for that day. Each day is different, and each day your needs are different. **Begin every day with an invitation to have God work His wonders through you.** Think of your growth and not as a child who expects to have things given to them.

Your daily prayers and meditations are important, because they will get you through the future. Early in the morning when you first arise, invite God to be in your heart and mind. Ask to listen to your world through God's mind, and then you will be allowing God to work through you as only He can.

The Brotherhood

Set Your Sights on Higher Levels
(Brotherhood, October 23, 1988)

Welcome to another session in Prayer and Meditation. We hope you will set your sights on a higher level of living. This is one of the reasons we are encouraging you to make this commitment to your own spiritual growth. Be fully present. When we speak of being here fully, we are speaking of your whole mind. Set your daily life aside to concentrate on your eternal life for a short period of time. This will open you up to more knowledge and understanding. You will be able to go about your daily activities with power and serenity. You will be better able to keep your mind on the positive or God side.

Come together to pray as a group. This will instill power into your life. Remember that Jesus told you that where two or more were gathered together in His name, there He would be. We know that you have not always stated that you were gathered together in Jesus' name, but it is the same, as you are seeking to know more about God. In searching for truth from the standpoint of God and Divine knowledge, you have called on all the Divine forces to come into play. Your gatherings are important to us and to many who are with you. This has added strength to your family and to each of you individually. For a period of time, you have set aside the world to concentrate on the eternal. As you pray, what you pray for is answered, for you have gathered a group of beings who are willing to help you pray and understand how this all works. Divine Love and all of the Power of the Universe is around you, waiting only for you to activate it. These meetings for prayer are being attended by many spirit beings, who are also concentrating on your efforts. This helps to activate All of God's many attributes in your minds.

There are many questions about the higher self and the over-soul. These two terms were brought up recently. The higher self is you as a whole, aware and spiritual being. The higher self lives in you as special cells or as your soul. It is also in the spirit world. It is the keeper of your record. But, as a spiritual self, it is in a group of spirits who are like-minded, in that they have attained the same level of spiritual awareness. The over-soul is what this conglomeration of spirits is called. As you become more aware and knowledgeable of spiritual things, you are expanding or growing in spirit. At times this is not obvious to you on earth. Remember that in this universe, everything is either growing or regressing. Think of the opening up of a rose and how each petal is loosened, until it becomes a full bloom and all the petals are opened. On earth this flower then dies as the petals drop off, and the rose is no longer seen. What remains are the seeds for more roses. You, as spiritual beings, could compare yourselves to a rose in the process of understanding and learning about spiritual matters. When you have reached a level of complete openness, you simply move to a higher spiritual level and start the process over again. If at any time you are not expanding and learning, you will begin to become smaller and regress to a point where you are dropped off into lower levels of understanding to learn the same lessons over again.

Each of you is expanding, some faster than others, but so far all of you are growing through these sessions and your daily meditations and prayers. There are many spirit beings present now, including the higher selves of each person meeting in the group. As your spiritual awareness grows, the higher self is able to progress to higher levels where larger groups of beings live. Allow us to give an analogy. Imagine that each being is a ball of light, and the more you learn in spiritual matters, the brighter the light inside you becomes and the larger the radius of your ability to shine. Then each higher level you reach is brighter by your own spirit and the spirits of the others in the over-soul. The over-soul is made up of a larger number of beings. As you see, each step gives you more power to shine and therefore the ability to understand easier. But when you fail to grow, you become bogged down in earthly matters and forget your spiritual self, then your light becomes dimmer and your higher self becomes smaller, and you drop to lower levels of understanding. Consider that the ability to shine is your knowledge. Then in your earthly life you will begin to make good decisions, as in your ability to find easier ways to make a living and to live life in happiness and contentment. Not only does your spiritual knowledge grow, but also your earthly abilities are activated. The struggle for a life of happiness and worldly goods will be easier. You will find the things that are important in life. You will know when to act and when not to. These decisions will come naturally to you, as you grow spiritually.

Our message to each of you is to continue in this good work. Prepare to live your earthly life more easily and your spiritual life in new, higher levels of understanding. Pray daily and ask God to give you more understanding. Pray that the light of knowledge will open your mind to comprehend what is given. Also we urge each of you to pray daily and to meet with this group weekly. Something powerful happens when a group comes together to pray and learn—it is good and wonderful.

Question us in your mind, or ask for our help; we are available to each of you at any time. We do not live in time and space dimensions. We love each of you and pray for you to open your minds to more and more.

The Brotherhood

Your Choice: Unlimited Growth in God
(Mary, October 23, 1988)

Welcome to another session, and I am happy that you have not forgotten to meet and pray. Meditation and prayer is what will get you through the coming times. I do not like to keep repeating that these times will be disastrous, but they will. This you already know. There will be storms and earthquakes, which will cause you some distress, but you my children, continue to pray and to meet. As you know, the Brotherhood and I and all the rest in spirit will be communing with you through your individual minds. Do not rely on any person on earth for guidance in these coming times. It will be up to each of you to open and learn spiritually what you can. **It will be your own responsibility to gain all the know-how you can, to open your mind to receive instruction.**

Today we will continue with what the Brotherhood has given you on the higher self and the over-soul. Understand that the higher self is you, and it can also be someone else. As you grow in spirit and have more abilities open to you, your higher self grows too. When you reach a certain level in the spirit world, the higher self can incarnate on earth as one, two or more people at the same time. It takes a level of competency to be able to grow in this way. The higher self must be able to maintain contact and keep an accurate record of each person's life events. Each thought and each action is to be recorded and kept up with. There could be another person on earth with the same higher self. Usually you will never meet this person, for in order to grow faster, the higher self will incarnate into different cultures, different sexes or different races. Also, in one life you may not be either rich or poor, but in other lives you could be one or both. The art of living in multiples gives your higher self a chance to advance at a faster rate of growth. It also is able to learn new lessons and practice new and, at times, old lessons learned.

The point in which your higher self could possibly do this type of incarnation is in a higher level and with the help of a larger over-soul. This is simply information for you about the spirit world and how it works. **The main point to remember is that you are always in a process of expanding or contracting.** It is up to you, through your choices, which way you will grow. The up or down is a metaphor, because in actuality there is neither up nor down. There is neither time nor space in the spirit world. We are above living in these limited dimensions. But in the different dimensions of the physical world is where you are able to practice your lessons. So do not think for one minute that we are putting your three-dimensional world down. It has its place and its purpose in your growth. It is important to your spiritual growth. **In spirit and in all worlds, there is only God or nothing.** And in nothing there is a void, and it is blank. This is the death you all fear. But understand that it is never necessary for you to die in this manner. It is your choice or because of your thought patterns, attitudes, actions or inaction that this occurs.

So you are to act, and act positively, in order to grow. You are to pray and meditate to facilitate your growth. When you act, there are consequences, but at least you are doing and learning. But to act with knowledge and forethought is to grow. When you do nothing but coast along on the shirttails of others, you are regressing and losing ground. All growth, as you know by now, takes place in your mind. All prayer is in your mind, and it is with your mind that you are able to meditate. Care for your thoughts. **Watch what is in your mind, and you will be guarding the door to the kingdom of heaven.**

As you think, so you will be! This has been said in many ways and in many languages. It is an eternal truth. Now allow us to consider your daily thinking and how it affects your life and spiritual growth. Assume you have a problem—money, health, school, work-related, or with your spouse. The type of problem has nothing to do with it; it is simply a problem. How do you handle this problem? Do you concentrate on the problem by worrying? Can you solve it by becoming alarmed and concerned? This is the way I hear some people pray: "Oh, Lord, I have this problem, _____." And it is repeated and repeated in detail in their mind. All concentration is on the problem and how terrible it is and how much worse it could get. "Oh, what if . . . ?" These are the words that should set bells to ringing and alarms going off in your mind. No amount of "what if's" will cure the problem. Seeing the worst of any situation will not alleviate it.

Now here is a better way to deal with your problems: Pray and tell God in one short sentence what the problem is. Confess your inability to solve it. Ask for guidance and for help. Quiet your mind until you can gain a sense of releasing the problem to God. Thank God for the answer to the problem, and continue to release the problem. Now here is the hard part. When you are prone to worry, instead, remind yourself that this is in God's

Hands and is being solved in spiritual ways. Soon you will see the results. God's result in solving a problem always comes in the right way at the right time, and for the good of all concerned. Continue to thank God and ask Him to help you to increase your faith, for it is by faith that your prayers are answered. Remember that Faith is the hope of the unseen answer to your prayer.

Not only are you asking for God's help and receiving it, but there are many spiritual beings on a higher level who have gained an interest in all who are seeking truth and knowledge. They are working to help you grow spiritually because as they help you, they help themselves. But don't think this is selfish; it is the way God works. So as you go about your coming days, you will have more confidence in your abilities, at work or at home. Your every endeavor will be strengthened by all this spiritual help you are receiving. Remember that we are not genies. However, we are in constant prayer for you and in this way you will see a difference in the coming year. You are growing and expanding; keep up the good work. Keep on keeping on with your prayers and meditations. The answers will come; soon one day you will simply know and not be aware that you know. It will be easier and easier with each prayer.

Mary, Mother of Jesus

Your Strength as a Group
(Brotherhood, October 30, 1988)

We are proud of the progress being made. Each person who prays and talks to God in his or her mind and heart, progresses.

We emphasize the family unit today for a reason. As a unit you have pledged to encourage your mother (Annie) in her work with Mary. It is in working with Spirit and with God that you are progressing as a unit. The group as a whole is progressing at a rapid rate of growth. There are some of you individually who are not as advanced as the others, but through the efforts of the unit you are progressing faster within this group. Alone your efforts would not be as powerful.

This is our lesson today—how as a family group and a praying group, you advance. God wishes to instruct you in prayer. He is aware of your misconceptions. Understand that prayer is set up to be activated automatically. It is activated by your sincere and earnest seeking of God. That is why, when you are in trouble or you are very frightened, your prayer is answered faster. It is the activating of the heart and mind in unison that opens the door to your answers.

In the beginning, when God set up the natural and physical laws of the Universe, He also set up your ability to seek His help. You call it prayer, but there is no magic in this word; it could be called petition or any other word. The act of praying is not what sets up your answer. The repetition of your prayers at times helps you acquire the right mindset, but this is activated in your mind by the uniting of heart and mind. When you have activated this mindset, then you will know what it feels like. It takes your desire, the agreement of your heart and mind, and faith that God will answer. The words or ideas of The Lord's Prayer are set up in such a way that they activate the opening of the switch, or the turning of the dial, to the answer of your prayer.

As you see, the idea of God as the old man who sits on a cloud and enjoys punishing you, and who at times grants your wishes and at times does not, is wrong. Like electricity, gravity and the law of relativity, the answers to your prayers are there when you make the connection. God does not desire for any person to be neglected or have hard times. **God is Pure Love. Because He loves unconditionally, He set up the rules or laws to ensure that you are cared for without interfering with your freedom of choice.** Prayer can be activated automatically, but there is power in the uniting of your prayers. For with a group as a unit, you have more power to turn the right knobs, or set the dial correctly, for the answers to your prayers.

It takes faith to receive what you ask for. At times the faith of one alone may be weak, and one may find it difficult to maintain faith. But in a group unit there is strength. That is why it is good to unite in a church. It gives you the ability and strength of the group. Let us use an analogy. Say you are one light bulb emitting light alone. There is light given off, but when you are joined by many light bulbs, what happens? There is much light, which can be seen even into the heavens. When your astronauts were up in space once, there was a city that turned on its lights as they passed over, high in space. The city was so illuminated that it could be seen in space. This was Perth, Australia, remember? As you unite to pray in a group, individually you are strengthened by the number and faith of your group.

Each of you will be seeing a renewal and opening of your home and each individual in it. There is progress both in spirit and in your rewards on earth. Remember, "Thy kingdom come; Thy will be done on earth as it is in heaven." As you seek God and set up the lines of communication, you are opening up the switches to have more and more spiritual good come into your life. Your mind will find ways to solve problems. New opportunities will come, doors will be opened and you will find an increase of All Good—All Good in the form of Pure Energy, which is God's Power. As you ask God to help you understand and live this life the highest and best way possible, you open doors that no one else could open for you. But, one thing for sure, you will find that your motives, ideas, desires and needs are changing. God can work with these changes. It's never too late to increase your spiritual learning.

Make a commitment today—to work with God in every-thing, to open the door to your mind and heart to God, to be led by God-power alone, and to give God the opportunity to teach you in ways that will be miraculous to your eyes. There is substance from which God can bring into your life all the good you seek for yourself and others. Now, as you desire this good, remember that what you desire for others is what you will be getting. So as you pray for yourself, always include others in your prayers, especially those who can harm you, such as criminals. Pray for relatives and co-workers. In this way you open the switch to your good. **Prayer is a two-way street; as you pray for others, it will be done to you.** If you are selfish or envious and pray only for others to help yourself, then you negate the good that God has prepared for you. Pray for your good and for each person on earth to receive their own good. There is enough substance in the Universe for everybody. There is no shortage. It is like electricity, as you use light and electrical power, you have not taken away from anyone else. Their house is lit also; they use their power in their own way and you use yours.

The Brotherhood

"Seek Ye First the Kingdom of God"
(Jesus via Brotherhood, November 5, 1988)

Today our "Big Brother," Jesus, will give the message. We are giving Jesus this status as our Big Brother to demonstrate to you the esteem and love that we have for Him. His life on earth was not an easy life, but He completed His life goals in that one lifetime. He was faithful and diligent to the end of that life. He continues to live and is continuing in His work, which is to demonstrate to each person or soul the way to live and complete its life goals. Big Brother is our term of endearment for Him. In truth and in reality, we are all children of God, and He loves each of us equally. Now, here is Jesus with today's lesson.

(Jesus)

Good morning, family. I have been in close communion with our Father God and am aware of all your individual and group progress. It is a pleasure to see that you have taken upon yourselves the seeking of God and His Truth. This is my whole ambition for every soul who has ever lived, to come into this close communion with our Source and Creator.

I give you words of Truth and comfort. In my lifetime on earth, I repeated this lesson many times. In the Bible it occurs only once. But believe me when I say, this is a very important issue to remember and take into your heart and mind: "Seek ye first the kingdom of God, and all these things will be added to you." This was almost a daily lesson that I gave my disciples and one of the most important lessons to learn. Each of you have committed to seeking the kingdom of God, which is found only within you. In setting your priority on God and His Words, you individually and as a group have activated His reward, that is, all things will be added to you. You no longer have a need to worry or become concerned with any earthly or physical issue—these concerns of your physical life, your finances, security as it concerns your family, and all responsibilities. As you continue to seek God and set your sights and eyes on God in your life, these are added benefits. God has the Power to provide All for you. Think on this one sentence again. **God has All the Power to provide for your every need.** This is an automatic process, which is activated only by your continual seeking of God and of how to improve your spiritual life.

Is this not wonderful? When you think of God as a Father-figure, you come closer to understanding the care, protection and love that He gives everyone. This does not mean you will not have concerns. It means you now have the assurance that God is providing for your every need. While I was on earth and traveling about the countryside to teach, the others in my group became upset from time to time and worried about earthly concerns like food, shelter, clothing, medical care, money, family left at home—all the things that you can still worry about today. This was the lesson that I kept repeating to them in that day, and one that is important for you to understand today. **Your main goal and your main mission will be com-**

pleted only as you seek to find God and activate His Energy into your life. Then you will have complete satisfaction and protection for you and those you love.

My Disciples were very human and had all the same concerns you have in this day. They also worried about their finances, loved ones, family, home, work, and what all this means. Remember, each of them had family as you do, but we did not have the telephone or any method of communicating with them. It was months and at times years before they visited their individual homes. When they did visit, they found their families were well cared for and had all their needs provided.

You are already aware of my love for parables and analogies. **You are to set your sights on God and the finding of Him in your heart and mind,** just as you do when you desire to hit any target. In many games, the only way to accomplish your goal is to set your sights on what you want. For instance, in bowling, your sights are set on the first pin, not on the back row. We will say God is the first pin—see how easy it is when you can understand? Another way to see this is in the games of darts or archery, where you set your sights on the center of the target. God is the center and core of All the universe. See, as you set your sights and your ambitions and needs on God, the rest is taken care of. But, if you start to look at the outer rings of the target, and become worried that you will not hit this small dot in the center, then you are losing sight of your goal. Do not look to the outer circles, which could be considered as all your individual concerns, but keep your eyes on the small core of the universe and your inner self. Remember always that this dot may be small to you, but it is indeed large, gratifying and satisfying in many ways.

There is so much to mankind that hasn't been found yet. You are as a target, in that there are many circles of lives and bodies. But **your core, deep inside you, is the way to God and All Life.** The largest and most obvious circle is the outer, physical life you are now leading. This is your career, home, loved ones and all the things that make up your individual lives. God is in the core or center of your being and is a part of each of you. As you focus on God and His Goodness, you activate many laws that give you many benefits. These laws will make you not only smarter, wiser, richer, but more spiritually aware.

My goal continues to be the same; I am as alive today as I was when I was on earth daily. My goal is to bring many (people) to the understanding of the Truth, which is God. I have the same feelings of love and concern for each of you as I did 2000 years ago. I have not been an active part of this group, but believe me, I am aware of your progress and work in seeking God. There are many way-showers in life and on earth. Sometimes they are not aware of their calling, but in true love they will include you in prayers and meditations, which activates in each person many benefits. As you each grow in spirit, your loved ones will be aided, in the physical and in their spiritual needs. As you continue to pray for your loved ones and the world in general, you become a way-shower, and this activates many spiritual benefits and earthly benefits.

This week I have felt a renewed hope in each of you; some feel it stronger than others, but as you continue to work with this group, you have the benefit of the progress of the whole. Release consciously your needs and concerns to God the Father, and have the assurance that He loves you more than your earthly parents could. He is aware of all your desires and needs. There is nothing impossible to Him, so you can release all your concerns to God and have the hope of good for all your concerns.

Now all this will not happen instantly. It could, but each of you must learn many lessons in this life. The good will come gradually as you become accustomed to giving all your attention to God and your spiritual life. When you come across a problem in your life, ask yourself this question: What spiritual lesson is there in this for me to learn? Pray for more wisdom in making choices, more understanding in your relationship with all people, more love for each person in your family and in the world.

Grow in spirit and in love. You have the prayers and good wishes of many, in many worlds, for you are a beacon of light in this part of the world. As more and more people come to seek God in their hearts and minds, there will be more peace and more of All good things.

This, however, does not mean that the coming events,[9] of which my Mother Mary has warned you, will not occur. These events were set into motion many millions of years ago and are now reaching earth. I came 2000 years ago because I wanted to show people that this was an opportunity to seek God and to advance in Spirit. The references to heaven and hell were to give the people of that time this knowledge. The ability to seek God and All His Goodness was as necessary then as it is today. Prepare for these events that will turn your world on its side. This will be a literal and a spiritual turning; all events are both physical and spiritual. When you understand this, you will have activated many "things" in your mind, life and world.

Today I wish to give you the same hope and love that I have been giving the world all these years. I pray that you will continue in this search for Truth in all areas of your lives. My blessings and prayers are upon you. My love is with you each day of your life as you continue to seek God and His kingdom. You are doing good when you seek to advance spiritually. Now comes your reward; you will see that those for whom you pray are being helped. Remember always how very much you are loved, Divinely Loved, and in God's Good, where we all are.

Jesus of Nazareth

---

[9] The coming earth changes.

CHAPTER

4

Pray and Meditate Daily

Daily Prayer: Your Lifeline to God
(Brotherhood, November 9, 1988)

TODAY WE WILL CONTINUE with Prayer and Meditation. We feel this is too important not to dwell on this subject. In activating your lifeline and your prayers to God, you will have more of everything you need in order to learn your lessons and live this lifetime. In practicing your prayers and meditations, you will not fail, as so many do.

This is what happened to the Greek immigrant's son who lost his race.[10] He began with earnestness and sincerity to seek God in all his endeavors. He had a good prayer line established, but he became engrossed with what other people thought, instead of what God thought. He lost sight of his God-view. His point of contact was lost and so was the race.

---

[10] Dukakis (Massachusetts governor, U.S. presidential candidate in the election of 1988)

And so, we urge you to keep the lines of your prayer life activated daily. This will insure your abilities to discern, to make good decisions, to see the truth in every situation and to "know." In "knowing," you will simply not become swayed by any poll or anyone's opinion. You will not seek to find your answers among men, but in the very word of God, as it is given to your mind and heart. You will not look to any person for their viewpoint, ask for advice from another human or become indebted to anyone but God. And remember, God forgives your debts as you forgive your debtors.

The other man,[11] who won, sought God's help and prayed much, as did his wife. It really was the wife of this man who instigated his ability to keep the lines of communication opened with the process of prayer. At the beginning of this race, he was behind and was giving in to too many different opinions and advice. It was confusing him, but he did have confidence in his wife. This is where he sought his advice. She reminded him of their ability to pray and seek God's guidance instead of man's. She was with him at every point and was in a constant attitude of prayer. True, she does not understand that prayer is activated automatically, but she did remain in constant prayer, lest God forget. In so doing, she activated the prayer lines and the process was set into motion. She was diligent and had the foresight to get the new President to seek God's help. This was not so much to win, as to be guided daily.

They are accustomed to the clatter of this kind of life. The other man was overwhelmed by the opinions of the so-called "experts." There is only one expert, and that is God. When you remember that everything that God is, is available to you, you win also. This man began to pray for the ability to use this power to help the world and to build a strong nation. He returned to the principles on which this nation was founded. The very nation itself, as a whole, was also praying for its continuation. This wife and new first lady is truly that. She is

---

[11] Then-President-elect George Bush

wise and loving. Her motives and understanding are for the good of every person on earth. It will be her influences that will be felt in this nation.

We urge you to continue to pray for the good of this nation and for good leadership to guide the affairs of the world. This is your ability to help establish the truth in all things. We urge you also to pray for your scientists to see the truth about this planet and to have a government which will act on these truths. Pray that you will be prepared for the coming events and that your nation will see and prepare, but remember to pray for the world and all nations to prepare.

Take this lesson and apply it to your everyday life. There is much to be gained, and your goals will be easier to attain. Allow us to begin with those who are working out of the home in order to provide money. Your responsibilities to provide for your home, family and yourself will be aided as you pray. Do not feel guilty about asking God for the money to provide a good life for yourself and your family. This is God's pleasure to give. As you activate the prayer lines and keep them opened, you will find new opportunities to live life, with more goods to make your life easier. This is good, to pray for the money to buy your family the "things" it needs in order to live without a struggle. It is not God's will for any of His children to struggle through life. Life should be a joy, and there should be all good things added to your life. Ask for new opportunities to earn more money and to fulfill your creative and internal desires to succeed. This is a good prayer.

For those who are in school, pray for your mind to open to understand fully what you are taught each day. Ask for the help to learn and to become the man you desire to be. It will be through your learning that you grow. Do not make the mistake of the loser in this presidential race. He forgot to seek God's advice and instead looked to his friends and those around him to advise and guide his actions. You are responsible for your actions; it will be you alone who suffers by any wrong decisions you make alone or with others. It is better to make your decisions with God's help and go against the crowd, than to be influenced by people who don't know any more than you. Learn to seek your decisions in your mind and heart. You will know what is good for you and what is not. This is the question you are to ask in all decisions: is this good for me, my loved ones and my future?

To all people, seek God in everything—your finances, career or job, future, decisions, desires, and for every good "thing." This is the way for God to answer your prayers. Remember that prayer is an automatic process that allows your good to flow through you as you grow in spirit and truth. Some people have been able to activate the ability to receive their good without too much effort, but this process was learned in other lifetimes. This is your lifetime. Find how to believe in yourself, your future and God. Keep the dials of your prayer line opened and flowing with All Good. It takes continuous prayer, and it must be a daily event, in order to keep the good flowing your way. Make this your utmost project: to stay in an attitude of prayer.

The Brotherhood

Your Prayer Activates Your Answers
(Mary, November 9, 1988)

I will give a message to the family, but it is Jesus who desires to speak now. My blessings are upon you as you go through the days of your life. I urge you to pray and give much thought to preparing your minds and hearts for the coming season of joy. This is my message to each of you: Prayer and Meditation. This sounds like a repeat of what has been given before, and it is, but it is a very important action and calls for much effort on your part. The action is the activating of your answer to all your prayers. In meditation you commune with God and His great mind, which guides you in all your ways. Now here is Jesus.

Judge Your Efforts by Their Fruits
(Jesus, November 9, 1988)

Dear ones, greetings from me and from the Father God. Our desire is to have you in close communion with us at all times. It is only in prayer and meditation that you will develop the abilities which will help you. Look at what has happened in your life since you have committed to prayer. It has all been good, has it not? Judge then by the way you feel and see this communication. Is it bringing you good results? This is how to judge what is true or what is not. The results are the proof of the matter.

The parable of the fig tree is what this issue is all about. Once, when I and my disciples were traveling about the countryside in what is now called Israel, we came upon a fig tree. This tree was barren and had not produced fruit. It would be good for you to read the story in the Bible, as I lived it and have not particularly read about it. I cursed the tree for being barren—that is, I stated it would be best to cut this tree down, for it was not bearing fruit as it should. (Mk 11:13-14, Lk 13:6-7) The Disciples wanted to know why I did this. It is by the end product that an issue or thing is known.

Now allow me to tell you this same principle in today's language. When you go to work and do a good job, you expect to be paid, do you not? When you buy an article or some material good, you expect it to perform, right? If you were to take the time to plant a fruit tree, you would expect this tree to give fruit. How do you judge your work, your material goods or your fruit tree? It is by the end results, is it not? The end result of your work performance is a salary. The end result of the purchase of your material goods is the performance of these goods. The end result of a fruit tree is the fruit, is it not? Then, of what use is a job, if it were not for the salary? Of what good are the purchased goods, if they do not perform as expected? And of what good is a fruit tree that does not bear fruit? It is by the results that you value and judge everything in your life.

These lessons and these teachings then must bear the fruit of being a help to each of you. It is in this way that you judge what is truth. It is by the end results of our work that you can judge truth. I urge you to judge these lessons and all that you learn and practice. When you are receiving the expected results, then you can say, this is truth. But if what you are being taught is not what you are receiving in end results, then is it truth? Everything is known by its end results, even truth. God is able to prove Himself to each of you. His teachings are worthy of the end results, which you are now receiving. Has not your understanding and knowledge increased? Have you not noticed a feeling of love and hope in your life? Do you see the good in all situations, or do you see negative results?

I think you are seeing truth, and this is proof to you. The feelings and blessings which you are receiving are proof of this way of life. By your fruits you will also be known. Everything is known by its fruits. How do you know your friends? By the way they treat you, is this not so? A friend would not cause you any harm, neither would your Creator. **Love is demonstrated by its actions.** God also demonstrates by His actions. Learn all you can, and bring me the questions that you do not understand. In explaining to you those things that remain a mystery, you gain much knowledge and wisdom. This is very good for you and this world.

Judge the answers to your prayers. Are you receiving what you pray for, or better? I know that when you have learned to pray rightly, you will. When you use all the keys, you will have the end results you desire. God does not cause you any suffering; this is a fallacy. God desires only good for each of you. It is His sincere desire to help you see the good in every situation. This is how to tell when you have contacted God.

Have faith in your inner ability to judge. Pray for wisdom and for knowledge to judge what is being given to each of you. It is your faith and desire to stretch your reach to God; that will give you the end results. **It is through you that God will**

answer your prayers. It will not be magic, but Divine. Your faith is what aids your answers to come quickly. Your expectation of receiving only your good is what will aid also.

Reread the key[12] that was given you recently. In this way you will understand more. Each time you reread and relearn a lesson, it goes deeper into your mind. In your mind it becomes strong, as its truth is connected to God's Truth.

Think about how you are beginning to understand more. Each week as you practice what you have learned, you grow, and it is only in spiritual growth that you succeed. Go with your inner feelings and thoughts. Ask God the Father to guide you and lead you. I am with each of you, as is the Brotherhood, which is the Holy Ghost.

Jesus of Nazareth

---

[12] "The Key to the Riddle" given Sept. 9, 1988 (pages 18-19).

5

The Thanksgiving Season

Give Thanks to Increase Your Good
(Brotherhood, November 20, 1988)

WE ARE AWARE that in your nation this week you are celebrating Thanksgiving. This is a good way to increase your good. Your forefathers must have been aware of the spiritual principle of giving thanks and being grateful. This is an important part of your prayer cycle—**to constantly be thankful for everything, and, most important, for this life and all its opportunities to grow spiritually.**

As you already know, prayer is an automatic response to your sincere seeking to grow spiritually. Take all you have learned so far and put it together to increase your knowledge of what is reality and what is an illusion. On earth your illusions are three-dimensional, and it is hard to know what is reality and what is illusion. But, through your seeking God and Truth in your mind, you are finding the answers to these and many questions. You are proving what is good and what is not. Have you not each found improvement in your lives—some in material ways and others in emotional and mental states? Your entire self will be improved. Your entire being, which includes the physical, emotional, mental, astral, psychic, protoplasmic, ethereal and spiritual selves, will show improvement. True, in some of these areas you will not have physical evidence of this improvement. But, believe me, it is felt and sensed by the inner you.

Being grateful for the knowledge that you have acquired aids the answers to your prayers. As you are grateful for what you have and for what is being sent to you, the answers will not stop. The more grateful you are, and we are speaking of sincere gratitude, the easier it is to receive your good. In the future your good will be in every area of yourself and on all planes.

How do you express your gratitude?—by simply having the attitude of gratefulness. See the similarity? Gratitude and attitude! These two thoughts are similar, in that **your gratitude is an attitude, one that keeps you inside the flow of All Good, which is God.** When you can maintain the attitude of gratefulness throughout each day, you are well on your way to growth, spiritually and in every other area. Your psychic abilities increase, your protoplasmic body is in constant activation and you grow spiritually. This also brings your emotions and mental attributes into alignment with God.

Appreciation is another way to show gratitude. What you appreciate and love comes to you in a big way. When you appreciate and love God in your heart and mind, you are calling on the Highest Power in the Universe. He is real and is only waiting for you to call on Him. God is the only One who can help you in every way. God is what we are giving you; it is an awareness of His Goodness and Love. Appreciate this wonderful love, which does not require anything of you but acceptance.

Activate your lines of communication with God-Mind through your gratefulness for all His Good gifts. Think—you have the Power of the Universe in your mind. Become an appreciative and grateful individual, and see how great is your spiritual growth. Do not wait for evidence of God's Love. It is evident in everything you see, do, feel, hear and are aware of. Look to the natural world; see the sun, stars, oceans, animals and plants. Look to the family unit and feel the love that can be in this type of group. This love is a part of your emotional well-being. This is God's Love. Listen to the music of your time and hear the harmonies as they are released into the air. Look to your homes, jobs, your children, pets, family affairs, friends; see the love of God in this arena. Be grateful for the awareness of your higher self and your spiritual self. There is much to be grateful for now—for the ability to think and reason, to create and enjoy, to love and be loved, to learn and perfect your spirit—these are gifts of God—for this life—for your knowledge of the eternity of life—for the coming together to meet with these loved ones, and to hear and learn.

Know that as you increase your gratefulness, God will be happy to give you more to be grateful for. God loves a happy and grateful heart. This is Truth. Do you not love to help those who are grateful for your help? Do you feel like giving to an ungrateful person? Remember it is an attitude, and not words alone, that brings the rewards of gratitude. This attitude is maintained by becoming aware of the beauty in your life, telling God in your prayers that you are grateful for All His gifts—family, friends, job, money, life, children, possessions, spiritual benefits and for all the wonderful gifts that are now being sent to you from on high. There is continuous flow of Good to you and for those in your prayers. As you ask and pray for others, you are rewarded. Keep a list in each home of people for whom you pray, and include the world. Open up your ability to receive wider, by prayer and an attitude of gratefulness.

We are in a constant attitude of gratefulness for each of you and for the spiritual growth that is happening in each person. Our prayer is for an increase of all good things in all your lives, but our main concern is with your spiritual life. When your spiritual life is healed and blessed, then all parts of your life are healed and blessed. Most of the problems of this world are caused by a lack of spirituality. This is true of every person and every life. Ask God for what will make your life easier. Ask for opportunities to grow spiritually and seek to know more of God. He will provide for all your needs. Learn to rely and depend on God for all things. Ask Him to help with those areas of your life that you wish to change. Be grateful for God and His ability to help you change.

Now go and practice this lesson in this week of your Thanksgiving. See your emotional and mental lives be the first to improve—but know that improvement is in all areas of your life. Our love, peace and prayers are with you each day.

The Brotherhood

Seek Good Daily for All
(Mary, November 20, 1988)

I have been aware of this day and of the importance of this week. The Brotherhood have given you a good lesson on the importance of gratitude in your prayer life, but allow me to urge you to become even more grateful for all your opportunities and challenges in the coming days. There will be many challenges, but know that you can learn through every experience. **Place yourselves in God's hands and allow His Spirit to charge and activate every area of your life.** As you go through these coming days, you will be better able to see hope and hear the inner voice as it guides you. Rely completely on God and on the spiritual side of your nature. This is what will be your physical and spiritual salvation. I am not talking of salvation in the same terms as it is used by many churches, for, as you know, your salvation is not dependent on any outer ceremony or confession. It is dependent on your sincere seeking, in your heart and mind, of God and His Truth.

Continue to hold your prayer daily and activate the process of good, which enters not only your life, but also your loved ones' lives. There is much good being released into the world. Be constantly grateful for every evidence of God's good in your lives. Know that as you pray for others and your world, you are first in line for all good. Do you remember Jesus' words to the effect that, "As you do it unto one of the least, you are doing it unto me?" (Mt 26:40) This is what he meant, that as you pray and seek good for other people and loved ones, you are helping Jesus in His prayers for this world and all people who have ever lived on it. As you continue to pray for this planet and the people of this world, you are increasing your staying power and abilities to survive all changes.

Keep part of your prayers as gratitude, because you cannot help but be grateful for all the answers. There is hope in every situation, no matter how dark or dismal it appears. Another time Jesus told the people not to look to appearances but to judge righteous judgments. What he meant was, know that what is on the outside is not all there is to life. You know that changes occur in the inner aspects of man. True changes are always from the inside out, not the other way. **Look for changes in your life to occur inside your heart and mind first, and then these same changes for good will appear on the outer edges of your life.** Be grateful for every small change for the better that you see, hear, or sense.

I am grateful to the people who are honestly searching. Their children and grandchildren will be aided. I ask that you add all people who you know and their children to your prayer list. Through your prayers, each person will be helped in their own way and through their own choices. Truth and God work through many different methods. They can be obtained in different ways and through different avenues. Do not feel that every person will find their good the way you do. It is the sincere seeking that activates the avenues to God. **There are many roads to God, and there are as many different methods to be one with God as there are people.** Each is unique and individual, and each will have their own way of searching for God. The proof is in their ability to love and be at peace. If you are receiving good, are satisfied and feel God's love, then you are on the right track. There is no wrong way to go to God. Is there a wrong way to go to a hospital for help? No, and so there are no wrong ways to seek God. **It is in each person's heart and mind that the connection to God is made, no matter what outer method is used.** All religions and all manners of prayer are good, as long as you are seeking God with a sincere heart and mind.

Because you search, you will be well prepared for the coming events, and your lives will be enhanced in every way. We are as grateful for this as you should be. Because you seek and open your minds to hear, we are able to give you Truth. We are as alive and real as you are. This knowledge should give you the assurance of how life is eternal and how alive you will always be. Your fear of death will leave and your fear of the coming events will dissipate, as the storm clouds do when the sun appears.

Do not fear opening your minds and hearts to God, for, as you see, He is only Goodness and Love. You cannot lose when you are using the Power and Energy of He who created it All. Meditate and pray daily. As some of you begin this busy holiday season, it will be hard to find the time, but know that it is important to you and your strength and energy physically. **Find the time, and do not allow anything to deter you from seeking God** and the spiritual help, which will be your easiest way of living through the busy season ahead and the coming earth changes.

There is much that you can do with your thoughts, for all life is lived in the mental and emotional level on earth. Think of this! You always have control of your thoughts, and as you learn to control your thoughts and feelings, you are progressing. I see God's good flowing through each of your lives. There is much to be grateful for.

Now, practice what you have learned in your mind, daily, and bring into your thoughts, prayers—for you, your loved ones, and your world. We also are praying for you and are interested in each of you. Our love, that is, mine and Joseph's, is with you as you continue to learn and to practice these lessons.

Mary, Mother of Jesus

The Meaning of Harvest
(Brotherhood, November 26, 1988)

We do have a special message for the family group. It will be in keeping with this week's time of giving thanks and being thankful. This is a very important part of praying and is a good way to pray.

During this week of Thanksgiving, you have had a good feast day in which to enjoy family, friends and also the good bounty of this year's harvest. When you live in a city, you forget about harvest time and the importance of having a good harvest. You don't realize what a good harvest means. You have a feeling of harvest each time you go to the store to purchase some item. It is not something you usually think about. In schools, this season is given a different meaning with the celebration of Hallow's Eve, and this day is also called Turkey day.

Allow us some time for a simple history lesson. In years past, when people lived off the land, this time of harvest was a joyous time and a time of much work, for the fruits of each plant remained on the vine or stalk long enough to ripen, and then there was a short time to pick and prepare them for storage. It was a time of long hours, of working side by side, and of everyone helping out. The signs of harvest were very visible to all. When the harvest was in the air, it could be smelled, tasted, seen, heard and felt.

In today's time, these pleasures are gone. You simply need go to a store, and all your bounty is provided you. There is no feeling of tiredness, or smells of ripened fruit and vegetables. The feel of grain in your hands is gone, as are the sights of trees laden with fruit. The laughter of people gathering together to reap the harvest is not heard now. This is sad, in that there was much pleasure from the harvest time and there were visible lessons to learn.

What we want you to do is to consider your requests as the planting time of the year. You enter your petitions to God through your prayers, and then you have faith that these petitions will be answered with what you have asked for, or better. In analogy, this is the springtime of your year, and it is the petitioning time for your needs, wants and desires. In the growing season of your earth, there comes the time to wait for the seeds to break out of the ground and to grow strong. This time requires you to do something. You must water, hoe the ground and watch for insects and other animals who will take the young shoots, but mostly you are waiting and waiting for the fruits and vegetables to ripen. Then the time of harvest comes, and there is much activity and more work than you can imagine. Soon all the work has been done, and the crops have been harvested and stored for the coming year. Then comes the time of reflection and planning.

Well, loved ones, the same events can be viewed in the prayer process. There is the time of planting, which are your requests. There is the time of waiting and of keeping the insects and animals from the crop; this is the time to use faith and watch your thoughts for any worry. Then it is the time of harvest, when your prayers are visible and usable to you. Later comes a time of reflection and planning. We will take each step slowly and give you pointers on how to be more effective in praying.

We will begin with the last. Remember Jesus' words to the effect that: the last shall be first and the first shall be last. This is a time of using the last part first, the planning and reflecting time. In this period of time, you are deciding what it is you need in order to live your life in comfort and peace. In what set of circumstances do you wish to live? Be honest and not extravagant. This is a serious time of reflection. **With God all things are possible, but in your mind you must ask for what is visible to you.** When you ask God for a set of circumstances, can you actually see yourself living in these conditions, managing the lifestyle you would like? Know that each set of circumstances requires its own payment. In order to have a business of your own, you must be willing to work hard to get it going and sustain it. You must also be willing to put aside your need for entertainment and enjoyment. It is all work, for a long while. This is how you are to look at your chosen lifestyle. Reflecting is simply a way to think. It means you are considering all the odds and all the evens to see the complete picture. Take this time, now, to plan each phase of your life. What do you truly want with all your heart? What are you willing to work for? Start with your body and its appearance, then go to your career or job, your home and all your possessions, your loved ones. Make lists of what you desire, and think on these desires for a few days. Then make another list of what you are willing to have, with all its required payments in time, effort, sacrifice and energy. Now you are ready to plant.

Next comes the planting time, or the time to seed your prayers with requests. Now that you have reflected and taken time to contemplate your earnest desires, you are ready to petition God and All His Abundance. Keep a list of your prayers in a notebook or tablet of some kind. Set the date of the petition on it, pray and tell God simply, honestly, and sincerely of these requests. Get quiet inside yourself and feel the presence of God as He listens to your petitions.

Now comes the hard part, the waiting and keeping your hopes high. Now is the time to use statements of faith and to read inspirational books, and the Bible, about faith. You will be talking to yourself much during this time. This is the time to be grateful and give thanks to God. This is a good time to count your blessings. How do you give God thanks? How do you bless? How do you keep hope and faith alive in your heart? First, count your blessings, such as your life, health, family, job, career, possessions, mate and life partner, parents, children, clothing, air, water, food, the ability to move about, your education, your ability to learn, your spiritual growth, love, peace, contentment, feet, your talents, your mind. These are only a few of the things and conditions that you can count as blessings. We are sure you will have many more individualized blessings. This is, in a way, making a statement of faith. **You may ask God to increase your faith.** You can also take a verse of the Bible about faith and use it as a statement or prayer of faith. Read the Psalms in the Bible, and there you will find many statements of faith by David. In talking to yourself, you may also simply tell yourself that you do have faith, and that with God all things are possible, because you are first seeking to find God in your heart and mind. A good statement of faith will be similar to this:

"I believe in God and I trust God to provide for my every need, want and desire in His own way and in His own time. I am ready to receive all the good God has prepared for me in this lifetime, now."

During this time, do not become worried or upset and begin to think bad thoughts about yourself or God. This is faith used incorrectly. It is through your thoughts that you keep the doors to your prayers opened. This automatic process needs time and faith to work out the details. One thing, always ask for your highest good and for all people to receive their own highest good. When you see someone with a home, car, or other possession you would like to have, tell God, "Look, Father God, this is what I want, something like this _____ or better." See, it could become a game; enjoy this time of waiting.

In this way you are not envying, or coveting anyone else's goods, and also you are keeping a line of communication open to God the Father, provider of All.

Now comes the fun part, the time of harvest and of reaping all your rewards of life. It is easy to be grateful when you are seeing the answers to your prayers, but be grateful always for these answers. It will be easy to tell God how grateful and how much you love Him at this time. Do so, and sing songs of Thanksgiving as they well up in your soul. This prayer of thankfulness should be one that is said daily.

Now you are back at the beginning of the process, the time of planning and reflection, the time to put into action your prayers once again. Of course, know that this is an ongoing process. Now is the time to change your mind, to change your request, or to perfect to your individual taste each petition.

Try this type of praying and see the benefits and rewards. It will not take much of your time, but it will take you being consistent in keeping hope and faith alive in your heart and mind. Of course this process is an ongoing occurrence. Do keep a record of all your prayers. Change these prayers and requests as you wish. When you have your desires firm in your mind and you have maintained the faith and hope, then look for the answers to come. This is not a one-time operation. Each time you become aware of some new need or desire, begin this process. With each desire or change you wish to make in your life, take the time to reflect and determine if this is truly desired. Remember, there is a price to pay in time, effort and energy for each request. This method is to be used to heal your bodies, minds, hearts and marriages. This very same process can be and should be used to increase your awareness, understanding and perception in all spiritual areas of your life. Each time you make a new request or petition to God, enter it with the date into your log. Ask all manner of things, circumstances, improvements in life, everything you desire or want. Nothing is impossible to God, but you also must be willing to accept what you pray for. If you pray for a million dollars and have a five dollar mentality, you see there is a problem. Ask according to your belief, attitude and vision. Ask God to increase your vision and mentality to receive all the good that is waiting only for you to claim it.

Practice each day some part of these writings. **These teachings are to be used and not simply read as a novel.** These principles will activate many new and wonderful procedures and rewards in your life. Forget the past and look now to the new you, the new person who is spiritually alive and actively praying.

The Brotherhood

Appreciate All
(Mary, November 27, 1988)

I am happy to give you some words on the great event (Thanksgiving) that you have just had, this setting a day for the express purpose of giving God thanks and for showing your appreciation. Do you realize that to show appreciation is the highest form of thanksgiving? Today we will speak on appreciation.

Think on the word APPRECIATION and allow all the images of this word to flood your mind.

(pause)

Now, think once again about the word APPRECIATION and feel this word and its meanings.

(pause)

See, words are not simply symbols, but they can and do bring forth from your innermost being, sensations. The feeling of appreciation is one you are to carry with you at all times. **It is this deep feeling of appreciation for all life that lets God know how much you love Him.** Now, know that I am not saying to allow your homes to become infested with rats, mice, or insects. What I am saying is to appreciate all life in every form, even in inanimate objects. Appreciate nature and all her glories. Appreciate yourself, this body you are now using to perfect your soul. Appreciate the mind that is you. Forget not one thing to be appreciative of.

When you show your appreciation to someone or someone shows their appreciation to you, how does this make you feel? There is a warmth and an openness in this relationship. Appreciation opens the lines of communication. It allows one person to be friends with the other. Even more, you are keeping the lines of communication open to God as you appreciate all His gifts. There is so much to be grateful for—your life, spouse, home, even your transportation. Yes, this allows me to give you a good example.

In the times when Joseph and I were on earth, we traveled by foot or by donkey. Do you have the slightest idea of how long it took to get any distance? Riding on the back of a donkey was not at all like riding in one of your automobiles. Today you have many advantages and comforts to appreciate. The car, streets and businesses that are along the highways, these are the comforts of your day and time. Thank God for all the comforts you have today. Feel the gratefulness in your heart, for here is the place you commune with God.

When you appreciate something or someone, you care and tend to this person or object. As you care for the body that you now occupy, appreciate it and care for it. As you enjoy the comforts of your home, care for them; keep them as clean and as well cared for as you can. As you wipe and clean each object, say a small prayer of thanksgiving for your ability to think, move, see, hear and feel. Appreciate the money that you use to purchase each object. If they are gifts, then handle the object with love, and appreciate the friendship and relationship that caused this person to give you such a wonderful gift. As you are doing your duties in your job or career, appreciate the company and the owners who have given you this means to earn money to care for your family. Appreciate those friendships you have now, because of this place of employment. Talk to your car as you drive to work and tell it you appreciate and love it. Even inanimate objects will perform better with a little appreciation. There is life in everything on earth. The metals have a life-force, the rocks, wood, even your new plastics have a life-force in them. This life-force is God, and as you appreciate wooden furniture, plastic goods, the brass bowl, you are giving God the praise.

Now, most important of all is to appreciate your spirit, this being who makes up the inner core of you. The life that lives forever—this is your spirit self. This is the Life-force, which is connected directly to God. Appreciate His great Wisdom and Love, which allows us to incarnate and return to learn and practice becoming more like Him. Be grateful for your entire life and not only this one lifetime. Be grateful for the process of incarnating and returning at this time. **You each chose to return at this time to be on earth**, to experience these great changes which are fast approaching. **You knew that at this time there would be many opportunities to learn and perfect your soul.** Appreciate your choice and remember, your most important lesson is to become one with God.

Now, none of the "things" on earth are as important as your eternal life. Your possessions are nice and good, but they will not in any way help you live life courageously or lovingly. Appreciate your possessions, but do not allow them to become the focus of your life. Prepare for the coming events by strengthening your prayers and your abilities to listen to God in your heart and mind.

I so love the words of Francis of Assisi when he asked God to allow him to become one with Him. **"Where there is strife, let me interject peace. Where there is hate, love. Where there is sadness, happiness."** This prayer I am sure is available to each of you. It would be good to read of this man's life and see how deeply he appreciated all of nature and all of God's gifts.

I have a special place in my heart for Francis. In his lifetime, I came and helped him to set into motion the art of truly helping people. Today people say, "I have helped my fellow man—I gave a beggar a small amount of money. See how wonderful I am?" This did not help this beggar, for tomorrow he will need to beg again to have food, clothing and shelter. Give a man a fish and he will return; teach the man to fish and he will care for himself. This is what is wrong in your country today. You are making beggars of many by not teaching them to care for themselves. The changes that make a responsible man out of a beggar come from within. When you give a beggar money, also pray for this man daily. This is giving him a new perspective. Pray for the children who are growing up to become beggars. True, they chose this way of life, but **you are responsible for praying for each individual on earth.** This shows God how much you truly appreciate all He has given you.

The simple words are what get the most attention, if they are said sincerely and with love. "I appreciate all you have given me, God," and then list all things, people and events.

Mary, Mother of Jesus

6

The Christmas Season

The Birth of the Christ-Consciousness
(Brotherhood, December 3, 1988)

OUR LOVE AND OUR BLESSINGS are upon you today and each day of this month, this Holy month in which you celebrate the birth of Jesus. We will be preparing you to see and witness the miracles of His Birth. This month we will take the symbolism of this Holy birth and make it come alive in your heart.

Parents of today have nine full months to prepare for the birth of their children. So you have had time to prepare your hearts for the birth of the Christ child in your hearts and minds. The preparations include the thoughts that filled your life and the feelings of hope and gladness. All parents, in every birth, hope they are giving birth to the one child who will do and become the greatest person in this world. This is the hope of every parent, to be a part of greatness.

Each of you is taking part in the greatest birth available to any one person, **the birth of the Christ-consciousness in this world.** You are a part of the great awakening. Be filled with hope, while all about you are dire predictions and dire warnings. Your hope is in Christ-consciousness and in God, who created not only this world, but all worlds. The preparations are to be as follows:

First prepare your mind and heart by cleansing from your thoughts all lingering fear, anger, envy, arrogance, jealousy, and any critical and condemning thoughts. These are to be cleansed with prayer.

"Now, in this very moment, I cleanse from my heart and mind all thoughts that keep me from seeing and receiving the full Hope of God."

You cleanse your heart and mind with thoughts. These thoughts are simply a word, such as "cancel, cancel," when you realize you have been losing hope, or are feeling anger or fear of any kind. This is a vigil that is ever with you. It takes practice and care in guarding your thoughts. It takes love and clear-mindedness to cleanse your thoughts and feelings. It is your ideas and thoughts that make up your mind. It is with thought that you decide which direction to take and which road to use. These are your conscious thoughts. The conscious thoughts you have with you at all times. The unconscious thoughts are hidden, and these take time to change, but the only door to use to change these thoughts is the consciousness and the awareness that is available to you with each thought. Your feelings, which rise up in reaction to others, to your thoughts, to the treatment you are receiving in any given moment—these are your heart.

Take conscious thought with you each day; guard your thoughts, reactions, your every feeling. Only in this method will you prepare your heart and mind to see all the wonders. What do you do when you find you are thinking negatively? Here is one good method: simply use the words "cancel, cancel," and negate the thoughts. There are other ways to do away with unwanted thinking patterns. Tell yourself, "I am now changing my mind to find God's Hope and Love in all places, in all people and in all things." Also, you can say to yourself something like this: "I no longer need to be fearful or envious, for I know in my deepest core that God loves me and is caring for my welfare. When I am able to lift up my sight to see only good in every act and in every person, I will be receiving this good." Talk to yourself; tell yourself the truth, which is:

1. **God is Pure Love, and you are in God's Pure Love.** It surrounds you, enfolds, caresses, cares for and oversees all you place in this Love.

2. **God is Pure Energy.** It is God's Energy that activates your body and causes your thoughts to give you a new perspective and a new viewpoint.

3. **God is Pure Trustworthiness.** You can trust God to care for all that is released to His care. Know that He is with you, and see His blessings all around you.

4. State, "I feel God's Hope alive in my heart. I see with new eyes and with a new understanding. Things make sense to me now. I see the improvement in my life and in the lives of those for whom we pray. I feel the hope of the world is in God."

You could continue this with all kinds of thoughts. These are prayerful thoughts. For what you concentrate on is what will be available to you in this life and all your lives. **Your concentration is powerful, and your thoughts are alive.** Be careful with your thoughts and feelings. Upon arising from your sleep, think with your whole heart and mind. Set before you the mood for that day. If you occasionally, as one does, get up on the wrong side of the bed, and you sense you're grouchy or irritable, begin to think of Love, Hope, Energy and of God. Ask for His help to turn these feelings and thoughts around to His viewpoint.

Now, then, this is the first step in preparing for the birth of the Christ-consciousness in your mind and heart. This word, Christ, is the highest thought, the thought that is nearest God and totally in God-Mind. So prepare for the "Birth" of this consciousness that is nearest to God-Mind. Birth is simply a beginning, and this is where you are, at the beginning. You cannot begin a journey without taking that first step. Now, as you correct your thoughts and bring your feelings into alignment with God-Mind, you will see much improvement in your life, beginning with the smallest things, and soon great and grand improvements will be visible.

End each day with a prayer and begin each day with a prayer. It does not have to be a long, wordy prayer. It can be a simple, grateful spirit that you take with you as you work, enjoy and live each day. Remain in an attitude of gratefulness to God and in an attitude of concern with where your concentration is taking you. Your concentration is like the end of your journey. It is the destination of each thought. Keep guard on your concentration, thoughts and feelings. This is our lesson for this week. We urge you to practice this daily, in preparation for the event of this month. Our love, prayers and hope are with each of you. God is available to each of you with love. Feel the concern, love and hope that we have for each of you.

The Brotherhood

Become Quiet and Receive More of God
(Mary, December 4, 1988)

I have much to speak of today. This is the glorious month of December in your world, the month that celebrates many things: the Jews celebrate Hanukkah, the freedom to worship God as desired. The Christians celebrate Jesus' birth.

The worship of God is always a freedom, for the true worship is in your mind and heart. This is the place no one but you can enter. This is your Holy of Holies, so to speak. Is this, your mind and heart, not your private closet? This then is the place to truly worship God. Every morning upon arising, enter your holy of holies. Be grateful and thankful to God for all you are, your life, sight, hearing, your ability to move, think and know. These small abilities are great in themselves. I call them small, because these are the very things that you on earth quickly forget. I call them great, because without them you would suffer. This is the way to prepare your heart and mind to receive more of God.

To receive more of God is not a sacrilege. This is your basic desire. When your complete being is filled with God substance, God-mind, God-energy, you will be a different person, yet the same person, only better. Enter the quiet place you have set aside as your temple. This quiet area is the place to enter to become one with God. In a quiet mood, open your heart and mind—this is done with your thoughts, or your imagination—and once again ask God to fill your being. This is true worship. Become quiet and wait on the Lord. In the Scriptures you will find, especially in Psalms, words to the effect of "waiting on the Lord." This is the method to wait on the Lord: In the quietness of your being, imagine God as a Light, which He is, pouring into your head, filling your heart with His Being. Sit and bask in this wonderful Light. Feel the unconditional love as it infiltrates every cell and every thought. In this manner, you open yourself to God and to All God Is.

Consider the All that God is and has always been. He is the Creator of worlds, nature, space, and all that is known and all that remains unknown to this day. Do as the Brotherhood have instructed you to do: identify God in terms that are available to you today.

Now, in this week, practice this meditation. You will receive instruction, gifts and an opening to more of yourself through meditation. While communing with God-Mind and God-Father, you will be filled to overflowing with All that God is—Energy, Love, Forgiveness, Hope, Peace and Power. These are simply a beginning of the ways to identify God in your heart and mind. Pray, dear ones, daily, and more whenever

possible. Pray as if your very life depends on it, and it does. This
I desire you to practice for one week; comply and see the
benefits to you, your family and loved ones.

Mary, Mother of Jesus

PEACE in All Hearts
(Brotherhood, December 11, 1988)

Faithfulness is the cause of spiritual growth—faithfulness
to your time of prayer and meditation. It is in the practice of
activities of the spirit that you grow in spirit.

Continuing with the theme of the coming season, we
speak about **peace on earth.** This is part of the story of the birth
of Jesus. Although it is not exactly true, it is in the spirit of the
story, in that there was much joy in "heaven," or in the spirit
world, and in all worlds, for a Way-Shower was born on earth.
The highly spiritual being who came to teach, instruct, love and
especially to give the Truth of God, had begun His life on earth.
Remember in the story, there is the singing of angels in the
heavens, "Peace on earth, good will to men"? (Lk 2:13-14) This
has been the prayer for eons.

Peace on earth lives only in the hearts of peaceful men,
women and children. So our lesson is, Peace in the hearts of all
beings. Peace is a feeling in your hearts. It is the quietness of
certainty in yourself. Peace is the assurance that what is
yours—health, abundance, wealth, love and all good—is yours
without struggle or fear. Fear cannot abide in a peaceful heart
or mind. As you eliminate fear and its by-products of envy,
jealousy, hate, anxiety, greed and a general bad attitude, you
will find that your heart and feelings fill with peace. You will no
longer be easily upset with others. No longer will you be afraid
someone will take advantage of you. **Your assurance is now in
the certainty of GOD and His Goodness.** Peace on earth
begins in each heart and mind, just as the song states, "Let there
be peace on earth, and let it begin with me." This is the first line

of a song in Annie's mind, one she loves. It also can be used as an affirmation. It simply is a prayer, in that it states, "God, allow peace to reign in the hearts and minds of men, and allow this peace to first begin in my heart and mind." Feel peaceful toward your home, loved ones and work place. When you begin to seek peaceful ways and peaceful means, you will surely find the way to bring about changes in your mind. The changes could be a change from an attitude of fear to one of calmness and confidence in self.

In this Christmas season, as you celebrate Jesus' birth, take with you the thoughts of peace on earth and peace in your heart and mind. Seek to find peaceful solutions to your problems. What you seek, you will find, remember? With peace comes hope, love, serenity and many good feelings and emotions.

You each know the process—what it is you desire in your life, you meditate on and think of. Think only the word PEACE; say this word to yourself over and over as a prayer. Begin to send out the thought to the world in this manner: "This day I send my thoughts of PEACE to every man, woman and child alive on this planet. I ask God to allow men to see His Peace in every nation and ask God to allow the leaders of nations to recognize His peace. I send thoughts of Love and Peace to my parents, brothers, sisters, spouse, home, workplace, to every person with whom I come into contact this day. I begin to think in terms of Peace. I seek Peace in my home and in my relationships. I send Peace out into the world and the entire Universe."

Do this exercise for one week, and see the benefits to you and your loved ones. As you interrelate with each other in terms of peace, you will be filling the atmosphere with peace. Start now, this moment, to send thoughts of peace to your heart in this manner. Concentrate on your heart area, and with your mind send thoughts of peace to it. Feel the peace as it washes over your body, your entire being. Feel the relaxation that now takes place in and around your body. See how the use of this word with concentration is capable of causing your body to respond? Understand that the entire Universe will respond to your thoughts of peace. Each person you concentrate on with thoughts of peace will respond openly, sooner or later. This is a simple meditation for peace. First you concentrate on yourself, your heart, your being, and then begin to concentrate and send the thought of peace out to those in your home, workplace and all whom you meet this day. Do this each day of this week. Daily and momentarily send thoughts of peace to your heart and to your loved ones. Tell yourself that each person you meet on this particular day will hear peace as it is emitted through your voice. Each person will leave your presence with the feeling of God's Peace as He works through you to give the world Peace.

Become the heart and mind of God. Allow only God to work through you. In this way you become a channel for God to give this world all His great gifts. **As you open your mind and heart to God and allow Him to use your mind and heart, the benefits will begin first in you.** Think on this great Truth!

(Pause)

By opening your mind and heart to God to send His great gifts of peace, love, happiness and All Good to the world, you are the first to benefit. You become more peaceful, happy, loving and surrounded in love. All of God's Good is yours to use first. This is a universal law, that **God will work only through men and will work His miracles only in and through the hearts and minds of willing men, women and children.** All your prayers and all your desire for good toward yourself and your loved ones will come first through you. God's Good to mankind is given as an answer to prayer. Your prayers are important to you, your family and friends, and to the world.

This week, bring this writing out daily and read it. Take it into your heart. Practice this meditation, which is easy and simple. Amend this meditation to suit yourself. The form of meditation is not important, but the sincerity and words you concentrate on are. Say to yourself these words: "I open my mind and heart to God, to use to benefit mankind with All His Good Gifts." Become a radiating center of God, His Love and

Peace. This is your task for this week. This is your assignment for the world and its inhabitants. Do this for your world and your planet.

The Brotherhood

PEACE Fosters HOPE
(Mary, December 11, 1988)

I address each of you in this group of faithful souls. You, who seek to find Truth and safety in the first and main place, know in your hearts that you have connected to God-Mind and to His Spirit. The Truth that is given is coming directly from God. Use these Truths to instruct, to cause your mind to expand into greater thoughts. Today the Brotherhood has given you a message of PEACE. I give you a message of HOPE.

As you build peaceful thoughts in your heart and mind, you will find Hope springing up inside you. Hope comes hand-in-hand with peace. When you obtain peace in your soul, you will find hope, and not an empty hope, but the hope of God— hope that will see you through the coming changes on earth with the assurance of one who has found Truth. You will radiate peace and hope. This aura of peace and hope will be as a lamp to light the way in the darkness of the despair that will overcome many on earth. This aura of peace and hope will open doors and open the way to your survival.

You are the hope of the world, you who seek God-Mind and All His Goodness. What you connect to in your mind and through your thoughts, you radiate. Have you not seen a person who is scowling and unhappy looking? That person radiates bad vibrations. He gives the appearance and feeling of anger and sadness. It is as if a dark cloud were upon him. In the same way, look at the happy person. See the light and happiness as it shines through his eyes. Feel the joy as you are near this happy person. You radiate what you are and what you think. You radiate your inner self for the whole world to view.

Concentrate on God's Peace, God's Love and God's Hope. As these thoughts take over your mind, you radiate these emotions, you attract these things to you, as a magnet attracts metal.

Take the lesson of the Brotherhood to heart. Practice it daily. Read it and think on it. Speak to each other nightly about how well you concentrated on Peace during your day. Give each other encouragement to think and feel these Truths. This is the way to help each other. Think in terms of advancing in spirit. These lessons are designed to help you do just that—advance in spirit. Learn to use what is given to you each week. Learn to think on these Truths, to use these lessons and to pray each day. In this way you are practicing and making an effort to aid us to help you. This is a two-way street. It is through you that God works, and it is by your efforts that we are able to assist you to learn.

Sit quietly and surround yourself with thoughts of PEACE. Then feel HOPE washing over you in waves. This is your duty; this will become your joy. Pray for yourself first, your family, friends, co-workers, then the entire world and this planet. Do this daily and hourly if possible. We will be doing likewise. You are now surrounded in PEACE, HOPE and LOVE. God is in and around us at all times.

Mary, Mother of Jesus

Awakening Christ in the Masses
(Brotherhood, December 18, 1988)

Today we speak of the true meaning of Christmas, which is giving Christ, or better yet, awakening Christ in the masses. The time is near when the Christ-Spirit will become awakened in the masses. It will come through much pain and agony. You who seek have, however, found the search for Christ most beneficial. You have not found this process to be agonizing or painful, because you search for truth before the coming changes.

Awakening the Christ-consciousness inside you is another way of saying, finding your God-Mind connection. Both
are the same! When you awaken the Christ-Spirit in you, you
are connected to the God-Mind. Is this confusing? The true
reason for Jesus' birth on earth was to bring the Christ-Spirit to
the masses. He was born on earth to show every person that
God is only Good. In those days, as in these, there was much
confusion, and many thought God was an angry God, one who
wreaked havoc on His people. Today natural occurrences are
still called "acts of God." This is a fallacy, an untruth! The
storms, earthquakes and volcanic eruptions are not acts of God.
Healing, Love and Peace are acts of God! The others are
simply nature restoring herself to equilibrium.

Jesus' birth brought the first good news: peace on earth,
goodwill toward men. Notice that it is goodwill toward men.
We in the spirit world always are sending goodwill to each of
you. God sends nothing but Good! Our good news in this day
and time is the same good news that was given on the day of
Jesus' birth. It is constant and continuous. God is All Good, and
we are made in His image and likeness. You are made in God's
image and likeness. You are to put away the errors of earth-
mind consciousness, which tells you otherwise.

The earth-mind consciousness is comprised of the "truths"
which everybody knows. It contains in it the erroneous idea that
disasters are caused by God to entertain Himself. It also tells
you that God is a vengeful God, angry and moody, who enjoys
playing jokes on you by sending you illnesses to make you
suffer. He also enjoys watching the "devil" play tricks on you,
causing you to believe this devil is good. It says you must have
darkness in order to enjoy the light; it is easier to do bad than
good; there is a heaven and hell, and if you "do good" by the
general populous standards, you get to go to heaven. It says
there is a devil or satan, who plays a game of chess with God,
and each of you are the pawns; that you have only one life, and
so you had better enjoy yourself while you can, by earth
standards; and that everyone is out to get you, including God!

These are errors that have been perpetuated by time. The longer people believe this way, the more they think it has validity. These ideas were false in the beginning and remain false today. Because you believe in a wrong idea long enough will not make it become true. Truth is truth forever, whether it is believed or not. Gravity worked long before anyone believed in it, did it not? The planet Earth was just as round in the beginning as it is now. No amount of believing in the flatness of the land made it so. God's Truths are always true, whether you believe or not.

These are the thoughts that Jesus came to erase. The Pharisees and religious leaders of his day were in opposition. The religious leaders of today are in opposition to anyone who gives you a different idea. Jesus' ideas and truths were considered a sacrilege, blasphemy against God. But it was God Himself who sent Jesus to tell the Truth, to give the people Hope, Peace, Love, and to put away the wrong concepts that interfere with each person making their own God-Mind connection. Today, many religious leaders think that the truths in the earth-mind consciousness are true, because "everybody knows it is true." A truth is not true because everybody knows it. A Truth is true because it is God's Truth and it is provable.

You who search for Truth have opened your minds to new truths, which are old truths. That is to say, you have opened your minds to God's Truths, which have always been truths. These truths are true for everyone in every world, and even after death these continue to be true. Jesus came to demonstrate and teach these truths. His stories and words tell continuously of these truths. Each story has in it many truths. If people could understand only a simple truth, they were better off. If people could understand that there were many truths in these stories, they grew even more. Take the story of the birth of Jesus. It contains many truths like these.

We in this world and all advanced spiritual beings send only thoughts of goodwill towards men and pray for peace on earth. In the innermost parts of your being there is a stirring that is awakening inside you. This is the Christ-Spirit, who desires to bestow on you a Christing, which is the highest connection to God. This Christhood begins in the smallest way and must be nurtured and cared for with love. You are to feel the purest and gentlest feelings of God inside you as you awaken to your truth, which is God's truth. The Christ-Spirit, which is your connection to God, is always with you, even in the lowest places. In those areas of your life that you think are too low for God, in these very places God has given you a connection to Him.

You always have many beings around you to help you. We are happy with your smallest progress and growth. The angels on high sing and give praises to God and to you for your smallest step in spirit. There are wise men in your midst to guide you and help you on your way. They come to instill in your mind the way to God. In the quietness of your mind, they speak and give you ideas to live by. They give you ideas to sidestep any dangers to your spirit. There will be those also, as the shepherds, who come to worship the God of your soul and the God-Mind who leads you if you listen. As Mary and Joseph were led to Egypt to avoid danger to the new babe, who represents the awakening of your spirit, so also will you be led to safety to avoid danger to the awakening of your spirit today.

See how this story can give you many truths? We can use this story of Jesus' birth and give you new meanings and new truths which you have not seen before. But as you read this story and think on it, these same Truths of God will awaken in your mind and heart. Feel the joy of this world as we see an awakening in each of you. Hear our song as we sing praises to God for your progress. Feel the serenity that is yours to command and that comes to you as you progress in spirit. We welcome you each to our world, as you welcome and are excited by the birth of each child in your family. As you smile and are overjoyed with each small step or smile of this child, so we are with your steps into Spirit.

Think of how precious and wonderful it is to see the first step, first word, first recognition of your child. This is also true of us, for we love each of you as our children, and with each recognition of God's truths, we rejoice and are happy. Our joy comes in giving you these truths. We rejoice each time we tell you how to find your connection to God-Mind and in seeing you use this connection for your good. Our greatest joy is in your progress. We see wonderful events in your lives, in the coming year of your lives, if you continue with your search for Truth. When you hold a newborn babe, your desire for this infant is only good. You wish and foresee a life of joy, happiness and greatness. Each parent wishes his child to be the smartest in the world. God also desires this for each of you, but He gave you the best gift, the freedom to choose your own life and everything that occurs in your life.

This is not an easy thing to do, as you parents know. To allow a child to make their own mistakes is difficult. But God in His wisdom allows each of you to make your own mistakes, to set your own goals. We help by working with your own blueprint of what you desire in your life.

Reread this in the days after your Christmas celebration. The following is a task we ask you to perform as you close this year of your life. Hold a session in which each person considers what he desires in his life for the coming year. Make a list of your goals and the achievements you wish to accomplish. These can be material goals, such as a better job, a new car, a better home, possessions, more education or more spiritual learning. If you have a spouse, take an evening or morning to sit quietly and talk over your New Year's goals.

But this week think on the awakening little babe inside you, who brings you All Truth and Love. Read the story of Jesus' birth and allow us to speak to your heart and mind with new insight. Quietly set aside time to read of this great event and bring the idea of how you can use the birth of the Christhood in your life. Pray and worship God in your heart and mind, as you shop, wrap your gifts and prepare your meals.

The Brotherhood

Give the Gift of Prayer
(Mary, December 18, 1988)

We come to instruct and give you a renewed sense of hope, peace and love. You cannot have too much peace, hope or love. Think on these words. Neither you nor your children can have too much love, hope or peace.

Today I concentrate on your families, homes and children. For those of you who do not have homes yet or children, these words will still apply. You have yourselves always and you have your future.

In this season of Jesus' birth, you give each other gifts. What does this mean? These gifts are representations of your love and concern for each other. In sending these beautiful Christmas cards, as is the custom, you are sending words of cheer and love to friends and acquaintances. You take time to select the appropriate gift. The gift is something useful or perhaps indicative of your love. The best you can give anyone is your love, concern and your thoughts of goodwill. As you give these gifts, give thoughts of love, peace, hope and goodwill. If you are unable to give gifts because of a shortage of money, give the best, which are your thoughts of love, hope and peace, and your prayers and meditations for each other. Allow God's Spirit to give His Love through you. Pray for your loved ones—this is the best gift. These outer gifts are simply representations of spiritual gifts.

I do not wish to demean the outer celebrations of your time and custom. They are wonderful. But remember that these are simply representations of spiritual gifts, which are everlasting and ever with each of you. Seek to send eternal gifts along with the earthly gifts. Seek to be a help to your friends through your prayers and meditations. Become an instrument opened to God-Mind to use, to channel and to focus God's Good to the world.

Now, my Christmas gift to each of you is the pride and happiness I have in my heart for your spiritual progress. I pray for your awakening to continue, for your spiritual gifts to become manifested on earth, as they are here. I pray for your mind and heart to open to new concepts and new perspectives, which are God's Truths. I pray that you will become all you are capable of becoming in spirit. As you each continue to grow in spirit, you are surpassing yourselves by lifetimes. You are growing to become capable and strong individuals in spirit and in truth.

Your are growing in goodness. You are to continue to seek God in your heart and mind, not for selfish reasons, but to be of help to mankind as you can. I see wondrous events in your lives as you grow in spirit. Your minds will become accustomed to the input of God-Mind as He instructs and leads you beside the still waters. Do you know what this means? The "still waters" is a set of words that indicates that your lives will be easier and you will have the "things" you need in order not to struggle for your earthly life. As you grow in Spirit and in contact with God, you will be able to see how He cares for your daily needs. Your life will become easier, in that you will have the right ideas and be in the right places at the right times. Much in this world is associated with timing. Often you have heard it said, "This person was in the right place at the right time." This is not an accident, but God can and does make events happen in perfect timing. You will find your money going further and making your lives easier. You will find the people around you to be pleasant and helpful. You will find your spouse agreeable, or perhaps you will be the one who is agreeable. In either case, your lives will be happier, calmer and more satisfying all around. This is what you have to look forward to by living in the Presence of God and seeking God in your heart and mind.

Your prayers will be answered in ways that will amaze you. Your good will happen in amazing ways, almost unnoticeably. These are not empty promises, these are Truths. This is how it is to live in God Presence. This is where your path is taking you. You are working with Spirit now, and these are the results. Continue to be faithful to this growth; take it upon yourself to start this new year with faithfulness and persistence in seeking God. Take it into your being to awaken in your spirit all the Truths of God. This is how to grow and to progress in reality.

Joseph and I urge you to continue to work with God. He is the answer to all your hopes and dreams. He is capable of bringing into your life all the good things, places and conditions you could ever dream of. You will not go wrong in this search; you will find God, because you have found God already. Depend on your own mind and heart to know and discern the truth. Each of you has the ability to perform miracles on earth. You can awaken in yourselves these latent talents—to know, to hear God's voice, to nourish, to replenish your storehouse and to have wealth. As God has given to others, He surely can and will give to you; it is all up to you. It is your belief and your faith that brings all manner of good. Think on these words as you plan for your new year. Think on past lessons as you set your goals in spirit. All things come first in Spirit and then on earth. The Lord's Prayer gives you this concept: "On earth as it is in heaven." In heaven all things are possible, all health, all wealth, all happiness, all serenity, all of every good thing you can conceive of.

Jesus wishes you to remember the most important thing: **God is Love, and as Love you are totally surrounded and live in this Love.** Each day feel the love, hope, peace and serenity that enfolds you. Each day be grateful for this Love, which is God. Walk in God's Love. Take this thought with you each day and into every circumstance.

Mary, Mother of Jesus

Jesus' Mission to Reveal God's Love
(Brotherhood, December 22, 1988)

We are prepared to give you words, as a message to give this special Christmas to the masses, to all who gather together on Jesus' birthday. We are happy to have a group of like-minded souls who join with us to celebrate Jesus' birthday. This is a special time of love, goodwill and thoughts of peace to all nations. We continuously send these thoughts to the world. We have been doing this for centuries, but every year during this season we are inspired by the goodwill that is in the hearts of men. Our message to you is one of Love, one of Peace.

You have been working to bring peace into your lives. We urge you to continue to bring peace into your life, home, workplace and especially into your family and friends. For the next thirty days we urge you to continue to meditate on peace and serenity. As you open your minds to the inflow of God-Mind, you will find these thoughts are natural and easy. Continue to quiet your mind with thoughts of peace. Send peace into your world and into each nation. Meditate on peace, serenity and love. This is the message of Christmas.

The word Christmas also means Christ to the masses, Christ in your heart and mind first. The Christ-Spirit is one of Divine Love and Divine Peace. As you open and expand your mind with these thoughts, you will find you are giving Christ to the masses and thus living the Christmas message!

Once, long ago in a stable, came a sparkling new and wonderful
     Spirit into the world.
With radiant face, eyes filled with Light, He smiled to all who
     came to see him.
In this child's eyes, the Love and Peace that filled his being were
     focused on the world.
Through his Birth and all that surrounded him, a story was
     being told.
Look into the life and message of this great one, from beginning
     to end.

And in every page, you will find it filled with Love and Peace.
He not only brought these great essences with him, he lived
    them and gave them to me and you.
On this starry night, as we remember his birth, let us pledge to
    live each day of our lives in Love and Peace, as he did.[13]

In this poem we have given, you will find the true message
of Christmas. Live each day as Jesus did, only you each have an
advantage—you also have His help, our help and God's help.
With all this power behind you, you cannot miss. Take a look at
love, and remember that forgiveness is a part of love. Make
sure your family and friends know of your love. It does not hurt
to say I love you to friends, or I appreciate you. In fact, if these
words were spoken more in the homes, you would have a
healing in the souls and spirits of each member of the family.

Take this week after Jesus' birthday and pledge to tell each
member of your family at least once each day of your love. It
can be simply a pat on the back and the words "I love you." It
can be a kiss on the cheek or a hug. Love yourself, and each
morning look at yourself in the mirror and thank yourself;
appreciate the body, the life and your soul. Love and appreciate
your own self, and then it will be easy to love and appreciate
others.

The gifts you give at this time of the year are tokens of the
love you have for each other. As you use the gift or hold the gift
you received, remember that it is a token and a symbol of the
love that person has for you. When you see your gift or you
think of your gift, send a thought of thank you and I love you.
Mental telepathy works, even though you do not believe it
does. People have a connection that is made strong with emotions. Love is the most powerful emotion there is. True love,
which is unconditional, unrestrictive and free of all malice, is
the strongest of all emotions.

---

[13] Byron and I gave this poem to our family and friends for Christmas.

Jesus came into the world with many missions. The most important was the revealing that God is a God of Love, that He only Loves each person and that he does not send anything bad to you. In fact, God takes all the negative situations given to Him in prayer and can turn them into positives. **If all you have learned in this past year is that God is Pure Love, you have learned a great lesson.** You have advanced much in spirit. This is the primary message that Jesus brought with him. He wanted you to feel comfortable in allowing God into your life. If it takes Jesus to help, he is willing and able to help you connect to God-Mind and put aside your fear of God.

Jesus is happy with your celebration of his birth. He appreciates the time and effort you have been making in learning about God and the Truth of God. He is here and sends his love to everyone. He is with each of you as you practice what you are learning, for it is only in practice of these truths that you will progress in spirit. Take all these lessons and review them as you can. You will find that many which did not make sense to you in the beginning, will now. You are understanding much in the way of spirit.

Our best wishes are with you, as are our prayers. We are ever with each of you and await only your call to help. It is your choice to call on us or not. We wait for this call, as does God.

The Brotherhood

PART 2

1989
Change and Correction

Beginning a New Year

Release the Past
(Brotherhood, January 1, 1989)

WE HAVE AN IMPORTANT MESSAGE to begin this new phase of your life. It is a ceremony to finish the old year and begin the new.

First, as you gather in your homes, take a calendar or write on a piece of paper the number of the old year, such as "1988." Place on this paper some rose petals or other fragrant essence. The old calendar will represent the burning of the old dead past. The fragrance of roses will represent memories of wonderful events that took place during the year. As you burn the old calendar, understand that it represents only the finality of the past.

The old year is over, and all that you accomplished or did not accomplish is completed. You cannot change the past with regrets. What happened is over, and it cannot return again. All the opportunities of that year are gone. What was accomplished for good will remain with you. What you lost or did not accomplish for good, is now burned and released. Never go back over any event with the thought, "I should have done this or I should have said that." This way of looking at the past prevents you from going forward.

Can you walk backwards at the same time you are going forward? Of course not! How silly, you say. No, it is exactly what many people try to do in their minds and hearts. They go over and over past events or conversations. They think of ways they could have acted or words that could have been said many times, to best or outsmart the other person. The words "if only I had" are useless and cannot change one thing. How much time do you spend in this useless pursuit?

This first week of the new year is the time to take stock of what you learned during the past year. It is the only time to look back through the year. You are to take this time to reminisce and consider what in this year was good. Be grateful to God for the completion of another year and for all your progress. Each person grows in Spirit and in Truth. Prepare yourselves for all coming events. We appreciate the effort and work that is needed to accomplish this. We love working with you and look forward to a new year of growth and closeness.

As you look back through the year, keep all the sweet memories of good times and good chats in your heart. These are your treasure. This is represented by the sweet fragrance. Then release the dead past to the past. Allow it to be changed as the paper and words are changed by the fire. Allow all of the past to evaporate into pure energy. Do not carry the dead weight of regrets. What happened is done. You can change the outcome through prayer.

Some of you feel that when we say pray, you think (in your own words) that this is "a cop out." This is not so! **Prayer is a powerful act.** You invoke many old and ancient powers of good when you pray. Prayer is automatic, in that it always gives good results. Perhaps you do not see the results as good at first, but have faith that good is what will be the outcome. Prayer will not give any other answer, it cannot. Prayer will help you grow in the new year; it will prevent you from making grave mistakes in judgment.

Good judgment is one of the powers of prayer. Judgment is good when you use judgment as God does, to discern and decide. Pray for the pure judgment of Truth to enter your life and give its good results.

Release your prayers to the Highest Power, which is God Energy. Allow it to work and bring the good that you expect. When you take your prayers back into your conscious mind and mull them over, you interfere with the Power of God, the power that could be handling your request. In this year resolve to pray with more feeling and to release your requests to God-Energy, which brings only good results.

Take your goals and pray on these daily. Release your goals to God-Energy to become a part of your inner life, which in turn becomes a part of your outer life. **Only that which becomes a part of the inner you will be revealed in the outer earth-world.** This is a major statement! Think on these words. Only that which you take into your inner life will be a part of your outer earthly life. These words are a key!

Take Love into your inner self; you will be loved and loving.
Take Peace into your inner self and live serenely.
Take Hope into your inner life and live in glory.
Take Joy into your heart and find happiness.
Take Knowledge into your life and live intelligently.
Take Spirit into your heart and mind, and live life fully.

We are, as are God, Jesus and Mother Mary, always with you as you live your daily life. We keep our word to you, to be available anytime and anywhere, to assist in your spiritual growth and to give counsel. We renew our pledge and our promise in this first day of your new year. We ask each person who desires this contact to come to us. Many will be able to receive their personal messages and write them down. It will not inhibit the weekly sessions, but add to them. We will give answers to what you do not understand, in language that is relevant to you. Come, listen and write down what you hear from us. We can talk to you in your mind, but humans seem to take notice of the written word. Our goal is to have each of you communing with us in print. Have a wonderful new year and new life.

The Brotherhood

Hope in New Beginnings
(Mary, January 1, 1989)

The beginning of a new year. The beginning of anything is always exciting—the new year, the new school year, or even a new age. A new beginning! How exciting a new beginning can be. How wonderful to have the hope of a new beginning. In reality you have a new beginning every day upon arising. But as happens so often, it loses its meaning. This new year seems to be another thing. There is much joy and excitement on earth as the old year nears an end. Oh, that you could look to the end of this era in the same way, with excitement and joy.

The Brotherhood has given you a way to release the old and to do away with the past. I will give you hope for the future.

The Beginning! How wonderful and exciting it can be. Look to this new year with all Hope, which is God, and with all Excitement, which comes from using God-Energy in your life. Feel the tingle of the beginning, the spurt of energy to commence.

Pledge to keep this excitement in your life. Pledge to keep the search for Spirit and Truth in your life. This is how to have an exciting year, how to grow in Spirit and in Truth.

Set your goals for this new year. Pray for the accomplishment of these goals. As you set your goals, you are doing three things. First, you are making decisions. Second, you are committing to focus your concentration on something. Third, you release through prayer the completion of the goals. This is another Trinity. One, two, three steps and it is done.

The setting of goals is the first step. If you have not done this, do it fast. It is a waste of time and energy to live one day without a goal. This is a form of abuse, abuse of time and energy. Look to every area of your life: spiritual, physical, emotional, mental, family, career and recreational. Perhaps some of your goals cannot be accomplished in this year. There may be steps to take this year, to progress to the completion of the goal. For instance, as a student, one of the goals could be the completion of education for a career. It will not happen in one year, but as the student works and looks forward to the completion of the goal, they progress. In other areas, look to the completion of the goal, no matter how long it takes. Another example could be a desire to become better parents. This is a task that will take a lifetime. It demands flexibility and honesty. It demands much love and compassion. It is not a goal that is completed in one year, but keep a log of this goal, and see how much better your relationship with your children grows.

Now, the second step is in focusing your concentration. When you can focus on a desired result, you will see the completion and the reward. It takes a focus of concentration in order to complete any task, but more so to keep the interest in your life. As an example, when you look into a pair of binoculars and they are not focused, what do you see? Blurred visions, half sights, these are the things you see. But as you focus the binoculars, you see clearly and are able to find the desired sight. Likewise, a life without a goal is a blurred vision. If you cannot focus on one goal, there is no hope of accomplishment; everything is possible and nothing is accomplished. It is true that everything is possible, but without a focus or a goal, nothing will be accomplished. As you focus on your goals this year, you will be better able to focus on a completion, or on the progress to a completion.

Third is prayer. Without prayer you will have a difficult time completing your goals. With prayer, ideas will enter your mind to make the task easy. Knowledge will come to the forefront, and you will simply know how to do, or what to do. Prayer answers in ways that are not always visible to you. Prayer can put you in the right place at the right time. You can find a search shortened for an item that is necessary for your progress. Prayer relieves your mind of stresses that are unimportant. Prayer will give you the know-how and the power to find the way to complete your goals. When you release your goals in prayer to God-Energy, you are using the Greatest Power in the Universe. You feel the satisfaction of knowing you are in line with your Spirit-self.

I cannot overemphasize the importance of the three steps. It takes all the above steps to be successful in reaching your goals. It will also take commitment, which is in place as you decide on your goals. It takes hope, which comes to bear as you pray.

I see in your future only Good as you continue to work with God-Mind, God-Energy and God-Power. Each of you will feel the tingling of God, as Love, in every molecule of your physical body. Become aware of the great potential that is in you. Become focused on the highest possible Love, which is unconditional. Give this love to yourself, your family, home, goals, and your life. Forgive yourself of everything; forgive your loved ones of everything. Forgive the world of all its ills.

Now as we have become excited about this new year, allow yourself to become hopeful for the new era. See the possibility of good in all that comes into your world. The storms are a warning and the earthquakes are a settling of the planet as it shifts into its new place in the universe. Feel the excitement that is ours in this plane. We find hope and good in all events, even in physical death.

Much will be revealed to you as you seek. Many answers to questions will come to you. You will find, in the unity of a group, a strength to endure and to outlast all others. As the group grows in spirit and truth, you will progress in your earthly life and your spiritual life. This certainly is good news, glad tidings. Continue with your quest to find your oneness with God-Mind. Continue to work with the Brotherhood of God as they reveal to you new ways to live. Joseph, Jesus and I pray for each of you as you go through this lifetime. We are happy to be included as you search for the Truth of All Times. Our love pours over every person. Feel the wondrous Love of God as we radiate it to you.

Mary, Mother of Jesus

Use Universal Power to Gain Goals
(Brotherhood, January 8, 1989)

You have had a few days to get your goals in place. Think them over. Be sure they are exactly the goals you desire for this year. This is your plan for the new year; it will be a joint effort between you and God-Energy. Without a plan for this year, you will simply blow in the wind and be taken one way and then another. A plan, as your goals are, gives your mind, heart and soul something to aim for. How do you think you would do if you were to shoot a bow and arrow randomly? Do you think you could score any points? Of course not, it takes a target, a place to aim your bow. Your goals give your mind a place to aim. Perhaps at the end of the year you have scored well in all areas—spiritual, mental, emotional, physical, career, family and recreational. Perhaps you aim at these goals and find you have hit perfectly in some areas and in others your aim was off. At the end of the year you will judge and decide how you did. The process of deciding on your goals, formulating them into words and then praying for the abilities to meet them, gives you a lesson which you could not have learned any easier, or with such great benefits. This is very important to your spiritual growth and to meeting your lifetime goals. Your spiritual life and physical life are lived simultaneously.

There are those who procrastinate and put off doing this type of mental work, because it is not required by a superior at school or work. This is for your benefit. This year you are required to perform certain tasks to grow in every way possible. We are a help, but understand that we are here only to HELP. We cannot live your life for you. If we did, then you would become puppets and would not be happy. In this manner you are learning to be self-reliant, self-dependent, self-motivated, self-confident and above all one with God. For as these attributes are brought forth from deep within you, you connect to the One who is in All and is the Great Motivator. This is how to have your prayers answered.

We will teach you to use the powers of the universe to gain those things you need in order to live life happily. This is a first step. You cannot proceed without taking this first important step. Plan your year by setting your goals.

Now, as you set your goals in place, be firm in your determination concerning them; pray for the abilities to accomplish them. We will teach you how to pray for the accomplishment of these goals.

Set your goals and pray to the One God of the Universe. Ask for these goals to be completed with His help; never ask again. It is set in God-Mind with the first request. Thereafter you will make statements of fact, or statements of affirmation, to instill confidence in your mind, heart and soul. God knows what is in your mind and heart. From these areas He answers your prayers. So keep the goals in your heart and mind daily. Allow God-Mind to bring the proper situation into your life to accomplish these goals. Daily affirm these as statements of truth in this manner: **"I have set these goals in my mind, heart and soul for the year of _____. God-Mind is connecting to my mind to help me accomplish these goals."** Also, you can take one goal; we will use the goal to lose weight. Daily awaken to these words or some similar:

"Today God is helping with my plan to eat sensibly. I am satisfied with my planned menu for this day. I work with my

body to feed it and care for it. My body is my gift from God. I love my gift and I show my gratitude by caring for my body with all my might, all my heart and all my soul."

See how you will not be begging God for what is already yours? God's desire is to be a part of your life. He wants to be a part of your entire life, not simply when you are in trouble and need help instantly. **God relishes being your Guide, Helper and Partner.** This is His true desire, to help you develop all your Godlike potentials. Here is an easy formula for each affirmation:

First, you are to agree with your goals and set them in your mind, heart and soul. There is a reason this is important. Remember Jesus' words, "Where two or three are gathered in my name . . . ?" (Mt 18:20) This did not always indicate people, but ideas also. Thoughts and goals are to be agreed upon in your heart, mind and soul. Then, through your soul, the connection is made to Universal Energy, which is God as Principle. As most of this group have prayed for more money, here is a good way, but not the only way to affirm more money in your life:

"I seek first the kingdom of God and am assured that all things I need are already provided. God's promise is to help me with money. I receive money, I use the money I have intelligently and I gain more money. This I am sure of in my heart, mind and soul. Thank you Father for your wonderful gifts."

As you bring God into the usage of money, you will find more ways to use your money wisely. Perhaps a better attitude toward your work will give your superiors the impetus to give you a raise. When there is overall improvement in your attitude, work habits and outlook on life in general, this will give your work-life new meaning, new interest and new joy. If there is to be a change in work, it will come about naturally and gently.

Second, after making the agreement with your heart, mind and soul, state your goal in your own words. Do not worry about how you use words. If there are better words to use, they will simply come into your mind. This will impress upon your heart, mind and soul that these goals are already accomplished in spirit, for **in God, when you ask believing, you receive.**

Third, always be grateful for what you are receiving. See how we state this—"WHAT YOU ARE RECEIVING!" When you agree in your heart, mind and soul that you are receiving these goals or "better," then you are using faith. Jesus' words are to be studied in these next few weeks. Look to Jesus' words on prayer. Some of his words you can easily find in your Bible. We will help also. Call on us daily.

The Brotherhood

How to Make Your Goals Real
(Brotherhood, January 14, 1989)

We have further instruction concerning goals that are already set. It is important that you continue to work with your goals to insure that you have them placed firmly in your mind—not only placed, but engraved into your brain cells so they may be able to reproduce. Only that which is real can be reproduced. Make these goals as real as you can. There are several ways to do this.

As humans you have five senses—eyes for seeing, ears for hearing, nose for smelling, mouth for tasting, fingers for feeling. Now in order to make something real, use as many of these senses as you can. Your goals may not be smelled, so we will eliminate this one. It will be difficult to taste your goals, unless one of your goals is to be a better cook. There are those goals which will not produce any noise. But you can use the eyes to see and the sense of feeling in a different way.

Now this may sound elementary, but it will work to help you use all your senses. In a notebook or on a large piece of colored paper, cut out pictures that represent to you that which you desire to receive from each goal. Since many of you have as a goal more money, allow us to explain how to picture this.

When a person has more money, or extra money, he is able to live in a larger house or have a luxurious car. Find a picture of someone of your sex and age, who can represent you, with money in their hand. If it is too difficult to find these kinds of pictures, place a picture of yourself on the paper and use play money to represent you; surround yourself in money. This exercise will work in two ways. It helps you use as many senses as you can to picture this in your mind. Therefore, this action engraves your goals further into your mind. This also helps you to think of the end result of your goal. There are those who desire to be free of debt, because this represents financial security. Think in terms of the desires you have in your mind and heart, because then you can feel excited about something pleasant. If your emphasis is on debt, then that is what is programmed into your mind, and you may well receive more debt. Sometimes it is better to reword your goal to one which says, "I am free of all encumbrances." Eliminate those things, conditions or feelings from your mind by replacing them with what you do want.

Some of you desire a better job. Picture a person of your gender in the environment in which you desire to work. This is an easy one. Do you wish to wear a uniform? Do you wish to be in a business setting? Picture a man or woman in such a setting. Write your name with the title you desire. These are mere suggestions. It demonstrates to you how you look in the end results, the very highest and best results you can imagine.

For family goals, everyone wants a happy family. This is an easy one to obtain, because every person desires happiness. Quickly there is an agreement between every member of the family. Find a picture of a happy family, in a happy setting. But understand that **in order to get to be a happy family, it takes forgiveness.** Many times there are old hurts which need to be healed. Allow the healing to come, even if at first it feels bad. Write under this picture the name of your family.

Help children set their goals. In helping them focus, it will be revealed to you what to do to help them this year. They should place on their bulletin board pictures of things they desire. Also, encourage them to draw a schoolhouse, or a picture of themselves with a report card and the good grades they wish to acquire on it. This is the way your world sees accomplishment in school.

If you can obtain colored paper for the background, here are some of the things each color represents. Red represents love; green—money; yellow—understanding or happiness; blue—peace; violet—transformation and renewal; white—all possibilities. Also you can draw balloons on your paper and include the words love, understanding, wisdom, reliance, self-motivation. Any condition you desire can be written in these balloons.

If you choose to have these goals displayed on a large paper, place this bulletin board in a place where you will see it daily. This is only for you or your family to see. This is not to be displayed for the general public. As an example, display your paper in your bedroom behind a door that is closed daily. This is so that you will see it daily and be reminded of your goals. If you choose to have a notebook, begin a new ritual before going to bed, that of thumbing through your pictured goals. This is for the purpose of engraving into your brain cells these accomplishments. When they are a part of you in mind, body and soul, you will begin to see results.

For adults, please do not think this is too childish and refuse to do this. The more of your senses you use, the quicker it will be engraved into your brain matter. This is the procedure to use for a few months. There will come a time to release and put away these pictures until the end of the year.

Another exercise is to write a letter to God. Tell Him **in detail** what it is you desire. Read this letter in an attitude of prayer and then put this letter away to be read at the end of the year. The more of these exercises you perform, the better these goals will be engraved into your mind, heart and soul.

Remember to think in terms of what you desire in the end. Give God the end results and not the steps you anticipate taking. Allow God the freedom to create the steps for you. You wish to be debt-free. Admirable, but difficult to engrave in your mind. It is better to picture yourself with large amounts of money, or to picture better still the possessions you would have if you had all the money in the world.

This is an important step for each of you. Allow your mind to create new ways to use all your senses. Open your mind to the suggestions that will come into it.

We urge you once again to follow through with these exercises, as it gives your goals a better chance to come into your life. Our prayers are with you as you live this life daily.

The Brotherhood

8

Changing Your Reality

In January 1989 Annie and I took a combination business and pleasure trip to Hawaii. This message was received upon our return:

Connect Your Inner and Outer Life
(Brotherhood, February 4, 1989)

WE HAVE BEEN WAITING to give this message for some time now. All of us in the Brotherhood are happy you (Annie) and Byron had a chance to visit the Motherland (Hawaii) and to receive the spiritual ions that are available to all who live there and visit there. We are calling these unseen particles ions, but in reality they are smaller than this. There is spiritual matter in the very land, oceans, rivers, foliage and air of these islands. You received many startling revelations and much information which you have not yet discerned.[1] In future

---

[1] We received some information in a "nonverbal" manner. This technique will be explained in a later lesson.

days new thoughts, which are spiritual in nature, will be coming to you. Today we will give an explanation of some of the conscious thoughts you received and explain them to you and to the family group.

The first realization you received was that **mysticism is simply another word for spirituality.** To become a mystic is to become spiritual. All people have the innate ability to be mystic, as each person has the desire to be spiritual. Being spiritual or mystic is the ability to see beyond the seen world to those areas of your life that are in the unseen, to become aware of your union with God-Mind and God-Essence. In becoming centered in the inner life with God-Mind, you are able to develop many qualities that are mystifying to those people who are living from the premise that all that is real is in the outer, physical world.

Think for a minute and allow us to take you through a scenario. You are now praying for those goals which you have chosen. There is a process taking place in your mind, heart and memory. This is being carried out now in the unseen world. Those people who live around you or work around you do not have any idea of your goals, neither should they at this time. They see you living your life in your old way, for the changes that are taking place are inside of you. Perhaps they are beginning to see a new attitude of hope or goodwill, but this is not impressive to them yet. As you continue to work with God-Mind and God-Essence in your inner life, these changes begin to materialize into the outer part of your life. You simply seem to be at the right place at the right time. There perhaps are promotions or new responsibilities in your work life. There could be disputes, but you remain in control of your inner life and work from the point of God-Mind and His Truth. Your prayers are being answered in small ways, yet in large ways too. Others consider you "lucky" or "leading a charmed life." You realize that your prayers are simply being answered and that you are meeting your goals with the assistance of the Most Powerful Source in the Universe.

You are becoming mystical/spiritual in your inner life and your outer life. You are connecting to God-Mind with a strengthening link-up. This then is our work—to help you connect to God-Mind and be able to use His Power in your life and life goals. When you become concerned that you are not in connection with God-Mind, call on us and have the assurance that we are able to work through your muddled thoughts and old beliefs. Our whole goal is to have you become dependent on God and to know the joy and peace that is yours in life.

The next idea that came (to Annie) in the islands was, **when you link up to God-Essence and God's Truth, you can change your reality.** Allow this thought to enter your inner mind, for there is much truth here.

To change your reality all you must do is to link up to God. This is our aim, to help you do precisely this. In setting your goals you have committed to changing your reality. Perhaps it is now only in the physical life that you seek change. But as you continue to seek God and All His Essence and Powers, you will be changing much, much more. You will change not only the physical life, but your emotional, mental and spiritual lives. You will develop many new and wonderful talents, which are innate in all people. You will become more psychic, more creative and more aware.

You will change your definition of reality! Reality is simply that which is happening to you at any given time. It was a reality that you were in school at one time and had many lessons to learn. It was a reality that you were a child at one time, but now your reality has changed and you are perhaps no longer a child and have put away childish ways. All things and conditions change, and **change is the universal code of life.** Make sure that the changes you seek are the best you can do or have. Making sure is what we are here to help you with. We wish to become a real part of your learning process.

Each of you could use personalized help with your individual problems. We have definite answers for your concerns. But without the ability to speak to each of you in a way that will be beneficial, we are at a standstill. If you are unable to write what you hear, then take time to listen and understand. The way in which you use this help is individualized.

Our concern is that you are not to think of us as genies. We are not here to perform magic tricks for your amusement or benefit. Our whole aim is to connect each of you to God-Mind and to His Power. It is always God who is doing the work and not us. We are simply a means to make your connection to God easier and stronger. We are aware that people have many ideas which are erroneous concerning their ability to work with God. He is still thought of as an angry God, a vengeful God. **God is Pure Love, and this Love is an Energy which is available to you** to use, as is electricity. The help we give is to become the conductor or the power outlet, for you desire to know God and All His Essence.

The Brotherhood

Depend on God for Everything
(Brotherhood, February 11, 1989)

Place all your affairs in God. Bring all your affairs to God. Allow God to be in charge of your life. The lesson is **depending on God the Father, for everything.**

Each person has different needs and is in a different stage of growth. This growth is physical, mental, emotional, and all people are growing spiritually. All are in different stages of maturity. But every person, no matter how mature or immature, needs to learn to depend on God the Father. Allow us to show you how.

Physically: there are those who have a need for a physical healing of the body. Some of you have become dependent on alcohol or other types of pleasures. God can and will heal this if you ask Him. But, you too must do your part. There is no magic wand waved to make it all go away in an instant. As you heal, there will be times when the desire is overwhelming. This is the time to call on God for help to resist that which is detrimental to your health. There are those who need to think differently about their bodies. Some of you have come to resist your bodies by not attending to its needs. Eat the foods that are good for this vehicle. Exercise the body, as this is what it was made to do—move. The body deteriorates if it is not exercised. This is an abuse of your own body. God, as you already know, does not like abuse in any form. You must care for the body with all your might. Then God will help you heal body and soul.

We are teaching you to depend on God for this healing. But if you are working against the healing by putting into the body those foods, drinks or items that are not good for it, then God cannot and will not heal the body. If you refuse to exercise and care for the body that is yours to use on earth, then why should God come to heal the body—for you to continue to abuse it? It takes your effort to receive any healing. Ask God to teach you better ways to care for the physical body. Pray for your ability to care for this precious vehicle. The body is the temple of God; this is where your communication with Him takes place. Consider that the body is Holy because through it, you are able to accomplish your lifetime goals. This body is a gift to be treasured.

Mentally: you are to depend on God to help you clear out of your mind all that inhibits your communion with God the Father. The old depleting ideas, attitudes, beliefs, thoughts and memories do not have to be recalled. **Pray to Father God to cleanse all that keeps you from reaching Him with a good, strong connection.** Ask Him to wipe out all memories that rear up from the past to cause you problems in the present. Change your attitude to one of complete reliance on God for all things. Some of you still rely on outer agencies, on career, job, talents or your parents. None of these will help you with the same capacity that God can. God can be the Source of all your supply. That is, He can and will lead you to places that will be for your best growth in all manners. Call on God to be with you as you make every decision. Call on God as you are led into new situations and new areas of growth. It is through your mind that you connect to God the Father and All Wisdom of the Cosmos. Use the Judgment of God in reaching all decisions; then you will make your decisions from the standpoint of Truth. Hold the thought that God, the Father, is your belief system now. Your desire is to be dependent on God, the Creator of the Universe, for everything.

Emotionally: as you grow in this lifetime, there are many emotions that can overtake you in an instant. Place all your emotions in God the Father. Bring your feeling nature into the realm of God-Mind to be cleansed, healed and held for all time. Place all memories of hurt feelings, broken relationships, misplaced loyalty, of childhood hurts, in the Love of God, the Father. Through His Love, you can and will be healed in your emotions. When you feel yourself being carried away by your emotions, call out to God for help. He is there instantly to calm you and bring your emotions into right thinking.

God, the Father, is the Spirit which activates everything seen and unseen. His Spirit is in everything and surrounds everything. As you already know, you have choices to make; we urge you to unite your spirit with the One Spirit of God. Spiritually, you can go centuries beyond where you are now. Many heartaches can be avoided by placing yourself in God. As your spirit grows and is united with God's Spirit, you will become more intelligent, wiser and more successful in every way.

Have total confidence in the abilities of God to correct everything in your life that needs correction. Bring yourself into alignment with the Spirit of God to fulfill your every need and many of your desires. Allow the Spirit of God to flow through your life, into your home and through you to those you love and contact. Give your ideas, attitudes, beliefs, thoughts, memories and everything you are to God. Place your whole being in Him for protection, growth and healing.

Our love pours out upon you daily. Our help is available anytime. God, the Father, waits only for you to call on Him. We will be there instantly to make your call to God a strong connection, so that you can receive all benefits from Spirit. Our love and our attention is yours.

The Brotherhood

Divine Love Cleanses and Corrects
(Mary, February 12, 1989)

Today I have some suggestions and requests of you. The Brotherhood of God has come to you with the request that each of you write[2] or, at the very least, begin to think of your ability to write. But this I say to each of you—it is in your heart, with your feelings, and in your mind, with your thoughts, that you connect to God, the Father of the Universe. I know that you do not comprehend all that is in the spiritual world. It is not too big of a mystery if you will hold one thought in your mind. The world and the Universe are greater than you can conceive of: **God, the Father is more powerful and more loving than you can begin to comprehend.**

All your requests are being acted upon immediately! What you desire is our prayer for you; we also pray for your continued growth in spirit. Now I ask that your prayer be this: to allow God the Father to enter your mind and heart to cleanse from your memory, attitudes and beliefs those ideas that prevent you from becoming one with Him. Ask Him for all that you desire. If your prayer is not answered as you wish, then know that there is something in your mind or heart that is preventing the answer. You hold the key to your success, and you alone have the ability to pray for the release of these disturbances.

I want you to know how very much each of you is loved. I will try to give you an idea, but know that this is only an

---

[2] This means "automatic writing" or, as Annie now calls it, taking cosmic dictation. Appendix One has more information about this type of writing.

inkling of the Love that is surrounding you every moment of the day. Remember the feeling of wonder and tenderness that overcomes you when you see a newly-hatched baby duck, or the wonder that any newborn causes? Think of how much you loved your first bike or first car, how wonderful and loving you felt on the first day of your marriage. Remember the commitment and the earnestness that was in your heart? Our commitment to each of you is even stronger. Our love is greater, for we love with God's Love, which is Divine.

When doubt or despair comes, remember that you are truly loved by many. You live in a circle of Divine Love. This is because of your efforts. Individually and collectively you grow in wisdom and spirit. As one person who seeks or as part of a group, you advance in spirit. This advancement will lead you into many wonderful areas and situations. When you seek or when you gather in a group for the express purpose of seeking Truth, you have attracted many higher spirits who pray for you and support your every effort in every area of your life. This support group is with you all the time. Have the confidence to know that every new endeavor is charged with thousands of prayers. Every effort on your part to correct any deficiency in your life is supported by this host of gentle and loving spirits. They are your guardian angels, your support angels and the gentle beings of the Brotherhood. You are not alone in anything.

These gentle spirits are not in any way judging you or your actions. They are simply points of love and help. They have your best interest in their souls. They surround you with Divine Love, which will heal all things in your life—Divine Love, which is an energy and a power for good. They simply multiply your efforts.

When you perform any service in thought or deed, it is as if this performance is given the energy of thousands. When you pray, your prayers are supercharged with Divine Love.

What I give is the love that you each deserve, the good report of your eternal advancement.

Our love, that is, mine and Joseph's love, is with each of you. Our pride is in your advancement, and our pledge is to continue to love you Divinely.

Mary, Mother of Jesus

Divine Love Heals and Strengthens
(Brotherhood, February 18, 1989)

Sometimes people become confused about praying with Divine Love as a healing balm. Remember that God can be both personal and impersonal. When you ask God or talk to God, you are relating to Him personally. To pray with the thought of Divine Love is to pray to God through His Impersonality. In this manner you are praying to God as He truly is, for He is All. To pray for a loved one or yourself, after your initial request, use an affirmation. A good example of an affirmation is like unto this: **"Divine Love is healing your or my spiritual, psychic, ethereal, astral, mental, emotional and physical bodies of all old angers, fears and hurt feelings. Divine Love now is renewing my/your life without this excess baggage. I am, or you are, now instantly healed."**

This seems like a long prayer and it is, but thereafter when you think of these dear ones, tell yourself and them mentally the following: **"Divine Love is healing you or me now."** In this way each thought of these dear ones or of your life becomes a prayer. No one can turn away from the warm, healing, soothing love that is Divine Love. It is a strong and powerful healing agent. Soon the choice will be to enter into this warm glow of God as Impersonal Love, or not to. As the person turns toward the warmth of Divine Love, the healing takes place. Also this is a good way to pray impersonally for those who fear God because of wrong conceptions of Him.

Jesus has some words of encouragement for the family, but allow us to speak first.

Good day, my faithful seekers. We are happy you are faithful. As you become strong in spirit, you increase your strength in all ways. Each will be stronger in body. As you strengthen the ethereal body and the protoplasmic bodies, the physical vessel is healed and made strong. That is, it will withstand the onslaught of disease. You cannot become diseased when your inner-self is "at ease." Germs, bacteria, viruses and such only take hold of a body that is in a turmoil. Perhaps the turmoil is in one of the other bodies, but this is the fertile ground that is needed for a disease process to take place. Now for those of you who have a disease of any kind, as you progress in spiritual growth and come into the healing Love of God, your disease will be healed in all ways and in every part of your being. This then is one benefit to each of you. If your body is not healed, it most likely is a choice made before birth. These types of choices are made for many reasons. Some are for the healing of mankind, others as a process of change, and some people are using a disease to rectify something in their life.

As your physical body is healed and strengthened, you will know internally where the safe places are. The psychic body will reveal warnings to you every day. For instance, when you experience problems with your automobiles, you will simply know beforehand and have these mechanical vehicles cared for. Or, as in cases of accidents, in the future you will simply change lanes or turn aside beforehand. This will take place without any great fanfare.

When the astral body is strengthened, you will simply be stronger in every manner. This part of you comes into play in trying times. It is that which keeps you on an even keel, no matter what is going on around you. Have you not seen a person who is in the midst of a personal storm, yet remains calm? This is the astral body, when it is in good working order.

Mentally, the old hurt feelings and deficient concepts that you hold on to will be healed. Many times you enter this life with mental problems from past lives. These can and will be healed as you progress spiritually. Allow God's Spirit to enter your entire being, and as you desire to know more of God and yourself, your mental attitude will change. You will not be aware of the changes, because they will take place inside of you. Your beliefs will change, and you will simply "know" deep within that God is Pure Love and Divine Protection to you in all situations. You will work mentally with God-Essence to improve not only your life, but your world.

Emotionally, God will be your stronghold and refuge. You will be stronger emotionally. The trials and tribulations of the world will not affect you. People who in the past could upset you will not have this effect on you. With a strong emotional foundation, you will remain calm and not panic as around you others do. With God as your foundation, you will have no fear, no matter what is happening. Your assurance will be in God.

As you grow stronger in your inner-self, you will be able to help loved ones become spiritually aware. New people will come into your lives for encouragement and to form a God-Mind network. You not only help yourself, but family members who are not looking to God now. You become focal points for God to work through. In working with us, Jesus and Mary, you are working with the spiritual network that Jesus set up long ago. **"Where two or three agree in my name, there I will be and so will the Father."** (Mt 18:19-20) This is a promise Jesus made to His followers long ago. Now here is Jesus.

Be Healed Within the Trinity
(Jesus)

Greetings. You are dear to my heart, and we infuse you in God's healing Love. My word to you is that I will be available to each of you daily. Call on me or talk to me about what concerns you. I will give you the explanation of the Bible verse concerning judging according to appearances. (Jn 7:24) Read this verse of the Bible. Continue to pray daily. Have faith in God the Father, but be aware that I am also using the Whole Spirit and Essence of God to pray with you and to pray for those people whom you love. My network consists of you, the Brotherhood, me and God. You are using the Whole of God-Essence in this manner. You are using the Trinity. View this Trinity as a pyramid, with yourself standing inside it. There is a spiritual significance to the pyramid. By using this vision, you will be healed and progress faster. In your meditations use this vision. In old Egypt a triangle was used, with an eye in the center representing the individual. This is you in perfect harmony with all of God's Creation.

You are continuously in this Trinity. We are All with you daily, praying, healing and agreeing with you as you grow spiritually.

Jesus and the Brotherhood

Truth vs. Appearance

"Judge Not According to Appearances"
(Brotherhood, February 26, 1989)

It is our privilege to meet with you. Our pleasure is in the advancement each person makes in their inner life.

A T TIMES YOU WILL NOT FEEL that you are growing, or it will seem in your outer life that you have not grown, but be assured that we have access to information not yet available to you. Our vision is clear and not clouded by feelings. So, no matter what the outer appearances are, you are growing and advancing tremendously when you seek God.

There is a small verse in the Bible in which Jesus spoke these words: "Judge not according to appearances." (Jn 7:24) Today we will concentrate on these words. All too many times we see and hear some of you lose hope and become despairing. The appearances of the outer life are not always in keeping with what progress is taking place in the inner life, so there is conflict between what is true and what seems true. We urge you to keep that which is true in your sights. Forget what "seems to be true." The difference will be the time it takes the outer life and the inner life to become synchronized.

Allow us to take, for instance, the world as it is appearing to the masses. It seems to be going along much as the world has for centuries. The seasons follow the same seasons. Winter will give way to spring, and the cycle will continue year after year. But in reality, you already know there are many changes taking place outside of this solar system, changes which will affect the world and upset the progression of seasons. This is the reality of what is true and what seems true; that is why many people think nothing is going to change. All this is, in their word, "hogwash." They think the predictions that are being made are scare tactics used by a few to bring notice to themselves.

The general population would like to believe that everything is going along as it should and nothing will ever change. It is comforting to mankind to believe that what he sees with his outer eyes is truth. Man says, "I see clearly and nothing is changing." But man sees clearly in one direction, with one perspective, and in one dimension. Mankind can see only what is visible to him in this one moment. Few can see beyond their physical sight. It is as if man holds a telescope in one place and in one direction. Do you understand how limited mankind's vision is? Can you begin to comprehend the abundance of other aspects of visions available to you?

Now allow us to become personal. Some people are experiencing money problems. If this is you, your sight is set in one direction, in the direction of the limitation. You are viewing the circumstances in which you find yourself in the present. Yet you have learned that there is a "lag time" when having your prayers answered. That which is happening in the outer world is not necessarily what is happening in truth. It is easy to become discouraged when you are viewing the outer circumstances as truth. Remember where your truth lies.

Your truth and everyone's truth is in God-Mind. The concept of discouragement due to outer circumstances is in living in earth-mind consciousness. It is very easy to shift down into earth-mind consciousness. This is the familiar and tried way of thinking. When you find you are feeling alienated and out of touch with God, simply recognize that you have shifted into earth-mind consciousness. For awhile, there will be the tendency to waver in between earth-mind and God-Mind consciousness. To recognize which mind you are using to think is advancement. Through recognition is how to shift once again into the higher, God-Mind consciousness.

Recognize what your mind is using to think with. Be cautious not to acknowledge outer appearances as truth. Return to the One premise—**GOD**.

As you view life in the physical realm in turmoil and perhaps in dire predicaments, maintain the thought that this is not truth. No matter how real it seems, **God is Truth**. Live in God-Mind consciousness; your every need will be met, at the right time and in the right way. Maintain that you are strong in faith, that you believe wholeheartedly that God is providing your daily bread. How you define your daily bread to God is how He provides it.

Talk to yourself and change your view of your daily life and how it is to be lived. You do not need to be in a stringent life-style. Ask God to help you increase your expectation of His Good and His abundance. Ask God to raise your viewpoint of how life can be lived. Begin by saying these very words, "**I ask God-Mind to help me elevate my standard of living today.**" See, you have not put off the time in which your standard of living is elevated to some far off, undesignated time. It is happening now, today, in this plane, in this world, without delay. Then say to the outer circumstances, or to each invoice for payment, "**God is in charge of my life; God is helping me meet these payments on time and with ease. I no longer feel hopeless or discouraged. My life is in God and in His Power to act instantly.**"

Speak these words to every circumstance in your life you wish to eliminate. To illness, or to pain, "**God is in charge of me** and all that affects me. My life, my body, my money are directed by God Himself." Speak to the very circumstances, to the requests for payment, to the aches or pains. Tell them, **"You are not true. You are only an appearance of truth and not truth itself. My truth is God and His Power."** Speak to yourself, to your body, to your money, to every part of your life. Speak words of truth. Deny what you see in your life that is not true. An addiction, such as alcohol, food or a person, deserves to be spoken with truth. Truth is God. Truth is what you see through God-Mind and God's vision. Remember always, there is more to life and to your world than what is seen, felt or heard with your physical body.

The Brotherhood

You Are Seeking Truth
(Mary and Jesus, February 26, 1989)

I am proud of each of you and the faithfulness with which you seek more Truth. Now when I say truth, I mean, to know more about what is real, what is unadulterated truth, the Truth that comes from God, the Truth of this universe, why it was conceived in the first place, how you as humans came to be and why you live. Is this not the truth you seek?

We, that is Joseph, Jesus and I, hear your thoughts concerning truth, concerning your life on earth and those elements in your life that affect you. Jesus will speak today to give you a message of hope. Here is Jesus.

The Restorative Power of God-Mind
(Jesus)

This is the model of what is to come in family unity. You are working with powers and principalities that are not understood on earth. There is doubt in the minds of some, but these doubts will be relieved. The Love that you breathe, drink and eat is the Love of God. With every breath, you breathe God-Essence. With each meal, you eat of the Life-Essence of God. With every sip of water you take, you drink of the substance of God.

God is personal and impersonal. God is principle and substance. God is All things; He is every contradiction. This is much for your mind to conceive, but this is truth, unadulterated truth. God is you, God is your life, God is the earth, God is the air, God is the water on this planet. God is the space between the planets and solar systems. God is the life in a drop of water. He is microbes and viruses that are unseen by the naked eye.

In working with God the Father, you are working with the energy of Life itself. You are using the power of the atom. In thinking with God-Mind, you utilize the Mind that creates all ideas, all inventions and all universal processes. This is a great and monumental system of power. This is the power to build and to destroy.

Think of the abilities that are yours through God-Mind—to rebuild your life according to the Truth of the Ages, to restore your life with the energy of ten thousand, thousand atoms. **Speak your words through the Mind of God and with His power: all will be according to your word.** Take a moment to allow this thought and idea to seep into your mind.

(Pause)

When you speak, speak with the Mind of God at the helm. Speak with the power of God, Creator of the Universe. Speak to those conditions in your life you wish to eliminate. Speak from the standpoint of God-Mind. Say to these conditions, **"Get thee behind me,"** much as I did in the wilderness. Repeat, **"Get thee behind me and bother me no more, for God-Mind is my mind and my world. I live in God, and nothing can harm me in this world or in any other world."**

Eat your food with the idea of this food being the life of God. What you take into your body will be God; what erupts from your mind will be God's thoughts.

Drink the very essence of God to satisfy your thirst. As you drink water, remind yourself, this is God's essence and you are nourished with God elements. As you bathe your body, use the substance of God to cleanse your outer body of all ills and to cleanse your inner life of all that needs healing, that which is known to you and that which remains hidden.

Hold in your mind the thought, **"God is thinking through my mind."** It is God who is activating in you a life of goodness, a life of wonder and a life of joy. Expect happiness, peace, love and plenty of good things. Through this expectation will come the answer. Expect to be led into the conditions and circumstances that are for your good. Bless every thought with Love. Bless every condition with God-Energy. Speak words of Truth throughout your life, mind, body and your days.

Today I say, utilize the Whole Body of Christ in your life. Utilize the Whole Essence of God in your mind. Admit you are at a loss as to what is true. Admit that you have questions that need answers. Admit you are at a loss as to how to utilize this Power of God. Then admit into your mind the answers, the knowledge, to create in your life goodness, joy, love, peace and happiness.

See, it is still the same today as it was 2000 years ago. Turn your viewpoint to God-Mind. Allow the idea that God is the Father of Creation. Then become aware of the creative forces which God can activate in you and in your life. Work with us—the Brotherhood, me and with God. This is how to find the Truth. This is how to receive answers.

The work you are doing, in writing in this manner to the Brotherhood, is important. Through the Brotherhood you will have a method to question, to receive specific instructions in how to conduct your life, in how to bring into your life the "things" you have need of.

Each of you can write to the Brotherhood. Question them if there is a point you do not understand. Bring to these gentle spirits all that you do not understand. They will answer with words and terms from your mind in order for you to understand. Concentrate your energies and emotions on God and all He is. Concentrate your energies on understanding more, on becoming all you desire to be. As with all mental and physical exercises, it takes concentration. Do not scatter your energies on unimportant issues in life. Bring into your mind the concentration that is needed to perform miracles, wonders and great advances. This is your heritage. This is your future. This is your Divine Right as a child of God, Creator of the Universe.

Jesus and Mother Mary

The Correct View of Problems
(*Brotherhood, March 4, 1989*)

We will continue with the same theme, not to look to appearances. We have several analogies we could use to tell you why this is disruptive. Looking to appearances, or what is happening in the world around you, is like looking through distorted glass. The events that are transpiring around you are a reflection of what you have been thinking, or what the earth-mind consciousness has been thinking. While you are on earth, there will always be problems to handle. This is the purpose of earth life. It is the reason you came into this world, to solve problems.

The occurrence of problems is a truth. When you accept that on earth there will be problems, you overcome one large misconception. **Many people thought that in working with spirit, all problems would be eliminated. Problems will not be eliminated, but what is eliminated is the fear that the thought of problems fosters in your heart.** You will not fear problems, because you are aware they are temporary. In accepting the fact that problems are here for you to solve, then you will get on with the business of solving them. Many people become fearful when problems enter their life. They become depressed and angry, first at themselves. They think problems are a symptom of some great defect in their makeup. Begin by accepting the fact that there will be problems. God's promise is not to allow any problems to overtake you, nor to give more problems that you can handle. **God knows your limits.**

Simply say to yourself the road is rocky for awhile, but soon it will smooth out and be easy to tread. As you become less fearful of problems and less anxious, you will find that problems will not stay around you for long. You hold problems to you with strong emotions. When you become fearful, angry, depressed and anxious, you are not only holding on to the problems, but calling more to yourself. Do not attach too much emotional energy to problems. Have faith that you can depend on God to show you the way to handle and eliminate problems. As you become less emotionally involved, you will find that problems will not be mountains, but simple inconveniences.

Remain strong in faith of God-Mind. Tell yourself over and over if necessary that **"God is in charge of my life,"** that **"God is Pure Love and nothing can harm me."** Not one thing on earth can take away your spiritual life, with the exception of yourself. But even that is a difficult thing to do, for God has placed deep inside every person a strong will to survive. Allow us to give examples of problems that face you on earth today.

Number one in prayer is the prayer for health. There seems to be much illness on earth at this time. Health is a matter of binding your physical body to your spiritual body. Health takes some effort on your part. Because of the day you live in, there are many conveniences that are detrimental to your health, such as the easy way you can purchase foods along the highways and byways. The amount of food in this country is overwhelming. Not all these foods are good for you all the time. Take a minute and read from the vast amount of information on nutrition, and then practice good nutrition. Drink plenty of water, not all these other drinks that are sweetened and carbonated. Too many sweets are not healthy.

Exercise your body, for that was what it was made to do in the first place. Would you take a car, store it on blocks and not care for it for a long period of time, and then expect it to run perfectly? Of course not, yet you do the same thing to your body. You have many opportunities to enjoy the pleasure in exercise. Once again, you have made the word exercise a bad word, one that brings to your mind the thoughts of agony, pain, dullness, not pleasure. Make your exercise a pleasure by participating in games you enjoy, regularly. It takes regular movements of the body to maintain good muscle tone. This will be important in the coming days of turmoil or if the need to flee arises. Keep your reactions quick by exercising your body.

The next prayer is nearly always for money. These prayers are often stated in despair and the emphasis is always on what the person does not have. Shift your attention to what you do have. See ways to use the money you have wisely. Make eating a pleasure: a picnic of well-prepared foods and a game for exercise can be a joy and can be money-saving. You will have more money! It does not take money to exercise and participate in most games. Now then, shift your attention to God as the source of your money. Can you not see that God can and will give ideas on how to use your money wisely? God can bring new opportunities into your life by placing you in the right place at the right time. Also, when you are looking to Spirit for your life, then it will not be so important to live by earth-mind standards. In learning about the eternity of life, many things that you thought were important become simple vanities.

It does not matter if you do not have the possessions that others have if you have happiness, joy, peace and love in your home. Find what is important in this life. Seek to see God in every situation, even in the financial areas of your life. Pray to God-Mind to help you utilize what you do have. Ask Him to give you more as you learn to handle what you do have. Is it really important to have the new car? Is it really important to buy costly clothes when you could wear clothing that is not as costly? But most important, keep negative emotions out of your handling of money. Bless and pay your bills with joy and say to yourself, **"God supplies me with money. I pay these bills in**

joy and peace because I know that God is now providing me
with much more money." See the difference in the emotions?
Remember that when you bring in fear, anxiety, despair and
anger in the use of money, you are calling for more problems to
come into this area of your life. When you think of your
finances, have faith that God is with you in this area of your life.

Next we hear prayers for relationships and how to handle
people. Begin to bring more love into your mind and heart, and
ask God to pour His great Love into all relationships. In relationships among men, or among men and women, it is love that
brings healing. Most problems in this area occur because one
tries to impose his or her view, will or standards on the other
person. Respect all people, even if they do not respect themselves. Love all people, and make statements that the love you
give is the Love God is giving you. You simply are a channel or
tube, through which God's Love is poured out to the world
around you.

Whatever is happening to you in the present is simply a
reflection of what you have been thinking. As you improve
your thinking and contemplate the use of God-Energy and
God-Mind in all your dealings, you will bring more good into
your future—not fewer problems, but the means to deal with
and handle the problems.

When obstacles arise in your path, you will look to God-
Mind to help by giving you ideas to bypass the obstacles. If you
thought we would make your journey through life a breeze, we
are sorry we gave that impression. It is simply that we see the
ease that living in God-Mind gives you. The problems will turn
into mere annoyances.

Put aside the anger and hatred of your circumstances in
life. These are the emotions that act as a magnet to attract to you
huge problems. Instead, build into your mind and heart the
thoughts and feelings of God-Mind as the activating principle
in your life. Allow God-Energy to heal all your ailments. God-
Mind thinks through your mind with new and wonderful
ideas; you will know what, how and when to do. Depend

completely on God-Mind for all your ideas. Remember always, **God is both personal and principle.**

Look at the good that is in you. Look for the good qualities in yourself, your partner, children, brothers, sisters and parents. When you look for good, you are looking for God. God is All Good in everything and everybody. Focus on the emotions that give you energy from on high. Focus on seeking God-Mind. When you are completely in God-Mind, you will have the answers to your questions quickly. Problems will be solved quickly, and your life will be a joy, filled with Divine Love.

Divine Love is so much a part of your lives. You live in God's Divine Love daily. Acknowledge it and bring it into your awareness. Be grateful for all the help each of you have in spirit. As you learn to live spiritually, your life will be easier. You have the wisdom of the ages, not the wisdom of earth.

The Brotherhood

Protection from Earth-Mind Consciousness
(Brotherhood, March 11, 1989)

Our topic is how to recognize earth-mind consciousness, and what to do to rise above this consciousness. It will be an ongoing process while you are on earth. After this many years of existence, the earth-mind consciousness is very strong. It's beguiling in the way it can enter your thoughts. When at first you begin to come into contact with God-Mind, there is a peace and joy that overtakes your heart. But, insidiously, the concepts of earth-mind consciousness creep back into your mind. Most often it enters as doubt. **Realize that in God-Mind there are no doubts, because all possibilities are opened to you.** So recognize that with the first doubt that enters your mind, you have slipped into earth-mind consciousness. These are those little thoughts that say something like this, "Is this all really true? Maybe these prayers are not going anywhere? How can I be sure that I am really talking to a group of beings who are representatives of God? Have I lost my mind? What if this is not true; am I fooling myself?" Now see how these doubts will raise other questions, which are a form of doubting? At times you think this way: "I'm tired of thinking only of God, heaven and the earth. I want to rest from this; I want to have fun. This is too much to consider."

Realize that when spirit begins to feel heavy and bothersome, you are slipping into earth-consciousness. This is a ploy to get you to put aside your prayers, meditations and contact with God. This does not come from any outside forces; it comes from you. It comes from the belief that God, Spirit and Heavenly thoughts are heavy in nature. This is an earth-mind consciousness thought, because Spirit and Spiritual thoughts are in reality the lightest. It is also very uncomfortable to change your beliefs. You all know that when you are learning something new, you are uncomfortable in the starting phase. This is not because there is an evilness in what you are learning. It is simply the process of learning something new. There are many little details to remember. How did you learn to drive a car? It seemed like you would never remember all the switches and maneuvers that needed to take place before you could begin to move the car. Now, however, each of you enters your car, starts the motor and drives away without thought. Is this not right? There is no fear in your heart as you step on the gas pedal. All the fear and doubt that were in your heart in the learning process are gone.

Now think, children, you are learning a new way to live, a new way to be. A completely new belief system is what you are learning. You are now taking action to change some very basic beliefs. Some of these beliefs have been in existence for centuries. The earth-mind consciousness is an old mind-set. When you were born into this world, these beliefs and concepts were instilled in your mind. Now realize, this did not knowingly happen. The system of beliefs that you are changing is very old and has been very much ingrained into the very fabric of your being, for example, the ideas that say, "God is an angry God; He will punish you." Now remember, when you were small your greatest fear was of being punished. It is the belief of your culture that God is the one who is punishing you for some misdeed. Or perhaps you overheard the adults in your family imply that some misfortune had overcome a relative because he had made God angry. As a child you learn in many ways: what you overhear adults saying, what you think is true, what other children tell you, and how you view the world.

It will take some effort for each of you to overcome the things you have in your mind that are earth-mind concepts. All effort should be in the form of prayer. Through prayers for yourself and your growth in God-Mind, it will be easier to overcome these old beliefs. We see that each of you has taken into your mind the concepts of prayers for others, but none of you are praying enough for yourself, or for your spiritual growth, understanding and knowledge. This then is our recommendation to each of you. It does not have to take much time, but if done daily it will become easy and pleasant. You will want to spend the time. As you bathe, or as you arrive at your place of work in the mornings, take a minute to do this simple meditation. Of course, this can be done any time of the day or night, but mornings are often best.

Become quiet, by holding your body still for one minute, while having a sense of a draining away of tensions quickly. Tell yourself the following or some words to this effect:

"I place myself in a white bubble of Light, which to my mind represents God-Mind consciousness. The outer layer of this light acts as a membrane, in that it allows into my mind only those truths I need today. On the other hand, it acts as a vacuum cleaner and removes instantly any thought or feeling that is not truth. God now surrounds me with His good. I am Divinely protected, Divinely guided, and Divinely successful today."

Then go about your day in confidence and love. If during the day you find yourself becoming tense and frustrated, simply enter into your short meditation of the morning and the idea of this great bubble of Light. Remind yourself of the wonderful love that comes to you daily from us, Jesus, Mary and, most important, from God.

Another affirmation we find good is: **"I am a radiating center of Divine Love, mighty to attract my good and to share my good with others, without attachment."** We found this statement of truth in Annie's mind. It was something she had read before. Any statement of this sort, which affirms in your mind the truth of God-Mind, is good. It must be helpful to you to be of benefit. Memorize these affirmations, which are simply little sayings or poems. Repeat these to yourself as you work, drive your car or wait in lines. The more you are able to keep your mind filled with truths, the more you will grow spiritually. When we say truths, remember that what is true of God is Truth. If all you can do is repeat what you know of God, like this: **"God is Pure Energy, Divine Love, Heavenly Protection, All Understanding, Pure Knowledge, Great Wisdom, Pure Intelligence, Alive forever and ever, Tenderness, Gentleness, Harmony, Pure Order, Joy, Happiness,"** this is good. See how you can simply repeat what you already know of God and enter into God-Mind consciousness this way?

The repeating of these simple statements of truth are for your benefit. Recognize that God does not become more Energy, He is already All Energy. God does not love more because you remind yourself that He is Divine Love. God is All Love, period! These are simply exercises for your mind to expand and to become accustomed to the truths. Now how do we get you to do these simple exercises? What method does it take to motivate you? We see the faithfulness of your efforts and believe that with time each of you will progress to the point where there are no lingering doubts.

Each of you have made it a point to learn more about life and how to survive the coming changes. Once again for this we praise God and are very grateful. It is with each small effort in thought and feeling that you grow.

Our message is not to be overcome by earth-mind consciousness. Now that you each know the truth, that God Loves you and wants you to be in closer union with Him, realize that doubt is simply a slipping into earth-mind consciousness. This is an error of thought, not something to punish yourself for, but something to correct with thought and prayer. The thought is this one: **"No, no, these doubts are not truths. The truth is that God is waiting for me to turn to Him."** This is the way to erase and to climb out of earth-mind into God-Mind consciousness.

The Brotherhood

10

The Lenten Season

Encouragement of Love and Blessedness
(Mary and Joseph, March 12, 1989)

MY LOVE AND JOSEPH'S LOVE is with each of you as you are cleansing your lives of all fear, anger, anxiety, depressions and such life-wrecking ideas and moods. We remember life on earth and have a great admiration for all you are doing. The fact that you are praying daily is admirable. The meditations that you learned are to be done daily as a reinforcement to the spiritual level of existence. The more you call on us and use our help, the easier it will all become. Soon you will be able to hear God's voice as He speaks to your heart and mind. Then you will be able to survive the coming changes well. With God as your guide, you will be led to safe places. You will be guided to perform and act in a manner that ensures your very survival. This is your primary purpose in this quest, to survive all the storms of life and to prosper, is it not? This also is our prayer for each of you.

My word today is love and blessedness; you do not need advice for now. What you do need is the **encouragement to continue to pray and meditate. Continue to write to the Brotherhood for your daily advice.** It is their wish to help daily with all that concerns you. Understand that their primary reason for being present is to aid you spiritually. This is accomplished by helping you live each day from the premise of spiritual connectedness. This gives you the highest and best perspective on life in general. There are spiritual lessons to be learned with each experience, as you already know. The Brotherhood will aid you in learning these spiritual lessons quickly.

This learning is much like a journey, in that you have the initial excitement of starting on the trip. Then comes the boring time, when you are on a long straight road. All you can do then is anticipate the next change in scenery. Well, dear ones, you are now on the long straight road, which can be boring. But know and understand that you are progressing well, that your journey progresses with each prayer and each meditation. This is how to keep going forward. Remember that in Truth you are either progressing or regressing. You want to progress, and so we wish this for you. Know that you are doing just as you should, but perhaps some of you could be praying more and meditating more. I caution you not to become complacent and think you no longer need to pray or meditate. Each of you would be better served if you would write and get your own lessons daily. Our love to each person. Our prayers are with each of you.

Mary and Joseph

Fast from Harmful Emotions
(*Jesus*)

This is Jesus of Nazareth. I come today to give a message of hope and love. Your progress as a whole is noted. We understand how difficult life can be on earth. We also know how easily distracted you can become in today's world. However, you have managed to maintain your level of attention on the spiritual matters. This is commendable; this is progress.

Many people in the world are celebrating the Lenten season. This is the time when they leave off certain food or habits that they enjoy. This is an error as to what is really needed. The Lenten season should in reality occur daily. What you are to omit are negative emotions, as you call them today, those emotions that cause so much harm. Fast from anger, fear, depression, anxiety, frustrations, jealousy, envy, avarice and all such emotions. Allow this fast to continue for a lifetime and not only for forty days. Through prayer you will be aided to eliminate these emotions from deep inside you. At times a person does not realize they continue to be exploited by these emotions. When you react to life situations in anger or fear, you can be assured that the other emotions are not too far away. Through prayer, these emotions will be eliminated. When they are eliminated, you will feel such a peace and a release that you will wonder why anyone would want to continue to hold on to these emotions.

Allow us to take the story of Easter as an example. During the fasting season, you concentrate on removing some small pleasure from your life; these can be dark and difficult days. I ask that you remove the emotions of fear and anger through prayer and any other means that is presented to you. Afterwards, there will come the day when you die to these emotions, the day these emotions are hung on the cross to be expelled from your environment. This is the time of cleansing yourself of all negative emotions and of all addictions, which keep you tied in knots of dark emotions. For now, fast from any emotions that cause you harm, from the addictions that prevent you from coming out into the open with your entire life.

For one week concentrate on this fast. For one week concentrate on cleansing your life of these conditions, which prevent your coming into the full glory of peace, joy and prosperity. So let this be your prayer: **"Heavenly Father, help**

me cleanse from my mind, heart and soul any emotions or
conditions that interfere with receiving your full glory and
joy."

To receive God's full glory is what you truly desire, for in
God's full glory is all the good your heart could ever desire.
This is the condition that allows you to live in peace, happiness
and health in every layer of yourself. Then you live in perfect
harmony with All Good. Instantly you have All the Power you
need to meet the situations that come into your life.

My prayer for each of you then is to be in God's full Glory,
to come into the same union that I have with God the Father.
This is a life of joy, peace, harmony and such immeasurable
Love that one is always in heaven.

Jesus of Nazareth

Faith Is Spiritual Currency (Spring Review)
(Brotherhood, March 18, 1989)

Let us review some of what you have learned. It is necessary at times to take a look at what you have learned. In
reviewing the material which has been learned, you may find
that there are still some areas which need more explanation.

The following you already know!

There is One Power in the universe, and this power is God.
He is the Creator of all worlds. God is All Power, All Energy.
God is the beginning and the end. Through God all worlds are
born. Through God and His total Essences we all live. There are
worlds within worlds, just as there are universes within universes. There was no big bang to create the universe. There
have been many big bangs throughout time. All life in the
universe is closely related. It is through the Energy which is
God that life continues.

There are no other powers or spirits which are greater
than God. God is Spirit, and it is in spirit and truth that you
worship Him. All that mankind needs to find God is to look for

Him with sincerity. God is found within each heart and mind. The connection to spirit is through your mind and heart. It is by prayer and meditation that you speak to God. Prayer is talking to God, and meditation is listening to God.

Now, allow us a minute to speak to you concerning spirits. On earth there has arisen much fear concerning spirits. This fear is part of the earth-mind consciousness and is what inhibits many from seeking God in spirit. The biggest fear is of some super spirit called the devil. **What the devil represents is man's turning away from God.** It is the selfishness which comes into hearts and minds. It is the wickedness of belief in demons. **There are no evil spirits.** There are, however, many mischievous spirits and lost souls who will play with your fears. They cannot harm you, except if you give them the freedom to do so.

If a spirit is lost and cannot find its way, or refuses to believe it has died the physical death, then it is a misguided spirit. Some misguided spirits seek to find a lost person on whom to deposit themselves. But understand, these are few, and the duplication of spirits in one body cannot be accomplished without there being some kinship. What we mean by kinship is like-mindedness, a kinship of thinking and attitudes and beliefs. So when you believe that God is the most powerful element in the universe, when you believe that God is All Power and All Loving and cares for you, you close the doors to the kind of thinking that is needed in order to be a part of this misguided scene.

Understand that when misguided or mischievous spirits are found, they are quickly invited to attend a school in the Temple of Knowledge. It is knowledge of God that is lacking in their soul. If they are not repentant upon acquiring knowledge, and deliberately refuse to stop their erring ways, then they are placed in a state of suspended animation. There are very few misguided spirits in this state, but the few who have caused harm to mankind have been written about and fantasied about much too long. How do you protect yourself from this occurring? You, dear ones, are protected the moment you seek God in your hearts and minds. The moment you turn your attention toward God, then you are no longer in the same league as these poor, misguided souls.

Evolution is the way of progress and evolution in spirit is true also. As a whole, our universes have grown. We no longer are living in the dark ages here, either. Therefore, to be frightened of a devil or evil spirit is a waste of time and energy. Most spirits are growing and progressing along the path of enlightenment. The few who are not are separated from us in a place or dimension of total darkness and total inertia. It is much as a state of suspended animation, in that they no longer are conscious. In this state of inertia, you could say they have been turned off, to heal, to rest, to allow the normal state of mind to reemerge.

Everyone has a normal state of mind which recognizes God as the Creator. We all know that there are no other gods before the One God, because there is no other power higher than God. HE is Total Love. With all His power and energy, HE is complete gentleness and compassion. HE loves us Divinely. We are His precious creations. We are His treasure. If you could just receive a small impression of the great love that is God's Love towards you, you would never doubt, fear or hate again. You could not. God's creations are encased in tenderness. **There is no love greater than the Love God has for His creation, which includes each of you.**

So then you know that God is Love. You realize that you are created in love, live in love, are surrounded constantly in love. You know that you cannot be apart from God or His Love. You also know that with God all things are possible; God will help you to perform all manner of good. There is no battle in God. The battle is in yourself and in your failure to recognize God in your life. You already know that God listens to and answers prayers—you have only to ask for help, and it is yours instantly. It is done through you according to your faith.

Faith then is the currency of the universe and God. With faith in God, all your prayers are answered. There are no problems in God; all problems lie inside you. When you have a need in some area of your life, God will be the answer. God answers with ideas, new attitudes and new friends. HE can move you or the people involved into the right places. Faith is the assurance that God is answering your prayer, even if you do not see the answer coming.

You know that you live eternally, that through repeated lives, you can rectify and amend everything. This world is a practice arena for living. How you treat people, how you care for yourself and your world, is how you progress. The most important person to correct is you. This correction is accomplished with much prayer and with God's help. To remove an old belief, replace it with another belief. To remove one attitude, you replace it with a new attitude. Your biggest task on earth is the alignment of your attitudes, beliefs and thoughts with God-Mind. You know that we are just as alive as you. The only difference is in appearance. We are not three-dimensional as you are. We are in the unseen world. We live and feel, just as you do. Jesus demonstrated this by dying on the cross and resurrecting on the third day. That was the whole emphasis of his death, to demonstrate the eternalness of life. We are all mental beings, and it is through our thoughts and our feelings that we move, live, love and become One with God.

Here is something new. All worlds and all beings in these worlds are connected to each other. As one world grows, that very growth pulls all others further along the path. As you grow in spirit, all beings grow. We are all connected to each other by God. The universe is interconnected, the one to the other. This is the reason the beings from the other planets (ETs, Space Brothers) will come to earth's aid. They wish for you to survive, because in surviving, you again have the chance to enter the union of planets.

You should know by now how very important you are to us. We love each of you and are overjoyed with your progress.

We are the Holy Ghost, which Jesus sent out. Our total aim and ambition is to assist mankind to find its connection to God. Each of you have your own special group of brothers, and we work with you to help, but never to take over your life. Therefore, remember that you must ask for our help in specific circumstances. We are continuously praying for you, as a group and individually.

Continue to pray for yourselves first and for your spiritual growth. Then pray for your loved ones and the entire world. Pray that God's total Being and Presence be felt by all. He is here, and HE is more alive than you are. Recognize the Love which is in this world. Meditate and ask the Father God to help you realize your goals, to help you eliminate from inside your being those things that prevent you from becoming one with Him.

The Brotherhood

Maintain Hope and Faith in Heart and Mind
(*Mary, March 19, 1989*)

Dear ones, I ask that you maintain an attitude of hope and faith. With hope and faith you will remain strong in your connection to God. These attitudes will see you through all the days of your life on earth and beyond. Your faith is the assurance of God's Love. There is nothing in the Cosmos to compare to the Love of God. It fills the Cosmos with all that is needed to start and maintain life—in stars, planets and solar systems. God's Love is forever with you. Recognize the Love of God in you and your world. This is all you need to be faithful, hopeful, and to have more good in your life. This is true no matter where you live. Keep faith alive in your heart by reminding yourself of God's great love for you individually and collectively as mankind.

Hope is the attitude which will see you through your entire life, both spiritual and earthly life. For now, concentrate on your life on earth. The physical life will be taken care of as you care for your spiritual life. See, as you bring order into your spiritual life, you bring order into your physical life. By order I am speaking of God's Divine Order. **Hope is an attitude that fills your heart with joy and assurance of things to come.** Look forward to living with hope. Maintain an attitude of good. Hope tells you there is so much more to life. There is more, and it is a grander life than you can imagine. What is important is what you keep in your heart and mind. This is where you live.

You think that because I have not lived on earth for such a long time, I have forgotten what it is like. This is not so. I hear the prayers of those who have lost all hope daily. I hear the prayers of the desperate, and my heart cries out to them: Awaken and know that there is hope, there is good, there is God. Open your inner eyes and look for Him in your heart and mind. I see the lives that are wasted by drugs and hopelessness. Many of today's people think that it is all over; there is nothing they can do to better their lives. They look at the material things and think if they had more houses, more or better cars, more money, they would not have any problems. This is not so. Real problems would come forward to be faced. See, you are facing the real problems. It is the issues that are in your mind and heart, that are real.

Learn to live from the heart and mind. This is where your real and true life is lived. When you face the real issues of life, you are the winner. Then you find that as you seek God and His rightness, as you seek to align yourself with God's energy, all these others things, such as houses, money, cars, your daily bread, will enter your life easily and will be the things you really need. Remember to put first things first. Seek God first. Look within your heart and mind; remove any attitude or belief that inhibits your alignment with God's total Energy.

When there is hope in your heart and mind, there is no desperation or fear. See, desperation comes from fear. So go to the heart of desperation, inertia, procrastination, laziness, and

see that it is fear. Fear and hope cannot live side by side.
Concentrate on Hope in God's Love and watch fear and its by-
products be eliminated. When you find yourself putting off
some task, realize that it is fear which is causing the delay.
When you feel desperation in your heart, realize that this is fear
in disguise. Say to these fears, **"Be gone, leave; I place my life
in God's Love, and there is no room for fear in my heart or in
my mind."**

Now understand that when I say money, cars, houses are
not the important issue, I do not mean for you to stop working
or providing for yourself. You are living on a double-edged
sword. One side is the earthly, physical life, and the other is the
spiritual side. What I am saying is to place your emphasis on
the spiritual side, to eliminate fear, anger, hatred from your
hearts and minds. Then you will find that as you align your
spiritual side, the physical side will be corrected.

Continue to work, for it is what the body needs in order to
live well. Now you will work with hope and Divine Love in
your heart and mind. Continue to set daily goals to accomplish
earthly tasks, but now you will set these goals with hope in
your heart. You have the faith to know that all can be accomplished through the Power of God and with His help.

**Daily, remind yourselves that you live from the stand-
point of hope and faith in God.** All can be accomplished on
earth with God's help. Tell yourselves there is nothing to fear
when you live with God's Love active in your hearts and
minds. You can do, you can learn, you can accomplish. This is
my message to you today.

I wish to have you continue to pray and meditate daily.
This is needed today to live life easily and to prepare for the
future. Pray for your spiritual enlightenment, for understanding to remain ever hopeful and ever faithful to the One God,
Creator of All. Keep the image of Love in your heart and mind,
the image of God's Great Love for us all.

                                        Mary, Mother of Jesus

Celebrate the Success of Jesus' Life
(Brotherhood, March 25, 1989)

(The following day, March 26th, was Easter.)
This is a celebration of the completion of Jesus' life goals. He was successful because he never wavered from seeking Father God's help. He was a vessel for God to reach the people of this world. He was a great mystic and a great demonstrator of spirituality. Allow us to give you some insight on the meaning of the death on the cross. This one event in Jesus' life has been misinterpreted for much too long.

Jesus' death on the cross was a public spectacle. All people in Jerusalem and soon in Judea were told of the death of Jesus. There was much controversy over his sentence to death. There were many people who held opinions on Jesus' innocence or guilt in defying the laws of God as interpreted by the scholars and priests of that day. It was imperative that it become a public spectacle, because that way more people would know of the events taking place around Jesus' death. Crowds of people were present and witnessed the dying of Jesus on the cross. It was necessary for this death to be viewed by as many people as could see it, because by being nailed to the cross as a common criminal, Jesus was placed side-by-side with those people who were common and who had erred. All people make mistakes spiritually, but not all spiritual mistakes are readily visible to others. Many spiritual mistakes are in beliefs, attitudes, or in conceptions of truths. Jesus was crucified with the common criminal, who makes not only spiritual mistakes, but is in error in his society. **The cross of itself holds no magic. It simply tells you that through the Power of God, all mistakes can be crossed out, erased or eliminated.**

Now the reason why more people were involved in this spectacle was to have more witnesses, not only to Jesus' death, but to the resurrection also. **The whole message of the death of Jesus was to tell everyone of the eternalness of life,** to allow you on earth to see that no matter what befalls you, even death, you continue to live. In reality there is no death. What happens to you in the dying process is simply to go from one level to another. You continue with life, eternally. Before this event of Jesus' death on the cross, life was eternal, but many people began to believe that when they died they would not continue to live. They thought this one lifetime was all there was. Many despaired and lost faith in the goodness of life. So Jesus demonstrated the eternalness of life to all people.

(Annie)

Why then did Jesus say, "If you believe on me you will have life everlasting?" (Jn 6:47) Did this imply that if you did not believe in Jesus you would not have life everlasting?

(Brotherhood)

Jesus spoke truths which had not been heard in that particular context before. Jesus said these words to get you (humanity) to believe that you live an everlasting life, and not only that life is everlasting, but that all the things that Jesus did on earth were previews of what you can do now. Jesus did not want mankind to believe only in him. He came to life to demonstrate the truths of God and to show what your potential is. But many people did not believe the words or concepts Jesus was giving to them. They said, "How can we believe this?" They doubted, much as you do today. So then Jesus said, "If you believe in me, if you believe what you have seen, what I have demonstrated, then you will have life everlasting." But even if you do not believe, you still continue to live, because this is the will of God, they were also told.

Jesus taught by demonstration. Look at the attitude Jesus held while he was on trial, to the faith Jesus had in Father God, and the communication which Jesus had with God. You will see how you are to believe, seek and act at all times in your life. Jesus forgave people. His words were, "Father, forgive them, for they know not what they do." (Lk 24:34) Jesus forgave all, and in forgiving he knew he was forgiven. He was aware also that this spectacle had to be a public demonstration of the eternalness of life. The people did not understand the truths of their beings and were following along a path which they did not understand. All went according to God's will.

In reviewing Jesus' life at the time of his death, look to the hope which he gave to all people. See the demonstrations of a spiritual life when he appeared to his friends after his resurrection. Read the life and times of Jesus as they are written in your Bible, but allow new thoughts to enter your mind. Allow yourself to view the attitude, the strength of Jesus' beliefs in God, to set the pace for your life.

In the spiritual world at this time, we celebrate the completion and success of Jesus' life. In one lifetime Jesus was able to complete his goals. He was human, just as you are. He had the same temptations and the same feelings as you. He could become discouraged; he could have become ill, but he didn't, because Jesus had a strong God-Mind connection. He and the Mind of God were One. Do you not see that you and the Mind of God can also be One? This is your potential! But returning to Jesus while he was on earth, he was just as each of you. The only thing different in you and Jesus is his sense of purpose, his connection to God-Mind.

You may not understand the concept of God-Mind. This is God in His pure, impersonal thinking. This is the Place where all Energy and all Creativeness are stored. Now Jesus was in direct communication with this Great Mind of God, and He was also in direct communication with the very personal Father-image of God. This then is the celebration—the celebration of Oneness with God, which is in your future.

Now consider the attitudes and the gentleness of Jesus. This is your potential, these will be your attitudes. Celebrate with us the success and faithfulness of your great brother Jesus.

The Brotherhood

11

Raising Your Expectations

Cross Out Error: Expect Good
(Mary, March 26, 1989, Easter Sunday)

YES, IT IS A TIME of celebration here (in spirit), as it is on earth. But our celebration is because Jesus completed his life goals in one lifetime. He did this by remaining close to God. Some people would say Jesus had tunnel vision, but at times it takes this type of vision to complete goals. Jesus had a mission. He was commissioned to speak Truth to the world.

On earth, religions have made this day into the spectacle it has become. They hold some truths, but deny others. There is too much emphasis on Jesus dying. Too much is said about his final words, and way too much stress is placed on the cross. These are simply symbols which have been symbolic spiritually for centuries.

The cross is symbolic of a crossing out of error. This symbol says to you, **sin is a spiritual mistake.** And Jesus died on the cross for many reasons, but it is the Father God who forgives sin. Jesus forgave sins on earth, because he was commissioned by God to perform to his fullest potential. All mistakes can be crossed out. There is nothing impossible to God, and so therefore it is as easy as crossing out, to be forgiven.

Jesus' body was not special, except that he realized His spiritual goals. But the body or the blood of Jesus was just as yours is. He was very human; he hurt when he bled. He felt pain, he felt tiredness and all other sensations. Jesus was simply a man, but when he kept his goals and began teaching to the masses, he became Christ. Now then, Jesus as Christ is special on all levels and in all worlds. Few have attained the level of Christhood, but all have the possibility of doing so.

In our time, the cross was a way of humiliating criminals. We thought that if a criminal was humiliated, it would deter others from committing crimes. It did not. Being killed by means of the cross happened only to common criminals, to the commonest, if you can use this word, of people. No one who died on a cross was an honored person. Jesus symbolically died on the cross to indicate that as Jesus he was a common man. As the Christ, he taught Truths, and he lived the truth of eternal life.

But rejoice and be glad. What Jesus Christ did was to prove to mankind that life is eternal. He took the mystery out of dying.

Look to Jesus' teachings and learn with the help of God to understand the true meanings in his words. As you seek God the Father, He appears in your mind and heart. He is Absolute Truth. Therefore He never wavers. What was truth in the beginning of time is truth now. Life has always been eternal. It will continue to be eternal.

Now I will tell you a little of what was happening in our family at this time. As you know, we were always attuned to the fact that Jesus had been commissioned by God to do this work. Not all of our children understood that the teachings were the work. Some of them kept expecting Jesus to settle down and marry. Others had questions as to why God wanted Jesus to live as he did, without a home or any place to call his own. In the few times we were able to speak to Jesus alone, he explained the following:

Father God wanted Jesus to live just this type of life, to be totally dependent on Him for all his needs. Thus he was able to demonstrate that God, as the Father, would take care of all needs, no matter how trivial. Man marries to have a mate, a partner, someone to help him with his life goals. In marriage, a certain life-style is set up, one that demands that the marriage or family come first. Jesus did not have time for this commitment. He was already committed to God and His lifetime goals. Jesus knew that his earthly life was a short one. He understood that in teaching the truths that had been ignored, he would upset the authority of the priests.

At that time, the earth-mind consciousness or race consciousness of mankind held many errors in thinking. This consciousness still continues to hold many erroneous concepts. It was the truths[3] in the race or earth-mind consciousness that the priests were looking to then and now. When a person makes a statement like, "All people know that," you can be sure that this is race consciousness. This is earth-mind consciousness used to receive truths.

Jesus also explained to us, his earthly family, that he would be among the common man in life and in death—not to believe in the appearances that were taking place in his life, but to pray for Divine Understanding to come into our minds and hearts; we would have the answers there, within us. He reminded us of the eternalness of life, that truth by earthly vision is not always as it is in spirit, that what is happening on earth is not always what is happening in "heaven," heaven being synonymous with God. Jesus stressed to his brothers, sisters and me that his love for us was unchanging. His appreciation of

---

[3] There are some spiritual truths in the earth-mind consciousness.

me as mother had not wavered. He appreciated his siblings and the life they had shared in childhood.

We as a family unit prayed much for Jesus and for his work on earth. We loved him dearly and always looked up to his knowledge and spirit. Jesus was our son, brother and uncle, as you are to each other. But also we knew that Jesus had been Christed, and that as the Christ he was to teach truths to the world, to demonstrate abilities to mankind, and instill potentials into the world that had never been taught or demonstrated before.

We still suffered and prayed to God for understanding when Jesus was nailed to the cross as a common criminal. It was the relationship or the appearance of his being a criminal that much afflicted us. When Jesus was not in his grave on that Sunday morning, I was overjoyed. He had proven the eternalness of life. All Jesus had ever said to me and Joseph had been truth, and now was no different. Jesus was alive and would return to earth to continue his work.

But it was soon apparent that he had returned to earth not as I had envisioned, but through spirit. Afterwards his disciples were able to heal in his name. They continued to give the teachings of Jesus as they remembered them. But the eternalness of life was apparent. Jesus lived and continues to live this day. Jesus had his body with him in spirit, because he uses this body to this day to walk on earth. Jesus is able to walk among you and talk to you. He continues to teach the common man about God. Jesus as the Christ has the ability to break into many fragments and still remain one. He is able to be in many places and on many levels and still be in heaven. It is this ability that he uses to be on earth in this day.

So today the lesson is a subtle one. **Do not look at the appearances of your outer life, but look at the reality of your inner life with God.** How much are you talking to God? How honest are you with God? Look at your expectations. Do you really expect God to provide for your every need no matter how trivial? He can and He does!

In your mind, use the cross to cross out all errors in thinking and believing. Cross out the race consciousness of mankind. Place your expectations in God-Mind. Use the cross in this way, with words: **"I cross out this appearance of (illness, poverty, or fear) from my mind with Jesus Christ's help. It is now erased completely."** From that moment on, tell yourself it is erased and bothers you no more, no matter what the appearance is. But the main lesson today is expectations. **Place your expectations in God-Mind.** Take a close look at your expectations. If you are to believe these words and have them provide the results you desire, then you must raise your expectations. This is what I mean:

Most people desire to have the appearance of what society today says is a healthy body. In my day a robust and chubby body was considered healthy. Today people look for a sleek and slender body. But if you (Annie) look out the window and see "things in the air," you panic and think it is time to become allergic to the elements. Bless the trees and all of nature. They are not your enemy, but your friend. On a cloudy day you expect to feel pain in your joints. These are the expectations I am speaking of.

Others of you pray for your finances, but you expect to be broke. When you think of your pocketbook, you expect it to be empty. When you receive a bill for payment, your heart skips a beat and your expectation is that you will not be able to pay it on time. Take the bills in your hand and make a statement of truth, like this: **"God is providing the money to pay this bill, now. All I have to do is to raise my expectations so that these words are truth."** See, it is not God who must do, but you. You need to get yourself and your inner life in agreement with God. The changes need to take place inside you. Pray for these changes to take place in your mind, heart and soul so that you can live life with God as your All.

Expect good. Expect health. Expect plenty of money to meet your every need. Expect spiritual knowledge. This is the lesson today.

                                                    Mary, Mother of Jesus

Drink In the Substance of God
(Jesus, March 31, 1989)

Hello, everyone. Expectations are your blueprint of life. What you *expect* to have in your life, will occur. When you plan to build a house, you have blueprints drawn up. Well, in the same manner your expectations are your blueprints of life. Your life will proceed just as you expect it to. This is not always how you want it to be. Bring your expectations up to your desires and then expect God to provide even more through you.

God the Father works through you and not for you. He works through your expectations. If you pray for health and expect illness, then which do you think will occur in your life? If you pray for financial wealth and expect always to be in debt, which will happen? Remember that expectations are your blueprint. Your prayers are important, and God answers prayers. But it is your expectations that determine how wide the door is opened to receive the answers.

Allow us to take health. Annie prays for health in body, mind and emotions. She now has brought her expectations up to a level where she is receiving emotional health. There was a time when she desired and prayed for emotional health, but her expectations were of tears, angers and fears. Now that she has begun to clear the angers and fears from her inner life, her expectations have risen. Her emotions are healed and she is stable emotionally. Now she must work on her expectations for physical health. Watch those little fleeting thoughts. See, when Annie notices the rain is nearing, she expects to have pain in her body.[4] She prepares her body for pain. This is an unconscious act. It is so ingrained in her mind, that pain goes along with cloudiness, that she is not aware she is tensing up. Take the time to do the inner work of eliminating unpleasant expectations from your mind and heart. Enter your temple, use lights in meditation to eliminate or wipe clean your expectations as you

---

[4] Annie has Anklosing Spondylitis, a form of arthritis.

would a chalkboard. Then fill your mind and heart, while you fill your expectations with all you desire. This will take more mental exercise.

Do not belittle the mental exercises I give; prayer is also a mental exercise. It is a mental process and one which you already know gives results. The thinking process is what connects you to the Divine. **It is through your thinking and feelings that you have the power to change your life.** Prayer, meditations, quieting the mind are all mental processes. Do you not see?

The ability to change your life circumstances is through these mental exercises. Challenge your mind, your thinking, to raise your expectations to the same level as your desires. When your expectations and prayers coincide, then you will see miracles in your life and in your world.

Now then, let us take a look at your finances. All of you pray for your finances. But look at your expectations. I used the example of how you feel when you receive a dun for money. Be mindful at that time and see if you feel a tenseness or a sinking feeling as you handle the dun. If you do, then your expectations are for lack and not plenty. When you think of your money, do you think, "I have plenty of money"—or do you think, "I'll not have enough money to _____"? If you are expecting to have a lack of money, this is the blueprint you are giving Universal substance to supply for you.

Watch your thoughts and words. Do you say, "This always happens to me," when some setback occurs? "I can never get out of debt." Or perhaps, "I wish I had a lot of money." These are thoughts and words which deplete your expectations. Your expectations are made up of all your thoughts, words and how you view yourself.

From this moment on, take charge of your expectations. Consciously make an effort to correct what you tell yourself about how you want your life to be. Take charge of your feelings, the little feelings that are present as you spend your money or think of your money. Here is how to do this.

Enter quietly into your special place within your mind. Give yourself a bath mentally and remove all fears and angers from your mind, heart and expectations. Mentally stand under a waterfall and allow the water to flow over you. In this case, water will represent God's Divine substance. Now turn your head up and open your mouth and drink the substance of God. Only in this way will substance work through you. This is my message to the world. God will not force upon you anything, not even your good. You must allow God to work through you. People who have plenty of money expect to continue to have plenty. If they don't have this expectation, they lose it. When fear, anger or hatred enter into the supply of money, there will be a lack. Perhaps they will have money but not happiness, something will be missing. Money will not be beneficial, but a source of pain.

As God's universal substance expands through your mind and heart, doors open to more money and more happiness.

Happiness is not in having great amounts of money, but in doing the Will of God in your life. **Complying with God's universal code of spiritual growth brings true happiness.** Expect to live happily. Expect to have plenty to meet all your needs. Expect to have your needs met; you are the only one who can define your needs. One person has need of a healthy body, another must have a large home, another could be comfortable or satisfied with a small home and few possessions. It is what you expect to have or to live with that determines what you receive. Consciously raise your expectations to a higher level. With God all things are possible. With God as your Ally, Mentor, you cannot fail. Open your mind and heart to all that God is. This is where your good lies.

For one week, do the exercise of the waterfall. Let the waterfall represent the fulfillment of all your needs and desires. Drink in the ability to make money, to be happy, to be what you want to be. Use your mind, use your feeling nature, to increase your expectations. I am available to help—call on me.

Jesus

Understand Your True Value
(Brotherhood, April 8, 1989)

We bless all the effort you put forth in seeking a spiritual awareness. Do not try to hurry your spiritual growth; it cannot be rushed. There is an awareness that first must enter your heart. This awareness is in finding out all you can about God-Mind and God-Essence, becoming aware of your place in the scope of God's plan.

Daily arise with this thought—take it with you as you live each day:

"There is One Presence and One Power alive in the Universe. That Presence and Power is God, who loves me beyond compare. I am made in the image and likeness of this One Presence. I am an individualized spark of the Divine. This One Presence and Power is my spark of Divinity."

When you can truly believe this, you will have progressed centuries. You will in this lifetime find your true value in life. When you realize, truly realize, that you are connected to God and All He represents, then you will have an idea of your true value. Your value can never come from you or anything you do or have. Your value is given by God.

For the past two weeks we have given lessons on raising your expectations. You each must come to an understanding of your true value in life. Few people have come to the realization of the words "made in the image and likeness of God." Become aware of who you are!

In a poem received by Annie some time ago, there was a line which made this statement: "Remember who you are!" When you each can recall your origin and your future, you will not have any trouble in realizing your true value.

Originally, we all came from God the Creator. So if we are made in His image and likeness, **we have the following attributes deep within us.** It is our choice to seek these attributes or to ignore them.

Love—a love deep inside us for all living things, for ourselves, for our world and for our future. If you did not have a love for your future, you would not continue to look forward to the future. The love which is inside us is Divine Love. This powerful Love heals, prospers and nourishes us.

Wisdom—the wisdom of the ages, it has been called, but in reality it is the wisdom of God. It is knowing all the answers and having an understanding of the best manner to handle every situation. This ability is deep within each of us. It is always within and awaits only our strong desire to have the ability awakened for our use.

Order—in all of God's Creations there is a permeable sense of Order. In nature, the ecology of nature is all in Divine Order. There is a food chain prepared for all creatures. This same food chain cares for this entire planet. There are many laws of nature and of the physical universe that were set into motion at the beginning. Deep within each of you is Divine Order. It will be through your thoughts, your mental conceptions and searchings, that you will find Divine Order and call it forth into your world. Become aware of the power of Divine Order in your lives. Make a statement to yourself like this: **"Divine Order is present in my life and in my world."** Tell yourself this over and over until you believe it deep in your heart. What is important is what you believe to be true. When what you believe to be true is united with Divine Truth, you will progress to the point of manifesting your desires.

Life—you are always alive. We all live eternally. **This is eternity, now.** You do not have to wait until another life to be or to have. You have all you need in order to live life fully now. Life can be lived only now; it's not later or past which holds life, and it's not in the future that life is lived. This is truth!

Strength—you are one with Strength itself. Your origin is Strength, because you come from God. Remind yourself: you are strong because you are strong in God.

Power—there is One power alive in the Universe. This Power is alive in you. You and Divine Power are one, a unit. Never think of yourself as powerless. Remind yourself you are One with God, who is All Power. You have more power within you than an atom does. Think about that statement!

Enthusiasm—you do not have to seek some drug or drink to give you enthusiasm and a zest for life. You are Enthusiastic because you are alive! Remind yourself daily of this enthusiasm which is deep within you: **"I Am alive and enthusiastic, because I am One with God."**

Will—the will to live, be and perform. This is an attribute which is yours, free, gratis. You do not have to muster up any will to live. Just let someone try to prevent you from continuing with this life, and you will see a tremendous will to live rise up from within. Remind yourself daily of the Will that is within you already. Here is how to direct your will: **"I will to do the will of God; God's will for me is only good."** This is another truth.

Understanding—this word implies that you already know. You already have an idea of what and how to do. This is another truth. You already know how to live, and you can instinctively know where to seek all your good. It is **"within you."** Remind yourself of this: **"I have the understanding of God within me. I can understand and comprehend what my life is about."**

Energy—you were made from Pure Energy. Your very being is comprised of Pure Energy. All you are and all you think is Pure Energy. Each thought and each feeling is a release of Pure Energy. Use this Energy wisely. Remember who you are! **"I use Pure Energy to create in my life the happiness, love and the situations which I desire."**

Remember that you are more than these few attributes, but if you can get a true understanding of your value by reminding yourself of your potential, then miracles will follow miracles. It is all up to you. No one else can do it for you. No one else can heal you or provide for you. **It is your responsibility to**

unite with the Truth of your being. Start here with these few attributes and become so immersed in these ideas that you do not have to remind yourself of who you are. You will have an assurance of your true value in spirit, in life and in eternity. The only way to incorporate these truths into your mind is by repetition. It will take many hours of thought to fully understand your place in eternity. Take this as an exercise to increase your expectations. Ask for our help to help you understand these truths. This is your spiritual bill of rights:

"You have the right to use all the power, energy, love, strength, enthusiasm, wisdom, life and understanding of the Cosmos."

There is one prevention: **this must be used for the good of the whole.** This power must be used to increase the spiritual awareness of the world. By increasing your spiritual awareness, you increase the whole world's awareness. We are all connected to each other through the life force. No matter where life is lived, we are one, a whole. All of humanity, of spirit beings, of beings on other planets, no matter where life is lived, as long as there is life, we are one.

Repeat these statements that have been given today. Or you can increase your awareness by making a statement to your mind like this: **"I am united with God through the following attributes. . ."** Then list these truths, such as, **"Divine Love, Divine Wisdom, Life, Eternal Enthusiasm, Divine Understanding, God's Peace,"** and so on.

This is how to enter into your mind these truths: Always call upon Divine Love or Divine Wisdom, because there is simple love and wisdom, but you want the powerhouse of Love and Wisdom, and this is denoted by placing the word "Divine" before the attribute.

All that is God is available to everyone at all times. It is by incorporating these truths into your life that you will be able to use what you are learning. Practice and practice more. These are lessons and not simply lectures. **You must take these into your inner self in order for these truths to be of use to you.**

This is also a good way to pray, by reminding yourself of **who you are!**

We will be with each of you as you practice. Call on us; use our assistance; this is our aim and our cause. Our whole purpose is to aid you in connecting to God-Essence, to help you use your full potential in spirit.

The Brotherhood

Practice Your Beliefs
(Mary, April 9, 1989)

There is always more to learn about God and about your spiritual life. I will simply reinforce what the Brotherhood has already given, the importance of taking these lessons and using them as a theme for your daily life.

Your entire purpose in living on earth is to practice what you have already learned. During your spirit life, when you are in the different Temples of Learning, your whole focus is on learning the principles of Love, Peace, Wisdom, etc. In the spirit life, as on earth, this is your choice. Most beings choose to be in the process of the eternal quest. This quest is for knowledge and understanding of the true nature of life, of which you are a part. You are always given a chance to rectify any error and practice to improve yourself. So your lesson today is that your entire purpose on earth is to practice what you believe. We all say practice, but suppose I give you some examples of how to practice what you have already learned. You already know many Truths, some of which the Brotherhood have given you today. Take these truths and repeat them to yourself daily. Suppose you are doing some task that is boring to you; take this time as you perform this task to use your mind and heart to improve your life. Do this by memorizing one Truth and repeating it to yourself until such time as it is fixed in your mind and then in your heart. Everything is learned first in the mind; it is intellectualized, and then it is taken into the heart and it is felt. Some people can incorporate these truths into their minds and hearts with speed. Others will be working on memorizing these Truths for a longer period of time. Do not compare how you do with another. **Every person is unique and will learn at their own rate and in their own way.**

The reason it is necessary for you to do this is that when you truly understand your value to God, your true worth, you will have progressed to the point of being able to use much of your full potential. Remember that Jesus told the world, "All the things I do, you will do, and more." (Jn 14:12) On earth today, many are living only to half of their potential. Many have not reached out to stretch to their full length in spirit. These memorizations and repetitions are for your benefit. Nothing can change God, because He Is. Do you understand that God is and always has been All Power, Pure Energy and All the other attributes to which we have given definition?

There are mental blocks in your minds, and it is imperative that you, with God's help of course, unblock these hard places in your mind. Allow an analogy. God is secure and stable as a very large tree. Upon this tree hang several ribbons. We will say in this analogy that the tree represents God as the One Secure and Stable element in your life. You, as people, are represented by the different ribbons. The wind is the circumstances of your life. When the winds of circumstance blow gently, then you as the ribbon are slightly moved. But when the wind of life's circumstances blows with more force, you become entangled by the winds and a blockage and a twisting occurs.

We could say this twisting and blockage of the ribbons happens in your life. As the winds of life's circumstances blow through your life, you will be able to use the very same wind to become disentangled. But always the tree remains secure and safe, a refuge and a rock in time of trouble.

To unblock the mental concepts that are keeping you from your full potential, you must become One, united with the security of God-Essence. Use the circumstances in your life to remove all tangled thoughts. **Use your life just as it is now to become One with God and All He Is.**

You are a mental being that feels. This is the truth about you and every other being alive. Angels, Saints and people alike, we are all mental beings who sense and feel. This is the truth about you. To change your mental concepts and your feelings takes much effort on your part. It takes repetition of truths to unblock and disentangle your life. These repetitions are another way to pray, because in reality God is not affected by our thoughts or feelings. He already is All. He remains All. It is people who are affected by what they think and feel. By using your mind and your heart, you can have the full power of your worth. To God, every one of us is priceless, a work of art. We are so precious to God that He would not like to have one of us suffer in the least.

So consider that you suffer because you do not have a picture of your true value. You suffer in life because you are lazy or disinterested in improving your life in reality. Remember Jesus' words, "Seek first the kingdom of heaven, and all things will be added to you." (Mt 6:33) This was true 2000 years ago and it is true now. As you come together to learn more about spirit and your connection to God, you are seeking the kingdom of heaven. As you practice the truths of which we are simply reminding you, your life will blossom as a flower; you will have true happiness and true peace, and all the other material things you need.

When you are discouraged, remind yourself that you are a spiritual being. You are not just flesh and bone; you are a mental and feeling being. You are an art piece in God's gallery. We all are made in the image and likeness of God. All you need do is accept these truths as truths about you.

It is through the words "I AM" that you are connected to God. Whatever you say after "I AM" becomes truth. Watch your words, your thoughts and especially your feelings. This is how to bring your expectations up to the top level, to your full potential and capacity. Be careful of the words that follow "I

AM." If you say, "I am tired," you are bringing this condition into your life. If you say, **"I am provided for by God,"** this is a Spiritual truth and will quickly manifest in your life, as soon as you truly believe the words with feeling.

Take these lessons and practice them, and practice more. It is through strengthening your mental contact with All that God Is, that you become strong. This is how to prepare for your future. No matter what comes into your future, you will be safe. As the storms come and the earth moves, you will remain secure in your connection to God. Through this connection, you will be guided to safe places at the right time. You will simply know how to care for yourself and others. This was Annie's original purpose in beginning this venture—to find out more about the future. It is through your connection to God-Mind and God-Essence that you will be safe.

Mary, Mother of Jesus

12

Seeking Out Your Lessons

The Blessings in Your Circumstances
(Brotherhood, April 16, 1989)

ESIRE TO LEARN more about spirit and God. This makes it possible for you to grow in all ways. There are many different levels of existence and many different parts of your entire being that can improve with every situation you face.

While Annie was reading a book, she was surprised to learn that **along with the freedom of choice comes responsibility.** Choice is a God-given freedom, and along with each freedom comes responsibility. Allow us to emphasize this by using the responsibilities you have as citizens of this country. You have many freedoms, and through these freedoms, you are able to accomplish and do many things with your individual lives. This is not available to people in other countries. But along with these freedoms, each member of this country has responsibilities. You are responsible for the selection of the leaders of this government. In order to continue to have these freedoms, you are the watcher of the ethics and morals of the next generation, of the leaders of this country and its judges. Every person is accountable for their actions. No one is above the law. In the past the citizens of this country have removed leaders from the seat of government when they have not abided by its laws. In few countries could this be accomplished. But how does this pertain to spirit?

God in His greatness has given each being freedom to choose. You can choose all details of your life on earth. You not only choose all the details of your life, but you also choose the circumstances of your life. You are the author of your life. You have the freedom to live life in poverty or in wealth. You can have a healthy body or one ravished with pain and illness.

This year we have been giving you lessons to change the circumstances if you do not like your life. Any aspect of your life or yourself can be changed for the better. You do not have to live life under any circumstance you find unbearable. It is within your power to change your mind and heart about anything. Along with this freedom to choose also comes responsibility. It is your duty to be constantly on guard to your goals, to find within you the items or circumstances which need improving. **You are the only one who can change your life. You are the only one who is responsible for your happiness, health or anything in your life.**

No longer can you blame life for what is happening to you. No longer can you feel helpless. No longer can you sit back and wait for situations to improve on their own. It is all up to you. How many times have you in the past made the statement that, "_____ was to blame for the mistake I made?" You fill in the blank with a name. Now you see this is a false statement. You are responsible for the mistake. No one can cause you to do, think or be what you are not—no one, not karma or any spirit. If there is something in you which needs to be improved, it is up to you alone to do the work to improve. No one *can* stop you; no one *will* stop you. This is your life. It is a gift from God. Understand that He will not live your life for you. God will not make your choices for you. The choices are made by you either directly or indirectly. If you make an effort to choose or to take responsibility for your choices, then you are in control. If you delay making the choices, then the choices will be made for you by circumstance. But any way, you have made the choice. You have control, or you can give up control to others or to circumstance.

What we are saying today is take control of your life. Change those things inside of you that need changing in order to have the life you desire. Stop blaming others for your situation. Where do you begin? In your heart and in your mind. All life is lived from within. **All changes take place within your mind and heart**. This you can do. It takes a decision made in earnestness and commitment.

Look at every situation in your life and ask it to bless you. Every circumstance has a lesson for you only. It is how you react to life that determines how you live life, no matter what the situation is or whom the event has affected most. If you are involved, there is a lesson for you. There is a hidden blessing for you! The blessing is in learning the lesson. **Ask the situation to give you information.** Then become quiet in your mind and allow pictures, words or thoughts to enter. You will find in this way that you can learn your lessons easily and quickly. Direct the events in your life now. Find the key to your blessing. **There is good for you in every event in your life, no matter how dark or dire the circumstance.**

Perhaps it is in releasing an emotion that you no longer need. Perhaps it is in forgiving yourself or someone else. There is a mental act or an emotional deed that needs to be performed in every situation.

Begin this week with this thought: **"I take control of my life and all the events in my life. I will react to my life in Divine Love and look for the blessing in every situation of my life."**

In making this statement, you are aligning yourself with Truth. You are in control of your life whether you like the circumstances of your life or not. You react to every situation in your life. By putting yourself in a straight line with God's Divine Love, you will take the blessing from every situation. This blessing is yours already. **It is not God or life who needs to change; it is you!**

By choosing to learn your lesson with the aid of God's Divine Love, all lessons will come to you gently, with tenderness. This is how to change your life for the better. **When you concentrate on the inner way or life, the outer circumstances and habits will fall into Divine Order.** The habits that are detrimental to your well-being will fall away. Those old ways of reacting will be replaced with improved methods. You can change. You can improve your life. You can be all you desire to be. This is Truth. This is the Truth of God.

We pledge to help you understand these words. For what you do not understand about this lesson, simply ask for clarity. With Love, we guide you to realize your full potential in God.

The Brotherhood

Find the Purpose for Each Event
(Brotherhood, April 22, 1989)

You are beginning to see that all events that happen in your life are there for a reason. Sometimes the reason is hidden within the relationship or within the interaction of people. But all events are in your life as a means to your spiritual betterment. Do not become too engrossed in minor details, such as which day will I see the changes? Or, will my friends see the differences today? Most important is to learn the purpose for the situations in your life. **If you are involved in any situation, take the lesson from it. In this way, you will find the good hidden in the situation.**

Take a look at the relationships in your life. Ask within, what is the significance of these relationships? We are not speaking of your marital partner only, but of all the relationships, the way you interact with people, the feelings between you and others. If there are unpleasant situations between you and another, know that the unpleasantness will be eliminated when you have learned the lesson, or if you come to a place of forgiveness. Then the relationship will either change for the better or the other person will leave quietly and without any hard feelings.

Most people do not understand this. They feel that people come into their lives accidentally. This is not true. Every situation is for your learning. People come into your life to bless you or to be blessed. They either come to learn a lesson from you or in order to teach you a lesson. A way to simplify this is to say, **"Every person comes into my life to be loved or to give me love."**

Love is utmost in importance. Love all people without attachment. Love all people, without becoming responsible for them. Love freely; love without any thought of return. Love because God loves all people. Love every situation in your life. If there is illness, know and understand that the illness is in your life to teach. The illness is calling attention to some area in your life that needs to be worked on with love.

Annie, you have the right idea about the illness which plagues you. It is a connective tissue illness, and so you are thinking your connection to God needs to be strengthened. Perhaps not only your connection to God needs to be strengthened, but your connection to family or certain family members, perhaps your connection to self or your connection to people in general? Every person, every being in the universe is interconnected through the Spirit of Life which activates us. Look at all connections.

For those who are depressed, look at why or what is so depressing. Perhaps it is you who depresses someone in some way. Perhaps it is your inner nature that you are holding down. See, to depress is to hold down or to mash down. Allow your thoughts to run away with the word depress. Look at all the different ways this word can be used. Within the word that describes the illness or condition is a clue. Then use the clue to look at how you interact with others, with yourself or with God.

Take an event in your life. We will use Annie as an example. She fell down and injured her ankle and a foot.[5] Look at this sentence. She fell down. At that time Annie was having a fight with her higher self as to what she wished to do with the information Mary was sending her. First, she had accepted to work with Mary, then she fell down in her commitment. So she fell down in reality. The lesson was, in what light do you make commitments? Do you honor your commitments? Do you follow through on your commitments? See, even if you are progressing very little, you have not fallen down on your commitment. You are still learning. You are still honoring your word.

Now then, perhaps you are disillusioned with people at your workplace. What spiritual lesson can you learn from the interrelationships you have with the different individuals? **Spiritual lessons are those which change you from within. They give you the opportunity to practice courage, patience, honor, valor, integrity, love, forgiveness and these kinds of spiritual assets.** When you are having trouble finding the clue, sit quietly and think about it. When this doesn't work, ask within, what is the lesson here? When you ask, allow any one of us to give the answer through your mind. That is, your higher self, us or God can answer your question. The answer will come! Depending on the individual, it could come with words, a train of thought, or perhaps through pictures or images. The important thing here is for each individual to ask their own questions and wait for an answer. **Every person needs to go through the process of obtaining their own answers.**

We advocate that these lessons be learned in love, love for yourself and love for your fellow man. Take your time, be

---

[5] In 1988 Annie fell down the stairs in our house and broke her left ankle and right foot.

gentle with yourself. You will learn the lessons that are yours to learn, if not this lifetime, then in another. You have eternity to learn. You could have a glorious life if you learned your lessons quickly. Then, as is true for a child in school, you will have the benefits. In school, a child is allowed to play, color pictures or is rewarded in some fashion for completing his work; sometimes it is just a paper star on his work. You are given something special for learning your lessons in a lifetime. There is atonement deep within you; there is more pleasantness in your life than unpleasantness. While you are on earth, there will always be lessons to learn. The joy comes in learning them quickly. The rewards are your power and pleasure. This is a way to meditate: contemplate your life, the situations in your life, the people in your life. There are clues in all of these as to the "things" you are learning. Perhaps it is forgiveness or integrity. Look for the common cord. This is a form of prayer. **It is in talking within that you communicate with the Almighty.**

We urge you with love to perform these tasks. It is in the doing that you learn. It is in performing that you advance. Be gentle with yourself and allow yourself time to learn the process. Take these lessons that are given weekly, and practice doing what we suggest. It is for your spiritual advancement that we are working.

The Brotherhood

Learn in Love
(Mary, April 23, 1989)

I welcome you into my circle of caring and faithful individuals. Each of you are becoming aware of the Love that is in the Universe. This Love is God. It is the Energy and Power of God that you sense deep within you. This is your connection to God-Essence and God-Mind.

At times I feel that we, myself, Jesus, the Brotherhood and Angelic Hosts, have given you the idea that we are not aware of you as individuals. Allow me at this time to reassure you that we are aware of each of you, individually. We see the progress you make. We help you with ideas and with love. **Love is the most important element in the Universe. This Universe is comprised totally of Love. God's Love was used to create it and sustains it.** Perhaps you don't feel this love is a part of you, but you are made in this Love Energy. Your entire being is made up of atoms of Love.

Today I wish you to see your world with love and in love. See that your entire life is love. You do not have to do anything special to have love; you already have it because your very essence is love, and you have had love since before your birth on earth. Be gentle and loving with yourselves. Allow Divine Love to make a difference in your life. You already have Divine Love in your life. It can make a big difference when you allow it freedom to guide you and prosper you. Daily tell yourself this Truth: **"I am made in Divine Love; my entire life is encircled in God's Love."**

Now then, take this message along with the message the Brotherhood has given. Use both of them together. Review your life with an attitude of Love. In love you can contemplate your relationships. In gentleness and forgiveness of self and others, you will accomplish much.

Love yourself; love your enemies. Bless those who desire to harm you. Place anyone who is hateful to you in a circle of God's Love. You do this with words. By saying, **"I encircle you in Divine Love and allow God to protect me and help you,"** you disarm your enemies when you pray for them. When you bless those people who are mean and unforgiving, you literally disarm them. Your enemies could be those who misuse your trust, or people who are simply uncaring in their approach to you. The word "enemy" means, in this sense, any person who abuses you, your trust, your love or anything to do with you. It not only means someone who desires to harm you but one who is uncaring and unthinking.

Forgive yourself of all mistakes. Forgive yourself of all there is to forgive. In life, you can be your own worst enemy. You can put others ahead of your own welfare. You can become so insignificant to yourself that you allow anyone to usurp your own authority. You allow others to use you. Forgive yourself of this sin (meaning this is a spiritual mistake). Forgive your past and your present of all that bothers you. Forgive family and acquaintances who in the past abused you in any way. **Forgiveness of self and of others will clear all emotional garbage.** When you are able to forgive yourself, you clean out of your life many useless emotions and situations.

Please do as the Brotherhood of God have requested in reviewing your life situations. Begin to learn all you can about yourself and your relationships. This is where you will grow, not only spiritually, but emotionally and mentally. My request is that you accomplish this task in love, gentleness and tenderness, that you forgive yourself, that you take it easy when dealing with yourself. Many people take these life reviews and use them as an excuse to berate themselves for being stupid. You are not stupid, but trusting. This is true of all people.

Trust is good. You need to trust yourself and others in this world. Perhaps some person has abused your trust. But this in no way denotes that you are stupid. It simply says you have trusted and been abused in that trust. Regain the trust that was placed in you in the beginning. Maintain this trust in yourself, in the inherent goodness of man, and especially trust God.

So to review, search for answers to the question of what lessons you are to learn. But search in love, forgiveness and trust. When you can love yourself, forgive yourself, trust yourself, you will be gentle and tender toward yourself. As you treat yourself with kindness, you will automatically treat others likewise.

It is true that in order to love another person, you must first love yourself—that is, if you truly desire to love as God does. In order to trust others, you must trust yourself. To know yourself is power, strength, and releases much energy. You eliminate fear and anxiety from within your heart. As you cleanse your inner life, this opens the way for spiritual blessings to abound.

Take these lessons and practice them. Keep these lessons that the Brotherhood have given you in mind. These lessons will lead you to survival in all manners and in all events. **The inner life must be put in order for you to be able to hear the directions that come to you. These directions are your survival physically, emotionally and spiritually.**

There is a message in these words for all of you. I do love you, as the poem[6] (below) implies. These words fit what I feel for each of you.

Mary, Mother of Jesus

Here is the poem:

I want to pick you up and hold you in my arms like a babe.
I want to wipe your tears away.
If only there were some way to let you feel the love I have
in my heart for you.
But if I can love you this much and want you to be happy,
How much more does God love us?
God in His wisdom allows each of us to face our hurts and to
direct our lives.
I will do the same, dear friend.
I will simply be here waiting, in case you need me.
I will wipe your tears in my mind and hold you in my heart.
Through my prayers I will love you with all that I am.

---

[6] This is a poem that Annie had received a few days earlier.

13

Renewing Commitment

A Life of Prayer and Gratitude
(Brotherhood, May 6, 1989)

WE HAVE A MESSAGE of spiritual value for each of you. What we see today is a need to reemphasize your prayer time. We see that each of you have been bitten with springtime, which to humans denotes playtime. The weather will continue to be unusual, but this will not in any way keep nature from showing her beauty. Enjoy your world. As you enjoy the beauty of nature, remember that God as Creator appreciates your love for His world.

Pray by being grateful for nature, for your life and for the era in which you find yourself. Pray by showing gratitude for all that you see, all experiences and all you are involved in. **Gratitude is a form of prayer.** Use gratitude to pray.

See, prayer is not always the requesting of conditions or things. There are many ways to pray. Realize that prayer simply is communion with God. Ask for God's help in every situation or condition of your life. We are sure that improvements will come as you pray. When you turn to God through your mind, all negatives will be converted into good situations. Now this good is your spiritual good. Ask God to help you learn spiritual values more easily. Ask His help as you go through this life and with your lessons.

We previously gave Byron and Annie a story of a life on earth of one of our Brothers.[7] They felt that they had learned much through reading of our experiences. We have another story of one of our Brothers.

We have a new Brother who last lived on earth during the time your country was mostly unexplored. He was brought over in one of the first ships to cross the great ocean. Here he is with his story. This will relate **how to live a life of prayer and gratitude.**

When I was a small child in my mother's arms, we came to this country because, as I was told, my father had been thrown out of England. He was a poor, lazy drunk who would not pay his debts. In those days England simply ridded herself of undesirable people by sending them to the new world. And so we came, father, mother, sister and me. Soon after we landed, there was another brother added to the family.

The location of the settlement was in what is now called New England. The weather was harsh. The people who already lived there were just as harsh. Most of these people had become disillusioned because of the conditions. The settlement was mostly primitive and the work was hard. In order to build, we had to cut down trees and make mud into mortar and then construct the small houses. Food had to be grown and meat had to be hunted and prepared for the long winters.

The native people resented us coming in. They felt we were destroying the forest and relying on the small animals too

---

[7] In another message, not part of this lesson.

much for food. Well as you can see, perhaps they were right
and somewhat foresighted. Since I had no recollection of civilization, I thought I was in paradise as I grew. I loved the forest
and made friends with the Indian children who lived near the
settlement. I loved to roam far into the forest to see what was
over the next ridge. What was behind the next tree was always
of interest to me. I learned to speak in some of the Indian
tongues. I also took pride in my strength and my physical body.
When I was a young man, perhaps age of twelve or thirteen
years, I went with the Indian tribe of my friends. Before winter
we went South and made camp in the forest near a great river.
It snowed from time to time, but the snow melted rapidly and
the sun would be back to warm our bodies. This was completely different from the harsh winters in the settlement. In my
father's home, they had no conveniences, not a barrel to collect
water or a place in the attic to store food. So winters had been
very long and very bad.

But among my Indian family, I was happy. They accepted
me as one of their own. I was called White Brother because of
my skin color. I sat around the evening fire and listened closely
to the stories told by the old ones. They told of the Great Spirit
which had made this world. They knew of other worlds that
had been before and told what they knew of these worlds.
Many of their stories had to do with the beauty that was in the
western lands, the red rock and the great mountains that were
so tall that you could see into heaven. My inner self longed to
see these great mountains and the beautiful rivers and lakes
that were in the western lands. I was told of an old tribe of
natives who had survived the last great flood, the great flood
that had destroyed the earth. These old natives had stories of
the nether world, the world that had flying machines and flying
stars. The stories sparked my imagination like nothing else
had. I began to want to find out where the Great Spirit lived.
The Great Spirit must live in the heavens that were seen upon
the great mountains.

As I was initiated into the Indian way of life, I was also initiated into a spiritual life. I was so intrigued with the Great Spirit Creator. I learned all I could from the old ones. I took the vision quest and smoked the pipe of knowledge. I saw great visions and spoke often to eagle spirit and wolf spirit. I made peace with all spirits as quickly as I could. I wanted their help to reach the great mountains. Later I told the old one, who had become my grandfather and mentor, of my plan. He suggested that I first go to speak to the ancient ones who lived among the red rocks. The oldest tribe alive had more knowledge of the Great Spirit.

So it was that I set out on the journey of my life, the search for the home of the Great Spirit. On the journey came my blood brothers, White Eagle and Running Wolf. Behind I left my love, Little Doe. Several days into the journey we felt that someone or something was following us. When we doubled back, we found Little Doe was tagging along. We held a tribal meeting and decided that we would lose too much time in taking her back to the tribe. Besides, she could cook and wash and do the other chores a woman could do.

The journey was very long in that it took us one year to reach the mouth of the great river. Then we were to follow a southern route into the land of the plains. Many of the tribes of natives had never seen a white man and were very curious. We exchanged our pelts and seeds. On the journey, we had very little trouble with other tribes. Some were friendlier than others, but on the whole we were greeted and allowed to travel through their territories. Some would ride a distance with us. By the second winter we were in the land of the red rocks. It was very desolate and a very strange land. Soon we came to the ancient ones we had heard of. We told them of our mission and the reason we had traveled so far. Many nights were spent listening to the stories of the last world, the story of the great flood and the time when the Grandfather Spirit who created the world had become angry. We stayed with these ancient people for one year. We learned much about the Great Spirit's method of being. We learned the rituals and to worship in the old way. We learned that indeed there were some mountains that were so tall you could see forever.

The great mountains were guarded by the great humped-back bear, who was very vicious and mean. These bears were relentless in their pursuit of anyone who invaded their territory. We learned to hold ceremonies to the great humped-back bear. We prayed, and I was led on another vision quest where I met the great humped-back bear in spirit. I was given a glimpse of the mountains and of the beauty that could be seen from the tops of these great mountains. I learned to be a medicine man with the ancient ones, because we were told that it had been prophesied that a new tribe would come to them to learn of the Creator Spirit. The leader was a man like none other ever seen before. His eyes would be the color of the sky and his hair would be the color of the sands. I was the leader of the new tribe. I had been seen in the past; this journey had been seen, and it was also told that the leader-to-be would have crossed the great ocean of the east and would go to the great ocean at the edge of the western lands.

We were quite impressed with this news. It took us by surprise. Among these old ones, Little Doe and I were married and blessed. From this tribe White Eagle and Running Wolf took their wives. So the new tribe was in part made up of the old tribe. Out of the old would come the new as prophesied.

As I felt a need to see the great mountains and to set up a new territory for my people, we left the old ones. To the north and the west we went, toward the great mountains; with valor and courageous hearts we hiked.

Through all the journey I was taken by the beauty of the land. I had not seen any land which was not beautiful in its own way. The trees and the shrubs were different in many of the places, but each had their own beauty. I was in a constant state of awe. I loved the land; I loved the animals of the land. The birds and butterflies were of such great beauty. In my heart I was constantly talking to the Creator Spirit of all worlds. Nightly I held a ceremony of appreciation for all we had seen and for safe passage the next day. In the morning we also held a small ceremony saying good-bye to the beauty of the land seen and greeting the new day that would take us into new lands. This became a ritual that lasted my whole life.

We came at last to the great mountains, and as we climbed to the tops we could truly see forever. We were higher than ever before. We were close to the Great Spirit Creator. The mountains were purple, a color we had never seen before. It was breathtaking indeed.

As we faced our first winter in the mountains, I was at a loss as to how to protect us from the harsh weather. I should have known that the Grandfather Spirit had seen to it that I would have a good companion. Little Doe settled us into a mountain cave facing the south. Here we were near running water, and there was a plentiful supply of deer, rabbit and moose. We had plenty of wood to build fires and plenty of food. In the winter months we used traps to catch the small animals and killed deer for food. The pelts were used to make clothing.

We stayed here for two years and in that time we tracked many new areas of land. Also, here we received into our new tribe seven new babes, four boys and three girls, a most auspicious number.

Throughout the years, we traveled mostly in the mountains of the great humped-back bear. We had little to fear because we were one with our environment. We held daily ceremonies to the Great Spirit and talked nightly to the spirit of the great humped-back bear. As our tribe grew in numbers we grew older. With age we became more aware of the unity of this world, of the true worship of the ONE Great Creator Spirit.

My best lesson learned in this last life was appreciation, to truly worship God as Creator and appreciate the beauty of nature. Appreciate all that you have, for even in this day all the buildings, the glass, the metals are all made by God, Creator. Not one thing on earth today is truly manmade, not even chemically-made things. All that is of this world is of God. **My message is to appreciate, appreciate and appreciate more, because through appreciation you are praying, worshiping and adoring God. This is true prayer.**

What you appreciate, you get more of. What you appreciate in your life becomes more precious. Appreciate your mind, heart, body, spirit, life, house, mate, children, spouse, work and talents. See, there is always much to appreciate.

Adore and worship God through appreciation of His world. Pray to God through your ability to appreciate. Appreciate the good in your life; appreciate the lessons you are learning. Appreciate your future, even if the future of this world is shaky. Your future is not shaky because you are becoming One with God.

Love your life and see it as an opportunity to grow in spirit. Love all that you have and all that you desire. Love God, the Father, because HE is Creator of All you see. Love your mate and spouse, children, parents, life, work and your opportunities to grow spiritually. Love causes more good to come into your life. Love and appreciation are prayers. Use this form of prayer to increase your life. Use this form of prayer to increase your spiritual awareness.

We of the Brotherhood of God appreciate each of you. We appreciate the opportunity to help you as you grow spiritually. We love you each and are waiting only to be called to assist you.

The Brotherhood

Strengthen Your God-Mind Connection
(*Mary, May 7, 1989*)

I will simply give a short message today. It is a message to urge you to make your connection to God-Mind strong. The perilous times draw near and it is essential that all people find the connection to God in their minds and hearts. You, who have the privilege of knowing beforehand of the peril, need to be especially faithful to your cause. The cause is the ability to survive all the coming disasters.

I see that many have become complacent in thinking that you will not face any of the coming disasters. You and your children will face disasters. **Your connection to God-Mind will give you the ability to remain calm and to hear His guiding voice in your mind.** You are to lead others to find their own serenity in God. The preparations are for your benefit and for the benefit of all people, because as you know, when you raise your consciousness, the race consciousness is lifted. This is not all. In the middle of turmoil and disaster, you will be the ones who lead others to calmness.

I hear through your thoughts that you do not always believe this is a good method to your survival. Believe me, it is the ONLY method to your survival. This is the very reason I have come to Annie. I love all people and all nations. But my concern is with this nation that depends on its technology. Machines will fail when the earth moves. All your outer preparations will be of no use. The cars will not move, nor planes, nor trains. These things will fail you. The wires that carry messages will be of no use to you in those dark days. I do not wish to scare you, but you must be aware of the enormity of the coming events.

Your only HOPE is in God. Your only chance of survival with any wits about you, is through God. It is better to know beforehand of the dangers, for in that day you will not faint. It is better to seek God now than in that last day, when all about you, others faint and die. Return to your old lessons and practice your prayers and meditations. **Pray in your own way, but pray. Meditate your own way; all ways are good that bring you to the presence of God.** Do not be lulled into a false sense of security. The events that approach earth will be felt worldwide. These are global events and happenings. No one area of earth will be left standing unharmed. All places and all nations will be involved in these disasters. Your technology will not save this nation.

It is imperative that each of you remain faithful to your spiritual quest. Through this strong connection to God, all information will be given in those days. It is my love for you which demands that I speak of this.

Mary, Mother of Jesus

Keep On with Courage
(Brotherhood, May 13, 1989)

We wish to give to each of you a word of encouragement, to keep on keeping on, in spite of the challenges that face you daily. It is persistence that wins out. You live eternally. Or in other words, you will go on forever and ever. So you have much time to learn your lessons. But as in every venture in life, it is to your advantage to persist. Only with a persistent attitude can you win and reap the rewards.

There are many rewards to this way of life. **The best is being in constant communion with HE who provides for you.** The reward we find best is the one that allows us to accept ourselves as God does.

Many people become discouraged because they do not see improvements fast enough. But life is not a race, it is a school, so that everyone who persists wins. But in the reality of God's Truth, all people will graduate with honors. It simply takes some people longer to understand than others. Do not allow your own personality to defeat you with discouragement. When you find yourself becoming discouraged and thinking it is no use or of no value, then be aware that this is the earth-bound consciousness speaking. This is the little you, who is lazy and childish. Instead of listening, remind yourself of the Great Love God has for all of us. Sense the sincerity and diligence which comes from God-Mind. Remind yourself that no matter what your crime or failings, you are Loved with a life-giving and pure Love.

Each person who is reading this has much help, so that when you pray, you do not pray alone; we are there. Any and every effort is aided by us and by many more loving spirits. We see your lives and your efforts to connect to God. These are all a vast improvement over how you had been living.

Each of you in the past had not been making any effort to understand your relationship to God or how to revitalize your spiritual life. Now we see people making an effort to understand and pray. You are having some success in connecting to God-Mind, praying to God, the Father. We see improvement in those who are faithful to their inner life. We see many changes coming to the inner and spiritual lives of the faithful as you begin to understand.

Simply remember that persistence and honesty of feelings with God and your higher selves will bring results. Remind your inner self of the love that surrounds you. No one is left loveless or alone at any time. There is a host of helpful spirits who are interested in your spiritual progress. Take a moment to quiet your thoughts daily and remember that you are indeed loved, honored and cared for. Every endeavor on earth is for your learning. You will continue to have challenges, but you will not meet them alone. You are to face life with courage and persist in making your daily God-Mind connection.

The Brotherhood

14

Overcoming Hard Emotions

Live from the Inside Out
(*Brotherhood, May 21, 1989*)

W E ARE NEARING the mid-portion of the allotted time for your goals. We wish to urge you to pray for these same goals. We will take a minute to give you some help with your daily life, because we feel that these goals have to do with an improvement in this earthly life.

Through prayer you connect to the Mind of God. It is in this Great Mind that you will find the "things" that make happiness. To place too much emphasis on the earthly, outer existence of life, is to limit God. **While on earth it is beneficial to live life from the inside out.** Too many people live life from the outer aspect only. This is not a balanced way to go through life. Realize that this earthly existence is temporary, that the goods of this world are not lasting. We speak of not lasting because they will not stand the test of time. All materials in their final use are returned to earth. From earth materials come, and to earth they will return. Few have stood the test of time; some like the pyramids are still standing but are not useful, except as a monument to the ingenuity of man. Placing too much emphasis on the material is to lose track of your real purpose in life.

Your true purpose on earth is to practice what you have learned and to learn to use your mind and heart more. We are not advocating that you abandon your earthly life by living away from society. It takes your active participation in this culture and society in order to stress the inner life. Your true purpose is not to be wealthy in the material way, but to be wealthy in the spiritual way, which can also include material wealth. See, this word "wealth" is like all words. It gives each person a different concept. So to place too much emphasis on wealth, as society denotes wealth, is to limit God in your life.

When you can release by forgiving the hard emotions like anger, fear, envy, resentment and such, you will progress in all manner of living. Your progress will be in the inner spiritual way and in society's outer method. You cannot become the person you desire to be with a heart and mind filled with old hard emotions. If you resent others they will know it, and your progress in the work place will be affected. If you are envious and resentful, you may fool some of the people some of the time, but sooner or later everyone will see these hard emotions as they surface.

We like analogies, and here is one: **You are on earth to reflect the Essence of God,** so consider yourselves much like a mirror. But God cannot see Himself in you because your outer life is smudged from the blurring of your inner life. You cannot reflect any image when the back or the inner part of the mirror is distorted. Your reflecting ability is limited and distorted. The reflection is seen perhaps in a comical way, as a mirror which appears to make the image smaller or larger, or thinner or fatter. Have you not seen this type of mirror? They are found most often in amusement parks. If the inner mirror is distorted, no amount of cleanser used on the outer surface will change the distortions. So in order to change the mirror and have it function properly, it must be resurfaced and aligned from the inner surface. No amount of work on the outer will suffice. Your life is much like the distorted mirror. People work and work on the outer. They lose weight, have surgeries to improve their outer looks. They buy clothes which are considered fashionable for this day. Many live in the proper home! You work and work on the outer life. But the distortions are inside, in the heart and mind, so no amount of work on the outer alone will suffice. The inner life needs to be cared for more than the outer. Many people will pray with emphasis on the outer life. "God, please help me get this job, or get this house, or lose this weight." You think this will make you happy, a better person.

Now that we have shown you the error in thinking this way, we are not saying that each of you have this problem. But every person has this way of thinking on the surface from time to time. So, in order to have you progress in the material earthly life and in the inner spiritual life, we say, do not limit God by concentrating on only one segment of you. Each person is made up of many levels, many facets. You can have progress in all parts of your life. You can have a certain degree of wealth. (It depends on the degree of wealth you can handle.) **True wealth is your ability to depend on God as the source of your income, your life force, happiness and health.** This is accomplished through prayer and meditation. It is accomplished through questioning your life and all the circumstances in it.

Pray to learn how to live. Does this sound like rubbish? It is not! You are only half living on earth if your entire perspective is on the outer life. In order to have a complete and satisfying life, learn more about your connection to God through prayer. Ask God questions. Your answers will come either through your mind, through reading, or through another person.

Begin each day with a prayer, even if it is as short as "God help me this day." End each day with a prayer of gratitude. Remove the hard emotions that block your ability to reflect the attributes of God. We are not advocating that you ignore your outer life, but simply that you balance it with prayer and meditation. Ask God's help to eliminate the hard emotions and thoughts from the inner self. Forgive all people and forgive the world. Forgive yourself; this is also important to your growth.

Return to a time of prayer for yourself, your goals and your life. Then pray for the world, all people in the world, for all of God's creations. Pray to strengthen your connection to God. Talk to God as you would a friend. There is no better friend. Be willing to change your inner self in order to be the person you desire to be on earth. All is good, the inner life and the outer. All is to be balanced with prayer and through your communication with God.

As always, we are available to help you. We will assist in your prayers and in your connection to God's Great Mind. What you bring to God is instantly turned into good.

God is good. We know you have heard these words before. What we are saying is that all you bring and give to God is replaced with good.

Give God your angers, and they will dissipate into contentment. He turns your fear into courage and ignorance into intelligence. Bring your thoughts of "I can't," and you will be saying "I can." Resentments will turn into gratitude. Envy will change into peace. Jealousy will change to trust. This is an automatic process of praying. All that is needed is for you to tell God, **"I no longer want these hard emotions or thoughts in me. I give these to you, God. What I have I give to God."**

When you find these in your mind—contempt, angers, fears, jealousy, envy, mistrust, anxiousness—give them to God. They will be changed instantly into trust, happiness, peace, gratitude, courage, honor, valor and truth. Whatever is in you, give it to God through prayer. **You do not have to change these things alone. You do not have to live alone or lonely. God is with you always, but awaits your recognition**

of Him in your life. We also are available to help you accomplish this task.

Once you can depend completely on God for all your life, your inner and your outer life, you will have time, energy and know-how to accomplish your goals. This is truly an easier way to live on earth. It is not an unhappy or difficult way to live. There is much energy wasted in holding on to these hard emotions, the energy to propel you into a new and more advanced way of life, energy which you could use to heal your body, to heal your relationships and to have a good life.

When we say a good life, be aware that a good life is dependent on your concept of a good life and on the concept which God holds of a good life. The good times are not always what you think they are.

To have a good life, there will be no abuse of body, emotions or mind, nor will any abuse of others be a part of a good life. So however you define a good life, if it agrees with God's definition of a good life, it is yours. **Pray to bring God's definitions into your life.** These definitions bring conditions which are good. God's definitions are love, illumination, light, courage, valor, trust, order, strength, happiness, joy, life, energy, power, wisdom and much, much more. These are the very "things" you are striving for. These are the conditions you desire to have in your life. Now we teach you how to have them, how to attain your goals. But we cannot do it for you. Neither will God, unless you ask Him to enter your life and aid you. **God will help, but He will not do it for you.**

Bring to your mind, heart and prayers all that you are. Allow God the freedom to change you and the conditions of your life. These changes will be wonderful, beautiful, glorious and good.

Our love and attention is with each of you. Our prayers are for your understanding of the words and concepts that we give.

The Brotherhood

Your Viewpoint Determines Your Life
(Brotherhood, May 27, 1989)

Several times we have tried to explain how we are here only to help you connect to God-Mind and God-Essence. OUR only purpose is to assist humans as they seek God.

In the past, the earth-mind consciousness of man became filled with fear, anger, hostility, envy, jealousy and now anxiety. It became progressively difficult for the common man to raise his thoughts out of the mire of such strong emotions. God became an angry and vindictive God, or the perception man had of God became thus. We, as the Brotherhood or as the Holy Ghost, have had the honor of being able to help man raise his thoughts past the fear of God and to resist the temptation of denying God.

Our help consists of taking the thoughts mankind individually has of God and surrounding them with our thoughts of truth. As people think of God and begin to question the validity of God, we are there. We help people look past their fears and go past the anxiety that is so present in the race-consciousness. The blocks are not with God. The blocks and barriers are set up in the individual's mind through fear, anxiety and hostilities. If an individual begins to fearfully question their concept of God, we are there to help their thoughts past their fear to the truth. We do not actually do anything except give Truth. We tell people the truth about God, as Jesus did while he was on earth.

There are still people who fear God. Some people think perhaps God can become angry and make bad things happen in their lives that they do not want. They consider the events in their lives to be handed down from God. When a person has some type of setback, the fearful one will think God is punishing me: "What did I do to deserve this?" Those who know the truth will look at their own past decisions or indecisions for the cause of the setback.

We help mankind go beyond their fear to see the truth of God, to view the Truth about God as the Creator, to see God as He really is and not as they fear He is. We are not here to help you by providing things for you, not even automobile parking places. Annie will ask God for a parking place near the front door of the store. So with this in mind, she seems to be in the right place at the right time for such an occurrence. But it is her mind that calls forth the ability to get a parking place in front.

We think you still do not appreciate the mind and all its capabilities. Through your mind you live life. Through your mind you call out of the Essence of God what you desire to have in your life. As you think, so you are. If you live life from a standpoint of fear, hostility, anger or anxiety, you are calling forth more situations to cause these strong emotions in your life. If you can simply hold on to the thought that God is Love, for instance, you would live your life from a loving and lovable standpoint. All circumstances in your life would reflect the Love of God. People would say, "My, aren't they lucky!" when in reality it is not luck, but your viewpoint, which determines the events in your life.

Some people say, "I try to live my life by being good." **It is not how you act that determines the quality of your life; it is how you think about God.** All life is lived from the standpoint of God-Essence. **It is what you believe about God that determines how you live life on earth.** This is a difficult and mind-boggling thought, because you say, "It is my education which limits me," or "It is the salary I am being paid that limits me." Or you look at your childhood and say, "It is my parents' fault that I am like I am." These are not truths! These are excuses man uses to put off something he fears, that is, to get through his own fear of God.

When mankind can keep the idea of a completely, totally loving God in charge of his life, nothing will be impossible to him. Then man will know that God and his life are good. He can begin to live from a standpoint of love instead of fear.

Oh, but some say, "What about the evilness of man? The ability of satan to lure me?" There is no satan or any other spirit who is limiting or luring you, except your fearful self. **You limit you!** Your thoughts are what are limiting you. The evilness and the idea of a satan are simply excuses of man to put off a task that is viewed as onerous. A misconception of man is that he is limited, fearful and easily trapped by spirits. Your mind is capable of many wondrous and great experiences. Through your mind you can change your life so that it would appear miraculous. By eliminating your fears, angers, hostilities and such strong emotions, you can literally change your life to one that is good, happy and comfortable.

How do you change from a fearful person to one who is fearless and courageous? Through prayer, through a deep belief in the Goodness of God. Through accepting the truth about God, that God and Love are ONE. We are speaking of unconditional love and not of love as your news media portray it. We say release and get rid of your anger, your quick temper, your ability to come back with a quick retort. Watch your words, watch your thoughts, watch your lingering feelings. This is the way to change your life. Put away the ability to say something nasty in response. Put away the nasty thoughts about others; we are all made alike, and what you do not like in another is often what you do not like in yourself.

Be quick to search out all the little thoughts and feelings that represent fear, hostility, anger, hatred, envy, jealousy, greed and selfishness. These negative responses limit your life. These kinds of thoughts and feelings are the limiting element in your life. It is by going past your fears, it is by seeing through your angers, that you will turn your life around.

Call on us at any time, we are not limited by time or space. We are always available to help you go past these strong emotions to find your connection to a God who is All-Love and All-Loving, all the time.

The Brotherhood

Self-Image and Self-Worth
(Brotherhood, June 3, 1989)

Today we are concerned with those who have a self-image of lack and for those who look to friends for all their self-worth. They are much as the prodigal son. Remember this story Jesus told while on earth? (Lk 15:11-32) The son asked for his fortune to go into the city to live. He spent his fortune in drink, party and friends. He was consumed with good times, with "friends." As long as he had money to spend, he had friends. There were many who joined him in drink and good times. But when his money played out, these so-called friends left him to starve. Sitting in a pigsty, eating food that had been thrown to the pigs, he began to think of home. He remembered his father's words of caution. He remembered the clean home and the good food that even the servants had in his father's home. He thought, "In my father's home even the servants live better than this; they have plenty of food, a clean bed upon which to sleep and some dignity. I will go to my father's house and beg him to forgive me. I will ask that he allow me to serve and live among the servants. At least there I will be cared for better than I am here. No one in this city cares for me. All my friends have abandoned me. They were only my friends as long as I could provide them with what they wanted. They were never interested in me, simply for who they thought I was."

This parable can be seen both in cases of people who look to their friends for self-worth and for those who believe in lack. Both have a negative view of their self-worth. Both live in different circumstances, yet this story can be applied to both. To seek instant gratification is to seek selfishly. To try to remedy spiritual concerns through material matters is to cause lack in your life. The young man in the story did not appreciate his worth, nor did he appreciate his life. He thought, as many of the young today think, in terms of *me* and *now*. They have no patience with life or the way it works. They want to be all they can be now and without much effort on their part. So they look to friends to fulfill their needs. They think having a good time, lust and friends will give them inner satisfaction. They expect their parents to provide them with the means to acquire their lifestyle, as they think they deserve.

In this parable the young man never considered that the father had worked hard, had managed his wealth well and increased it. Nor did he see that his father was not only a good steward, manager and had a business-like approach to life, but he was also a good and caring man. It was only after the son had spent the fortune that his father had given him, in wild, riotous living, that he began to see clearly. It was after he had by-passed many opportunities to better his life that he began to see what life was all about. The father tried to give the son knowledge and learning in the art of becoming a righteous man, but it did not take. The lessons fell on deaf ears. The words were not taken into the mind and heart by the son. He thought, "This old man doesn't know what life is all about today. He's living in the past. I'm of the new generation. I'm young. I have a right to have fun. This is my opportunity to be with my friends. They like me more than my father does. All my father did was restrict me and give me his old-fashioned views. I don't need this. I can make it on my own."

So away the son went into the city with his low self-esteem and his misguided concepts about life. He fell into the "good times" and found many friends. Everyone praised him and told him lies about how wonderful he was, how smart he was, how intelligent and how lucky to have a rich father. He prided himself on the fact that he didn't have to work. He had it all. These attitudes limit and restrict more than any parent. Looking to others for your self-worth is futile because no one is interested in you as much as you and your loved ones are. No person or so-called friend who is with you in "good times," is really with you. The young man found himself down and out, no friends, no money, no food, no bed, no place to call home. He put away his arrogance, his pride, his self-importance. He took a good honest look at his life, a good honest look at his inner self and the values and conditions that had brought him to this place. Here in a pig's sty, fighting the swine for a bite of food, he reflected on his earlier training. He began to see that his father was very wise, very astute and a good manager—he knew how to hold on to money, he knew how to manage his life, not only for his benefit but for the benefit of the entire family. The son became very remorseful and wanted to ask forgiveness. He would only ask that his father allow him to become a servant.

What the son found was humility, honesty and truth.

Well, what happened? The minute the father heard that the son was returning, he was very happy. The father ordered clean clothes of the finest be brought, a hot bath and a ring for the son's finger. He ordered a feast to celebrate the homecoming. **The son saw the truth of his life and acknowledged that he was wrong.** The father did not give him a place in the house as a servant, but returned him to his rightful place as son and heir.

Now let us look at how this applies to self-esteem and self-worth. To look to others for your self-worth is wasteful. It wastes not only your inner resources, but your life's energy. To try to have a good time is a waste of time, money and energy, because the best of times is that time when you are in true communion with God. You by yourself are nothing. You could not give yourself life-energy. This is a gift of God. **You are valuable and worth much because of Who created you, not because of the money you have in your pocket. You are worth much because of the mind and heart that God placed in you, not because you can have a "good time." Your value is in the inner recesses of your mind. Your talents are those that God gave you in the beginning. Look at your life with a clear eye. See that you are of value, because you are of value to God. See yourself in truth.**

To inflate your self-worth is as bad as to negate your self-worth. These are simply two sides of the same coin, the coin that says you are worthless on one side or that you are better than someone else because of outer trappings on the other side.

The money, the car you drive or the clothes you wear do not make self-worth. **God looks only at what is in your heart and mind**. He sees into those places where you hide and squirrel away your little faults. Take a good look at yourself with honesty.

To negate and belittle yourself with anger, hate and strong words is wrong. This is not having a true concept of your value. When your mind chatter is saying things like, "I knew I would screw up; I can't do anything; everything bad happens to me. I must be a bad person to deserve this in my life," or "I'm afraid I won't make it. I don't have enough money," or "I can't handle my money, so I will party. Why does this happen to me and not to someone else? God doesn't love me like He does those who have money," you are belittling the gifts God has given you.

To limit yourself is to limit God. You close the door that God could use to help you. Your limiting thoughts are prayers and bring with them the same situations. So in reality you are praying for the conditions you are in now. **Gratitude for what you do have opens your mind to new possibilities**. Gratitude must be sincere and heartfelt. See your worth as a wonderful creation of God. See that in your Father's house are many mansions. See that it is your Father's pleasure to give, but you need to come home in order to place yourself in the right place. When the prodigal son returned to his father, he found not only the little bit he was asking for, but plenty. When you rely on God as the source of your income, your life (your physical life as well as your spiritual life), then you will receive a full cup.

So we say, pray today to see yourself as you truly are. **Appreciate yourself as a creation of God**. See that this inner life is what you are desiring, what you look for in life. The good times are the times you spend with God in prayer. The hard drink and drugs of this generation are limiting to the user and to God's ability to give. Begin today to tell yourself over and over, **"I am a creation of the One God.** He is providing for all my life, money, cars, education and my welfare." When you find yourself inflating your self-worth, or negating it, then stop immediately. Tell yourself you do not have to look to anyone else for your good. It is God's pleasure to give you all you need. Trust and pray. Have faith and pray. Eat and pray. Sleep and pray. But pray without fear. Pray with love for yourself, your life and your world. You are the prodigal son who has returned to his father's house. You are welcomed with open arms, rings for your fingers and treasure.

These are our words and our prayer, that each will identify their own true worth as a child of God, that you will live life aware of the love that surrounds you always.

The Brotherhood

15

Praying as a Family

Let Prayer Be Your Motto (Mid-Year Review)
(Brotherhood, June 24, 1989)

YOU WHO HAVE BEEN FAITHFUL to the prayers and learning of spirit and truth, we call you to continue to work to improve your understanding of the Universe. One half of this year has passed, and in this time you have been praying and meditating according to your inner will. We ask that you remain faithful to this life, remain faithful to the search for truth. We ask that you make a pledge this day to put more effort into your search for truth and God.

Our whole objective is to help you connect to the Great Mind of God, to have you receive His input in your lives and in your day. As you open your mind and heart to receive more of God-Mind and God-Essence, you find that you are becoming more perceptive and intuitive. You will simply know that you know. You will find that your mind and understanding are

opening to new ideas and new flashes of thought. You are not
simply mirroring what you have read, but it is now becoming
internalized into the fabric of your being. The truths that you
are learning are now helping you to understand more about
life. These truths are bringing with them an opening of your
consciousness to new ways of thinking and new methods of
praying. As you grow in spirit, you find many things changing
in your life, and yet there will be constancy, which is rewarding. As you change in the inner recesses of yourself, your life
will take on added meaning. Your prayers are now being
answered quickly. Those for whom you pray are being healed.
They are regaining their inner sight. The lame will walk. That
means the ones who were lame from addictions or negativity
will walk in a new light, which is the light of God.

We ask each person to make a list of the names of their
loved ones and friends. List all people who are members of
your earthly family, list all friends and list all enemies. In this
way you will be complying with Mary's wish for prayer for this
world. Start with your family and loved ones. Through love the
connection will be made quickly. Through your love, which
will connect to God's Love, your prayers will be answered so
that the best outcome in each circumstance will be done. **Daily
pray for all the people in the family prayer basket.**[8] Understand that only through prayer and in meditation will you
grow spiritually. Only through spirit will your connection be
made to All Good, which is God.

Now let us give you a glimpse of what's to come for this
family group. You are unique and unusual because not many
families can gather together in peace in this day. Not many
families even live in the same area in this nation. That you can
come together to pray and learn of God is truly a wonderful
thing. It deserves being held up as a model for all people. Take
pride in the fact that each of you gathers together in this group
of family members, not only in peace but now in love; that you

---

[8] The lists of names were put into a "prayer bowl/basket."

can put aside your differences and see into the inner nature of your family members, that this group of beings who has gathered today is blessed and will be a blessing to all people.

We ask that each family member take notes of the events in your life that have changed because of the gathering into one unit and praying. We ask that Annie and Byron compile a book[9] describing the gathering of their children and children's children. We wish for you to serve as a role model to others, that through the story of your individual lives and how you pray the one for the other and the world, more people will do the same. You are in reality a family unit. But understand that to become a family unit in the future will take only the will and desire to pray together. **All people are one family on this earth planet. Therefore, as people come together to pray, they will become each a unit of spiritual family.** But you as the role models are not only family in spirit but in earthly terms also.

Soon you will have been meeting for one complete year. In this year each of you has grown in spirit and in truth. Perhaps you cannot detect it yourself, but with careful thought you will appreciate the changes in your life, the mellowing of angers and fears, the courage and the integrity that is now a part of your inner self. Perhaps you have become more gentle and more loving or patient. Perhaps you have released not only hostility but anger, fear and envy. Perhaps you no longer are jealous of other people, but are satisfied with your connection to God. These are the subtle inner changes that have been occurring in your life. We encourage each of you to keep notes of your personal changes. Annie and Byron will compile the message we wish to give to the world—the message that it is imperative that family members pray, one for the other, that prayer become the motto for all people. Let your prayers be for the planet and for a gentler turning of the earth.

The Brotherhood

---

[9] That became this book.

The Urgent Need for More Prayer
(*Mary, June 24, 1989*)

How I love each of you; words cannot begin to tell. I know that you have never considered me a part of your lives. I choose to work with this family who has never revered me as many people do. The reason I have chosen you is to demonstrate through you who are not connected to any particular church. You have varied backgrounds, and through your past religious training you now choose to learn the truth. **I request that you take seriously my request to help me pray for the world, as a planet, as a people and as your home.** I sense the limiting time factor. I have a sense of how short this time is to prepare for the coming events and to help others prepare. You know how fast these last few months have flown by. Consider that in a few short years, the trials and tribulations will be upon earth in earnestness. It is to this end I request that you help me, through prayer for this lovely world.

Understand that the need for prayer is urgent, that because of people just like you, we can have a gentler turning and not the turmoil I foresee. Ask God to help you with the praying. Tell Him everything that is in your heart. Learn to put aside the angers, fears and hostilities that only add to the violence in the atmosphere. **I ask that each person pray one hour per day. Know that this hour can be broken into parts.** You may pray fifteen minutes in the morning or perhaps thirty minutes. You can then pray the rest of the time at night. Or you may pray for ten minutes in the morning, twenty minutes upon entering your home and the rest before bed. See, this is how to set aside time for prayer. Understand also that you can pray at work; when people think you are lost in your thoughts, you will be lost in God's world. The prayers can be said throughout the day, but to meditate will require some set time. Perhaps you can commit to praying only fifteen minutes per day. This is fine, but increase your prayer time as you learn to pray.

Pray for all people, for those you know and for those who are merely a part of this life on earth. Pray for your enemies. Ask God to help you forgive them. Ask God to bring into your heart thoughts of love for all people. Pray for those who have spoken badly about you, those who perhaps have been nasty or mean. Consider that they do not know their true worth as children of a loving God.

Perhaps it will be well worth your learning the prayer of Saint Francis of Assisi, he who asked God to make him an instrument of His will—to help him plant love where there was hatred, to bring peace where there was strife, to bring joy where there is sadness—see, this is how to pray. There are many ways to pray. Take note of prayers that have endured the passing of time. If you cannot think of any other way to pray, repeat over and over The Lord's Prayer. In this way you will be opening up your mind to project good into the world.

Your thoughts are powerful, as are your words. Be careful how you use your thoughts and words. Make use of these powerful elements, which you alone control. Pray by speaking the words love, peace and hope to all people and to all nations. Simply **meditate by concentrating on the words hope, peace and love.** As you send out these thoughts of love, peace and hope, think of them as balloons filled with these essences. See these balloons of peace, love, and hope going through the air to all parts of the world. Send these thoughts to people, oceans, rivers, animals, mountains, and to plains. You could easily spend much time with this one method of prayer.

This is my request today. Do not think that I come simply to request, but **understand that the reward is in the doing or the accomplishing of the request. God will bless you as you work with me on this project. I have requested of God a special blessing for the people who will work with me. Your prayers will be filled with miracles, and those for whom you pray, those whom you love, will be healed. Understand that the healing comes from God.** The opening of doors comes from God. As you continue to work with me and with Spirit, you will be blessed and a blessing to all people. But most especially you will bless your loved ones, without them knowing how or from where the blessings come. **Keep quiet about all things.** Talk only among this group of the answers. Do not try to portray yourselves as holy but only as seekers of the Truth.

I thank you for listening to my call. I am grateful to have such wonderful people as you to work with. My love is ever with you.

Mary, Mother of Jesus

Meditate on the Spiritual Dimensions
(Brotherhood, July 9, 1989)

We are happy that you continue to meet and gather together in the name of God-Mind and God Almighty. This is a great testament to your faithfulness. **Faith is the cornerstone of life.** As you grow in spirit and truth, you need faith to energize your life. As you go into the next decade, you will need faith to survive. Remember to begin to gather your thoughts and words for your input into the next publication. We desire to have you give testimony of your growth in spirit. Many will be inspired by your faithfulness to prayer and meditation. Begin today to be faithful to even the smallest thought that enters your mind.

This week we gave your mother and father the words **Eternal—Infinite—Energy. These are the three dimensions of Spirit.** On earth you live in time, space and depth. But when you can begin to live from a spiritual standpoint, you progress to your spiritual limits. Even on earth you can live in the spiritual dimension. It will not only be beneficial to this lifetime and your physical needs, but at the same time it will enhance your spiritual life. **As you live your physical life, you are also living your spiritual life. These are lived simultaneously.**

You do not put your spiritual life on hold while you are on earth. In spirit and in truth, you live on many levels and can live from the standpoint of Eternity, Infinity and Pure Energy.

This week we wish for you to take these three words, concepts, and allow them to grow into your awareness, for all people live in these three dimensions. All of life is lived from this standpoint. Take these three ideas and use them to energize your life, to energize a sluggish pocketbook and to energize a sluggish life. Concentrate on these words and keep them with you.

Simply by repeating the words, it will give you the open-ended idea of life. See, time is eternal. There is no limit to time, but while you are on earth you become mesmerized into believing that this is the only life you will ever have, when in reality it is but one small lifetime, one small part of your entire life.

Not only is God eternal, but as His heirs and children, we live eternally. What did Jesus say? "In my Father's house are many mansions. I go to prepare a place for you, so that where I am you will be." (Jn 14:2-3) Do you not see Jesus was telling us **we live in the same time, space and frame that God does, which is Eternity, Infinity and Pure Energy.** Jesus used the word "mansions," because this is the biggest place you can conceive of living in. So to say "in God are many mansions," it gives us the idea of the infinity that is available in Spirit.

When Eternity is your time concept, then you can begin to live in Truth and in Spirit, because all things progress from the standpoint of Eternity. Your life is eternal. Eternal are your opportunities. Eternal is the time in which you truly live.

Just as eternal is your time concept in Truth, so **Infinite is your space. Infinite are your possibilities. Infinite is the space you live in when you have awakened to Truth.** You are infinite in concept. You are not limited to this one lifetime. There are infinite lifetimes to be lived. **Lighten up and don't take this one lifetime so seriously.** Take a light hand in dealing with yourself. Be gentle with your inner self and begin to change the perspective from which you think. See the endless potential that is within you. But this does not mean you can become lazy and wasteful in this lifetime. Waste, in any form, is not rewarded. It is an abomination to waste a lifetime, to give in to idle pursuit of short-lived pleasures. Take care that you are always grateful for the infinite space in which you truly live and allow this idea to give you the gentleness to live in love. The only limits are those that you place in your life, for everyone could be more and do more than he or she is doing. Every person could pray more and seek more Truth. Realize that you have just begun to live, now that you are understanding Truth and your endless possibilities. Remove the blinders, barriers, and the limits. **Take time to pray, for this is your lifeline.**

Energy is the third dimension in which we all truly live. Pure Energy is in the air you breathe, if you take the concept with you. If you will breathe with the thought that this is Pure Energy, then it will be. See, there is no need to become depleted, because there is always Pure Energy in the Universe. Nothing is wasted in Truth. When an idea or a thought is no longer useful to a person, it simply transforms into Pure Energy. **Pure Energy is the presence of God.** So to live in the three spiritual dimensions, you live in the presence of God at all times. You live from the point of Truth. Now then here is a good way to energize your life, your pocketbook and home. Take everything and hold it with the thought of Pure Energy. In this manner, say you have the idea to change your life in a small way. Think, the idea to change my life is filled with Pure Energy. As I understand it, to leave off this habit, I am energized with Pure Spirit. Hold on to this thought. As you confront the habit or impulse, you are imbuing it with Pure Energy and in this way it is changed into new energy.

Over the next two weeks take the ideas **ETERNITY— INFINITY—ENERGY. Meditate on these words.** Allow them to bring into your mind all they imply. When you cannot meditate, keep the words in your heart. By repeating them you will open your mind to endless possibilities and opportunities. New hope and new faith will infuse you. New ways to live will fill your mind. See, it is a mental world. What you think is important. Where your mind lingers is important. So watch your every thought by giving your mind something to think on. Fill your mind with these three words and see what opens up to your mind. See what ideas come into focus in your life. Each person will have a different experience. Each person will have different ideas and concepts. But remember, this is your individualized mental world. It is your individualized help.

The Brotherhood

16

Facing Yourself in Truth

Examine, Admit and Forgive Your Mistakes
(Brotherhood, July 22, 1989)

ODAY, let us take the story of the woman who was brought before Jesus to be stoned because she had been caught in fornication. Remember Jesus' reply? He said, "If any here be without sin, let him throw the first stone." (Jn 8:7) Jesus was reminding us that **all who are on earth are here for correction.** The whole purpose of coming to earth is to work through some area that needs to be changed. Not everyone's need is visible, but everyone has corrections to make. On earth it is customary to show your best face to the public. You allow others to see you only at your best. **God sees into your heart, and there the truth of you is seen.**

Perhaps you have hidden the truth from yourself. Perhaps you truly do not see anything that needs correcting. **Pray that you may see the truth about yourself, because only in truth** can you see what needs correcting. Only by facing yourself in truth can you grow. It takes a big person to admit his mistakes. It takes one who is mature and able to take self-scrutiny. This is a requirement in order to mature and grow in spirit. Every person on earth has an area that is in need of correction and possibly elimination. This is our lesson to you: **take time in your meditations to scrutinize your inner self,** the self you show only to God. This is the way to make amends, before any drastic event brings you face to face with yourself. Allow this to be your prayer for the next fortnight, to take a good look at your own weaknesses, your own behaviors, your own habits and your own thoughts, because all events proceed from your thoughts. To correct a behavior may require help from people who are trained to help you. To overcome a bad habit perhaps takes the aid of others of like mind. **All corrections begin with prayer, with the desire to change. All bad habits are eliminated because of the individual's desire to put this away forever.**

This theme of going within to look at yourself is one that is recurring in your Bible. Jesus gave many lessons on looking within. **To look within is to look to God and to look at yourself in reality.** Seek to improve your outer life by correcting those habits that are not needed. Perhaps they are endangering you and others. Perhaps these little habits are not as bad as they are uncontrollable. In order to be clear about yourself, you need to correct these habits, behaviors or desires for the betterment of your inner self.

Do not become dismayed, because you have much help. You have us and you have God-Essence to help you overcome all manner of useless, time-eroding habits. If your behavior causes anyone else anguish, or if it is not a habit you could think of as "in heaven," then realize that it is useless. Be honest with yourself. Be honest with your scrutiny.

Let each one correct their own mistakes and give others only your prayers. Pray for each other and for your entire family and friends. Open yourself up to God-Mind to be infused with the light of knowledge and inner illumination. Remember always that each person has been made in Divine Love, that your very being is composed of this Great Love. As you open your mind to clear away any debris that hinders your spiritual progress, understand that this task is to be made in love. Never allow yourself to remain in a state of remorse or depression because you are "bad." This kind of thinking is detrimental to your spiritual growth. It is good to be remorseful and sorry for any mistakes, but then you are to forgive yourself and forgive others. **Take Love, which is your truth, and allow it to flow into your every thought.** Bring love, compassion and forgiveness into play.

Here are the steps to take in eliminating any bad habit, behavior or condition from your lives. *First* **and primarily, pray that you may see yourself in truth,** that you can recognize those areas that need to be corrected, eliminated or redirected. Pray to see yourself in truth, not to berate yourself, but to correct any behavior that causes you to stray from God-Mind. Often people do not see their own shortcomings. Understand that all have these areas to correct. So first pray to see what needs you have.

Second is to recognize the "evil." **Take this word evil and let it stand for that which takes you away from God-Mind.** Know that you of yourself cannot do anything about it. It takes a mature person to say, I cannot do this alone. Ask God's help in eliminating or correcting this condition.

Third is to **forgive yourself for your mistakes, not to dwell on the error but to dwell on the Love of God.** Forgive yourself, and then forgive others for their part in this condition. Release this habit to God-Mind to correct. **God will not judge you, but He will take all you are and make it better.** When you come to God in fear, He takes the fear and gives you courage. So to come to God with a condition or habit that is not good is to give this habit or condition to God to be changed into one that is beneficial to you and others.

Learn to love yourself, not as you think you are, but as you truly are, with all the areas that need correcting and all the conditions that could be improved; this is how God loves us. This is how God works to help us. Love yourself as God loves you.

The Brotherhood

Correct Yourself in Love
(Mary, July 22, 1989)

I come to implore each of you to give more time to prayer. Consider that it is now your need to pray. Through prayer you connect to the One Great Mind of God. In this connection, you are all you want to be. In this great connection, you become all you desire to be. This is the only way to live life easily and spiritually. **Your first obligation is to your own spiritual growth. Next comes your obligation to your loved ones, and last you are obligated to pray for the world.** I remind you that each has taken upon themselves the need to increase their spiritual learning. Each has taken upon themselves their own needs and their own communion with God Father.

If there is one thing to remember this week, it is to pray to feel the love that surrounds you. This is how to live success-fully. The Brotherhood has come this week to give you understanding, in that each person has a need to correct themselves. I come with a similar message: **Correct yourself in love, view yourself with love, and think of yourself as loved,** for each person on earth is loved by Father God. Every person who takes the step to connect with Father God is not only loved but appreciated and helped.

See, you do not have to live this life alone. You do not have to make these corrections without help. These are the reasons you came to this earth life—to correct and to polish your spiritual self. But this need not be a lonely journey, nor does it need to be a difficult undertaking. The difficulty comes from trying to go it alone. You will find as you work with Spirit or with Father-God, your learning is easier and your connections will be made faster. Understand that each has a hidden agenda for themselves. Each one of you has some inner hidden area that needs to be improved. For some, it is perhaps a habit that hinders your complete release to Father-God. For others, perhaps it is in being critical of others, or in not being patient or understanding with people. See, every person on earth has a need for correction, to refine and to polish some area of their lives.

Prayer is the easiest way to change. Pray and give up to Father-God all that you are, including those situations that are detrimental to you. This is how to overcome those habits, conditions or situations. The giving up is also the ability to surrender all you are to Father-God. In His own way and with His many abilities, Father-God will help you face the truth of your being. He will cause you to see those things that need changing. This allows you to give final approval to the releasing of these habits. Father-God will not take away anything you desire. If there is a habit that is detrimental to your spiritual growth, Father-God will simply bypass this situation until you are ready to do away with it. He continues to give you spiritual increase in knowledge and understanding, for as you grow in knowledge and understanding, you will then see the need to change. When you change, He will help you change from old, useless habits to new and improved ones.

By surrendering all you are to Father-God, you help Him create in your life those situations that are for your growth. Understand that learning can come gently or it can come with difficulty. You do not have to become ill or have accidents to get your own attention. **Give your attention to God and allow Him to guide you gently in the changes to make.** Many times a person must come close to death in order to realize that there is a need to change or improve, but understand that this is not always necessary. Learning can come to you in gentler ways if you will surrender yourself to Father-God.

This then will be your prayer: **"Father-God, help me see myself as I truly am. Help me correct those areas in my life that are correctable, and help me accept those areas in my life that cannot be corrected."** This is much as the prayer of Serenity, which states: **"God grant me the courage to change the things I can, the serenity to accept those things that cannot be changed, and give me the wisdom to know the difference."** See, this is all you are to pray for. As you daily surrender to God all that you are, the things that need to be changed will come to the forefront of your mind. The reality of the conditions in your life will be seen in truth.

Many times people worry about things that are not important, like their looks or their clothing, or perhaps their age. Now take this example. You can change your looks with work. You can improve your clothing. But there is nothing you can do about your age. You simply are what you are, so accept this with serenity. You cannot change your height or your intelligence or your abilities. If there is not the creative artist inside you, you can take lessons and learn to paint or draw, but you will not become a Michelangelo. As far as your intelligence, you can always learn more, but you will always be what and who you are. Concentrate on those things that can be corrected. Concentrate on the important issues of life.

The most important issue is your spiritual growth. This is your real life. This is your true goal on earth, to improve your connection to Father-God. Learn and practice surrendering all you are to God. Allow Father-God to be your guide, your help and your life. It is through prayer that you connect to Father-God. Through prayer you are able to speak to Him. Through meditation you listen to God-Father. Take this seriously and practice your meditations and prayers. **Begin each meditation with a statement that you are listening to the input of Father-God. This is the purpose of your meditation.** Understand that your spiritual self will connect to Father-God. Through all your prayers you are connected to God, and this is the Source of all Good.

My dear children, I love you and I would have you pray daily for your own spiritual growth and for this world. Soon it will be imperative that you have these lines of communication set strong. You will need to hear the Voice of God in your soul. Practice this daily. Simply commit to your own spiritual growth. Then be grateful and pray for the world.

Mary, Mother of Jesus

The Origins of Abuse
(Brotherhood, August 13, 1989)

Good morning. Do you remember the layers of bodies you have? First in the inner core is the physical body, that which you see and are aware of on earth. Then, as layers, each body surrounds the physical. There is a place in the body where there are points, also called Chakras. Each body is able to interconnect and transmit information in the form of feelings and thoughts. Now here are the different bodies that you possess in Truth: the inner core is the physical body, the next layer is the emotional body, mental body, psychic, astral, protoplasmic, ethereal, and surrounding it all is your spiritual body.

There is an illness that is rampant now on earth and is manifesting itself in many forms. Due to this, people believe there are many diseases, when in reality there is one major disease of the spirit. There is the original mistake which is the cause of this process.

Annie heard the doctor at the rehab hospital[10] say that there was evidence of alcohol in the year 6000 B.C. This is not entirely true, because the origin of abuse began long before that. In the land of Peace (today this is referred to as Lemuria),

---

[10] Annie's son was in the rehab hospital for recovery of alcoholism.

there were eons of peace and happiness in which mankind lived as one with his environment and himself. He used all his senses and was free of all abuse to himself, earth and others. There was much happiness and peace in the world in those days. Drugs and alcohol were definitely used only for illness. These were the medicines of that time. Man did not have very many illness except for an occasional injury or illness in very old age. This was the time when man lived for hundreds of years in good health and strength. A man of 100 years was considered a young man, much in comparison to your 30-year-olds of today. Man had a long and happy childhood and time in which to learn about his feelings and the power of his thoughts. Humanity was in the time of greatness.

Alas, someone began to use medicines not only for healing of physical ailments but for relief of emotional ailments. The first reason to abuse yourselves was shame. This is the root of all abuse of this day. First came shame, then fear, anger and selfishness. Then, these emotions fragmented into many other kinds of emotions, such as rage, anxiety, depression and on and on.

What you are experiencing today is the end result of the original sin for which mankind was banished from Eden. Man came to abuse not only himself, his family and the environment, but was on the brink of destroying the planet. The technology was far more advanced than now. There were many conveniences, but none of the work that these conveniences cause now. The government of the people was easy. Each person was in tune to God-Mind and received their relief for mistakes (sins) from God directly. The voice of God was upon the land, and everyone was able to hear God speak to them individually through their thoughts and feelings. Also God spoke to the masses and all people heard Him. Man used the powers of his mind in order to provide for himself, to entertain and to learn. There really was no need for vehicles, because you could levitate and transport yourselves to any area you desired through the use of your mind. There was no need for fuel, and the climate was perfect. There was no use of secrecy, because all were brother and sisters. To rob from one was to rob from yourself openly. Since each could read your thoughts, there was no deceit, conniving or obscure plans of attack.

Before this era ended, God warned the people Himself. He spoke to them and tried to reason with them. God had given man the freedom of choice, as you already know. All God could do in His goodness was reason, teach and exhort. But man liked the feeling of intoxication. Mankind refused to heed the warnings. This was the first denial. Humanity said, "God has never punished us, and He is always there to take care of us. He would not let us destroy mankind." God said, "Listen to me, the course of action you are taking will lead to mankind's destruction. You are now abusing not only yourselves but all future generations." Mankind didn't believe, because it was in a state of denial. Humanity continued to say, "God would not do that. It's all a threat." Man, much as a young person first entering adulthood does today, ignored and didn't believe God. So came the first turning of the axis. All things on earth were shaken and turned upside down. Only those of a pure heart were allowed to live through the event.

But through the genes was carried the potential for abuse. God did not do this as a punishment; it was the result of their behavior. When you abuse your body, you also abuse all future generations, until the time comes, as today, when children are being born addicted at birth. Those were the beginnings of abuse. Today is the time for the healing of all abuse on earth for generations.

Today all people carry the gene of abuse, and it manifests itself in many ways. Most of the time each individual experiences the disease of abuse under many different guises, such as alcoholism, drug addictions, food addictions, obsessions, compulsions and anything used to keep you from facing yourself with all your faults. There are people today who are abusing their inner selves through strict religions, strict diets, strict rules of conduct. Then you have the people who are abusing themselves through no rules, no code of conduct, through perversions of all kinds. Every area of life is being abused in this day. The physical body is abused in many different ways, through dieting, overeating, drinking, drugs, exercise that becomes an obsession and sex.

The emotional body is abused by not allowing yourselves to feel. When you do not feel pain, you cannot feel relief or true love. When you do not allow your feelings of anger to surface naturally, they will come out in unnatural ways, such as physical, mental, emotional, psychic and spiritual abuse to children, wives, mothers or fathers. The mental body is also being abused, not only from neglect but also from overindulgence. The mental illnesses of today are a result of this root cause. The spiritual body is being abused by strict religions and rules that inhibit your ability to contact God directly. When people look to others for their idea of God and their spirituality, this is abuse. Not one human on earth today is exempt. All people are abusing something or someone. All people are abusing earth.

Now then, in the physical body you have the core of all abuse. The first place you evidence abuse is in yourselves, when you do not allow your emotions to surface and leave your inner self. These emotions we have described as depleting for this reason: they are depleting your energy. First you deplete your physical energy, and there is physical illness. Then you deplete your emotional energy, and you have emotional illness and phobias of all kinds. You deplete your mental energy with these depleting emotions when you do not let go. Instead you ponder and think of the incidents that caused the anger, fear, guilt or shame. When you dwell on the feeling of depletion, you are abusing your mental body. People have abused their psychic body to such an extent that now those who are in touch with their psychic abilities are considered rare. Man has abused his astral body and cannot use it to transport himself, levitate, or perform any of the feats that you could if your astral body were whole. The protoplasmic body is in a state of extreme illness. The evidence on earth is in the form of cancer, AIDS, arthritis, cerebral illness, retardations, handicaps and illnesses of all kinds. For centuries there has been blindness, deformity and deafness in the world. Now you are experiencing many new diseases and many new variations of old diseases. The medical community is fighting a losing battle, because they have not touched the root of all illness.

The remedies that are prevalent today are not working, because all people are in a state of denial. How many times do you hear this type of comment? "Well, I'm not as bad as John Doe, because I only overeat," or, "I only drink a little," or, "I attend church every Sunday." People go to church, but they never realize that church—or the teachings of church—does not go into their hearts. You have those people who think, "I am thin, and so therefore this is not for me, but for all the fatties in the world." Or people will deny their depleting emotions and say, "The Devil made me do it. Satan is loose on the world and we must fight him." Satan is inside each of you in the form of abuse. The battle against satan and satanic works are in the inner person, and only each person can work on himself. The idea of a being who is unseen and powerful was invented to place the blame outside of humanity. In the guise of the devil and satans, mankind had an excuse, an alibi for his abuse. One form of this illness is not better than another. The alcoholic is not worse than the overeater or the exercise addict or the religious addict. All actions that are truly only reactions to anger, fear and shame are the same.

All mankind is guilty of abuse. The only way to stop abuse is individually, not wars against crime, poverty, drug dealers or anything. What you battle you give power to. How to stop all abuse is for each individual to go within and make amends to God the Father. He has already forgiven man for this abuse. What earth is suffering from today is forgiven by God, but **each**

person is responsible for his own healing. Each person must take care of his mistakes. When each person is taking care of his mistakes, he doesn't have time to worry about anyone else. You are not responsible for anyone else's actions, not those of your children, parents, spouse, brothers, sister, friend or mankind. This is a problem that needs to be solved now.

Dear children, this is the way you will be role models for others. You will each learn to give support, love and prayers to others in this group as they search inwardly. **Each person is responsible for the release of all depleting emotions in their own way.** We can help if you will speak to us or God through your mind and writings. Each of you can do this in the name of humanity. See, **in the next 1000 years, only those who have been healed of addictions will survive,** because, in order to survive, you must be in close touch with your feelings and thoughts. You must be able to hear and sense the directions you will be given. Not anywhere else will you receive your directions. No book or map will be provided for safe places during the turning of the world. It will come into all minds and all hearts. Only those minds and hearts that are free of abuse of all kinds will be prepared to hear the instructions. For your own survival, you must get in touch with your feelings, attitudes and beliefs. Humanity must clear the mind and heart of all abuse. Man must get sober and serious about his own inner life.

Now is the time to come out of the state of denial. No one is exempt, for all have depleting emotions locked tight within themselves. We would say, if you drink, go the route of group meetings with like-minded people, other drinkers who have the desire to stay healthy and sober. There are now on earth many self-help groups, books, seminars and classes. There is no reason to stay in denial. If the abuse is not overt, then be thankful, and get it all out in the open. Do not wait to hit bottom. You do not have time. Go somewhere and get the help you need. If you are using drugs, then clear yourself of this abuse. If you are relying on food, clear yourself of this abuse. If you are using sex, clear yourself of this abuse. If you are relying on religion, then clear yourself of this abuse. Any crutch you use to avoid clearing out the depleting emotions is abuse.

There is so much help available to you, both in spirit and on earth. If you have been a victim, attend a group for former victims of abuse. If you have been raped in any form, not only sexually but emotionally, mentally or spiritually, go within and clean out of your own mind and heart the angers, frustrations, shame and guilt. The people who have been healed of abuse will be the survivors.

This will be the reason for peace during the next era. This next era is a rest period for mankind. Those who deserve the rest will be allowed to incarnate; the others will have to wait for 1000 years before they will be allowed on earth. That is why in the Beatitudes Jesus said, "The pure in heart will inherit the earth."

Now our request is that every person purchase a notebook. Begin to write your own journal of daily thoughts and feelings that you would like to change. If you do not think you have any depleting emotions or addictions, then pray, because you are in a state of denial and cannot progress until you open yourself to the depleting emotions you are hiding. The depleting emotions must be released into the outer as they surface. You cannot keep these depleting emotions inside you any longer. You will not only lose your physical life, but you will be spiritually handicapped when you come back to earth. You will be spiritually handicapped for a very long time. This is not God's will, but your will. This is not God's choice, but yours. If you are too lazy or too much into denial to think, it will be your downfall. Each person is responsible for himself. You cannot do it for your children or husband. You can help them only by helping yourself. No one can say, "I do not have these addictions." Every person has these, because every person on earth carries them in their genes. Pray to God to have your shortcomings revealed to you. Ask for His help in changing the mistakes of the past.

In the last lesson, we gave you an idea of how to change, accept or know the difference. The things you cannot change are those things that have become so rooted into humanity that no individual has control over them. Only by changing the depleting emotions into replenishing emotions can you help humanity. What you do not have control over, accept. Your age, culture, sex or sexual preference, talents, intelligence, stature—these are simply some of the things that cannot be changed. The angers, shames and fears in your heart and mind can be changed. In this notebook, write about your shortcomings and admit that you are at a loss as to how to change. Ask God-Mind to reveal the ways in which you abuse. Perhaps it is simply by being controlling of another person. God does not control. Neither can you. Perhaps it is by being critical. God does not criticize; neither can you. God does not make your choices, neither can you choose for anyone else. Such are the attitudes and beliefs that need to be changed. From the smallest to the largest, mistakes are to be ferreted out of your heart and mind.

Take your regrets, shame, guilt, depressions, angers, and write to God about them. If you know the cause, then write about it. If you no longer know why you are feeling sad, angry, or overreact to others in a negative way, write to God. Tell Him you no longer remember. Pray to have a release of the inhibiting emotions. Write your heart out to God-Mind, and in this way allow a healing to begin in the soul.

Each person is to pray, the one for the other, and never criticize or point out someone else's defects. But in all honesty, one on one, you can tell the other what concerns you have about them. You can say, "I see in you this depleting emotion because I recognize it in me." Love and pray together. As each of you corrects himself, you are helping all the people whose names are listed on your prayer list. Add to the list each week the name of the person who this week caused you to feel a depleting emotion. Add names as you meet people and as you get to know others. Soon your basket of prayers will be a large

one. All people whose names are listed on your individual prayer list will benefit by each step you take to heal your soul.
The Brotherhood

Pray for Help and Expect Results
(Brotherhood, August 27, 1989)

Today is the beginning of many happy times for us, you and God. Today we repeat a lesson that we have given in the past, that is, expectations. Let us link the thought of expectations with the lesson that we have been giving you on correcting your thoughts and feelings.

It is your choice to live life in anguish or in peace. To live in peace simply takes you concentrating on your personal progress as to your thoughts and feelings, then choosing to let go of all depleting emotions and replacing them with Divine Love and all that God is. It is always your choice and yours alone that is in command of your life and the circumstances of your life. Many times people will blame parents, their career or education for their mistakes. Understand that this is your choice! All events in your life are your choice: your career, your education and/or your attitudes toward your parents.

First in light of expectations is choice. **You choose what to expect or what to expect your life to be.** Expectations must be based in reality. It is not real to expect to wake up one morning and be as rich as Forbes or the Kennedys. So base your expectations in reality. **Expect to get better in health, in finances, in happiness and in personal progress.** Personal progress is used today to denote your ability to eliminate depleting emotions. It is the depleting emotions that stand in the way of growth. You cannot grow if you harbor angers, fears, resentments and envy toward anyone. You can grow through them, however, by praying to God to help you eliminate these emotions and replace them with His love, peace and wealth. This is the key to success in this process.

It is only through the ability to release all these emotions that deplete your energy to God, that you are able to grow spiritually. Understand that this is not a process that you can do in one day. It will require your conscious thought for a period of time. It requires you to lean on God and on us to help you in this process. It is not an easy process, but one which will bring you many added benefits. The most important will be your ability to hear the Voice of God as He guides you to safe places.

As an example, there are people who will walk with a large radio on their shoulder blaring as loudly as possible in their ear. Do you see the isolation and complete loss of reality that happens? They are not aware of their surroundings or of the lovely people who are walking beside them—and, most important, how can God get their attention, or whisper guidance? It would take this type of person much to become quiet within themselves. Only in the quieting of the mind and heart can God speak to you.

Now let us say your depleting emotions are the same as this large radio. You carry a running tape in your mind and heart of all the things that have happened to you, that hurt or caused you anger. Your mind and heart are filled to excess with these depleting emotions and a recital of all the angers, fears, and more and more thoughts of "poor little me." To pity yourself is not only depleting your energy but zapping it quickly. This concentration on angers, fears, envies, resentments will be what keeps you from hearing the voice of God.

In order to stop this vicious circle, you are to pray and ask God to help you get off this merry-go-round. **Pray that God will not only help you face the emotions that need to be faced, but to eliminate them.** There is one action that will prevent you from progressing in this very important exercise—that is, the ugly head of denial. Do not think for one moment that you do not have these emotions deep inside of you. They are there, and it is easy for these types of emotions to rear their heads inside of your mind and heart. Before you know it, you will be giving in to their game. If you think, I don't have these emotions anymore, you delude yourself. If you think you have completely cleansed your heart and mind of all depleting emotions, you are deluding yourself, because these are so ingrained in humanity that it will take herculean efforts to rid yourself of these emotions.

Do not despair, because you have He who is capable and willing to help you, that is, God the Father, Creator of All. Daily pray for yourself and for others who are seeking God. Pray for others who are involved in this process. Pray the one for the other and, through your combined efforts in prayer, all will succeed. But understand that this will be a daily undertaking. It will not be one of those prayers that will be answered once and for all time. The ability to think in depleting ways is in your genes. It is the illness of which we spoke last time. It is caused by the original souls, who are you who turned away from God in the first place. Now you must combat centuries of learned response. You must combat millions and millions of years of practice. It is only through God and His help that each of you individually will triumph.

Pray first to recognize these depleting emotions in yourself. These types of emotions are very capable of disguising themselves in your eyes. This is the process of denial! It is that which says, "I'm not as bad as old Joe or old Jane. They are the ones who are really in denial. I can easily see their fears, angers and resentments." **Understand that what you are seeing in others is simply a reflection of what is inside of you.** If you see another's anger easily, it is because anger is in your heart and you recognize it. If you see fear or denial in another, it is because it is also in your heart and mind. It may be disguised as a good fear, like the fear of fire or the fear that cautions you to be careful of heights. Perhaps you have these fears in an exaggerated form. This is still an unrealistic fear. It is one that is out of control in appearance or feeling.

After you recognize that you are also in denial, as are many people, you will be better able to pray for yourself and for all who live in the world. Pray to be released from your addictions or shortcomings, and begin to ferret these out, no matter how innocent they appear to you. Then you will be working to clear your mind for the time when you will need to be able to hear the Voice of God, that time when it will be essential to your survival to hear His guidance. Only each individual can do this work for themselves. Parents will not be able to perform this task for their children. What the wife has done to clear herself of addictions/shortcomings will not benefit the husband. No one can become complacent or lazy in this task. It is one that each person must do for themselves. **All you can do for your loved ones is pray that God have mercy on their soul and on their being. Pray that they will come into the Truth of their being.**

Take heart; give thanks that as you gather together to prepare and to learn to prepare for your future, you have many spirits who are also praying with you. You have spiritual entities who are interested enough in your personal progress to be of assistance to you at all times. As you come out of the fears, angers and resentments, we will be there with love to fill these spaces immediately. Call on us to help with this all-important task. Call on us to give you warnings of slipping into old ways of thinking. We love each of you for the desire to prepare for the future in reality. Understand that these are only spiritual preparations. It is time for spiritual preparations, for inner work, and soon you will hear the Voice of God guide you to what is needed on earth to prepare.

This cleansing of self is so important that God is giving this idea to many, in many different walks of life. In religions the idea is coming through. In self-help groups this process is taking place. In schools this is being taught to the children along with their lessons on reading, writing and math. This is the ability to choose and to say what is to happen in your life. The program of "just say no" to drugs is a part of this lesson. It gives the children the first thought that they are in control of their lives and do not have to buy into the times or into the ways of their peers. This same lesson is being given to those who are working to cleanse themselves of their addictions. It has been proven vital to work with this concept of self-control and self-choice, but only with the assistance of a Higher Power.

Now you are to take this same message into your heart and mind. Expect this process to work. **Expect good results. Now is the time to clear from your mind and heart anything that will prevent you from hearing the Voice of God.** Understand that this is your goal. This is your aim—to be able to prepare for the times ahead when the earth will tremble and shake. This is how to prepare for the time when there will be chaos on earth. Because of this inner preparation, each of you will remain calm and secure in the knowledge that God will guide you. You will always be in God's Love and Care. Pray much for yourself and for others. Pray for each other, as all work to eliminate anything that will prevent the Voice of God from reaching you.

The Brotherhood

17

The Power of Prayer

Help Others Best Through Prayer (Fall Review)
(Brotherhood, September 9, 1989)

THIS IS A TIME TO REVIEW all that you have been taught. There is always a need to review and remember the truths of God. These things you have already learned and have, we hope, internalized as truths:

God is the Creator of all that is seen and all that is unseen, all that is known and all that is unknown. HE is at once Pure Energy, Pure Love, Total Light and much, much more. God is more than anyone can imagine and is much more loving than you can realize. God is in everything and is everything. God lives in all worlds and is in every creature at all times. God is the Life Force that animates His worlds. God is both father and mother of the Universe. God is Spirit, and it is only in Spirit that you can contact Him.

Your true life is spiritual, and you are only on earth for a
short time. Life as you know it on earth is a living education.
This world is a schoolhouse for you to learn your lessons in
spirit. There is the law of cause and effect, which governs the
world and all worlds. This is a spiritual law and as such it is
immutable. **What you think on earth is what you will live.
How you feel on earth will determine the conditions of your
life. Life is ongoing and eternal.** You have lived since the
beginning of time and have been many personalities. Throughout your lives you have committed many acts and deeds, which
are reflected in your life today. You are an accumulation of all
you have learned in time. The conditions of your life have been
determined beforehand.

**You have complete freedom of choice. This is your right
and your obligation—to choose for yourself.** This choice is a
God-given right, which cannot be denied you at any time. **It is
because of this freedom of choice that God will intervene in
your life only when you request it.** And then, God will do only
what you request. He will not take over and live your life for
you. This is the part that is not only your obligation but your
Divine right.

Time and space are issues you must deal with on earth and
are not a part of Spiritual Life. These are not an issue for God,
and so therefore **when God answers your prayers, He always
answers now. It is always NOW in spirit.** It is always now in
which you really live, even while on earth, but you have the
perception of living in the past and the future. This is a part of
the three-dimensional life you have on earth.

Your main obligation is to your own spiritual growth.
Understand that this is not selfish but leaves you open to be of
help to others, with the correct frame of mind. As you progress
in spiritual growth, you are also helping the race consciousness
to heal. As you work on your own thoughts and feelings, you
are clearer in mind, thought and deed. In reality, understand
that you can correct only yourself. You have no control over
anyone else. **The best way to help others and loved ones is**

through prayer. Remember that you are to correct those issues in you that can be corrected and to simply accept that which is not correctable.

Remember also that you are never alone when you call upon God the Father to help you. **You can have Divine intervention at any time.** This intervention will come in ways that are known only to God. As you daily call on God the Father to be with you, He will help you accept, correct, and give you knowledge to know the differences. You will be much better in spirit and in truth. You have the ability to connect to God if you will eliminate all fear, anger and such emotions from your inner self.

You also know that the best way to overcome fear, anger, jealousy, envy and such depleting emotions is to give them up to God. Allow His Spirit to intercede and intervene in your life. **Surrender all you are to God, and allow His great wisdom to enter your life.** You also realize that this is an ongoing process and one that is to be undertaken daily.

You also understand that the words in your Bible are filled with truths that will guide you if you will but think upon them. Ask God to explain, through your mind, the message that is in every word. Man has the ability to hear God speak, through his mind and feelings. This is how God speaks to us all. You also remember that prayer is the process of speaking to God and to All God Is. Meditation is your ability to quiet your mind and hear God speak.

This is your mission, while on earth—to seek to know God and to make contact with the Father through your mind and heart. You are to surrender all you are to God: that includes all feelings, all thoughts, all beliefs and all attitudes. You do not have to become anything beforehand to contact God. **God loves you just as you are at this moment in time.** God does not expect perfection from you, only willingness. God is willing and able to perfect in you what needs to be perfected. You are to concentrate on God and on your spiritual contact with Him. Do not worry about money, friends, loved ones or conditions.

These issues in your life will be taken care of as you surrender yourself to God.

Your priority in life is the contact and sustained connection to God. When you can live life from this standpoint, your life will be enjoyable and durable. Remember these words of Jesus: **"Seek ye first the kingdom of God, and all these things will be added unto you." (Mt 7:33) This is the first rule, and it is the most important rule.**

Understand that all you need in life is to make a strong connection to God-Mind. Seek to have God-Mind help you live this life spiritually.

The Brotherhood

Prayers for Well-Being
(Mary, September 9, 1989)

The love that is in my heart is there because God first loved us all. **It is in reality God's Pure Love that we pass around through His worlds.** Yes, I have a request—you might say, as usual—but in reality it is the same request I have been making for months. I request prayers for yourselves, your loved ones and the world population. I request that this prayer be in this form or some such form like this:

"Father God, I request per Mother Mary's wish that you send your Love into the hearts and minds of all men, women and children of this world. I ask that you forgive us all of our erroneous thoughts and beliefs. Forgive our ignorance, our mistakes in thinking there are many gods, when in reality there is only You, Father.

"Help each of us on earth to open our eyes to the mistake we make in abusing our land, our minds and our hearts. Help each of us as we seek to correct the conditions and thoughts that prevent us from seeing the Light, which is your Love.

"Father God, help each of us to correct in our own lives those areas which need to be changed, to accept those parts of our lives which cannot be changed, but most of all Father God, give us the wisdom to see the difference. We ask, Father God, as each of us works on himself, that this will help the collective consciousness of mankind. May this soon be the normal way of thinking, that mankind will think only of You and your Love.

"Send your peace into the world and into those areas of the world that are torn apart with wars. Help each one to reflect Your Peace in his or her heart, mind and life. I surrender all that I am to You, Father God. I surrender all that I hope to be and all I can be to your Love. Thank you, Father God, for hearing my prayer and for your answer. Amen."

When enough people have released from their minds and hearts the effects of the disease that is abounding on earth, each will have freedom. This freedom will be spiritual freedom and spiritual release. Then your mind and heart will be clear to be infused with God and All that God Is. People will see you infused and beaming in light. The light will be God, as HE lives in you.

Truly, God is Light, and there cannot be any darkness where there is Light. Take this literally. When you have seen me, you will see that I have been infused with God's Light. It is not simply a reflection, but the Source of All light that is in me. The Light of God removes all dark, depleting emotions, sickness and crime. The addictions of this world will be gone, and so will the effects of this disease of addiction. Not only are addictions an effect of this primary disease, but also are all physical, mental and emotional illnesses that are on earth today. Mankind will be free of all illness and all handicaps. Man will be free from all forms of depletions: hunger, starvation, illness, wars, crime and corruptions. This is real freedom. None of these conditions can have validity in the Light of God. These are conditions of darkness, and this is the darkness that will vanish in the Light of God.

Meditate on Love, Peace and Freedom with these words in mind. **Meditate on your connection to God-Mind; this will help all men connect to God.**

I also ask that each of you pray for the release of my message to the world.[11] I understand that not all people will believe this is my message, because it will be viewed as too strong. People think of me in loving terms, and this is good, but even the most loving mother at times must become stringent in her approach to her children when those children are in danger. There is also "tough love" in spirit. There are times when a mother must say, "Awake child, and see which road you are taking. Reconsider your life and listen to my counsel." Help me pray that the people of this world will heed my warning and will see the truth in my apparitions.

Understand that as this family group grows and more people come to hear the messages as they are given, this growth will increase in the race consciousness as acceptance. Pray much for your loved ones. More and more people will begin to turn to their own inner concept of God. Never ridicule or say anything against another's method of worshipping God. There are those who are too caught up in the outer elements of their religions. Instead, **pray that each person on earth will see with spiritual eyes the issues that are important.** Pray for all Mormons, Muslims, Jews, Hindus, Shintos, Buddhists, Catholics, Protestants and all people. Pray for those who are agnostic and atheist, for those who follow their own way of seeking God.

There is but one God and one heaven and one Spiritual Realm. All people will enter this realm sooner or later. Not one soul will be lost. We have all eternity to wait for the progression of souls. But as each of you and each of us prays, this time will come sooner. This time of unity with God will come in a flash, because when the race consciousness takes hold of the idea of Oneness with God, it will happen in that moment.

My concern today is for the physical and spiritual well-being of the people of earth. If too much fear is inflicted in their hearts and minds at the time of the changes, they will digress in

---

[11] The book, *Mary's Message to the World* (Blue Dolphin Publishing, released in May 1991).

spirit. This fear needs to be eliminated before they can progress. Because of this fact, I pray much for the people of earth. I pray that each one connects to God and to His love, which is pure. It is for this reason that I request your help in prayer, because **prayer is cumulative in nature, and all prayers help toward this end.**

My love is with each of you. Jesus and I are willing to help you, and we are grateful for your help with this great task. It is within your ability to help, and it is for your own good to help. Pray daily and nightly for my message to reach the world. I thank you for your efforts and your help.

Mary, Mother of Jesus

Life Is a Game: Cheer Yourself On
(Brotherhood, September 24, 1989)

Our joy is in you and with you, as is our love. We sense we have given you a large task to complete. Do not think you will be able to enforce the changes within your own personality soon. This is an ongoing task, one which will take a lifetime to complete. But it is also one that you do not have to accomplish alone. God, as Divine Love, is always with you during any change. He is ever present and ever aware of your struggle.

We ask that in the changing of self, you bring in joy. Live each day in Joy and Love. In this manner, the issue of changing the things you can will be accomplished slowly and without much outer effort. The changes within yourselves are to be made first and always with God's help. We are also on hand for instant help, but you must call on us and on God. Live each minute as if it were your last minute on earth. Live each minute close to Father God, Jesus and us. In this manner, you have much help with your daily tasks. Live for the minute or the hour, and do not worry about how you are doing. **This method of living in this hour will get you through many changes. In a short time you will have made an adjustment or shift to**

living in the here and now. You will have made this without difficulty. To live in the hour, you will make this hour a most complete spiritual experience.

Now one word of caution: never, ever berate yourself. Treat yourself with kindness. If there is a lack of motivation, you will not become motivated with berating. Become your own best cheerleader. Make up some affirmations, much as these young ladies of today do to urge their team on. You, Jesus, God and we are a team. **Cheer yourself on with affirmations.** Give yourself something to cheer about. Even when you are down, cheer yourself on. We like this analogy of cheerleaders. You are the team as you live each day to the fullest. You are the cheerleaders, and God-Mind is your coach. We see at this time of the year much emphasis on this sport. Think of yourself as living a game. It is the game of life; it is lived only for a short time.

In this game of life there are certainly periods of time. There is childhood, teenage and young adulthood. There is the period of raising children or of living a mature life. Then there is the period of old age. Each person is their own referee or judge. In reality you play every position, but by allowing God-Mind to become the coach, you will be guided into the best methods of overcoming the opponent. **Consider that the opponent is not some bad or evil spirit but simply the aspects of your personality that need to be changed. The battle is within yourself.**

We simply ask that you live this period of time (in your life) with the excitement and joy of an interesting game. When one side is badly beating the other, the game becomes uninteresting. Or, when the opponent is winning, the game is not only uninteresting but boring. All have a tendency to berate the team, but not the cheerleaders. They yell on encouragement. They say, "Come on and get out there and win. We know you can do it. Fight, fight, fight. Keep trying. You can do it. You can do it." This is the encouragement of joy. This is the encouragement of love.

Encourage yourself with joy and love. Become aware of your progress. Perhaps the yards of this game are difficult to come by, but, as the cheerleaders, keep on rooting for your team. Maintain loyalty, trust and faith in the Coach. Understand that there are those up on high who can see every play: this is us. Work with us, and we will give personal messages to help you in this great task. We can do this only by communicating with you privately. We now ask that each person learn to write, so that we can help you.

Understand that each of you came into this life to polish some aspect of your inner self. **You came with a purpose and this purpose was NOT to correct your loved ones, but to correct yourself. You came to work on you!** Remember to pray for yourself above all. Daily ask Father God to be with you during this day, to live the day in an attitude of change. Live in an attitude of encouragement and love. Concentrate on what it is you wish to accomplish. Leave the thoughts of shoulds, failure or berating, alone. When you hear yourself falling into this pattern of thought—the one that says you are so stupid, you failed, you should have done this or you are bad—STOP. These thoughts you must instantly eliminate by replacing them with a cheer, something like this: "You stumbled and failed, but get up, pick up the ball (which represents your goal); keep on running towards the goalpost. Go, go, and don't look back. Keep your eye on the goalpost."

Keep in mind that you are going to change only those parts of you that can be changed. So first decide if this habit or way of thinking can be changed. Perhaps you are trying to tackle a phantom. If the habit, trait or issue cannot be changed, you are wasting energy, time and effort. Decide first who is the opponent. Where are the goalposts? What are the rules of the game? These are the guidelines that will determine how you play the game of life. These are the guidelines that will set you into right thinking. Listen to your cheerleaders. Listen to your cheers for encouragement. This is the excitement of life. We also are your pep squad. We are cheering each of you on, because it is important to us and to the race consciousness that you win the game.

Literally, we ask that you come up with some affirmations in the form of cheers, that daily you encourage yourself with these cheers—something as simple as "You can do it. You can do it; you can live today in _____." Fill in the blank: it could be sobriety, compliance, peace, abstinence, love or joy. And understand that you are never alone with your goal. You can live this lifetime to the fullest. You can accomplish the act of clearing out of your mind and heart all angers, fears and depleting emotions. You can clear your mind and heart to hear the very Voice of God.

The Brotherhood

Prayer Is Cumulative
(Mary, September 24, 1989)

Dear children, I come today to give my love and assurance to you as you gather together in faith and love for Father God. Soon the days of trial and tribulation will be upon you. I ask that you remain faithful to your calling. Remain faithful to your inner search for a clear communication with God. It will be those who have affected a change within themselves who will hear the voice of God leading them to safe places. I understand that changing is not easy nor pleasant, but the rewards of accomplishing the changes will be great. It will not only benefit you but your children and children's children—that is to say, even if you do not have children or ever have children, the future generations will be affected by the changes that are now occurring in each of you.

Remain faithful to your search for God-Mind and God-Essence. Remain steadfast in your pursuit of survival. It is in this method that you will accomplish much spiritually. **Understand that prayer is cumulative, that each prayer is added to past prayers that you have said and that we have said.** Pray daily, not only for yourself but for the cleansing of the minds of men, for the cleansing of the minds of governments and of leaders of the world. I pray that as each of my apparitions is viewed by the people of this world, they understand that I come to warn, to alert and to give notice of the great changes, which shall surely take place.

Already governments are being alerted to the changing climate. The nations are beginning to see that something is happening in that part of the world which cannot be affected by humans. Already the storms have begun to grow in strength and in frequency. There is cause for alarm, and I have come to sound the siren of alert. I come to call the faithful to prayer and service, the service of changing themselves, in order that the world may change gently.

The massive amounts of money spent in studies is a waste. Studies do not foretell. Governmental studies do not accomplish anything except add to the confusion. Do not pay any heed to the warnings of man, but listen to the still, small voice within you.

As you are concentrating on the changes that you can effect, remember to pray. **Remember that through prayer and meditation many things are accomplished in the ethers.** Make a statement of fact, of intentions. Say, "I will pray The Lord's Prayer this many times, and in so doing I will be praying for world enlightenment." Or pray for world peace or for elimination of hopelessness. Pray for Divine Love to enter each addict and to speak to him of change. Only in this method will true change take place.

The governments of the world are concentrating on punishing the sellers of drugs, but they should concentrate on the user. When the user no longer uses the drugs, the sellers will not have a market. When enough addicts have changed their ways, more will see the light of encouragement and hope. Many in today's societies are hopeless. They say, "This addiction is stronger than I am. I feel weak. I don't feel confident that I can change." There is much denial in every person. They say,

"Soon I will change. Soon, in a week or two, I will think of the consequences of my actions." But little do they know that time is short and change of this magnitude is a long, slow process. Pray for the minds of those people who are hiding their little addictions and for those who openly abuse their bodies to see the light. When the light of Truth has entered the minds of men, then they will not deny their habits.

Pray for the addict, for governments of the world, for family members of the addict, for the society of the world. Everyone is affected by this rampage of abuse. Every sector of society is harmed; even those who do not have anything to do with drugs and alcohol, abuse the body with food, sex, work or any habit that takes over one's life. People can and do become addicted to their individual religions. When a person spends more time on matters of their individual religion instead of in prayer, that person is abusing his mind. It does not matter which religion has the most people in its churches or the most money. It does not matter the clothing or the fixtures of the church. What does matter is the Spirit of the religion. It is the Spirit of people that matters.

Mary, Mother of Jesus

Unselfish vs. Selfish Prayer
(Jesus, October 7, 1989)

Hello, dear children, this is Jesus. I wish to speak to you about prayer. I understand there is much confusion about this subject. Praying is speaking to God either formally, as in The Lord's Prayer, or informally. Either way, you are indeed praying. **It is a matter of heart and not of words. It is a matter of intentions and not simply phrases.** God can and does look into your hearts at the time of prayer and sees your true intentions.

Now throughout the past few weeks, Annie has had in her mind to ask about selfish prayer and unselfish prayer. She wanted to know the difference. It seems that the organizations (AA and Al-Anon) she and David belong to advocate unselfish prayer. This she did not understand.

It is all quite simple. What is selfishness in general? Wanting all for yourself, desiring that only your needs be met. Selfishness is a total and complete involvement with and in yourself, to the disregard of all others, to have the feeling that someone or something owes you your desires. You would selfishly feel that what you want is more important than anything else in the world.

To pray selfishly, you would want your needs, desires and hopes met without anything being required of you, simply because you asked for it. You would never think of anyone else. Their desires or needs become unimportant. It is you, first and foremost.

Now, in order to pray unselfishly, you need to understand that everyone on earth has the same kind of needs and desires. What you think is important, everyone considers important for themselves. In praying unselfishly, allow God to give what you truly need and desire. At times you do not know what you need or even what you truly desire.

Everything has a price! In order to pray unselfishly, you must be willing to pay the price. The price is not always in terms of money, but in terms of conduct or consequences.

As an analogy, a woman prays for a baby to come to the family. Perhaps you desire to become pregnant and deliver the child yourself. The consequences are that you must accept the pregnancy with all the possibilities of danger. Then you must accept the role of parent with all its responsibilities. Also you must accept this child underfoot and in your care for eighteen to twenty years. This is the price for the answer to your prayer for a baby.

Or perhaps you pray for a business. Are you prepared to work long, hard hours without pay in the beginning? Are you prepared to be responsible for your workers' welfare and to be their guide during the business hours? Are you willing to put aside your home life for your business? Are you willing to have no days off in the beginning?

Everything has a price, and you must be willing to pay the price for your prayer in order to receive the answer.

Now, we will return to the unselfish prayer. In praying unselfishly, you ask that as you receive your desires, all people have their prayers answered. Be willing for others to have creature comforts. Pray for everyone to have health, wealth and happiness. This is the unselfish prayer. You must be willing for all people to have their prayers answered.

I prayed unselfishly, when in the Garden of Gethsemane. I prayed, "If it is possible to put this cup (the crucifixion) aside, let it be so." (Lk 22:42) And then I prayed for courage to see me through the task. **This is praying unselfishly—when you allow God-Mind to made the final decision.**

At times, some people need to hurt from physical ailments in order to align their karma. In this case, you would pray that you have the courage to see this task through. Or perhaps, as in the case of Annie,[12] she must forgive and release angers that have been held inside her for many years. But first the pain needs to be remembered, in order to be forgiven. In this case, a *selfish prayer* would be, "I do not want to hurt for any reason, and please just take the hurt away, even if I do not learn anything." In order to pray unselfishly, she would say, "Give me the courage to withstand the pain, in order that I may forgive."

God will answer the unselfish prayer first. God gives courage and allows the time of hurt to be shortened when the prayer is unselfish. God will give the child to the parents who unselfishly are prepared for the long-term responsibilities.

To pray *unselfishly,* pray for others first and foremost. Then ask what you may for yourself. If you are confused as to how to pray, ask to be guided in prayer. If there is confusion in

---

[12] In regard to Annie's incest recovery.

what you truly desire and you need direction in making a decision, ask for guidance and direction. **Nothing is impossible to God, except a closed heart and mind.** God cannot enter the mind or heart that has sealed itself off. God cannot communicate with the heart or mind that is looking to itself for all answers.

Remember to pray for all people to have their needs and desires met. Pray for their spiritual healing first and foremost. This is the real unselfish prayer. Pray for your loved ones and especially your enemies. Simply pray for all people who criticize, ridicule or insult you. This is the purest prayer of unselfishness. Pray for your home planet Earth. Pray for all people.

God will not take over and give you what is good for you against your will. To do this, God would be making robots out of you. God would be taking away your choices and your self-government. This would be breaking a promise. God takes His promises to all worlds seriously. He will not break His word or promise. God suffers when his children do not heed the warnings that are given. He suffers when people turn away from Him, because God knows that each one of these people will suffer much for eons. He would have each person on earth be free of the consciousness of addiction to drugs and all harmful habits. These addictions are the end result of the first souls turning away from Him.

The highest form of prayer is simply talking to Him as you would a loved one. Speak to God about all your concerns, your worries, your cares. Tell God what bothers you, what you would like in this lifetime, what you would like to accomplish. Speak to God simply, in your own words. Speak to God of troubles, of joys, needs and desires. Most of all, ask God your questions. He can and will answer all questions. Pray to God formally and informally. Go to any church and worship God, or simply sit in nature and worship Him.

Now to the word "worship" God has given this meaning: in this context **He wishes you to worship—to become ONE with HIM.** Strive to put out of your mind all chatter, to become quiet with the forethought that in doing so, you and God will meet and unite forces in Love.

God realizes that you have different ideas of Him. But understand that God is all things, so He is what you envision Him to be. But also, He is what all people envision Him to be. He can become small or can be Himself, very large. He can be felt as an energy or simply as acceptance. God accepts every person. He understands your (Annie's) anguish and knows that you desire for all the children to learn what you are learning. But, Annie, pray for these children and allow them the freedom to follow their own direction.

God does not promise to make your life easier. He does promise to be with you through every part of your life. He will give you what you ask for in terms of help. **Understand God will wait for you to ask for His help. He will be waiting for you to call on Him.** Before God gives you "things," mere possessions, He will give you things of the heart and mind.

First, you will receive understanding for your problems, love for your enemies, kindness for all people and compassion for family members. God gives ideas to help you improve your work, home and life. God gives you interest in subjects that will help you to work out your own problems. This is your first help.

Many people pray as the song, "Oh Lord, will you give me a Mercedes Benz." This is not how God works. He will not simply give, but He leads you in the correct direction. God will provide teachers to give you instruction when you are prepared to receive the information. He shows you the way to help yourself. And, most important, He sets you in the right place at the right time. This God promises. He helps you achieve your heart's desires. It will be your inner heart's desires and not the heart you think of, when you think of desires.

Remember always simply to talk to God in your own language, in your own words. This is true prayer. Worship and become One with God.

Jesus

The Joy of Commitment
(Brotherhood, October 21, 1989)

Today we will speak of commitment and what all this entails. This is not a lesson that will make you feel bad; it should be one that will renew your commitment to yourself, to God and to each other.

There is much joy and celebration after a commitment has been made. Take for instance the joy and celebration that occurs after a wedding. All people love this type of celebration, because it is also a new beginning, the start of a new life together. Even those who have been married for some time will sense the commitment and the joy that follows by renewing within their hearts their own marital vows. Then there are other types of commitments and initiations, which are very similar to marriages, simply because they will denote a passage into a new life. Take, for instance, the celebrations at christenings, graduations; in some religions there is Bar Mitzvah, girls' fifteenth birthdays. These are all celebrations of a passage into a new life.

Each of you have made a new commitment to yourself and to God as you have progressed into this new life of seeking spiritual messages. For many months now, you have been seeking to better understand yourselves, your world and your future. In so doing, you have come to know more of God-Mind and all His Essences. You understand now that life is in reality a school to learn and practice. You understand that in reality your life is lived in spirit and not on earth. We ask that you renew your commitment to yourselves and to God. Begin with renewed interest to seek spiritual knowledge and understanding.

Perhaps we have given you more than you were ready for. We do not think this is the case. It is simply at times overwhelming and too much to take into your minds or your conscious minds. Your subconscious mind understands and recognizes the Truth. **The Truth is that you were conceived in Love, you** live your life in Love and will continue to live spiritually in Love. This Love is God or Divine Love.

Now, in this moment, make the commitment to remember each day how very much you are loved, how very much love is within your every thought and feeling. At times each person on earth gets caught up in the daily routine of their earthly life and forgets. You forget that this is a school and take this life too seriously. You forget that this is practice and each day is a practice session. You get caught up in thinking that this lifetime is it. You hear the words and do not understand or internalize their meaning.

Now, each person renew your commitment to yourself. Commit to live this life in joy and with patience. Commit to remind yourself daily that you were conceived, made and live in Divine Love. To do so you will understand that what you think of as serious will be less so. What issues are perplexing to you will be revealed. The mysteries will be revealed and this life will be lived in joy.

Father God did not want any of you to suffer or become so caught up in this life that you forget the realities. This is school and as such there will be lessons given on different subjects. These subjects will be lessons in patience, forgiveness, reliance, trust, honesty, tolerance and love. These lessons are not only spiritual but real. Where there is tolerance, there is forgiveness and love. Where there is patience, there is tolerance. Where there is honesty, there is trust and openness. There are many more lessons of this type. But remember that always, always you are Loved. It is not only the lesson of forgiveness; this is how you are treated by Father God.

Rejoice and see that what you have been given as information is Truth and is now becoming reality in your life. This is the beginning of the end. There will be more large earthquakes and storms. The lesson then is to put your emphasis on the spiritual and not only on the earthly.

How do you incorporate this into action and commitment? Commit to live your life spiritually and in Divine Love, reminding yourself daily, or momentarily if need be, of the Great Love that is your inheritance and is yours now. Do all you can to live life comfortably, and seek to expand your spiritual understanding. Do not place too much emphasis on worldly goods, because in a few years these will not be as they are now. This will all change!

Live this life to its fullest, remembering always what is real and what is not. Now some have a problem in determining career goals. Do all you can to make the money you are capable of. Do not get caught up in who is best or who is the leader. The lessons on earth are to get along with your fellow man, to become more understanding of those who do not have the information or education you have. Earn and strive to earn all you can, but not at the expense of your time to spend in meditation and prayer. Place your emphasis on the spiritual always.

Remember always the importance of prayer and meditation. Allow nothing, or no one, the opportunity to interfere in this. The ability to pray and to meditate on spiritual issues will get you through the coming times. Already the earth begins to shake and tremble. Already the climate is of concern to those who in the past chose not to see the changes. It is late dear children; it is coming close to graduation time. Prepare and be ready for the last test, the test of Trust in God the Father.

Daily, and each moment if need be, forgive all people in your past and present of any slight or indiscretion. Forgive all manner of attacks—verbal, emotional and physical. Forgive all people instantly. Forgive those who do not realize the Truths. But most of all forgive yourself, love yourself and be tolerant of yourself. **Commit today to love as you are loved, to forgive as you are forgiven, to be understanding as you are understood. Commit to live this life in joy and peace and love.**

Commit to increase your understanding of spiritual issues, to practice the spiritual lessons you have already learned. Practice relying on God to be your guide, to lead you in Truth and always in Love. Rely on God-Mind to increase your knowledge.

Some of you have lessons that you think of as very difficult. The difficulty is releasing them to God, to a Higher Power
than yourself. These lessons that we have given to you in this
past year are real. The words have all been Truth. And as such
we urge you to review these lessons and recall what has
already been learned. Now take these lessons and practice. But
understand that there are no bad grades in this school. You will
not be reprimanded or punished in any method. The punishment comes from your turning away from God-Mind and
relying on your own power. Your power will not be enough.

Many are confused as how to live this life now, with the
knowledge that you possess. **Live this life to the fullest. Place
the emphasis on spiritual issues, but understand that spiritual issues are practiced in life issues.** It is in releasing your
control and power to God that you gain. It is in giving of
yourself that you are given. Upon arising daily pray and give
thanks always to Father God. This places your mind and heart
in the proper perspective. This aligns you with All Energy.
Then take the day and perform your tasks in love.

Plan for this week and ask God the Father to provide you
with the means to live this life as you desire. But always
remember that Father God gives opportunities and gives subtle
hints. It is up to you to work with them. When a thought arises
as to a change in either employment or career goals, pray on
this and ask for enlightenment. Trust your inner self to reveal to
you what you need to do or the way to act.

Care for the body and do the things that will strengthen it.
Care for your mind and think the thoughts that will strengthen
it. Talk to yourself and tell yourself of the Love that is in you.
Talk to yourself and tell yourself of the Power that you are
connected to. You can accomplish all things, but it will take
reliance on God and trust in God the Father. Pray for the
understanding to discern the real from that which only appears
real. There is much fool's gold on earth. With help from God the
Father, you will be able to find the real gold in any situation.

Commit to living this life from this day forward in reality of Spirit. Commit to a life of prayer and meditation. Commit to placing your emphasis on Spiritual issues and learn all lessons in Love. Commit to better yourself, to no longer abuse your mind, body or heart. Put away all abuse of self and others. If this seems difficult, pray much for strength and for enlightenment.

Remember always, abuse is the one thing that God abhors. Use love instead of abuse. Use spiritual means to live on earth. Take good care of your inner self and seek the inner guidance that is available to each person on earth. Treat yourself with love and treat all people with love, even those who have offended you. Forgiveness is essential. Love is essential to you on earth, as it is to us in "heaven." Use whatever prayers work for you. Use whatever meditations that work for your inner self. Always remember that we are, as are Father God and Jesus, only a thought away. Instantly we are with you when you call. But you must call for us as you must call out to God the Father, Creator and Almighty.

The Brotherhood

18

God's Extraordinary Love

You Are Loved, No Matter What
(Brotherhood, November 4, 1989)

TODAY, we will once again speak of God's tremendous love for each person. We repeat this lesson because we feel you have not internalized this message. You know the contents of this lesson in your mind, yet you have not truly made the connection of knowing it deep within your heart.

Understand that simply to know something mentally does not constitute knowledge, as God gives it. **The heart and mind must agree, and then you will "know it." This "knowing it" means you will never forget.** The knowledge will become as much a part of you as your morning routine. When you "know and recognize" the Great Love that is yours unconditionally, then you will live in freedom, the freedom to live your life with confidence, assurance and self-esteem. Do you need to take a few minutes each morning to remember how to

walk or talk? Of course not. You do these automatically because you have internalized them. They are now a part of you,
and you are a part of these abilities.

To "know" that you are loved Divinely will also become
internalized, and then you will be free to love yourself, to
forgive yourself and others. It is difficult to love another when
there is no love for yourself. It is even more difficult to forgive
your fellow man if you cannot forgive yourself. The answer lies
in recognizing that each person is loved unconditionally. This
means that no matter what you have done or thought or
attempted, you are loved. This Love is the most powerful Love
in the Universe.

We request that each one take this message and daily take
the thought, **"I am loved no matter what. God loves me
today."** See, dear ones, the Love that is yours will set you free to
live this life in totality. Nothing will be difficult for you. Nothing will be withheld from you, because you will know the
secret to living life joyously. Live life in Divine Love. This is
your goal. You already live in Divine Love! But you do not
remember that you are loved, and forgetting is the cause of
your many doubts and anguish.

Always think of God as Good and Loving. This is Truth,
for in reality God is all this and more. He does not punish or
cause you to do anything you do not want to do. You live this
and every life in complete freedom of choice. If at any time you
find God to be harsh, then remember that this is your old
concept of God and not Truth. As you read the Bible and find
God represented as a harsh and angry God, understand that
the writer was then giving an earth-mind concept of God.
Likewise if you think of God as angry or harsh, this is your old
earth-mind concept that has reared in your memory. It takes
time to completely clear out the memory of all these old concepts of God.

At times people feel restricted by God because He has
given guidelines by which to live happily. These guidelines
come in the form of the Ten Commandments (Ex 20) and Jesus'

Sermon on the Mount. (Mt 5-7) These are simply God saying, "If you live by these rules, you will surely find happiness and freedom." Many people who are in jail say, "God does not love me. Look at the bad times I have had in my life. This is not love." In reality, each person chooses how to live his or her life. It is not God who has stopped loving this person, but themselves. When you cannot love yourself, you wonder how God can. God sees past your mistakes and sees you in your entirety and in truth.

In the olden days, God told the Israelites how and what to eat. He taught them all things for their health. He taught them to be clean and to wash their food, because in past times people did not always wash. Today God does not need to give such explicit instructions. In the past you have bought into the concept of an angry and punishing God. These concepts will harm your inner self as much as not washing yourself or your food will harm your outer body. Always remember these are simply rules by which to live happily. God will not punish if you choose to ignore them. The punishment comes from not living by the rules.

The most important thought in your life is this: **"I am Divinely loved by a gentle and caring Heavenly Father." Remind yourself daily that God's Love is free and unconditional.** There is nothing in this world one need do to have it. It cannot be bought or stolen. God loves you as much when you do not recognize His love as when you do. God's Love is unwavering, strong and true.

All the thoughts and deeds of the past do not interfere in God's Love. Divine Love is like the sunshine. It falls on the good and wicked. Like the sunshine, it is there if you recognize it or not. Internalize this concept! Take it into your heart and mind. The mind is quick to grasp new ideas and concepts, but the heart must mull over and over the new concept. Nightly and daily remind yourself of God's Love and become grateful for what this truly means. Become aware of Divine Love in your life. Learn to rely on the concept of Unconditional Love.

When you feel downhearted and distressed, remember that no matter how you feel, you are loved. When your life does not flow easily, remember that you are loved. Outer situations in life are lessons and have nothing to do with God's Love. Your success in the eyes of the world has nothing to do with the Love that is yours from God the Father. He is ever-present and ever-true. He is unyielding and steadfast. He is not influenced by anything on earth. Whether the person recognizes or loves God does not influence God's Love for each person. God loves the one who recognizes His love as well as those who do not.

Be cognizant of the Great Love in which you live. Become grateful and recognize this love. You will begin to feel when you have internalized this concept. You will become free to be all you can be. This is true success in life.

The Brotherhood

Internalize God's Love
(Mary, November 4, 1989)

Work to internalize the concept of Divine Love in your life. Take this concept and chew on it as a dog does a bone. In this manner, you will internalize the concept. This is what I mean. Notice that a dog will take a bone and lick it, chew on it and sometimes even fall asleep with it under his chin. He keeps the bone close to him at all times and even when he does leave the bone, time and again he will return to see if it is safe. Take this concept of Divine Love and the example of the dog. In this way keep the idea with you until you have internalized it.

You will sleep with the idea of Unconditional Love— when you settle into bed for sleep, remember you are loved unconditionally. Review the day and all its activities. Perhaps you will have regrets on some issue, or you will feel happy about some situation. The last thought to consider is, **"I am loved Divinely."** Keep this thought with you as you drive on the highways or as you work. This is the way to mull over an idea or concept.

The chapter in my book on Love[13] is good to review. I have told that Divine Love is healing. You can use the words Divine Love and visualize the Love of God as a pink light or in some other method you devise. Use this visualization and the words, **"God's Love is healing this now,"** as an affirmation. Allow the Love of God to heal old hurts and pains. God's Love can heal your life situations.

Allow me to explain how God's Love can be used to energize your life. Perhaps you and your mate are not getting along: there is some difference of opinion. Then use "Divine Love" as an affirmation to heal the division. Perhaps your child is needing to feel more love in his life. He is attracting attention in a negative manner. Hold this child while praying the words, "Divine Love surrounds you and me." Having financial problems? Again, hold your paycheck or bankbook and visualize God's Love as a light pouring into your account.

Upon awakening, sit quietly and visualize God's Love streaming into your heart and body in a healing light. Then begin your day. As you go through your washing routine, think, "God still loves me. God has been with me as I slept and will continue to love me through each minute of this day. I can be energized with God's Love. Divine Love and God's Love are one and the same. Divine Love is energy, pure energy. It can be used to heal, to set the future into the good and to guide. Because of Divine Love, I can and do love all people. I forgive all people, including myself. I can do this because God loves me and forgives me."

Mull over and over this concept of Divine Love, unconditional love. Always think of God as alive, active and loving you. Make this a part of your system. Make this concept as much a part of you as your speech. When you have accomplished this, you will find Pure Joy and Divine Peace, a peace and serenity

---

[13] "The Subject is LOVE," chapter 4 of *Mary's Message to the World*.

which will hold you steady and strong. When you have fully accepted and internalized this concept, you will lean on it and let it guide you every moment. You will never feel alone. There will be the security of Divine Presence with you.

When you have fully internalized the Love of God, then you will begin to live life successfully. There is self-confidence and self-assurance in the internalization of Divine Love. This self-confidence will give you the edge in many situations. You will not have to be loud or demanding, for all the Love of the Universe is yours. You will have a commanding aura much as Jesus had.

People listened to Jesus when he spoke, because He had self-assurance and much confidence in his inner self. This assurance and confidence was there because **Jesus knew he was Divinely loved.**

Consider Jesus' life on earth. Read his words and read between the lines of his stories. He told much in his tales. He told of God's Love and of all that is Divine.

In the Sermon on the Mount (Mt 5-7), Jesus gave some attitudes to hold. He told of the rewards of holding such attitudes. There are lessons within lessons. **The first internalization that needs to take place is living daily in God's Love.** Internalize the knowledge of living in God's Love. Become so sure of this concept that there is never any doubt. No matter if you feel it or only think you realize it, God Loves you unconditionally. When you can internalize this idea, your eyes will open to much, much more.

I appear to many on earth because of Divine Love. I come not only to recall each person to his place in God's Love, but to remind you that we are all Loved Divinely. Not just the Saints and Angels, but all of Creation, are Loved Divinely.

Make this concept personal and internalize it into your inner self. In this way you will digest the idea and become one with it. Only through this process of internalization can you proceed to deeper meanings. Only then will you have a gentle spirit and a gentle soul. You will handle yourself with love and compassion. You will live in compassion with your fellow man.

Stay with this one concept my children, for it is an important concept. Keep this idea with you for one week and see the progress in your inner self. The feelings for yourself will be gentle and peaceful. All relationships will have a new, gentler air about them. Your work will be satisfying, and your life will become more inspired.

I request that each pray for himself and for his world, that each pray daily for the healing of the planet and the people of this planet. I wish for each person to feel the Love of God and also the love that comes from gentle spirits, who are daily at your service. They wish to be called into service. They request you place in their hands some issue that is close to your heart.

Now I thank each of you for listening to my request and to my words. Understand and internalize this fact of truth—you are Divinely Loved.

Mary, Mother of Jesus

Believe in Yourself and Your Abilities
(Brotherhood, November 18, 1989)

We have given the message of God's extraordinary Love for everyone alive. We ask you to use the affirmations daily and remind yourself of His great Love. **God is both personal and principle. His Love is such that no one on earth could begin to imagine the quantity or quality of it.** Work with the affirmations daily.

In the past we have told you that life on earth is a school. During your lifetime you are learning many lessons, some subjective and others objective. These lessons are overt and occult. This simply means that some lessons you will or can be aware of and some lessons are hidden from you until you return to the real Spirit world. Each can progress by taking this life with less seriousness. You are in school, and not everything about school is serious and heavy. **Life is a joy and can be lived with lightheartedness.**

When faced with an issue that is overwhelming, remind yourself this is simply a difficult lesson. Do not give in to despair. See what in the situation can be alleviated with a change of attitude, what in the situation can be used for growth and what is not changeable. Let us give an example. We will use the situation with Byron. What is happening in Byron's career now is a blockage. It has nothing to do with his previous actions or is in any way connected to punishment. He is learning to use his whole self. He is learning to sell his services,[14] and this is not easy. There is much rejection involved in this type of work. Remember that God is not rejecting you and neither should you. Now, no matter who is selling their own abilities, there is this difficulty. Byron must have confidence in himself and in his ability to perform the work that is being offered. This is not comfortable to him yet, because he is expanding and reaching out to surpass his previous limits. Now his horizon is further out and his abilities are many. Remember that you can do anything your mind can conceive and believe. This then is the lesson. But your faith must be strong, and faith can be increased.

Believe in yourself and in your abilities. It is imperative to believe that you can perform the work you are offering to others. Byron noticed that although many were needing this type of work, not many were contracting his services. Why? Because his faith was teetering. On the inside he was unsure of his abilities. He was selling himself short. He was much more qualified than he allowed himself to think. He could do many things besides sell. He could motivate and instill in others a sense of fairness. He could work with mathematics and could

---

[14] Byron was an independent business consultant, specializing in high technology companies.

talk sensibly with vendors, bankers, accountants and others. But it was not comfortable. Understand, the discomfort is good. It is growth. It is stretching and exercising your confidence. **First you must believe! Each person must believe that he has within him many abilities.** Many people today are selling themselves short. You do not believe in yourselves. You see yourselves only as a clerk, salesman, floor nurse or simply as a worker.

Today we ask that each person believe in themselves and in their abilities not only to survive but to live. Believe that you are connected to a loving and caring Father God. Take inventory of your abilities and desires. Ask first in meditation if you have listed all your abilities. If you are unable to question your inner self, then ask someone who is of like mind and is of your liking to assist you in this inventory. Make a list of what you wish to accomplish. Make a list of the desires that are in your heart, not anything outrageous, such as to be an instant millionaire, but good and productive desires. Perhaps you wish to have a larger income. See ways to change the inner you to accomplish the desire. First, each of you needs self-confidence. Each person must be honest and open with himself. Do not allow any false sense of personality or underestimation of self to enter into this list. We could take each of you one by one and tell you what is needed, but then it would be us doing your lessons and your homework. Next do the same with what you must change on the outside to accomplish your desires. Perhaps there is more formal schooling needed. Do not let this stop you. Seek what and where and how much this will take. Make a budget and allow yourself to see the possibilities. If you think there is no money, there will not be any money. Think instead, it looks like a money problem, but I will ask Father God to show me how to accomplish this. Then look into grants, loans and scholarships. If what is needed is self-improvement, then find ways to accomplish this, and always do everything with prayer.

Be grateful for your abilities and for an expanded horizon. The stretching of self-confidence is a lesson. Be grateful most of all for God's Love and care. Remember always, you are not alone and the help of the universe is with you. At times we feel that not everyone makes use of the extra help that is available. All your daily activities are lessons, some large and others small. Even the keeping of a routine is a lesson. The coming together of this family group is a lesson. It is a lesson in faith and belief. Now take this lesson in faith and belief and use it to enhance yourself in this world.

You live in this world and you live today. Each is learning lessons, not only in order to survive the coming earth changes, but to live daily in confidence. **When you live in confidence, you are honoring the life God gives. You are honoring the abilities God has given.** When you can use your whole self to enhance the life that you are aware of, then you will be doing the Will of God. Do not live for the coming earth changes. These are already happening. To live only for that day is a waste of a lifetime. Live daily and learn all you can each day. As you learn the overt lessons, understand that many lessons are taking place within you on levels beyond your awareness.

Here then is our desire for your daily living:

Live in self-confidence, with love and gratitude for God's Love. Expand your horizons by stretching into areas that are a little uncomfortable at first. The old, earth-mind consciousness will be saying, who are you to think you can do this? Who do you think you are? You can't do this! In touching your feeling nature, the old earth-mind consciousness will tell you this is uncomfortable because it is wrong. But understand that earth-mind consciousness does not like to have you expand and grow. Note each time you stretch there is less discomfort.

Daily meditate and pray for God to help you grow in spirit and on earth. Ask for help to perform the task you have set. If you need to seek another job, do not go alone. Go armed with God, Jesus and us. We are all here to help you live daily. Remember that most problems can be overcome with a change of attitude.

We ask that each day you remind yourself that you are in school. Look for the lessons you feel you are in the process of learning. Some will be on learning to forgive, but most will be about learning how to have confidence in yourself and your abilities. Each circumstance is an opportunity presented for your learning. Each day you will solve problems, see with new insight and build more confidence. Each day is for learning and for fun.

Love yourselves and appreciate who you are. Appreciate what you are. You are the loving child of a Great and Loving Father God. **Seek to find your inner connection to God, not only for your spiritual growth, but for your everyday life.** This life is a gift.

To have self-confidence implies that you have confidence in God. This is the important reason to increase your faith in yourself. Seeking to better yourself on earth is to better yourself in spirit.

Many will look to life as it is being lived on earth today and wonder why—why all the drug abuse, crime and abandonment? These are issues of growth and spirituality. These are opportunities to grow and expand. This is a period of opportunity to overcome abuse in many forms. Do not look to the world and its problems as excuses for your lack. See the good in everything on earth. See the good that is available to all people. Become aware that the accumulation of power and money are in vain. There is power in overcoming. There is power in growth and advancement of daily living. Forget the issues of the world, except to pray for the world and all its inhabitants. Prayer is your duty and your opportunity.

Live each day in the Love that surrounds you. Live each day in joy and prayer. Live each day to improve yourself, either inwardly or outwardly. Reach out and use all the resources that are available. Reach out to God-Mind and allow us to help you. We await your call. Nothing is too small, and no issue is too great or ugly for us or God. Abuse can be left behind. Earth-mind consciousness can be quieted. It is possible to live this life daily in God-Mind. It is possible to accomplish your desires. It takes faith, work and prayer.

The Brotherhood

Be Your Own Best Friend
(Mary, November 18, 1989)

Hello, my children. How much you are loved from this side! We, Joseph and I, wish you could understand this. You each are in our prayers. Continuously we pray for your growth in Spirit and in truth. We understand how difficult it is simply to live on earth. This era is even more difficult than previous ones. There are many ways available for abuse of self and others. Your only recourse is to pray for people and include them daily in your loving thoughts. No one in reality is a lost soul. All can and will eventually be made whole. Simply through our prayers we ask that it be sooner than later.

If you could perceive the love that is directed toward you from God the Father, you would never feel lonely or sad. No one would ever doubt their capabilities or opportunities. This is the reason we tell of the great love that we hold for you. We hope to impress upon your mind and heart the truth of this Love.

My dear children, think well of yourselves. Be good to yourselves and think of the love that is in the air you breathe, the thoughts you think and in each functioning of your whole self. When a thought or feeling of sadness or anger creeps into your mind or heart, remind yourself of this Love. When you feel you are too tired to continue, remind yourself of the full potential of your life. **Be your own best friend;** have compassion for your entire life. **This is how to love yourself:** Remember always that each part of your life is for growth. Each thing you overcome is overcome in Spirit. Each time you depend on God, you win, not as the world views winning, but you win in more ways.

Perhaps in the past you have suffered. Jesus also suffered while on earth. He showed the way to overcome suffering by forgiveness and through compassion. Do not dwell on the suffering, but in the lesson the suffering brings. Dwell on the good, always. Dwell on the learning and not the difficulty of the lesson.

These next years are "Years of Grace." They are an opportunity to overcome anger, envy, jealousy, hatred and all depleting emotions. **This is the time to learn to depend on God the Father. Now is the time to learn to love, first yourself and then others.** It is time to stop all forms of abuse. Do not abuse with your thoughts, words or deeds. Now is the time to have compassion and to be good-natured. Learn to look for the good in every situation. Stop all wild pursuit of worldly goods, the frantic buying of items that deteriorate and perish. Seek to find the "goods" of the heart, which will not perish or tarnish with any passage of time or events on earth. This time of Grace is given to all who will listen with their heart and pray with their whole soul.

Mary, Mother of Jesus

God's Love Is Greater Than You Can Imagine
(*Brotherhood, December 9, 1989, Advent*)

Good day, family members. Welcome to another season to celebrate Jesus' birth on earth. During the last few weeks we have requested that each person think of the Love of God. We continue with this theme because of its importance. It is the reasoning behind all the aspects of your life, the answer to many questions and a help to everyone in this lifetime.

To review, **God loves humanity with such a Great Love that He has allowed man to know the concepts of Divinity, which are: to be creative, loving, forgiving and responsible.** You are not robots. As free-willed individual cells, you have the privilege to create whatever you will. Man is the creator of his own life circumstances. You have opportunity after opportunity to rectify mistakes. Allow us to speak on your ability to create whatever you will.

Every moment of each day you are creating your life with every thought, attitude and belief. These determine how you learn your lessons. Some will learn easily and others will make it difficult for themselves. The question is how to learn easily, how to live life without the abrasive incidences which can occur.

First, remember daily that you are living in God's Love, whether you are aware of it or not. You are a part of this great Love and can rely on Father God for all your needs. When you have a sense that you are far from the Love of God, this simply means you have lowered your sights and are using earth-mind concepts. You are using the erroneous thoughts of humanity for your truth. Begin by making statements of fact. Declare to yourself daily, **"I live in God's Love whether I can sense it or not. I rely on Father God for all things and all issues. God's Love is greater than I can imagine."** These are affirmations made in a positive mode.

Now we will explain the difference in making statements in the positive as opposed to negative mode. A negative statement would be something in this vein of thought: "I know I must rely on God, but I don't feel Him near me and I can't do this." Or, "The Brotherhood says God loves me with a great Love, but I don't feel it." This is relying on a sense of earth-mind truth only. Perhaps you can see a mental image without the connecting sense. To use the mind without the heart is not making the connection. Instead make your statements of fact in this manner: declare to yourself, either in your mind or out-loud, but with powerfully felt words, the following, **"The**

Brotherhood assures me that I am Loved with a great Love from Father God. I may not be feeling it now, but it is Truth and I will have a sense of this Great Love in time."

Do not depend on what you can feel or think, because mankind has built within himself many ideas, beliefs and attitudes that are in error. Rely on us to help with your connection to God-Mind truths, which can be proven. These are truths that are provable and so can be relied upon.

We have given the reason for Jesus' coming to earth, to demonstrate to mankind its own potential and to recall to each person the Great Love that is God. And yet, 2000 years later, you have not reached your potential. You have not claimed your spiritual inheritance. Man is still much as the prodigal son who went away into a far country to spend his inheritance. (Lk 15:11-32) You are far removed from God as a whole, simply because you have relied on other men to give you your attitudes, beliefs and faith. Too many rely on other people to give them their own interpretation of the Bible. The Bible holds truths that are applicable to many different situations, and as such there are many truths in each word.

Father God is much as the father in the story who waits and looks daily for a sign from the son who is far away. He waits for some slight hint that, individually, man wishes to be near Him.

In the story, the first thing the abandoned son did was to recall the love that his father had for all people in his household. He recalled that even the lowliest of servants had more to eat and were clothed better than he. The son spent all his potential, felt not only lonely but unloved. He found himself in a pig's sty living among animals. Now let us look into the meaning of this from a psychic standpoint.

To live away from your Source, which is Father God, you will live as an animal, merely working for your daily bread, not realizing any goals, nor seeking anything greater than what is in front of you, seeking only the pleasures of the moment. Today mankind finds himself in this mentality. He thinks what he is told to think, he expects what he is told to expect and he conforms to mankind's dictates. Who is this person or persons who are controlling? It is the collective thoughts of man. Today it is the merchant who dictates and the government. This is a commercial world, and it is commerce that dictates your morals, your desires and your hopes. There is more to life than "things" or status. Now, "things" and status are good, but not when they are your whole life, the reason for your existence.

Begin by recalling the Great Love that is God. **Bring to mind daily that God and the spiritual life are more important than anything else in this world.** This in no way denotes that you are to live life without "things" or status. We simply say put your trust and your worth in spiritual issues and in spiritual values. Recall that this life is not your only life. Because of God's Love, each person has been given many lifetimes to learn. Appreciate the Great Love that is yours.

Now to return to our story: the spent son made a life decision. He decided it was preferable to live as a servant in his father's household than as an animal. He would go and offer himself as a servant to his former household.

As the father was accustomed daily to watch for the son to return, he was seen from afar. The father, in his love, wanted nothing more than to aid, assist and welcome the son home. The father had a feast prepared and received the son into full rights as heir and not as a servant.

God's Love is greater than this. His desire is that no one should suffer. In God's great wisdom, He understands that in order to give free will, He must allow man to make mistakes. God is our Father and Creator. He is ever-present to help each of you. If it is understanding that you lack, then ask for understanding to comprehend this Great Love. If you lack motivation to live in God's Great Love, ask for motivation. If you lack anything, God will give you what is right for you, in the circumstances of this lifetime and in your spiritual life.

As you make your preparations for this season, **remember that the most appropriate gift of all is Love. The most**

appropriate gift to mankind is daily prayer for the lifting of consciousness. In order to help your fellow man, pray daily that he learn whatever lessons there are to learn and that these lessons be given clearly and with hope.

Annie had thought to help the homeless with a gift, but we say help the homeless through prayer and not only through "things." During this season, it is customary to give gifts, but we say give the gift of Love. Daily give the gift of prayer for each person on earth. It is not only the homeless but the addict who is in need. The scourge, or the plague, is upon you, and it is the desire for instant gratification. It is seen in the addict mostly, but this same plague can be seen in the need for instant gratification of all kinds, in the desire for power, as is seen in abuse. It is in the turning away from God. People are relying on drugs, money, status, prestige and on many different issues to give them their worth. **Your worth comes from Spirit. It comes from what you carry in the deep inner recesses of the mind.**

We say it is not necessary to give items to the homeless, unless it is put in your heart by God. But it is necessary for you to pray daily for the homeless, the addict, the abuser, the robber and the murderer. This is how to help your world and mankind. It will take more than a few items to help the homeless and imprisoned. It will require education, honorable work skills and housing that is geared to the needs of the poor. The poor will always be with you, because the poor are in this life situation for a reason. The plight of the homeless will individually be relieved as each person works on their own lifetime goals. Through prayer you help these people to learn what it is they are to learn. Through prayer you help more than through the giving of items. Hold a special prayer time for the homeless, the imprisoned, the abused, those who are fighting.

Most important is to recall the Greatest Love in the world, which is God. Remember your full potential as demonstrated by Jesus while on earth. Understand the power in your words, in your thoughts and in your basic attitudes. Read how Jesus calmed the storm and how nature obeyed his word. This is your potential! You also have this power in your words and in each thought. Watch those thoughts. **Be forgiving, loving and prayerful. Live out the situations in your life to the best of your ability.**

Do whatever is before you with all your heart, all your might and all your mind. We will use Annie as an example. She is currently working through some old issues of abuse. There is deep-seated anger in her body. Not only is your mind capable of holding on to thoughts, but also the body holds many ideas, beliefs and attitudes. At times it is difficult for her to proceed, but this is her task in life. This is the lesson, one that will help her to eliminate some old hurts, angers and resentments. Many of you do not have such dramatic circumstances to live through, but whatever is in your life is dramatic to you. It is important for you to give your all to the completion of each circumstance in life. Through the circumstances and situations of life comes power to overcome, to love and forgive. Forgiveness is something that is more than words or attitude. It is spiritual. It requires an elimination of anger, envy, resentment and jealousy.

If your heart is telling you that some issue in your life is to be worked on, then do it, because this is the next step in your learning. Sometimes it may be a simple thing, such as an increase in your education. Or it may be a change of attitude, or perhaps to trust yourself or others. These are the circumstances of learning. You can advance through prayer and meditation if you use these issues to increase your learning. Meditate by blanking your mind, then recall the Love of God, the lessons and affirmations that we have given. Then enter the temple of your mind and talk to God the Father. Talk to Him as you would a loving parent. If in this lifetime you have not had the experience of a loving parent, then use your ideal of such a parent.

Next, you must trust that what you receive in your heart and mind as ideas or feelings are the answers to your meditations. Perhaps you have a feeling to give some item or time to others; then pray more and ask Father God to reveal the answer to you clearly. Perhaps you are in need of a structured church environment. Then go and find the appropriate place through prayer. **Each of you is individualized and will have different needs, different issues to settle, and different circumstances to meet. It will be through prayer that you will find your answers. It will be in meditation that you commune with the Father.**

Now enter into this season and bring into your home the sense of Love this season brings to the world. For a brief moment the world is a happy place, a place filled with love for many. Pray for this same spirit of love, sharing and joy to fill each moment of life. This is the season that aids you in recalling the Love of God as Father. The aim of all is peace on earth and goodwill towards all men. This is our prayer daily. This is the prayer of many good spirits and angels.

Fill your mind, heart and body with Love. Fill your home with love, and send loving thoughts to each family member, even those who oppose you. Concentrate on Love!

The Brotherhood

Your Potential Is as Christ
(Brotherhood, December 24, 1989, Christmas Eve)

Welcome and allow us the time to send more love, more joy and more peace into your lives. We enjoy the feeling of joy that comes over the world at this time of the year. Our prayer is that this same feeling can be held every day.

On earth, this is the time to celebrate Jesus' birth, but we say celebrate this day as the day man was shown his full potential. Jesus came to earth to show the way, to lead mankind out of the darkness of despair into the light of love, peace and knowledge. His message is one of hope and goodwill. He came to teach man to communicate with a loving and powerful Heavenly Father.

Over the past few weeks we have insisted that you concentrate on the Love of God. Make this Love, which is alive and healing, a big part of your thoughts. Rely on the Love of God-Mind to fill all needs, heal all illness, and bring peace into the soul. It is this same Love that Jesus came to proclaim. As you already know, the people of Jesus' times believed in a God who was harsh, punishing and angry. Many people of this day still believe in that concept of God. But you know and understand that God-Mind is not punishing, but allows the working out of His laws of behavior. He allows each person to live their own life with full rights to all decisions. Each man is allowed to make his own choices. But what man has forgotten is that with the right comes the responsibility of living with the choices he makes. Today many in the world call this karma, or cause and effect.

What Jesus teaches is that **by relying, believing and trusting in God's love, you can overcome the effects of karma.** You can reach up to new levels and new heights. By seeking the truth of God, you can learn new ways of living, which include the use of all the powers that man possesses already. You have the same abilities that Jesus had while on earth. You can levitate, multiply your sustenance and heal your own illness. This is your full potential; these can be developed only through concentrating on the Essence of God. **Each person has the responsibility of staying in close contact with God and relying on God to provide for all their needs.**

Jesus taught man to pray, and he gave what is called The Lord's Prayer. The words invoke many levels and open your inner powers. The words teach you to believe that God is the source of All—that you do not have to sacrifice, beg, plead— but simply to trust and be grateful.

Every person is responsible for their own growth and seeking. The prayers of the faithful will heal. So continue to pray the one for the other and most of all for the world. Remember that this is the greatest gift of all. The things or trinkets of this world will vanish. **The prayers of the faithful**

will endure and bear fruit. These prayers will be answered. So concentrate both on the spiritual and on your physical needs during prayer, but remember that most important of all is your spirit. **Your spirit-soul endures and lives forever.** The things of this world will become dirt and enter the cycle of regrowth on earth.

Rededicate your search for the spiritual. Reaffirm in your mind and heart a listening for your directions from within. Seek to make your contact with God-Mind powerful and direct. In this way, you will have the assurance that what comes into your mind is from God, the Heavenly Father. Set for your goal the meditations of the heart. Do not waver from this goal, for your very survival depends upon it. In the coming decade, there will be many who will come saying their way is the right way to God. But if it does not lead you to an inner contact with God-Mind, then be very wary. Be cautious in giving up anything of a spiritual nature to anyone. Jesus' method was of inner contact with God-Mind.

Jesus taught that to make contact with God-Mind, you were to enter your closet and pray to God in private. (Mt 6:6) God answers you openly, for all to see His power. The closet you are to enter is the closet of your mind. This simply means to go within. Meditate and take your petitions to God in private, and allow God-Mind to decide what is best for you. You do not need to confess to man or to give your prayers over to anyone. Do not give your inner instruction over to anyone else. **Do not depend on another to receive your inner instructions.** What you need to know will be revealed through you, but first you must practice the communication, and this practice is best achieved through meditation.

Look at what mankind considers miracles. These are simply the working of greater laws, the evidence of belief, the revealing of trust. Jesus did not waver in his trust of God. He felt sure that God would answer His prayers. Why? Because Jesus was in constant contact with God-Mind. He talked to God through his mind and heart. The trust was real, the belief was power and the love was present at all times in Jesus' heart. This is your aim, to trust this much, to believe and feel God's Love in this manner. This is why Jesus was born.

Celebrate his birth by loving all people, including your enemies, as Jesus did. Bring the peace that is so much a part of this season into your meditations, and understand that peace as Father God gives is more powerful. Take on Jesus' attitude of love, trust and peace. It is all a matter of attitude anyway. This life is lived from the mind out. Take on the attitude of love, trust and peace. When you become upset, meditate and return to Father God to become balanced in love, trust and peace. Trust Father God to help you live this life to its fullest. This will not be as the world sees fullest, but as God sees fullest, spiritually. Trust God to provide you with the situations that will enhance you spiritually. **Bless every situation that enters your life. Every situation carries with it a learning, spiritually.** This is how to celebrate Jesus' birth.

During this week, look over your goals of last year and begin to think on what you wish to accomplish in the coming year. Remember always our love and help. Understand that Father God is very aware of you and is loving you even more than we do.

The Brotherhood

PART 3

1990
Your God-Mind Connection

19

Communing with God

Learn to Visualize
(Brotherhood, January 6, 1990)

THIS IS THE ENDING DECADE of this century. It is also the decade of completions. Understand that as this century ends, a new one begins, and each beginning is a time of expectations, of hope. This is the decade when each of you will perfect your listening skills.

The next century will be lived from the mind. Much of the new technology will have to do with the mind. Your scientists and educated will learn to use the great powers of the mind. This is why we urge you to get a jump on this process by practicing it now. These great mental powers can be used now, but it takes practice. How do you practice or develop these? They are a natural development of meditation. As you progress in learning to meditate, you will find yourself becoming more and more psychic. This is the best way to perfect these powers.

Now understand that these potentials are in everyone. Everyone can develop them through meditation, but meditation should not be used for this purpose. **Here is the "catch": use meditation to commune with God-Mind only. As you develop the ability to commune with God-Mind, your mental and psychic powers will be increased.** They will evolve naturally.

Since your aim is to develop mentally and spiritually, we urge you to learn to visualize. Understand that each of you can become proficient in the use of this mental power. **What you can visualize and believe to be true will BECOME TRUE IN YOUR EXPERIENCE.** We ask that you begin to use visualizations that we will place in your mind. Here are some simple rules to follow:

1. Always start your visualization with "the problem." That is, begin with what is bothering you. If it is physical, like an earache, you will enter your body (mentally) through the ear, and begin to clean it out and use healing agents. If your problem is finances, then you will enter your checkbook and ask what it is you need to "see." If you do not have a checkbook, then take your pay, as money, and build a house in your mind with the money. Enter the money and ask it to reveal what you need to know. Then sit inside the mental house or checkbook and become quiet. Whatever you see, feel or hear will reveal the problem to you. Arise, find a bucket filled with money in the corner of a room. Begin to take money and use it to add on to your house. As money is pulled from the bucket, more springs from the center of the bucket. Fill your rooms with this money, then sit down and sense the feeling of satisfaction. Then open your eyes.

2. Everything is possible in visualization. You will always find a way out, an aid or convenience. If you find yourself in a well, there will be a ladder for you to use to climb out of the well. If you are in a dark place, light will come from the tips of your fingers. Do not analyze this process.

Simply use whatever means are available to you through your visualizations.

3. If at first you think you are unable to visualize, then simply tell yourself this is happening in your mind. Remember, your mind will speak to you through every sense available. It will speak through your feelings, hearing, taste, sight, smell or voice. As with all new lessons, it takes practice.

4. Use visualizations to see the completion of your goals. Simply see and sense how you will look, feel, smell or be when this goal is completed.

5. Always sit in an upright position with feet comfortably on the floor. Take three or four normal breaths through your nose, and let them out through your mouth slowly. Then state your intention for the visualization or meditation. Say to yourself, "My intention is to see my completed goals." Or, "I intend to learn from this earache, or this heartache, or this lack of money." Whatever your intention is, claim it in your mind.

This process will help to improve your meditations. **Begin each meditation with your intention.** If your intention is to commune with God-Mind, then say it to yourself. If you have a need or a problem on which you wish to meditate, then state this intention.

Now comes HOPE. Hope, as we define it, is the expectancy of a positive answer. This is part of your visualization. Expect to find the right answer or to have the problem dissolved.

We would like for you to look at your last year's goals. Note which goals have been reached. Congratulate yourself and see the things you have accomplished. Add what you have accomplished that isn't on your list. Then review the list. Do these goals still interest you? Do you think they are important to you? Do you still wish to have these goals on your list? Revise them as you desire, or eliminate them completely. This list of goals is your guide to how you are doing. It is a way to measure your accomplishments and to give yourself credit. We rejoice with you over your accomplishments.

Now we are increasing our communication with you through your mind; if you hear us speaking, please acknowledge. It is our way of helping you to increase your mental powers. Use these exercises daily or, at the very least, every two days. You will see many benefits in the coming months.

The Brotherhood

Define and Develop Your Goals
(Brotherhood, January 20, 1990)

Remember to work on your goals, as time is passing. These goals are the target you are aiming at this year. Remember to include goals in all areas of your life: spiritual, emotional, mental, physical and others such as in your marriage, career, school or in recreation and hobbies. Begin looking into hobbies that will teach you some new ways of coping with your environment, such as hiking, camping or perhaps swimming. This way you learn and have fun at the same time. Pay attention to all areas of your life. Life becomes boring when you fail to live it fully, or if you concentrate on a few areas of your life and neglect others. It is important to your health to pay attention to all areas of your life.

Visualization is handy in getting you into the right mindset for your life. It will help you see results or solutions. This way you will be exercising your mind and spirit. Allow your mind to dominate your life, because it does anyway. You live from a mental standpoint and not from a physical standpoint. Yes, you must take care of the physical body, but this can be fun, if you allow it to be. Make games of caring for your body. Have fun living life. It not only is a school, but a pleasure too. Understand that visualization is a tool to make your life easier. It will help to focus your mind on the end results and not on problems. Remember, whatever your subconscious receives as your desire, that is what it will work towards. This is the danger in worry, because you give your subconscious the wrong idea of your desires. Through creating specific images, it gives your mind clear pictures and direction of what you desire. Leave the end result and the unfolding plan to God-Mind. Allow Him to give you this or something better. Allow God to make the last decision as to what is best for you. This way you are able to release the solution to God-Mind. As you release and give it to God, He will be free to give back to you what is best.

Become still in the closet of your mind. **It is now time for you to use this stillness to communicate with God-Mind and to strengthen your ability to communicate.** It is imperative that you learn to use your mind to get information and guidance. And in order to do this, you must strengthen the mind by using it. This is why we continually give you mental exercises to do. From time to time it may be necessary for you to go off into a quiet place to commune with God, but for now this is your lesson. The lesson is to set up a good line of communication with God-Mind. We urge you to follow Jesus' lead and example of going within to commune with God. You may want to go to a solitary place to pray. Read in the Bible and find all the passages that tell of how Jesus went alone to pray, as in Mark 1:35. Even Jesus, who had the greatest connection to God-Mind, needed this quiet prayer time. You do too. Jesus was in constant, direct communication with God; at times even he found it necessary to go alone and pray. Notice the time of day when Jesus went alone to pray. Most always it was during the night, early in the morning or late at night. There is a reason for going alone in the night. During the day there is much activity in the world and this emits vibrations. Your very body is activated by the vibrations of all this activity. Most animals are day animals for this reason. Each person has a magnetic field, and this acts like a magnet and is quickened by the activity of life. It causes your heart to beat a little faster, your breathing is a little quicker; all your reactions are hastened. During the night, on the other hand, the pace is slowed down. The animals sense this and they become drowsy and will sleep. (Of course we are aware of the animals who have a reverse time clock and hunt at night.) But notice the level of activity at night and how very quiet the world becomes. It is during this time that your magnetic field, reactions, even the autonomic part of your brain is turned down. It is much easier and more effective to communicate with Spirit. Once in a while, try getting up during the night to pray and visualize. The results will be amazing. **This is your task for the coming year: to strengthen your ability to communicate with Spirit.**

In the last few days Annie has been hearing (in her mind) the words, ". . . and ye shall have dominion over them." We will use these words to give a good lesson. It is one that is true and well timed. What you have dominion over are your thoughts, words, actions, attitudes, all issues of your life. In the story of creation, it says, ". . . and they shall have dominion over the birds in the air and over the fishes in the ocean, over every living thing man will have dominion." (Gn 1:28) Now use your inner self and decipher these words. The birds of the air are your thoughts. The fishes of the sea are your attitudes, urges, perhaps even your addictions, those things you wish to or already keep secret or under cover. The animals who roam the earth are your wandering thoughts, your wandering eye, or that which is within you that leads you astray.

Now this verse of the Bible simply says you will have dominion over every area of your life. So visualize all the good that you desire in your life, and begin with your spiritual life. Give it the importance it deserves. In visualizing the increase of your spiritual life, use something like this: allow the bright sun to represent God-Mind, and see yourself sitting in a meadow or by the sea. Next see the sunrays coming toward you. The sunrays will become an elevator and take you to the sun, which has represented God-Mind for ages. In the beginning of this visualization, give yourself **the intention of becoming one with God-Mind and all that God is.**

Do you have some area of your life that troubles you? Bring this area to the temple in your mind and pray about it. Is there some person who troubles you? Do the same. Is there something you have need of? Visualize the results you desire, but first take it into your temple and pray. **Prayer is your ability to communicate and speak to Father-God.** Visualization is an exercise for your mind and heart to agree on the results you desire.

A good way to begin each day is with gratitude. What you are grateful for, increases in your life. So be diligent in giving praise (gratitude) to God-the-Father. For every small thing be grateful. This is a good way to communicate with God-Mind. **Begin each day with, "Thank you, Father God, for this day and for my life on earth."** As you dress, be grateful for the clothes you wear, the home you live in. Many people forget that **"all good things come from the Father."** (These " " denote words of Jesus.) (See Mt 7:11, Lk 12:32) And give thanks for the smallest blessing. This is a habit to promote in your life on earth. It is an easy way to increase your communications with Father God. It also has the ability to change your attitude. **Man cannot be sad when he is aware of all the "Good" in his life.**

See, little children, prayer is more than simply requesting. Tell God-the-Father what concerns you about your loved ones. Is it that they are unhappy or ill in spirit? Tell God-the-Father all that is concerning you. Use both kinds of prayers, the formal, such as The Lord's Prayer, and simply speaking to Him as a father. What concerns you about world affairs? Pray for this too. What concerns you socially? Pray for this also.

Remember, you have dominion over your world, and this planet is your world. Take command of your ability to pray and the effects that you can have upon the planet through prayer. Take command over your inner life and effect changes through prayer. Your dominion, abilities, effect on your world, are more than you had envisioned.

There is power in you, placed there by the Creator. Use it for good, because you will not want to use it for bad. There is a

Powerhouse of Good that you plug into. Through prayer, meditation and visualizations you are able to use this power. **The power is God-Power.** It is the Creative Energy, which is God. The ability to use this power is how you are like God. This is what He was speaking of when he said, "I will make man in my image and likeness." (Gn 1:26) It is in your ability to create in your dominion. It is your ability to use this Creative Energy to heal, bless, enjoy and have dominion over.

Take this lesson, which is an important lesson, and *reread it daily for seven days.* Allow the time necessary for the words to seed your mind and heart. Think on these words and concepts. Ask Father God to give you any explanation you need, then become quiet and listen. When you least expect it, the answer will come. We are already speaking to your minds—have you heard us? It will be through your mind that you will receive direction. Begin to practice by asking us questions and listening for our answer, which will come through your mind. Put away fear by praying constantly.

The Brotherhood

Strengthen Your Powers
(Brotherhood, February 3, 1990)

The wave of pure energy is now visible to your world. It is apparent to the scientists and learned ones that there is something huge happening in the universe and that this will affect your world. It is bigger than anything anyone could ever imagine. They are in dispute as to what is happening and how it will affect your world. The agreement is that it will eventually affect this planet and this galaxy. It is wonderful; it will be a new and glorious world after the wave of energy has passed. This is how we want you to look at the coming earth changes— as a new and wonderful event. There is growth and expansion of the universe, and you will witness it. Do not allow any fear to enter into your thoughts because you know what will happen and how it will affect the world.

Your attitude and outlook is to be one of hope and anticipation. It is similar to giving birth: it is a blessing. **This is why you have chosen to be on earth at this particular time in history.** Understand that you have very little time to work out the problems of your life and prepare for the coming events. So do not waste any time from now on. Here is how to prepare. This is truth and not platitudes.

Only those who are prepared will survive. It will be the ones who have fashioned out of themselves a quiet place within to hear all instructions, who will survive. This is why it is imperative that you become quiet and meditative. The preparation is to make your very own God-Mind connection. Prepare a quiet place to commune with God the Father within your mind and heart. It is through repetition that you learn, and this is why we repeat and repeat. It is so important that God is now using every available instrument and means to give this same message to all people. **It will be through prayer, meditation and quietness that each person will receive their own instructions.**

Use this method of meditation—visualization. It is a method to allow you to use your mind and heart in unison. By visualizing, you are strengthening your connection and ability to become quiet. It is simply a tool to use, to make your work easier. It is much like an exercise to flex your mental muscles. Yes, there will be a need for you to be strong, both in body and in mind.

We have for the past year or two been concentrating on strengthening your mental and emotional powers. Each person must rid themselves of many false beliefs. These beliefs are concerning yourself. **Believe yourself to be strong, powerful, energetic and, more important, a survivor.** Do not hold on to fear, anger, resentment, jealousy or grief of any kind. These depleting emotions take up space within your heart and expend energy. These emotions use so much energy that is need-less. When you think only of what you wear, eat, drink or drive, you are wasting much energy. **It is imperative for each person to stop all self-abuse.**

Each person is training for a *great meet*. It is real and will take much fortitude. This great challenge will take all you have to survive. It will require you to be in superb condition. We are not speaking simply of looks, but of physical, emotional, mental and spiritual condition. All aspects of the whole being must be in good shape and condition. Prepare mentally and emotionally; this is what you must do. If you harbor any resentments to any man (this of course includes women and children), you must reconcile and forgive. It is better to forgive than to be weighed down with these emotions. We will ask that if this is true of you, write out all the unpleasantness, all the anger or feelings that caused you to be angry or in fear. Continue to write about these emotions until you have arrived at a place of forgiveness. Understand that forgiveness is not just words but emotion, that when you forgive you release from within any ties to this person. If the person is aware of the disagreement, then write to him or her and simply say, "I forgive you." This is a good way to prepare emotionally. If the person is unaware of the hurt or anger, then use your mind to see yourself speaking to the individual, saying to him or her all the words you have written down. Visualize how you will look as you forgive. See yourself even wearing a halo, to give yourself a good feeling.

Now we speak to those of you who are not taking care of the physical body. It is just as imperative to be in good physical condition as it is to be in good spiritual condition. This is a great event and will require everyone to be in top shape. If you do not like to exercise, use your visualizations to see yourself enjoying exercise. If you need to lose weight, use visualization to assist your diet. No matter what shape you are in, you need to condition your bodies. Give the physical body good foods, foods that build tissue and not simply restrict your calories. Calories are not as important as people on earth think. **It is the**

choice of foods that is important. Do you eat the kind of food substance that gives nutrients and vitamins, or is the food you eat empty of nutrients? Simply to take in sugar is not good; to overindulge in fats alone is not good. You must study and see which foods are good for the body. Think of yourself as separate from your body. Look at this body as it is in reality, a vehicle and not the real you.

In the aftertime,[1] there will not be the modes of transportation you have now, nor the conveniences, nor the ability to have someone else do your work for you. It will be up to each person to pull their own weight. There will be no freebies. All people will earn their living. We urge you to enjoy what you have now and do not think of the parting in sadness, but think of the joy of new times. This is why it is important for each person to have a body that is in good physical condition. It will be better in the aftertime, and it will be different. For a short period of time there will be confusion, because people have come to rely on others to provide for them. People are used to going to a store or restaurant to get food. In the immediate aftertime, this will not be so. There will be much confusion. So now is the time to prepare, by studying and spending time in the wilderness. Study plants and see what can be eaten and what cannot. Find the raw materials that you will need. Use this as a game or as practice. Understand that you will receive all instructions at the appropriate time. In the aftertime, each one will find ingenuity coming from within.

But for now, we urge you to begin to prepare for the coming events with determination and the proper mindset. It will happen as foretold; it is happening now. There are three areas of concern which need your attention now. **You are to prepare mentally, emotionally and physically.** Do not leave off one to concentrate on the other, because all three are important. It is once again a trinity; one is just as important as the

---

[1] The Aftertime is also known as the Thousand Years of Peace. It is described in detail in Chapter 9 of *Mary's Message to the World*.

others. **Be in the best condition possible; use all the informa-tion available now to help you.** This is the age of information, and it is imperative that you take advantage of this age.

The Brotherhood

Expansion, Increase and Renewal (Spring Review)
(Brotherhood, March 4, 1990)

Once again it is the Lenten season on earth. In spirit, of course, we do not have these seasons. This is a time to contem-plate the purpose of Jesus' journey through life on earth. We will simply review today and allow your mind to open to an expansion of ideas. Many times in reviewing you become aware of questions, doubts, or of misconceptions.

Also you find that with the season changing to Spring and the plants and trees coming into bloom, your whole attitude will change for the better. It is again proof of the renewal of life. It is the season of hope, but remember that your hope is in Christ Jesus and in our Heavenly Father who loves us.

As you go through this season of blossoming and budding trees, recall that you too live with the same life energy that brings these seemingly dead trees to life, that you and nature are one in God. Recall that all the issues of life are simple. It is man who makes them complicated. Religion has made all kinds of ritual and all manner of sacrifice necessary. This is man's way and not God's. If you like or feel better practicing these rituals or sacrifices—do so. You will not be punished with hell and damnation if you do or do not. **Keep all rituals of your religion if this enhances your worship of God the Father.** There is no harm: the benefit comes from the concentration on God and not the practice of earthly rituals. We understand that some religions have their members refrain from items of plea-sure. Each is allowed to give up what they wish for this Lenten season. Instead we urge you to give up angers, envies or jealousies, which keep you from true communication with God the Father.

This is how to perform this: when you become angry with another or yourself, simply pray in your own words, "Father God, I wish to be changed, to be cleansed of these angry feelings. Help me to forgive myself and the other person, and to put this issue in the past and leave it there."

Recall that the Father is Goodness without equal, Love without limit and Pure Energy. All that you deposit in the care of God will be changed to Pure Energy, Divine Love and complete Goodness. The only way to feel good is to give your feelings over to God. The only way to have true energy is to bring your whole self and deposit all that you are in God, knowing and understanding that all you are is made whole in God. Wholeness and Holiness mean the same. We say wholeness when it pertains to people or beings and Holiness when it is God.

Keep all your communications with God simple. It is as simple as speaking to yourself, for God the Father is within you, as is His Kingdom. Do you understand that Jesus, while on earth, did not wish to scare people or cause them anguish over his words, so he said, "The kingdom of heaven is within you." (Lk 17:21) Now if the kingdom of heaven is within you, God is in His Kingdom, which is within you, and so God is within you. He hears your every thought, your every nuance, and knows all your inner questioning. God knows you better than you know yourself. God is aware of all your motives and your whole life, which includes your past lives.

See how useless it is not to pray about all things and not to include God in your entire life? He is already aware of you as you truly are and not as you present yourself to the world. He loves you and He cares for you. In His total Goodness, His only desire is to help. You are in complete control; He must await your request for His help. All you need do is simply say, **"God, help,"** and it is done.

We urge you to bring all the trash that inhibits you from seeking God the Father with all your mind, all your soul and all your might. Bring the issues that are inhibiting you, controlling you or which you have given a portion of yourself to. It does not matter what you think of them; they will change, and you will change when you allow God the Father and Christ Jesus to enter into your daily life. During this Lenten season, bring your entire self and allow God to cleanse for all time any lingering hard emotions, bad habits, addictions, compulsions, obsessions or anything you are ashamed of, because what shames you is keeping you from being completely open to all God has prepared for you.

If there is something about your personality you don't like, bring this to God or to Christ Jesus. Some of you have the habit of not being completely honest with others, and we say this is a bad habit, because it allows you to hide things, issues and habits from yourself. You who are aware can no longer use the excuse of being human and being in a human condition. Bring everything to God the Father. If you are not aware of anything that inhibits or prevents your complete openness with God, then pray by saying something like this: **"God, I am not aware of anything that is causing me to hide from You or myself. Father God, I allow you to cleanse, to change all areas of my entire life. I am certain that all changes will be for the better."**

This is how to prepare for direct communication with God, a communication that is so clear and open, you will have the assurance of only Good in your life. You will view all events of your life with hope, all people in your life with love and all circumstances of your life as Divine. This does not mean you will not have problems. It means you will know where to go for help. You will be able to understand and hear the words of God as He speaks to you through your mind. He will speak with ideas or a change in circumstances; you will have the assurance it is all working together for good. The feeling of assurance and certainty is your increased faith.

This is how to prepare not only for Christ's resurrection, but for your resurrection in spirit. **Pray by opening up your mind to the inflow of God as Energy, Love and Wholeness.**

The Brotherhood

On-Going Communication with God
(Brotherhood, March 17, 1990)

Communication with the Father is an ongoing process. It is like living life. To live life, you do not do it one day only and then put life on automatic pilot. You live daily in life, doing, thinking and performing. This is true of your communication with the Father. There is no plan of salvation that would allow you to perform certain steps and then be saved for all time. **To be in true and open communication with your Creator is a moment-by-moment process.** It requires you to question and seek to be near Him.

Many people take it upon themselves to live life without the Father. Bring God into every part of your life and allow His Divine Will to be done. Give Him your problems, but give them up completely. Give them to God the Father with the thought that you are happy and content with His Will. **Understand that God's Will is always Good. God cannot give anything but Good.**

Some people look at the world and all its problems and say, "Where is God?" Others view life as a onetime event and neglect to see the wholeness of life and its many lifetimes on earth. Many people do not believe there is eternal life for all. God will not leave anyone out of His Eternalness and Bliss. Precious metals and gems are made only from great heat and pressure. This is also true of you. Only the person who is compliant and willing to learn all lessons and give himself to the will of God will not suffer the great heat and pressure of an earthly life.

The compassion in your hearts is good, but look at the workings of God. All events in a lifetime are for the refining and fine tuning of the soul. The violence that is seen in today's society is the violence that is in the race consciousness, the centuries of hate, anger, resentments and envy. It will take a new race consciousness to eliminate the violence of this world. How do you help? It takes each of you praying to eliminate the anger, hatred, envy, jealousy, resentments and even the snide remarks from within you. As one changes, there is a small change in the race consciousness. As one prays for himself and for his world, it is done for all people. Still you do not understand how this process works. **Everyone and everything is interconnected.** Every thought is taken in by the earth-mind consciousness. Every action is retained by this consciousness. As in the theory of relativity, every act and every thought begets a like thought and act. This is true of prayer and of good thoughts.

When you begin to think kindly of others, it too enters the earth-mind consciousness. When you begin to love yourself, you can love others. When you are honest with yourself, you are honest with others. Likewise, as you change all these depleting emotions, thoughts and deeds, so likewise the earth-mind consciousness changes. This is how to help. It is not a simple act or thought. **It takes concentration and determination.** Because of the overwhelming amount of violence in the earth-mind consciousness, it is constantly pulling towards complacency, disinterest and neglect of thought. This kind of life is not as easy as you thought. You cannot pray once and be done with it, for that one prayer has entered an abyss of hard emotions and deeds. One lonely thought becomes lost and overtaken by the violence in the earth-mind consciousness.

When you read or hear of a murder, do not regale against the murderer. Don't think and feel hard emotions towards them; instead, pray for the murderers as well as the victim. One prayer for one murderer will not take care of the core problem, which is the earth-mind consciousness. Many prayers prayed

for the violence in the world could take care of the core problem. Do you want to put only a band-aid on a fatal wound? Or
would you like to stop the bleeding and take positive steps to
save the wounded? What you have in the earth-mind consciousness is centuries of small family feuds, small tribal wars
and the very large world wars. These are the cause of the
violence and the abandonment of self in drugs and addictions.
Pray for the instigator and the victim, because everyone is a
victim of the violence in the race consciousness.

Now, in order to help, cleanse your mind of all violence
and all addictions, no matter how small. We say anything that
keeps you from God is detrimental to your well-being. **Pray for
yourselves, but also pray for God's Good will to be done on
earth, just as it is in heaven.** Think awhile on this statement.
You repeat it in The Lord's Prayer, but you do not understand
it. What is your idea of heaven? Understand, in reality it is
much more than you can envision. What conditions do you
expect to live in, in heaven? They will be better. Read how John
saw it in the last book of the Bible. He described heaven as
having streets paved in gold. (Rv 21:21) John could not find the
words to describe the beauty and grandeur. Not only the outer
beauty is to be considered; also consider the inner peace and
great love. This inner peace and love is yours now, but it will
not come easy, nor will it stay with you without some effort on
your part. The ease of heaven is available now, if you will think
seriously about the words you say in prayer and mean them.
Prayers said in rote mean nothing. It is the connection of mind
and heart that makes a prayer.

Allow God to perform in your lives. Pray for the murderer
with love and for the victim with compassion. See the good in
all people. If you cannot see good in a person, then know it is
buried deep inside. Pray always for God's Will and not for
man's will. Man can kill to avenge a killing and double the
consequences. God forgives and eliminates the whole act.

Pray to increase love of yourself and your fellowman.
Pray to rid yourself of all hard emotions, and then watch how

you will change. When something goes wrong in your life, you will no longer regale and complain about the deed. You will not tell anyone about the wrong in your life or dramatize it. Instead you will release it through Divine Love and prayer. **What you send out returns to you.** If you are angered by others, and hard emotions are released into the race consciousness, then you have tuned in to race consciousness and it will be from this point that the events in your life will come. **When you tune in to God the Creator through prayer, the events in your life come from God-Mind, and all will be good.**

Allow us to give an analogy. You could say that the different consciousnesses are like the different frequencies on a radio. The dialer is your thought. The fine tuning is your emotions. Now do you see how you bring into life what you are thinking and feeling? With the thought of vengeance and the feeling of anger, you instantly tune in to the earth-mind consciousness and bring into your life all the violence that is there. But through prayer, you once again set your dial into God-Mind and bring into your life stability, peace, love and contentment. When you pray for God's Will to be done in you and your life, you are fine-tuning to God-Mind.

Through daily prayer, you release more love into the race consciousness. Then you will see a true decrease in crime and addictions. **The more you tune in to God-Mind, the more Divine Love is released into this world.** God works in this world only through individuals. It was His promise to mankind at the beginning of time. **He will only do for you what He can do through you. As more and more people are tuned in to God-Mind, then more and more peace, love and compassion are released.** You are already beginning to see the effects of prayer in the tumbling of controlling governments. The people of these individual nations have been praying for many years, and now it is happening as quick as a wink. So do not think we are simply giving you the same old message. This is an important message and one that is needed today in this world.

Remember always that we love you, and our sole purpose is to help you connect to God-Mind. The Father waits for your call daily. **What happened yesterday is gone; it is what is happening now that is important.** The prayer of today is the one to say, the prayer of yesterday is in the race consciousness already. **God loves you more than you can know, and His Good is more than you can envision.** Remember, this is not good as the world gives but Good as God gives.

The Brotherhood

Find Answers Through Your Seeking (Easter)
(*Brotherhood, April 7, 1990*)

Welcome to the most important thing in your life—the learning of Spirituality. This is a time of new beginnings. It is time to celebrate the resurrection of Jesus. We have taught that Jesus' mission on earth was to eliminate the futile fear of God, death, each other, church authorities, governmental authorities and any other element that causes fear. His whole life on earth was a demonstration of Divine Love, Justice and Life.

Jesus, as the way-shower, is always available to any who seek him. He is and can be a guide to the spiritual development of every individual, or he can simply be your elder and loving brother. It is all a matter of individual choice. As you prepare to celebrate the resurrection, remember that it was not a supernatural event, but a natural one. It is for all people, and even if you do not believe, you continue to live. Since you are alive on earth in this time period, it behooves you to learn as much as you can. There is a reason for so much interest in the supernatural. People are looking for answers; they are ready for answers. **Each person will find their answer through their own seeking.** It comes through every mind and heart. It will not be in cards or books, although those things will be used to interest people. **Answers come in the form of thoughts and** feelings and are personally geared to the circumstance of one's life.

It is time for everyone to connect to their own version of God. Each individual will have their own concept of God, heaven and life. **The beauty of God is in the individuality of each person. The Love is in His ability to use who you are and what you have to teach.** Every person will be led on their own path. Everyone will have their own work with and for God the Father.

Pray for knowledge of your life work and of issues that need to be resolved. Seek to help through prayer, because this is the best way. God speaks through you to each person in your life. Do not preach, but be open to say the words to each individual that come to you. Do not censor your words, because your words may be the turning point in someone's life. **Meditate daily to open your mind to the inflow of God-Energy and Divine Love. Spread this love to all people without exception.** See similarities and not differences, see love and not contention.

Love and renewal give energy and hope. List all the ways God loves you and this world. God gives the sun to warm, rain to water, clouds which shade, flowers for beauty. This is all simplistic, but this is how to begin to appreciate your world.

List Divine Love in your life—a home to shelter you, a car to make your coming and going easier, food for nourishment, loved ones to share with and teachers to give knowledge. There is more to list. Daily give account of the Love that is manifesting in your life.

You could verbally list your good—a new day to live, prayers to pray and time for meditations. There are temples to build in your mind and words of comfort to give to others. Through growth there is always hope and energy.

The Brotherhood

20

Using Affirmations

Affirmations and Acceptance
(Jesus, April 21, 1990)

HELLO, DEAR ONES, it is Jesus of Nazareth. I bring a lesson in affirmations and acceptance. The Father, who is the Greatest Creative Power, is ever ready to give what you need in order to live life successfully. Now understand that success is defined in spiritual terms first, then in earthly terms. Here is what you already know about life. Life is eternal, and you live after a physical death. In the state after death, you keep all you have in your mind and heart. The feelings you hold in your heart go with you. Thoughts, attitudes and beliefs are with you in the eternalness of life. Internalize the truths you are learning, in order to be fruitful in demonstrating your good. **Internalize simply means you must use what you learn daily, just like you use your instincts.** I will teach you how to forgive and release all manner of issues or all kinds of obstacles.

God is both Principle and Personal. He relates to you in a personal manner by loving you, just as you are now and as you will be. You are given freedom of choice and, in order to retain your freedom, God relates to you as Principle. That means He set up the Universal laws to work whether you believe in them or not. These laws are automatically set into action with a thought or act. Before you entered into this life you committed to lifetime goals. You also made a "wish list" of all the things you would like to accomplish. You chose circumstances, places, culture, and named some vocational desires and educational desires. Now, the educational desires were of life issues and not schooling. God the Father, as Principle, answers your prayers in life. What you concentrate on is what you receive. He is impersonal and unemotional about this, as principle. This way all people are given the desires of their hearts. This requires you to concentrate on what you want and to make a decision. The decision is one that is made with your mind, heart and soul.

Concentration, then, is the key to opening up to what you desire. It must be a *firm commitment* to what you desire, and it must not be harmful to anyone else in order for the good to come from God. Do you realize that when you worry, you are concentrating? And, when you become depressed, seeing only the negative, this is concentration? I will teach you how to change your inner mind to what you desire for your future.

All the Good you desire is already prepared for you by the Father. His energy and creativity are constant and never ending. **There is no limit to God or to His Supply.** When you receive from the Father, you are not in any way depleting His storehouse of good, nor will you be taking away someone's success, money or health. There is plenty for every person who has ever lived and who will ever live. Put out of your mind the thought that there is a limit to God or to His Good.

The ones to convince are yourself and the inner workings of your mind and heart. **These affirmations are not for God's**

benefit, but for yours. God knows His potential. It is mankind who is ignorant of his potential. Therefore, it is your mistakes in reasoning that inhibit you. I will show you how to release all old negative ways of looking at your life. **Your job is to convince your mind and heart that God is wanting to give and is willing to supply you with all kinds of Good.** You can have what you desire, as long as this desire is in keeping with your own lifetime goals, and what you ask for will not interfere with your goals in this life, nor will it cause harm to you or anyone else. So, the following affirmations are for you. Use them to agree in your mind, heart and soul with what you desire. Always end each prayer time of affirmation with the statement of allowing God's Will to be done unto you. **When you can allow God the Father to perform His perfect Will in your life, all circumstances and all people will be put in your path without any worry or concern on your part.** It will just simply happen before you know it. First, I will list the areas of life that we will address. You will be solving old problems and bringing into your life health, wealth and happiness. You can bring into your life success, creativity, money, honor and release from anything that would deter your growth.

Begin with statements of Truth about God the Father and you, such as:

- I believe in God, Creator of the Universe. I believe in Jesus, His son, and I believe that through the power of the Holy Ghost I communicate with the Father. I believe in Eternal Life, forgiveness of sins and communion with all worlds.
- I release all fear, envy, resentment and negativity from my mind, heart and soul. I seek only Divine Love.
- My heart and mind are in agreement with God's perfect Will in my life.
- I request the Angel of Divine Love to enter my heart and heal me of all that deters my success in this life and my spiritual growth.
- Divine Love heals my body, mind and heart. I go in peace, knowing that all is well.

- Divine Love protects me in all circumstances of life. I am Divinely Protected, Divinely Guided and Divinely Healed.
- Through the Power of God the Father, I am capable of success in life by my definition.
- My Heavenly Father is supplying me with all the money I need to meet all obligations, the money to shelter, dress and feed my family. I no longer fear receiving bills or fear any need for clothing or food.
- I am Divinely Guided into situations that will enrich my life with money, love and peace.
- I stand in a circle of Divine Light to be healed of all ailments now.
- God is working His perfect Will in my life. I am at peace.
- God's Will is only Good, so I call on God's Will to be my will.
- I call on God the Father to place me in the right place at the right time, in order to be financially successful. God wants me to be a success by my definition. I release anything that hampers me from obtaining this success.
- I allow God's Will to spur me into action. I have all I need within me, to be all I want to be. I am grateful.
- Through the Power of God, I can be healed. It is God's desire that I live this life in perfect health. Therefore, I release all fear concerning my body, mind or feelings.
- The Truth of God is opening my mind to all possibilities. I am healed in mind, body and soul. I do not need to do anything in order to deserve this health; it is mine by the Grace of God.
- I can be loving, kind and warm because I am filled to overflowing with God's Love. I am patient, kind, friendly, concerned with my world and myself. I will be kind, loving and concerned with others, as is the Father.
- I seek to be in close communion with God in order to be all I want to be.
- I am always in God's Love, but I do not always know this. I will tell myself I am always in God's Love.

- I give the problems of this day to God to adjust and bring into order.
- I release all concerns to the Power of God, to set in Divine order. I walk this day in God's Light and am always in perfect tune with Him.
- I am a radiating center of God's Love, mighty to receive my good and share my good with others.
- All the good I desire is wanting to be in my life. I release anything that detains my receiving this good. I accept my good, and I ask that others realize that their good is waiting for them to claim it.
- I go forth this day in peace, love and happiness. I am happy with my life, home and family. All differences are ironed out in the Name and through the Power of God.
- This is the day the Lord has made. I will honor this day with a cheerful attitude, a happy heart and a grateful mind.
- I am truly thankful for my life, work and health. God adjusts every situation in my life with His love.
- There are angels who watch over my coming and going. I am always in the company of God's Angels. They are with me to help instantly with any need.
- I love the Lord my God with all my heart, all my mind and with all my soul and strength, and I love my neighbor as myself.
- I send the Angel of the Lord before me to prepare my way. Every person I meet today is my friend. All my daily transactions are conducted in peace, and I am Divinely protected.
- I call upon the Angel of Love to heal this situation. My home, loved ones and my life are healed now.

Dear children, **these are examples of affirmations that will change your life.** They will change your life because they will change your inner thinking. It is you who is in charge of your life. If you have something you fear to face, ask your own Angel to go before you and pave the way, make the road smooth and bring peace into your life. When you are in the throngs of fear, call out to the Angel of Divine Love to come to your aid. This will happen instantly. When you are in pain, call upon your Angel to bring your thinking into Divine Order.

Now if you have a problem with another person, you may write to the other person's guardian Angel and ask for help to heal the situation. If you are concerned with another, ask for Divine Love, or the Angel of Love, to open that person up to a healing. If the concern is negativity in thinking or negative beliefs, ask for the highest Angel of the individual to bring into full inner view the errors which concern you. This is the best way to help another.

All these affirmations can be used for others simply by replacing the "I" with a "You are." This is the way to affirm for others healing, love, peace, wealth, health and happiness.

Today, take these affirmations and your individual prayer list. Before beginning, make adjustments in the prayer list by adding names, and beside the name add one word to indicate what you are praying for, such as "Annie—health" or "Byron—protection in travel." Begin by declaring for yourself and then declare for those people on your list. Do this every day and see results.

Practice this method of changing your mind and heart. Understand that what you are doing is adjusting your thoughts to agree with the Truth of God. When you can agree in mind, heart and soul on anything, then it will happen in your life quickly.

Jesus of Nazareth

Watch Your Thoughts, Feelings and Words
(*Brotherhood, May 26, 1990*)

Today we speak on Freedom of Choice and the Power it contains. This way of life is to be lived daily and not just on weekends or special occasions. **The daily practice of turning to**

God the Father within is what is needed in order to come into your full potential. This is the potential of all men.

Freedom of choice is yours continually. You are constantly making choices on how you feel, what you think, what your beliefs are and how your day is going. Understand that small insignificant remarks bring results as well as thoughtful remarks. The inner self is always listening and gives what you want without asking directions or explanations. When you arise in the morning and declare, "I do not feel good," then you will most likely not feel good that day. If you think, "I do not feel good," it is your choice. How to avoid this is to say, truthfully, "I do not feel good now, but the Father within gives me the strength and healing I need to live this day in health." This is how to use affirmations to program your inner mind to what you desire. There is a residual effect in thoughts, feelings and words. This means the beliefs, words, thoughts and feelings of the past do not magically disappear when you change your mind. There is a residue of attitudes and beliefs left from old words and thoughts. They have a place in your mind and heart and will not easily give up that place. Words, thoughts and feeling are things, just as your clothes, cars and homes are.

How to eliminate the residue of old beliefs from your mind and heart is to USE different words, thoughts and feelings to change your mind. Watch your thoughts, feelings and words. This is what Jesus meant with the parable of the virgins left to tend the lamps. You can read this in the Bible. (Mt 25)

As you have read, the ten virgins were given a chore to do. They were to watch for the bridegroom and be ready for him with their lamps. Five were lazy and did not prepare properly. Then at the last minute they wanted the other five, who had prepared, to help them. But the wise virgins said no, go and seek your own oil.

The virgins represent the thoughts of the future, the feelings, beliefs and attitudes of the future, those that will come into your mind and heart tomorrow, and all the rest of the tomorrows of this life. They are what you will decide to do with your freedom of choice. The five lazy virgins are unguarded thoughts. **The word is WATCH!** This is the word today. WATCH! **Watch what you are thinking, feeling and saying to yourself and to others.** Do you tell yourself the truth of your full potential, or do you see the illusion you are living today? Are you watching, in the sense of monitoring your thoughts, beliefs, attitudes and words? Are you watching what you say about yourself and others? Are you critical? Do you respect yourself and others? Do you affirm daily your uniqueness, your allegiance to God the Father? Do you tell yourself TRUTHS?

The oil which the virgins used to light their lamps were their words. **Use your thoughts and words to guide your feelings into right action.** They will set you in alignment with all you can be. Use your words daily by affirming and denying. That is, rebuke or deny the fear, anger, hostility and aloneness that you feel. Say, **"I deny, rebuke the fear that is lingering in my heart and mind. I ask my Heavenly Father to replace this emotion with His Love."** See, this is how to use affirmations to replace old beliefs and attitudes. In time, as you daily watch your thoughts and words, and change them through affirmations, these old fears and angers will be replaced. As we have said, thoughts, beliefs and feeling are things that take up space, just as your home, car and body. So to have room for your new thoughts you must rebuke or erase the old ones.

The bridegroom is representative of the new life you will have when truth is wholly in you—the new life free of old fears, angers and resentments. When this time comes, you will not let down your guard on these inner thoughts and words; you will continue to WATCH! But the door will be closed, and what comes into your life afterwards will be from new thoughts and words. The new beliefs and attitudes will dictate your outer life.

Jesus was cautioning men to watch their every thought and word in order to be prepared. Change these thoughts and attitudes with your words. Your words are the oil and wick in the parable. You are to sit by the door of your mind and heart, watching your words and thoughts in order to be prepared for the new life.

Now understand that the affirmations that we gave were examples and not the only ones you can use. Use the ability to affirm everything, every day. When you think a thought that will not bring the results you desire, then immediately cancel it and replace it with an affirmation. Every thought can be an affirmation. If you are feeling confused, state, **"I no longer desire to remain in confusion. I seek the Father within to bring His wisdom and knowledge into my life, now."** Or you can affirm, **"I watch my words, thoughts and attitudes. Those that are not in keeping with my new image are replaced with spiritual and uplifting ones."**

There is **POWER** in your choices and in your ability to choose. Not only is it a freedom, it is a **POWER** ready to be used to improve your earthly and spiritual life. By aligning with all that is Good, you align with God.

We urge you to keep a log of your work with spirit and God. We encourage you to write how you see your day and its events; keep a record of your thoughts, attitudes and feelings for that day. In this way you are able to monitor how you progress and, if you are not, why. In the future it will encourage you to see how much you now understand, how much happier you are and how much healthier you become. Not all things will be seen as improvements at first. Perhaps you carry within you attitudes you see as good, and they are not good for you as you become healthier in body, soul and mind. Or perhaps there is simply a newer way of looking at life, which is better. Changes are constant, and what you want is to change for the better, spiritually and physically.

Where there is Power, there is Energy. As you release and rid yourself of old fears and angers, you will be releasing energy. The way to live life with energy is spiritually. The way to improve your life is spiritually. By spiritually, we mean in the presence of God. We have some suggestions on how to use this lesson.

This is an example of how to use energy. Upon awaking in the morning allow five minutes to make contact with the Power of God within. Simply say to yourself, **"Today I choose to live in the Energy of God the Father."** Then pray your morning prayer. This will set your mind in the direction of the Father within. Arise and stretch your body as you stretch your mind toward Good. Take time out at intervals to monitor your attitude and words. Perhaps when there is a lull, ask, "Have I been using the thoughts and words that represent the conditions I want in my future?" With your noon meal take a quick moment to think, **"I will stay in contact with the Giver of Life."** Before retiring for the night, write about your day, and include the events that you want to be rid of. Perhaps it was an unusually good day and you are grateful. Or perhaps there was some dissension and you need to forgive. When you forgive, all you do is *give up* the resentment, fear or other depleting emotion and *give* a word of encouragement. You will face your new day free of all past regrets, fears and depleting emotions.

The reason we refer to negative emotions as depleting is because they continuously drain energy, as opposed to the lighter emotions, which continuously give you energy such as love, peace and happiness. Now maybe you can understand why these emotions are to be replaced. It will redirect energy, which you can then use for what you enjoy—to be creative and happy. Negative emotions take up room and have weight; this is why they use energy. People who are steeped in negativity use much energy and are under much stress. They soon find themselves with many diseases. Yes, there are other reasons for disease, too. Fear and anger deplete your inner reserves of energy. This inner reservoir of energy can be replenished as you erase and rid yourself of fear and anger; then energy continuously replenishes you.

We pray you will use this lesson to your benefit. We urge each to try this new way of preparing for your future with energy and power.

The Brotherhood

Mind-Heart Agreement
(Brotherhood, June 9, 1990)

We continue to concentrate on affirmations. Use affirmations to change your mindset. There is no magic in affirmations, except the magic of your mind and heart connecting to Spirit. When your mind and heart can agree with the concept of the affirmations, they will produce results beyond your expectations. Take for instance **the Truth that God is within you. When you realize this Truth deep within, and your mind and heart can agree on its Truth in spirit, you will have connected to the same power that Jesus used to work miracles.**

We will expand on this Truth. **Deep within each person, the Father waits to be a personal guide.** He is not particular about the name used to call Him. He simply desires that man seek Him where He is located, deep within every heart of hearts. Many people seek Him in church buildings or in a religious leader. **God the Father is within every soul.** He is continuously giving life, love, beauty and peace. Completely accepting His gifts is another thing. Take words of Truth into your mind and heart as an affirmation until you believe them without thinking about them. They must become the same certainty that you have of your gender. No one has to think about which gender they are; everyone is sure of this. Believe the affirmation, and be as sure of it as you are of your name. This same certainty is needed by the mind and heart to see results.

The Father is within you. Understand that upon entering into the heavenly kingdom you can claim all the good you desire. You are God's offspring, His heir and His love. **Whether you are feeling it or not, God is loving you and is within you.** Whether you can understand this or not, God is waiting for you to choose how you wish to live this life. You live by choosing your future. As an example, if health is what you desire, *the very first step is to concentrate on finding God within you.* Go into your inner temple and ask to be in union and communion with God the Father. Do this daily, until such time as you begin to have a sense of the Father. Understand that the Father is not difficult to reach. What is difficult for man is to silence his mind and heart. It is difficult to reach beyond the earth-mind consciousness of fear, hostility and resentments. Daily upon entering your temple, forgive yourself and others, using their names. Forgive everyone of all wrongdoing. This clears your mind, so you can rush through the race consciousness to the inner quietness. If a memory comes to mind, forgive the incident or be grateful for it, whichever is appropriate. Finally will come a sense of peace, a sense of something special. When you have reached this level of consciousness, then use affirmations for health. If you desire health, simply state in the affirmative, "I desire to live in complete health," or, "All of God's Energy is within me, healing, adjusting and making me whole and healthy." **Whatever comes to your mind as a request, state it in the affirmative.** Instead of begging the Father with, "Oh God, please make me healthy if you will." Change this into an affirmative statement, which is closer to truth, in this manner: **"God, Father, I choose to live in health with agility and limberness. It is God-Energy that is my Health. I am grateful."** Now repeat this until you can sense the connection of heart, mind and spirit. It is your heart and mind that take the time. Do not use your feelings as a guide; simply continue to pray in this manner. **You are not responsible for how your healing comes about.** It may take the form of working with a specialist of medicine, or a body trainer or a dietitian. How is not your problem or concern; simply follow the direction given to you. **Making the connection to the Power of God is your responsibility.** After the connection is made, there will be a sense that this is complete. Now is the time to give thanks. You will state again affirmatively, **"Thank you, Father, for my perfect health, my limber and agile body."** Continue to affirm in gratefulness until the health you desire is what you feel daily. **Remember, there is a lag time between the time your prayer is answered in spirit and when it appears in your physical reality.** This is a method to use to receive all that you need. Simply change the word "health" to meet your need.

Now be assured of the Truth that the Father is within and willing to give you all manner of Good. When this becomes a total reality in thought and feeling, you will bring forth your request instantly, as did Jesus.

The purpose of affirmations, as opposed to pleading prayers, is that it is your mind (attitudes) and heart (beliefs) that need to change. The changes are easier to attain when you make statements in the affirmative. To plead your prayers indicates to the mind that there is a possibility of rejection. **God does not reject; He simply gives. He is continuously pouring out to all people of all worlds His Love, Peace, Joy and all He is.** Remember, it is the race consciousness that inhibits through fear. The race consciousness will say, "God punishes and can withhold your request." This is not Truth, but an illusion that is activated through belief. If you believe that God can withhold, then this is what you receive. **When you affirm that God is within you and always giving, then what you say and what you hear is TRUTH.**

We wish to speak about the difference of your inner life and outer life. Remember to differentiate between the events that affect your inner life and those that are merely a part of the outer realm. Words, thoughts and attitudes affect your inner life. What you believe about others or events is what will become a part of your earthly life. **View all events as coming from goodness, even if you cannot see the good in the beginning.** Declare all events in your life as good, and they will produce good results.

There has been much interest in what was (in history and/ or past lives). This has given people food for thought. We do not in any way say this is wrong. **Remember that you live only today.** Take the scenarios of past lives/history as a way to see how great and wonderful God is. Continue to ask questions about the past; these questions give us an opportunity to give Truths which will help to expand the mind. The future is always of interest. But since Mother Mary has given you the predictions,[2] we say **concentrate on learning all you can to promote your inner contact with the Father.**

When you can be assured that the Father is within, then the circumstances of your life will not be terrifying. You will be sure there is life, love and all goodness within and without. This is how Jesus lived on earth. Remember that as the Christ consciousness, He is the way, the truth and the life. This means that through the Christ consciousness, which is within everyone, you will find the Way, Truth and Life. There is no magic in the way Jesus lived, but it has always been seen as magical. **Jesus, as the way-shower, came to demonstrate man's full potential.** He came to break the habit of living in fear. Let us explain. Man is confused and fearful about all things. He fears wars and depressions of economy, and all manner of fears are lived. He feels alone and sees only the futility of living simply to work, eat and sleep. This is man living the earthly life. It is truly an existence and not living fully.

But the man who is seeking the Father and all the Father has to offer is living life eternally. He knows and understands that life is eternal. He is assured of love, peace, happiness and all manner of good. There is a mystical and magical quality about him. Every person benefits, because this type of man lives from the inner to the outer. He understands his relationship with his Creator. He has found his inner temple, filled with the light of understanding, and has insured a loving quality of life. Did not Jesus live such a life? He was truly as the lilies of the field, in that he did not worry about the things of earth. He did not accumulate worldly possessions, because he wanted to demonstrate that the important treasures were the treasures of your mind and heart. **Jesus needed to make a point, and this point was that all you need is provided by the Father within.** God is a loving God, and when people use the laws that He set up, they have the energy to heat homes and provide nourish-

---

[2] In Chapter 2, "Mary's PREDICTIONS," of *Mary's Message to the World.*

ment to their children. There will be no need to tear the ecology to provide roads, cars or to pollute the earth. You can use levitation and teleportation, and many other of your innate powers. Remember all the things Jesus did are only a prelude of what is available to mankind. He simply came to give a preview of your inner abilities. These inner abilities can be obtained only through connecting to God, who is within. This requires a strong belief, a stronger connection and a firm conviction.

Our aim is to help you make this strong connection, but it can be made only through you. We cannot do this for you. Our part is to help every person go past the race-mind consciousness and through their fears, hostilities and resentments. We help you differentiate between what is inner and what is simply of this outer world.

Choose each day to make these Truths your conviction. Choose each day to live in the Presence and only through the Power of God the Father. Become so assured of His Love that you do not doubt it for one moment. Know within, to the core of you, that God is interested only in your thoughts and feelings. This is where to begin. **When the inner is cared for first, the outer will be adjusted accordingly. It is your inner life that needs care.**

The Brotherhood

Today's Thoughts, Tomorrow's Substance (Mid-Year Review)
(Brotherhood, June 23, 1990)

This lesson will be a review. To some of you this is new knowledge, and to others it is a time of reflection. We represent Jesus as a spiritual body on earth. We are also known as the Holy Ghost—Holy, which is another way of saying whole, complete within itself. We represent the Whole Spirit of God the Father. Ghost is another way of saying spirit. Our duty is to assist people on earth to connect to the Father. We simply maintain you in correct alignment, so that you can go past fear, hostility, anger and the hatreds of all time. Fear is an illusion. By going through the illusion, you conquer the fear. We will speak first of the Father.

God is both principle and personal. As Principle, He is the laws of nature, such as the law of gravity, aerodynamics, physics and ecology. As personal, He is our Heavenly Father, who is All Love and our Creator. **God is much, much more than anyone could ever imagine. He is Greater, Grander and more Loving than you could ever know.** God does not punish! But you can receive what appears as punishment when you go against the laws He created. For instance, if you do not hold on to a railing in a high place, such as on a mountaintop, and stand near the edge, the law of gravity will cause you to fall. Depending on the height from which you fall, the injury could easily be fatal. There are many laws in place, of which you are not aware. Only in recent history have people become aware of the laws of aerodynamics. So realize and remember that God does not punish, but you can be harmed if you go against a law that has been set in place.

God is very much alive and active in the Universe today. God is your life. He is the life force that energizes you daily. He is the Spirit that is alive in nature, as trees, plants, minerals and animals. **God not only watches over you; He is in you and you are in Him.** When you can realize this, then you will find the peace that passes all understanding. God is the only Spirit that is alive. God is Life and His Life is eternal. This means that we have eternal life. We live and live and continue to live. There is only one way to abstain from living, and that is to be placed in a state similar to suspended animation, where you are not actively alive. This also is your choice, but it is usually a choice that is not made actively, but passively.

God is so very wonderful, in that He has given us all the power of choice. You are fully capable of choosing all that affects you. You have chosen to live on earth in this time frame. You have chosen the culture, parents, type of home, gender and many more choices that affect your daily life. Let us explain again that you live life eternally and are always making choices. As you see, we speak of reincarnation, as it is called. Do not be fooled into thinking you could return to live as anything other than a human. You will not live life as a plant, mineral or animal. You were made in the image and likeness of God the Father in spirit.

God is Pure unconditional Love. **He is always loving and, as a personal God and Father, He loves us beyond all reasoning.** Begin to sense the love that the Father has towards all His creations. When you can attain an inkling of this Great Love, you will have touched your connection to Him, and through this connection you receive all instructions, answers, healings and peace.

To facilitate connecting to the Great Power of Divine Love, first you are to pray with a sincere heart and an earnest desire. This is all it takes to be in touch with the Father. We have instructed many, through the writings we have given to Jean Foster,[3] to build a temple in their mind. It is through the mind and heart that one is able to connect to Spirit. Build this temple lavishly and make it all you want. This is your temple; only you will worship the Father in this temple. God is a great and wonderful God, so do not build a small one, but make it as grand or grander than any on earth. After awhile, if you choose to change it, that is all right, since it is your special place to worship. If you have trouble building an imaginary temple, then recall a beautiful place that you have seen, and use it as a temple. Some people like the ocean and others like a mountaintop. Realize that this is your special place, and no one will ever enter it but you, God and spirit beings whom you choose to invite. You may invite us, angels or Jesus to enter your temple. We cannot and will not enter unless specifically invited. In your temple, you can ask all manner of questions. Tell God whatever is on your mind. We recommend that you empty your mind

---

[3] Within the book, *The God-Mind Connection,* by Jean Foster.

and heart of all that bothers you daily, since these issues are what interfere in your connection by acting as a filter to your connection to Spirit.

Not only do we recommend that you pray daily, but we also ask that you meditate. Relax your body, and then continue to use words, or a word, sound or chant to silence your mind. Then enter your temple and worship by talking to God. Allow a moment, or preferably more time, to listen. You may or may not hear anything. Most often the person on earth is not aware that God is talking to their soul. You may feel the communication, because you receive nourishment and energy. Later, when needed, it comes to your conscious mind as an idea or a flash of knowledge. Then you will have the answers to questions and solutions to problems.

Remember, everyone is using words, attitudes, beliefs and thoughts to sustain their quality of life on earth. **As you think in your inner mind, you will become.** Release all fear, anger and resentment, and find the energizing Love that is God. Use forgiveness to eliminate all depleting emotions. To forgive means simply that you will give up anger, hostility or fear in order to receive Love. As you forgive, you are forgiven. Forgive all people and no longer harbor any depleting emotions. **If you cannot forgive, then ask God to help you forgive. He is willing and able to do all things.** Secondly, remember that no one needs to face anything alone. **God is in you and He is not judging anything you do.**

One word about sin; this word simply means **a mistake of the spirit.** Do you punish a child for not understanding a lesson in math? The loving adult does not; he simply helps the child. This is how God acts toward each person. The unforgivable sin is to turn away from the Higher Power, who is alive and at work in the Universe. We say Higher Power, because on earth God is called many different names. But there is only One Spirit and One God. Even the unforgivable sin is forgiven when the person recognizes there is something or someone greater than himself. This is the extent of Divine Love. To correct any mistake (sin), simply ask the Father within to help you with knowledge and understanding.

Fear, anger, hostility and resentments, envy, jealousy, avarice, selfishness—these emotions and thoughts deplete not only the body, but the spirit. They play havoc in peoples' lives. They deplete your ability to live life actively. These are the great sins, because they act as filters and blocks on your side of the connection with God. See, God is constant and always emitting Love, but these depleting emotions can keep you from feeling His Love. People who have turned away from God will often be the ones who are ruled by these types of emotions.

In order to clean these emotions from within, pray and ask the Father to help you see how to do just this. If you are facing any fearful situations, pray by turning your thoughts to the help that comes from within. Simply say to yourself, **"God is my help. He loves me and is not punishing me in any way.** This is an illusion which will soon pass. The more I think of Divine Love and all its attributes, the faster the illusion vanishes." In the beginning, when you are still living with fear and jealousy, say to yourself, "This is an illusion; I will not judge by appearances, but I will judge by Truth. **The Truth is that God is Love, and He is alive and active in my life now."** Soon you will realize that you are not as fearful or as jealous. This will be the beginning of Truth and Love active in your life.

Jesus said, "Judge not according to appearance, but judge righteous judgments." (Jn 7:24) This means that what is happening in your outer life is what was active in your mind, not what you are thinking today. **There is a time of delay; the thoughts of today are the substance of your tomorrows.** Your beliefs, attitudes and words today bring future circumstances and situations into your life. As you change your attitudes, words and thoughts, your life changes, and so do your beliefs. This does not mean you are to have a life without problems. It means you will be strong in spirit and able to face anything that enters your life. You will see beauty in everything, because you will see with spiritual eyes. You will see wealth in the midst of poverty. There is courage, understanding and wisdom in all situations. Simply remember that **God is loving you in all situations.** No one can buy spirituality (closeness to God); it is earned through your sincere desire to be close to God. The moment you turn to God and ask for Truth, you open your mind to Allness and unconditional Love.

Take this lesson and meditate on it. Ask questions of us, and through your thoughts and feelings we will give answers. Do not worry, simply meditate and pray.

The Brotherhood

Success Depends on Faith
(Brotherhood, July 7, 1990)

In this lesson we will concentrate on faith. Faith is spiritual currency. It is needed in order to have your prayers answered. It requires faith to succeed in life, marriage, business or in any life event.

Faith is believing. It is a belief, an attitude and a strength that is deeply ingrained. **When you are faithful to yourself, you are faithful to God.** To be faithful to yourself requires that you believe in yourself. Many people do not believe in themselves. They live in fear and anger, which deprives them of faith. This type of faith does not require words, but a good sense of self. Today it is called self-esteem, but it could also be called belief in oneself.

The people who have suffered neglect or abuse of any kind will find it difficult to have faith in themselves. Often there is a need for a healing to take place. They must learn to believe in themselves. This can be done by looking back and finding those times when you did persevere. Even when drastic measures were used to cope, it took faith in oneself. Never look at the abuse or neglect, instead look at the resourcefulness that was used to survive the trauma. For those who are finding it difficult to live today, look at the many ways you have survived the experiences of life. When you look at the past, you will see how much faith you have had in order to live.

Faith is akin to hope. Where there is hope, there is faith. Hope is the ability to look forward to a better understanding, a brighter future. **Keep hope alive in your life, and you will have faith in yourself and others.** Faith is a lot like trust, in that when you trust yourself and others, it is easier to have faith in oneself and others. Faith is not simply a belief but a feeling, a desire and an ability.

Faith can be increased through prayer and faithfulness. As you pray for others and your world, you will increase your faith. **To insure its increase, ask the Father within to increase your faith.** All that you desire is given by the Creator, the Father within. Everyone needs to have more and more faith, to believe in themselves, their ability, future, career and spirituality. Faith can also be increased by remaining faithful to your set time for prayer and meditation. Stay interested in helping yourself and your loved ones through the use of Spirit. As you see results in yourself and your loved ones, it will cause your faith to grow. Then you have proof of your faith and abilities.

Here is how we recommend that you meditate and pray. **Set a separate time for meditation and one for prayer.** Perhaps it can be that you meditate early in the morning or you pray early in the morning. **Use a meditation to begin your day.** In meditation you will first still the body; you may find this easier in the early morning or late at night. State what your meditation will be concentrating on. **Meditate on one thought, such as peace, health, love, wisdom or understanding.** Your meditation need not be long time-wise, but it must be unhurried. Use your imagination to cleanse all negativity from your mind. Do this quickly with words and with an image of light. We recommend that you **sit upright to meditate,** to prevent you from falling asleep. Visualize a green cleansing light, or use the color of your choice, but afterwards always use this color for cleansing. Stand in a circle of this color of light and think, **"I am being cleansed of all negative thoughts, fear, anger and hidden resentments. As I am cleansed I forgive all people, and all people forgive me. It is done, it is accomplished."** Silence all thoughts and then mentally stand in a circle of white light to be healed, protected and guided for the day. Repeat the word for this day. The word in this case could be Forgive, Peace, Cleansed, Love, Accomplish or Blessings. Remain in the state of meditation for a few minutes. Then awaken with the thought of feeling energetic and ready to meet all the activity of the day. This will not take long. It is an exercise of the mind to cleanse and heal. Throughout the day, as people come to mind, forgive them and say the word of the day as a prayer for them. If for instance you are using the concept of PEACE, then you will bless everyone you meet with peace in your heart, in your mind, and immersed in your aura. If the word is LOVE, then do the same. You can say, "I send PEACE to you and forgive you of all transgressions." **End all meditations with a short prayer for the day.** Say something like, "Father, please be with me today and bless all the people I see." Or, "Father, give me the strength to find peace in my heart and in the faces of others." Use the word for the day as a prayer.

Set a time in the evening for prayer. **Be faithful to this time,** and pray daily in this manner. First, you will ask that all thoughts, deeds and attitudes be forgiven in you and in those for whom you pray. Then pray for your loved ones, and be specific at this time as to how you perceive their needs. Realize that God sees All and knows All. Then pray for the people with whom you work, you play or meet. Pray for areas of the world by continents and by religions. Pray for those who do not believe in God the Father, that they may be enlightened. Weekly change the way you pray, so that it will not become rote and lose its meaning. Also change the place you pray: sometimes use the outdoors and sit in nature to pray. At other times you may want to drive to a lake or pond of water to pray. Pray in a different room, change the clothes you wear or the locale,

but **do not change the time.** Remain constant in this and see
your faith increased.

Another method to use to increase your faith is to begin
each prayer and meditation with a statement of faith. Many of
the Catholic and Protestant churches use the Apostles' Creed.
Each person can use their own version of this or simply their
own words to say why and how they believe in God the
Creator. We like the words Annie uses in stating the Truths that
we have given concerning the Creator. She says, **"I believe in
God, Creator of heaven and earth, He who creates all known
and all that is unknown."** This is Truth. The words carry much
power. Use words of truth to make your statement of faith.
Perhaps you would like to create your own Creed. If you are
meeting in a group, this could be a group effort. For a group, set
a date when everyone brings their statements of truth. Then in
the next session have each read their own statements of faith.
Use these different statements to incorporate into the Creed of
the group, or each time allow a person to read his or her own
creed. It is better to use your own words, because they take life
in your soul more easily. By repeating your Creed of Faith, you
increase your faith.

Remember that Jesus asked the people who came to him
for healing, "Do you believe I can do this?" Then he would say,
"According to your faith it is done." Listen to these words. First
you are to make a statement of belief in God's ability to heal,
then state, "It is done," which finishes the work. So you could
say, "Dear Jesus, I believe that you walked on earth and still
walk among men. I believe that we have been able to speak
directly to you. I believe that God the Father can heal me and
my loved ones through you. I believe, and it is done according
to my faith." This statement says first you choose to be healed,
or choose to have a healing in a loved one. Then you state your
belief that it can be done because you have faith in Jesus'
abilities. But, more important, you believe in the Father Creator. You finish the work with a statement of completeness.
This is another form of prayer to use. In time you will make

your statement to God directly, without Jesus' intercession. This will happen as you become comfortable with speaking and listening directly to God.

Each time you repeat your statement of faith in prayer or in meditation, this increases your faith, and soon many miracles will be evident among those for whom you pray. Many miracles will happen in your lives and in your loved ones' lives. When this way of praying is used in a relaxed and easy way, you find that your prayers are answered easily. Release the prayer without worry of how it will come about. This is how to have the faith that moves mountains.

Another recommendation is that the group make a list of specific prayers for themselves and loved ones. Then pray for the people on the list, or as a group pray for the loved ones of everyone in the group. Details do not need to be revealed; use simply a word or short sentence to describe their need, such as physical healing, guidance, substance (money), a change of jobs, emotional healing, and always ask for your own spiritual healing.

You are doing a great and noble work by praying, and it will be unifying to the group and powerful for the individual as well. **This will be your new purpose.** You will have reached a new level of spirituality. It is time that you use your faith and knowledge to increase good in this world. Pray to prepare those who will survive the coming earth changes. Pray for immediate needs, such as healing of a specific illness, or for any difficulty that is overtaking minds at this time, such as a world event or a national event.

Now miracles can begin to happen. **Understand that miracles are simply the use of the higher laws of Spirit.**

The Brotherhood

21

The Seven Energy Centers

Bringing the Entire Self into Balance
(Brotherhood, July 27, 1990)

Our lesson today is about bringing the entire self into a state of balance.

THERE ARE MANY ASPECTS to each person. Each has many different bodies that are interconnected and interdimensional. There is the physical body, which you inhabit as the personality and identity and which is presented to the world in this lifetime. There is the higher self, which resides in the real world of spirit. This is your conscience and the keeper of your book of life. In between are layers or tiers, from the physical to the spiritual—the emotional, mental, psychic, astral, protoplasmic and ethereal bodies. As you see, there are several bodies, which in reality are more like layers of skin. Each one has a function, and each is of great use to enhance life on the earth plane. Each keeps memory and each affects the outcome of your spiritual life goals. These different layers need to be in balance, and the best way to bring all aspects into balance is through meditation and prayer. In meditation, you are able to align the different elements and receive a total and complete healing. Each body is different and each is alike. This is a paradox, of which you have learned there are many in life.

Within the physical body are centers of energy or, as they are called today, "chakras." There are seven of these centers, each corresponding to a body. All the centers lie along the inside of the spinal cord. That is, they are next to but not connected to the spinal column, laying within the body facing both the front and back sides of the physical body. Each has a corresponding color, which is connected to the color spectrum of light; a musical sound, which is connected to an electrical current; taste, which is used to savor life; aroma, which is linked to the magnetic field; and sense, which acts as a radar or sonar unit.

The lower is the base center and its corresponding color is red, deep red, the color of un-oxygenated blood. From this center, life and strength are activated. This is the center of the physical body and it is linked to the testes and ovaries, from which life springs on earth. Through this center, one is grounded to mother earth via the feet. There are rays of energy that pour out of this center through the legs and into the ground. Through this center you are able to plant your feet firmly on the ground and utilize all the energy earth has to offer.

Next up the spinal column, a little below the navel, is the second center, whose color is reddish-orange. This is the center that controls Universal Order and Balance, the order and balance that links you to all Universal laws and laws of physics, like the law of gravity and such. It is the place of origin in the development of the fetus. Through this connection, the mother feeds the child through the umbilicus. Here is the element that gives the baby and the mother a special connection. The connection to the physical body in the woman is through the womb and in the male through the prostate gland.

The third center is in the solar plexus, a center that is below the breastbone. Its color is yellow, and it is the center of Wisdom and Knowledge. The mental body connects through it, and it's the reason that when you are frightened or receive a mental shock, the reaction is felt here. When there is a huge shock that involves the mind and emotions, you will react in this area and it will spread to the lower emotional center. There are many gland cells in the stomach, liver, kidneys and pancreas that connect this center of the body.

The fourth center is located in the center of the breastbone and connects the psychic to the spiritual body, as does the third eye. This is the center of Love and Divine Will. This center keeps you aligned to the higher spiritual levels of life. The corresponding color is twofold. For the physical heart and the issues of Will, it is light green. For the issues of Love, it is pink. The gland that links this center is the thalamus. When both are in balance, you will emit an opalescent color.

The fifth center is at the base of the throat, and it is the center of Power and Zeal, or as zeal is known today, Enthusiasm. The color is light royal blue, and it is linked through the thyroid gland. When you give away or misuse your power, there will be trouble with the throat. This center gives power to your words. As you speak words, they are brought out of the power center and charge forth to bring into your existence that which you speak. If you criticize anyone, the power of your words will also bring the same into your life. If you use words to praise, what you praise will be brought into your reality. Words of love bring more love into your life from all areas.

The sixth center is located in the middle of the eyebrows and is called the third eye. It is the eye that one uses to see perceptively. Its color is midnight blue, and it is linked to the pineal gland. This center is the seat of Divine Understanding and Divine Imagination. When you understand something, the

term used is "I see." This center also links all the five senses of
hearing, sensing, smelling, taste, as well as sight. When a
person is using his imagination to fret or worry, he will invari-
ably get a headache. This center connects to the heart center and
is your connection to the Cosmos. This is a very important
center to use as you learn to trust your intuition.

The highest center is located at the top of one's head and is
called the Christ center by many today. We call it your Cosmic
Spiritual center. Its color is purple, ranging in color from light
to dark. It is also connected to the pineal gland at the top,
whereas the third eye is connected to the pineal gland at the
base. This center and the third eye are used in meditation and
connect one to the highest realms of life.

Each center connects you to a different dimension and a
different plane of life. It is through the entire whole self that life
is lived on earth. You came to earth to have expression in life.
On earth is where you are able to overcome more quickly the
erroneous thought patterns. It is here that you practice using
your entire self.

Do you understand how much more a person is than his
personality? Each person is important in the universe. Everyone is linked through these different centers to all of the
Creator's realms of life. How can this be? Consider that each
person is in reality many different identities on earth. He is a
son, brother, father, grandfather, uncle, friend, salesman or
whatever career personality, nationality and cultural personality. Likewise, in spirit you are many more identities. Each of
your aspects is enhanced by the other. As these centers become
aligned, you will hear the voice of God as He guides you, savor
the fullness of life, see all events, people and circumstances in
Truth, sense coming events and prevent those that can be
prevented. Also, you will feel Divine Love more fully, smell
truth and honesty in people as well as in events. All areas of life
will become enhanced, and you are more serene, courageous,
wiser, more understanding and loving. This is a better way to
live, an easier method. You will learn to forgive quickly and

bless others as did Jesus. All fear will be eliminated in a quiet and gentle way.

The importance of aligning your entire self is to bring you into a greater use of all the talents that are inherent, to bring out your greater potential as a son of the living God, to find your ability to use God Power to heal, levitate, see into the future, read minds and to do all the things Jesus showed as your full potential on earth. Remember Jesus said, "The things I do, you can also." (Jn 14:12) This requires some work on your part. It will require a routine of daily meditation and prayer. This requirement also states that **your meditations and prayers are solely for the purpose of connecting to God.** All these things are simply added benefits. If you seek to meditate to develop these abilities because you want to be known as a great psychic, you will not find these abilities. No matter how noble your intention to become a great psychic, it will not happen. It will happen only because you want to connect to the Father within.

Life is lived in cycles. Use this knowledge to enhance your meditations by keeping a set time for meditations. We feel that you do not understand the importance of maintaining a set schedule. It is important to you to keep the set time, because as the time nears, the different aspects or bodies of which you are made begin to come together with the purpose of meditation. Your whole self gets ready for you to meditate and pray. Be faithful to your commitment to meditation and prayer. Prayer is not simply the requesting, but a time to express your beliefs in God and in yourself. It is a time for you to express Truths about yourself and about your loved ones. Each person is more than the personality you see. State this in your prayer. For instance, when praying for a loved one, such as a parent or child, say the person's name and state Truths like this, **"Mom or son, you are a child of the living God. He placed in you many aspects to enhance your life. You are strong, courageous, loving, powerful, understanding, enthusiastic and perceptive. Your life is in Divine Order, and all events in your life** are healing your entire self." Make this type of statement about yourself and others, because all these potentials are true of every person. Everyone has the ability to be more perceptive, loving and enthusiastic. When you make these types of statements, the higher/whole self instantly is linked to the physical body, and there is joy. A greater degree of healing enters the body when statements of truth are spoken than happen when you beg for a healing.

Once again we ask that you take this very important lesson and read it often, referring to the instructions for meditation and the reasoning behind the instructions. Be faithful to your set time of prayer and meditation. Then wait for the results. Make allowances for timing delay to take place and be patient for the rewards. It takes time to notice differences. Affirm, **"I will be faithful and patient in my meditations."**

The Brotherhood

Qualities of the Energy Centers
(Brotherhood, August 25, 1990)

We are so very proud of each of you for seeking the light of God's Love. **Understand that all things in life proceed in an ebb and flow pattern.** At times you may not feel very spiritual, and at other times you will feel very spiritual, but in reality you are always seeking to find "the way." What you are doing in this lifetime is very important and can help you advance in your real life by centuries. We know that there is no way to prove this to you in a manner that can be seen by earthly terms. We feel that every person will come to an understanding of this truth with time. Remain faithful to your quest, so that you will be prepared for all future events. When the time comes, you will know how and when to act. This type of seeking brings many benefits to you, but not the type you are specifically looking for today. The benefits will be of the type that are for your highest good. In time this will prove to be true. In gentleness and understanding, we are always ready to help. It is our pleasure to await your call for help. This call is not always a conscious call; at times your subconscious now calls for help. Remember always that whether you realize it or not, if you feel it or not, **God the Father is loving you today.** Listen to the inner stirrings and inner promptings; these will be from your higher self, us or the Father. These inner promptings will not always give you the answers you want, but they will give the answers you need.

We will discuss the energy centers because they are important and will open your inner self to all possibilities. These energy centers within you overlap and intermingle. It is not so important that you learn their exact locations as it is that you learn the qualities that they bring into your life. The colors are a way of identifying them; this too is not an important issue. **The importance is the flow of new energy and the clearing away of depleting emotions.** Allow your mind to focus on the meaning of the words that represent the energy. At different times these words will mean different things. Do not dispute the flow of thoughts that arise as you meditate on the words Life, Wisdom and such. This is an opening to your inner self and an opening of new horizons.

As you have learned, there are ways to meditate and call forth these energy centers to become more active in you. **Always begin each meditation with your intent to communicate with the Father within.** Recall why you believe and how you believe in God. Do this by reciting your creed of faith. It can be one learned in childhood or, better still, one in your very own words, such as, "I believe in God the Father, as taught to me by the Brotherhood or by my religion." Or, **"I believe in God, Creator of the Universe, and in He whose life I see activating throughout the world."** Put into your own words what you believe to be truth. This is better than reciting someone else's creed. **Truly meditate and pray in your own words.** Understand that the affirmations or statements we give are only as examples. You may use them until you feel comfortable creating your own versions. There is no magic in the words we choose as opposed to words that you will use. The magic is in your faith. To increase your faith, state that you desire to increase your faith. Say, **"Father I desire to have greater faith in order to receive all that has been prepared for me."** It is simple and easy. There are times when you may not use words but feelings; God understands this too. You may also allow your inner mind to commune with God in silence, understanding that it will reveal what has been received when needed.

Now as to the energy centers. Think first what these words mean. We asked Annie to look up these words in the dictionary to get the full use of all words available in this language. (This is because we can use only those words we find in her mind.) It would be good for each of you to read about the meanings of the words that describe the different energy centers. We speak of the words "strength," "life," "order" and such. This will give your mind more information to work with in bringing to you new thoughts and new ideas of how these energies apply to your life. You will know how to invoke the flow of energy when you have need of it. It is all through the use of words. Each individual word brings to mind many sensations, feelings and mental pictures. These are the ways your inner mind communicates with all the different elements of your entire self. The reason you need to activate these energy centers is that these energies are depleted by the emotions of anger, hostility, fear, resentments, envy, jealousy and such. To overcome these depleting emotions, you will find that the more energy of the opposite element you have, the better and quicker you will come out of the depleting emotions. You will rise out of these feelings, like the sun rising out of a mist. It will simply happen, and you will not have any sense of struggle. It is the same as when a light is turned on in a dark room, except these inner changes happen slowly and insidiously. Before you know it, you find that you are losing the feeling of anger or hatred. Be aware that anger can also disguise itself as depression, physical illness, or even as a vague feeling of discomfort. Each of these depleting emotions can use the form of illness to disguise itself. Meditate daily on each energy center, and then concentrate on the energy that is needed. **If you are feeling unloved, then concentrate on the center of Love and allow all this word means to conjure ideas or thoughts to heal you.** It will not happen in one meditation, but with time it will come about. Be patient and persistent, and it will pay off in great benefits.

The base or root center is Life and Strength. Think of life and what this word implies. **Where there is life, there is activity, an ability to adapt to surroundings and differing conditions.** There is sparkle, light and effervescence. Life denotes interest, seeking or a search for survival. See how these words conjure up some interesting images in your mind? Doesn't everyone desire sparkle in their life, career, marriage and all phases of life? Imagine what an increase of life energy would do to your confidence. What will happen in you is to know that you individually will survive all things. Understand that there is the ability to adapt and change. It is never too late to change. Yes, you can learn new ways of thinking and feeling. Be persistent in your search for a better life.

Think of strength. These are some of the words that describe strength: courage, might, force to withstand, an ability to support, vigor, firmness, potency. **Strength as we use it is the ability to last, endure, and the capacity to perform.** When Divine Strength energizes, you have the strength of the universe. You are able to withstand and bear all things that happen in life. You have the courage to do what is really needed in order to survive. You have the courage to face yourself and to resolve problems. You have the courage to surrender to God and to allow yourself to better your life. There is support for you spiritually and in all ways. Your physical strength is increased as well as your emotional and mental strength. All aspects of you are increased. There is psychic strength. You are able to use all your talents and potentials. Dwell on the word strength and on all its meanings when you are feeling weak.

The second center is Order. **Divine Order is the highest
and best order possible, anytime or anyplace.** Words to describe order are: an authority, control, choice, status, harmony.
It is the ability to have things in their proper place, to command,
supply, regulate, conduct and manage. It is the same order that
holds the planets in their proper orbits. It is alignment in its
proper perspective. This opens up the energy to harmonize, to
take the authority to choose. You have the innate ability to
manage and regulate your life already, but perhaps it has been
depleted through concentrating on the wrong emotions. As
Divine Order is brought into play in each life, there is stability,
harmony and peace, which inhabits all aspects of life. One part
of your life will not overpower the others. You have time to
work, play, and to pray and meditate. You are free to choose,
manage and regulate your own life. As you call forth the energy
of Divine Order into all parts of your life, it brings about a
harmony of its own. Evoke Divine order into your marriage,
relationships, career, finances, even into your choices of what
to buy. When you bring into your mind the thought of Divine
Order, it will protect you, allow more self control and give you
a feeling of status.

The next center is the center of Love and Will. Love is
forgiveness. To love is to forgive until the number seven plays
out. You forgive, forever and ever. You forgive all people and,
most important, forgive yourself. This is the essence of love.
Love is tolerant, adoring, loyal and freeing. When you truly
love, you release and give up all control. Love is never inhibiting or selfish. You have many feelings and thoughts of love, but
understand that **Divine Love is not controlling or manipulative.** It is used only with the highest and best results. Allow this
unconditional Love to invade your inner life. God is always
loving each of you, even when you do not feel it.

In this manner, allow the mind to bring what the words of
the different energy centers mean to you, individually. What
does it mean to have Divine Will working in you, or to have all
the Wisdom of the universe at your disposal? What does it

mean to you to be Powerful and full of Zeal and Enthusiasm? How would you feel and act if you had all the Understanding of the Universe and all the Imagination? How do you feel when you concentrate on the top of your head with the thought, "Spirit of God?" These are the energies that are already active within each person. They can become filmy and depleted as the person concentrates more on hostilities, angers, envies and jealousies. When you wallow in self-pity and despair, you only deplete your own energies. It is not that God is punishing you, instead it is that you are punishing yourself by what you concentrate on.

Please do your inner work and follow the instructions we are giving. If you only think of them, it is good, but if you actually meditate in this manner, you will find, in time, old resentments leaving as you become patient, loving, understanding and wiser. The very ability to choose wisely will bring relief from the oppression of overspending. You will have a better understanding of your finances and will find ways to use your money wisely. Remember that the traders of commerce tell you they have your best interests at hand, but in reality they are selling you ideas to buy their products. **Only you and your higher self have your own interest at heart.** This is why it is important to rely and trust your own inner self. In the coming lessons, we will continue to give more information on opening the energy centers. Each time we will expand on what has already been learned and stressed.

During your meditations, concentrate on the different energy centers. Take the knowledge within you and use it to increase these energies. Perhaps at first you will not feel or see any differences, but in time there will be deep and permanent changes. Annie and Byron went to see a movie *(Ghost)* that gives an illustration of many Truths. It is a film that has been made with help from higher guides. The people who created and produced this movie may not be aware they had help. It came as they prayed for ideas. The movie gives a good illustration on how love can transcend death. Not everything in the movie portrayed truths. There were a good many truths hidden within the story.

A word about movies and storytelling. The people in the stories are all representative of different times (referring to past lives) in your life. Every person has at times been victim and victimizer. Each person has been the good guy and the bad guy. This is why fairy tales are so popular. People identify with them. A child will identify with the heroine. Everyone has been Cinderella, Snow White and Juliet, but also every person has been the wicked witch, the wicked stepmother and the closed-minded parent. Look at all stories as portraying different times in your own inner life.

The Brotherhood

How and When to Use Each Energy Center
(Brotherhood, September 15, 1990)

We continue with the energy centers. It is important that each person open to the inflow and outflow of energy and understand that all energy is God. These energy centers represent the different aspects of the Father within. They enhance life on earth. As you open the flow of these energies, your life comes close to what is your ideal. Your spirituality is activated in your daily life. As the energies are activated, you will see differences in your reactions to life and people. At first you will not notice these differences, but soon, if you reflect, you see that you feel differently and react differently to life. The changes will be subtle and insidious in nature.

Meditate on these energies and remember that it is for your good and not ours that you meditate. Our aim is to help by bolstering and supporting your efforts to connect to the Father within.

To review, **the center of life brings the ability to change and adapt.** Use this energy when you are faced with changes that need to take place. If there is a change in jobs, you will call upon life energy to help adapt and adjust to new people and new routines. If there is a move of residence, you will call upon life and strength to aid in all adjustments to environment, climate, home, people and routines. **Use Strength for the ability to endure when you are faced with something that is out of your control.** Or use Strength for the potency to work and act in an effective manner, such as when you need to make changes in habits or thought patterns.

The center for Order is the same Universal Order of the planets. When you feel disharmony or find yourself in a condition that seems unmanageable, **Divine Order is the energy that can help you find harmony and the ability to cope.** This is your ability to command your attitudes, beliefs and habits.

Wisdom and Knowledge are located in the pit of the stomach. This is your ability to sense the Truth. It is often called "gut feeling." When you open this energy center, you will have the ability to judge properly and take action when needed. **Knowledge gives you the ability to use spiritual Truths and Divine Intelligence.** This is the seat of common sense and the ability to know. When faced with the need to recall certain facts, use this inner energy center. When faced with questions about beliefs or attitudes, you will know how and what to say. **All the Knowledge in the Universe is within you, in this energy center.** It is through this energy center that every person will receive their own instruction.

If faced with a job interview, you will be instructed in what and how to reply. So do not waste energy worrying about how you will do in an interview. Simply call upon the energy of Divine Wisdom and Divine Knowledge to speak through you. In this manner you will be relaxed and give a better first impression. You will be surprised at the way you answer all questions with honesty. You will put yourself in the best light without seeming to be a braggart. If you are called upon to speak before a group of people, there is no need to become tense. You have the ability to use Divine Wisdom and Divine Knowledge to your advantage. Your talk will be concise, filled

with good information and given in a way that all will understand. If you are in any situation in which you do not know
what to do or how, use this energy to help you decide and act.
This is the connection to universal information. It is a way to
use more God-energy, here and now.

Next is Divine Love and Will, the energy that is most in
use today. People do not realize that Love is an energy and
think of it as an elusive feeling. **Divine Love and all love is
much, much more than a feeling. It is an energy like electricity.** It has the capability to heal, protect, guide, direct and
influence. When you are "in love," you can be swayed easily by
the love of your life. Love is also devotion, forgiveness, tenderness, loyalty, consecration and reverence. It is the ability to
attach, and it is passion—passion, not only of the sexual kind,
but the passion of an artist or a religious leader.

Use Divine Love to heal bodies, relationships, finances,
business, nations and the planet. Concentrate on Divine Love
and visualize the person who needs a healing. In this manner
you are asking Divine Love, which is God the Father, to heal
this person. There is no need to plead or beg, you have the
ability to use your mind and heart as did Jesus in prayer. Jesus
said at the end of his petition, "Thank you, Father, because you
have heard me." He was sure of God's ability to hear him,
because he was aware of this inner connection to God's Love.
You can heal the family by stating that Divine Love is flowing
through you to all whom you love. Use love to forgive, first
yourself and then others. As you forgive everyone in this
lifetime, you are forgiving all the residue of past lives. It is good
to forgive all people and all events of past lives, because **you
stop the wheel of karma by forgiving.** When you first begin to
forgive past lives, there may be a short period of pain in which
the memory cells are emptied. But continue to forgive, and
soon there is a release as there has never been in your life.

**Divine Will is the ability to choose, deliberate, take
action.** It is purpose, determination and persistence. It is your
Divine right to choose all situations in your life. If you do not

choose, you are left to the effects of the past or to karma. **The best course of action is to will to do God's Will,** because God's Will is always good. God wants you to be as successful as you desire to be. He wants you to be healthy, wealthy, happy and satisfied with your life. It is in aligning to God's Will that you find shortcuts to these states of mind. Pray to have God's Will active in your life. Say often, **"I will to do God's Will."** Or, **"God's Will for me is only good, so I choose to have His Will active in my life."**

The Power and Zeal center is at the base of the throat. It is through the throat that you give Power to your words. Most important is what is brought through this center. It is the ability to do, act, control, command, to magnify. It is completed work, effectiveness, force and authority. Power also means the amount obtained by multiplying any number by itself, but think that what is true of the number is also true of you. There is more power in magnifying yourself through God. Some people are powerful in their demeanor and speech, because they have learned in the distant past to use this energy. Everyone can consciously learn to use Power to enhance any situation in this lifetime. For instance, if you are faced with a lack of motivation, you can call on Divine Power to flow through you to motivate. Or, if you think you are not demonstrating all your potential, call upon Power to show your effectiveness and authority.

Zeal is enthusiasm, diligence, interest, eagerness, ardor and avidity. Daily call upon Divine Enthusiasm to flow through you to increase your power to move, act and be effective. All these energy centers are interconnected and flow one into the other. When you are lacking in zeal, you are lacking in life, power and love. If you must start with only one energy center, start with zeal. It's the most readily available. It will demonstrate the proof people need of the existence of these centers of energy.

The third eye has always been magical. It is the seat of Imagination and Understanding. **Understanding is the ability** to perceive the meaning of any situation, the ability to grasp ideas from Universal consciousness, to comprehend, realize, believe and use all intellectual faculties. By concentrating on understanding, you will see Truth in action and have the ability to perceive the unseen. When you need ideas for your life, concentrate and release this energy. Use understanding, not only when you must see someone else's point of view, but when you wish to see Spiritual Truths. If there is a need for new ideas or to bring stability to your family, call upon Divine Understanding.

Imagination is the most exciting of all energies, because it gives you the ability to paint pictures of your future. Remember to leave everything up to God to give what you picture or better. Through this energy center is the ability to see yourself as God sees you—beautiful, energetic, filled with enthusiasm, kind, loving, understanding, powerful, forgiving, wise, knowledgeable, alive, strong, intelligent and successful.

Quiet your mind by breathing out three times. That is, concentrate on the breathing out and relaxing during the out breath. Then fill your imagination with pictures of the life you desire. Next, release these to God's Divine Will. This is how to use this magical center of energy. You can also use imagination for your loved ones by simply saying in your meditation, "I see you as God sees you," and then list all these qualities. This is a very powerful prayer. Use your imagination to paint the pictures of life. When you desire to have new friends, rejoice in your imagination with them. When you need a new work experience, see yourself coming home tired and happy from your new job. **See the results, the finished picture.** Or, better yet, see yourself banking the money you earned from the new job. Let this be your prayer. Use your imagination to see peace in the world. Use this faculty to see headlines in your newspaper of **PEACE** in large bold letters. When you need a healing of the physical body, see yourself (in meditation) enjoying perfect health, doing the things you would do if you were well, playing games with family and friends. Or, if you need anything, see (in your imagination) the thing completed or done, not the process but the completion of the request. Leave the process completely up to God the Father.

The most important energy center is the Spiritual. This is the seat of your connection to God. It is at the top of your head. Spiritual in your language means vital principle, breath of life, conscious incorporeal being, supernatural, brave vigor, the essence or active principle, idealism. But you know that **spiritual means All that is God, all that is known and all that remains unknown.** You are more alive in spirit than on earth. You are alive for eternity. This is your connection to Divine Potential.

By concentrating on the spiritual center of energy, you enhance all energy centers, because they all are interconnected and interdependent, the same way all things on earth are interconnected and interdependent. If you will simply look at nature and the laws of ecology, you will see evidence of this. Not only is there an ecology of the natural planetary world, but there is an ecology of spirit. The ways of earth are also spiritual. The natural world simply reflects the spirit world. The Spiritual center is your connection to the REAL World; it is your ability to use all that you are, to enhance your life on earth. By concentrating on this center, you activate all of God, as Principle, in your life. You DO NOT need to know the exact manner this is activated. What you desire are the results. This will happen as you bring spiritual energy into your mind, body and affairs. If there is a lack of time to meditate, concentrate on the Spiritual center and allow it to activate all centers within you. Then go in peace and "know" that deep within is all that you need to face any situation in life. See inwardly and feel the spiritual center shower your entire body with its energy.

We pray that you will heed our teachings and use the lessons to open these energy centers daily. This will help every person open to the Father within, hear His instruction and receive all the good He has prepared for you. **These lessons do you the maximum good only if you practice them.** Allow time for daily meditation and prayer. Learn to rely on the Father within for all your needs. He is loving you with a love and interest greater than any in this world.

The Brotherhood

Nature and Uses of the Energy Centers
(Brotherhood, September 29, 1990)

We will explain more about the energy you receive through the energy centers. This energy is more than the simple energy to propel, more than the concept of energy that is held on earth today. It is not only the energy to activate but the energy to access. It is pure energy, which can be used to mold in your life what you desire and what you need to reach your lifetime goals. Do you realize what pure energy is? **Energy is the substance of God Himself. The Father used Himself to create life, worlds and universes.** It is the raw building blocks of the universe, all that is known and all that is unknown. This is the energy you access, mold and shape to give your life meaning, health, wealth, fortitude, power and anything you have need of.

Many people become engrossed in the world's view of how things should be. They are not open to the mind-expanding nature of God. Use this energy to open your mind and heart to All that is God. Access all that the Father has prepared for each of you. **There is the ability, through life-energy, to adapt and change.** Realize how wonderful this is! You no longer need to remain stuck in the same old rut. Every person has the ability to break out of their mold and spring into a life of power, courage and raw ability. Everyone can change old, depleting thought patterns, attitudes and beliefs. Everyone can become all that they were meant to be. No one must tolerate the depths of depression, no matter what the cause. You have the ability to change this occurrence in your life. You cannot fight the depression by berating yourself. Instead, continue to remain faithful to what you have learned. In the midst of depression, say over and over to yourself, "This is not real; what is real is the Love that the Father has for me. I will concentrate on what I know about God, the Father within, and simply know in my heart that these feelings of depression are old memory cells releasing bad memories."

Now this is not the only use of life energy. Allow us to begin at the top of your head, with Spirit, which is your connection to all that is within Spirit. Can you realize what this means? It is your ability to use the power and talents that Jesus used on earth. For now, simply know that within your mind and heart is the ability to calm the raging climate. You can heal and call out of death, life. You can rearrange molecules and change water into wine or whatever you are in need of. This is your potential, as it is every person's on earth. No one person is better than the other. Every person has these innate abilities. As you concentrate on Spirit, you release the most potent power and energy in the universe, a power and energy greater than any atom or neutron-yielding bomb.

You do not need to know how this works; simply align yourself with this power and call it forth into your mind, heart and life. This is the power to expand, grow and heal earth-mind consciousness. By doing so, you help the entire world and all its inhabitants. You can bring into play spiritual values and see miracles be wrought within you and your world. These energies can only be used unselfishly.

We will go on to imagination. In Annie's meditations, she paints the pictures of her life with words. Her life is painted in hues of love and with colors of wealth. She paints pictures of happiness, health and plenty of good—good friends, money, good clothes, a smooth-running car, a nice home and all manner of goods and time to enjoy them. Paint the pictures of your life in this manner. Use words to describe the conditions you desire, but not in detail; simply use generalities. In this manner you leave it open for the Father within to create the situations and circumstances of your life as He wills, which is good.

Health, wealth, riches, happiness, plenty of good friends, time to enjoy life, plenty of money to use to make your life comfortable, plenty of health, wisdom and power to live life fully. See, you are not dictating how and when you desire your good to come, but are simply making a blueprint of what you desire and leaving the details up to the Father.

Use the energy of understanding to help you see through the eyes of spirit into the inner workings of all circumstances and all people. Allow the energy of understanding to bring into your world peace, serenity and fullness of life. **What you understand, you comprehend; what you comprehend, you become.** Allow the energy of understanding to open your mind and heart to a surging of Spirit in you, your life and your world.

Within everyone is the power to know, perform and act with diligence and force. You no longer need to wait to see what others do in order to find the way. Those who release this Pure Energy will be leaders, by following the way that is shown within. Nor will you need anyone else on earth to give you guidance. **Within every person is the power to access the Father within, who gives better guidance, more understanding and more abilities to live this life.** When you activate these power centers, your words and prayers have potential and power. You will have charisma, that elusive quality that all great leaders have. You will have the ability to see into the future and to know the trends that will follow. Begin simply by speaking words of life, like this: **"I activate within me the Power that I need in order to be all that I can be,"** or words to that effect. You can list these abilities of power and say, "These are active in me," and you have activated them. Use your words to activate all that the Father has prepared for you. Use them to live life fully and potently.

We cannot say enough about Zeal, because this is a real, motivating energy. It is the bounce of life, the ability to enjoy life. It will give new meaning to your work (career), home, love interest and to your everyday world. Zeal as enthusiasm is the quality of great leaders. People who are at the top of their career have much enthusiasm. **Zeal is the spark that motivates.** It is the energy to run the engine of your body, your world and your future. Take a close look at the people in your world; you will be able to tell who is enthusiastic and who is not. Enthusiasm colors the people who have it with happiness, contentment and the energy to move and propel themselves through many activities. They are busy and interested in what they are doing. Not only are they able to move themselves, but they can light a fire under the most idle of people. **Zeal/Enthusiasm is kindling. It takes hold of a small spark and lights up within you a raging fire of energy.** This energy takes you through every event and circumstance of your life, with energy to continue on. Every morning, say words that ignite within you a fire of Zeal and Enthusiasm. Simply say, as you are rising out of your bed, **"This day I will live enthusiastically."** When you have convinced yourself that this is real and this is your goal, it will happen. Then watch out, because you will be a dynamo of energy and accomplishment.

The center of energy that we use the most is Love and Divine Will. This is an equalizing energy, in that all people love something or someone. Most people do not love the most important person in their lives, themselves. Look at loving yourself in this manner. Where would you be without you? Who would you be without you? How far would you get without you? It is not egotistical to love yourself; it is egotistical to think you are the only one who knows, thinks and feels correctly, and that only what you think, feel or do is important. **To love yourself is to love what God has made.** It is the ability to appreciate the life, body and mind that have been given to you as a gift. Loving yourself is an appreciation of what and who you are, knowing that all of life is One. You have eternal life, and this lifetime is one of your choosing. It is the role that will help you achieve spiritual growth. Life on earth is a classroom, and the events of your life are lessons to enhance your real self.

Love gives you the biggest eraser there is in the Cosmos—forgiveness. It is through forgiving that you erase events, hurts, abuse, trauma and all manner of ills. **You break the chain of karma by forgiving.** Through forgiving, the lesson of abuse will be completed and learned for mankind. Man, individually at first, will have the freedom to go on to other lessons and other achievements. Forgiveness is freeing, because what you forgive is accomplished, done and over with. There is no need to return to a life that reflects the same old patterns. Forgive and understand that when you forgive, you release yourself to higher and better things.

Divine Will is Energy that will heal, guide, protect, enhance, enlarge and prosper. These are simply the things which the Father has already set up for those who surrender to His Will. Divine Will is freeing, energizing and elevating in all ways. **God has more good for and in His creations than you can imagine.** No one has the capacity to envision the Good that is in the Father's storehouses. As you seek to have Divine Will established in your life, there is an uplifting of your inner self. Soon all fear will be gone, all angers will dissipate and all resentments will be but a bad dream. Pray to have Divine Will active in your life. When you believe that Divine Will is All Good, you will be amazed as miracles follow miracles and wonders will never, ever cease.

The releasing of these innate energies is important to you; it is for your betterment that we teach this. Learn it and learn it well. This is our prayer.

The Brotherhood

Seek Ever to Improve (Fall Review)
(Brotherhood, October 13, 1990)

We support your search for the Father within. We will review what you have learned so far.

All your imagination and mind could never conceive the wonder and greatness of God the Creator. He is more wonderful, loving, giving and powerful than anyone can imagine. He has given everyone many gifts.

The first is the gift of eternal life. You are here on earth to learn and practice what you have learned in the past. Real life is lived in spirit. The life you live on earth is temporary because this is a schoolhouse or a laboratory. The circumstances of your life are twofold. They are a product of your attitudes, thoughts, words and beliefs. They also are a chosen path to a greater understanding and learning. All you are seeking on earth is for the values and privileges you have in spirit. The security that everyone desires is what is considered in spirit a normal happening. Each person lives many lifetimes in order to perfect and fine tune his personalities and his real self. Death is but a returning to your real life. It truly is a homecoming. Everyone has lived many times on earth and has died many deaths. Death is not to be feared, but considered a normal part of life.

You have been given the gift of choice. You can choose anything you desire. Along with freedom of choice comes responsibility for your actions. Every thought, word, deed, belief and attitude is revealed in your life. Be careful of what you desire; it will become yours, and not always as you envision. People are often like little children, in that they want one thing and then quickly change their mind and desire another. This kind of desiring only delays your good. There is a lag time between spirit and earth. When your desires are heard in spirit, your higher self and the Father confer in spirit, where everything happens quickly. These desires must be viewed with your own lifetime goals in mind. Sometimes they may be granted with some amendments. At other times they may come just as you desire. It is always your higher self with your lifetime goals in mind who makes the final decision. God allows each soul to work in their own way and at their own pace.

You are loved with a love that is greater than anything on earth. **God is the love and the act of loving. He dearly loves you with a love that is all-encompassing and healing.** Illness and all experiences in life are simply a method used for your learning. God does not punish anyone. He does not need to, since people are harder on themselves than God could be. You are on earth to learn to love by forgiving first yourself and then others. If you could hold but one thought in mind until it becomes a part of you, **hold this thought: God loves me, now, just as I am.** Simply to allow this love to encompass all that you are and all that you desire will be healing. **God does not judge; He loves.**

God is not only your life, but He is also the life that is in the trees, minerals, animals and other people. He is Life, Love and All Good. Remember that Jesus gave a new commandment to people: **"Love the Lord God with all your heart, all your mind and all your soul, and love your neighbor as yourself."** (Mt 22:37, 39; Mk 12:30-31; Lk 10:27) **This is your true purpose.** Many people have difficulty loving themselves. As a result, they have difficulties loving others. To love yourself is not selfish. It is the ability to show an appreciation for the life energy that animates you. Loving yourself is freeing and releasing in nature. It gives you the energy to live life with kindness and compassion. When you love yourself, you will be compassionate, kinder and more patient, because you learn to be so with yourself. Selfishness is the act of thinking only of yourself and of not loving yourself. Selfishness is the fear that you will not get what you perceive as your just due. Selfishness is fear, pure and simple. Appreciate the life energy within everything and make a conscious effort to become one with this life, for it is God the Father.

Appreciate your choices, and understand that if God were to enter your life and set events and circumstances, it would become His life and His choices. You would be robots without choice. Now do not confuse surrendering of your choices to the Father and wanting God to set things in certain order. When you desire for God to work and give, you want without any effort. That would be asking the Father to be a genie. But when you surrender to God your life and choices, then you are asking God to help you learn your lessons quickly. You are giving the Father all that you have. This is good. **It is the total surrender to God that brings much growth spiritually.**

You have learned that you are on earth to practice what you learned. In spirit you do not have the concrete evidence of your beliefs, attitudes and thoughts as you have on earth. All is mental in spirit. While on earth you do not see that the circumstances of your life are due to your beliefs, attitudes and thoughts. Words describe thoughts, attitudes and beliefs. They bring into your life these types of situations. In this manner, if you think thoughts of negativity, that is, in thinking only in terms of bad, evil, being dismayed and critical, this is the type of circumstances you will have in your life. Because it takes time for these attitudes, beliefs and thoughts to materialize, people do not make the connection. However, you have learned that all events are in your life for a learning experience. This is your way of becoming more alive, spiritually.

You have learned that you choose before birth many things—parents, culture, race, nationality, gender, financial circumstances and education of the family. You choose body size, coloring of hair, eyes and such. You choose how healthy the body will be and how rich or poor you will be in the future life. All these choices are made with a certain life goal in mind. These situations help you learn the lessons of this lifetime more easily, for instance, a need to learn to love yourself more. There are many ways to go about this; we will demonstrate two. One, you could enter a very loving family and from them learn to be accepting and gentle with yourself. Or you could enter as the underdog in a culture and learn to overcome with love and patience. So, with this in mind, do not fight against your choices in life. Take what you are and where you are, and increase and grow in spirit, personality and in every way. Always seek to improve and better your life situation. Understand that money and the possessions of this life are here for you to use as a learning experience. They are not the ultimate goal, but simply a method to motivate certain lessons. While you seek to improve, you are learning some very important lessons. Growth and improvement are spiritual methods to get people motivated. Understand that living is doing and accomplishing. Be easy with yourself, and seek to understand yourself well. In this manner you will grow spiritually.

People are not always aware they are learning, because life is lived in many dimensions at the same time. Each person is very deep and can accomplish much simply by seeking to better themselves. As you change, the circumstances of your life change. What thrilled you in the past will no longer be attractive. It is as Jesus said: "When I was a child, I spoke as a child; now that I am a man, I speak as a man." (1 Cor 13:11) As you grow educationally, mentally, spiritually, you outgrow some old thought patterns and rise to new levels. Always seek to improve yourself and your life. Education gives the best method to improvement. Education can come through reading or learning new skills, and not always in a school setting.

Seek improvement in attitudes, thoughts, words, and you will see an improvement in your life. It will come insidiously and slowly and will be a strong growth. If you take but one or two thoughts from this lesson, it must be these: **God loves you irrevocably and always. Watch your words, because out of YOUR mouth comes YOUR life-style.** Words are powerful, strong, and they bring to bear fruit of like conditions. Seal these two thoughts deep in your mind. Recall these words, and they will help you live on earth at this time.

Our primary goal is to have you open your mind to the inner learning that is available to all people. Through the inner mind will come all instructions for your survival on earth during the coming events. Continue always to improve your connection to the Father within and pray, little children, pray much. Pray as you have been taught. Then allow time for the input of the Father into your mind. Understand that you will not always be aware of His input, but allow time for Him to speak to you. Feel His Great Love for you, individually and as a people. When events in your life seem overpowering, recall that these are in your life as a learning experience. Say to yourself, **"This too shall pass, for only the Love of the Father is constant and never ending."**

Keep these words in your mind and take them into your inner heart. Allow the Father to help you. Remember that HE only helps and will not live your life for you. To receive His help, keep on doing what you are doing now and ask for His help. It is yours, as long as you are the one initiating and performing the task.

The Brotherhood

Spiritual "Knowing" Through Understanding the Energy Centers
(Brotherhood, October 27, 1990)

The lessons on energy centers are important lessons, because they teach you to "know" within the magnitude of the Spiritual aspects of your life. All you learn about spirit and how it works will increase your understanding of yourself. When you can understand these different aspects, there will be many benefits. You will be more understanding of others and yourself, more patient, kind, tolerant and more trusting of your God-Mind connection. You will be able to call upon the different aspects of your REAL self to aid you in living on earth. Most of all, you will be honest with yourself. A popular saying is, "Above all, to thine own self be true."

Use what you have learned daily by calling on these centers to remain open. Allow the inner awareness of these different centers to open your mind to new ideas, new abilities and new life. Those who have been praying, meditating and practicing will have many life improvements. There will be more activity that is beneficial. This activity is good to and for you. It will be pleasing to your inner and outer self. As you use the different centers to live daily, you will find more power in your abilities, more strength and conviction in your life circumstances. Here are some suggestions on how to use what you have learned.

When events in your life seem overpowering, out of control or out of kilter, simply call out the words "Divine Order," over and over, until you feel a calm and peace enter your heart and mind. Then you will have the assurance that truly Divine Order has taken place and all things will be "right." These words will bring to your heart and mind the remembrance of proper alignment, the ability to manage and cope. You will know that there is a Higher Power setting events, people and things in their true place.

When you are faced with the need to explain anything or to give a talk, call upon Divine Knowledge. The release of eternal knowingness will come alive with the right words, phrases and tones. Or, if you need to have strength to face any situation or person, call upon Divine Strength, and the energy center will release a jet stream of strength to see you through any situation. It will also give the ability to face any person, no matter how difficult. If you are in need of motivation to carry you through some situation, call upon Divine Power to release its jet stream of energy, and you will have the necessary strength, gumption and power to do anything.

As Divine Life becomes active within, the tempo of your life will pick up. New and interesting people will enter your life, and there will be better living situations. Strive to improve your life in spirit, and it will be improved on earth. Life is interconnected with all dimensions and planes. Heaven is not separated from earth. **Spirit is not a separate life from the life you are living on earth. It is all together and ONE.** So, as you pray and improve your spiritual life—by trusting in God and having faith in His Powers and Abilities, your earthly life will show vast improvements.

Many people improve their earthly life and in that way improve their spiritual life. Improve your spiritual life, and your earthly life will become much better in all ways. Whatever you do to improve yourself will improve your entire and real self. Remember that if you are not growing, you are digressing, and digression is death! **Keep your focus on prayer and meditation, then all things will be added to you.** This is Jesus' promise to the world. He said, "Seek ye first the kingdom of God, and all things will be added unto you." (Mt 6:33) This means to put first things first. **Begin by seeking the Father within.** Then all the events, circumstances and situations in your life will be improved. It would be good to read this entire sermon[4] of Jesus' as it also includes The Lord's Prayer and much, much more of what we have been teaching.

These "added things" are those events, circumstances and situations that will help you achieve your life plan—and your life will be improved as you get unpleasantness out of the way. When you find yourself in difficult situations, simply ask God to help, then all Power, Strength, Wisdom and whatever you need will flow within you. **God works through you and the situations of your life.** In unpleasant situations, ask to learn the lesson of the event quickly. Then look forward to peace of mind, happiness and good. As you learn the lessons of this life, you are rewarded in your spirit life. Power and strength come from within, because they come from the Divine Source of All.

Stay in an attitude of prayer, and keep your meditations daily. The events, situations and circumstances of your life will change in grand and magnificent ways. The biggest changes will be within you. **As you change inside, the events of your life change dramatically.** At first it may be difficult to notice the changes, but in time you will see great changes in your attitudes, reactions and in the simple way you live life on earth. There will be slight changes at first in your health—mental,

---

[4] The Sermon on the Mount (see Mt 5–7).

emotional and physical, in this order. Then those people who are no longer in line with your new outlook on life will leave gently. You will not react to people or events in the same old way. New activities and situations will be in your life. There may be a complete change of friends because you will be attracting to yourself like-minded people. As you seek to remain in connection to God-Mind through prayer and meditation, there will be improvements in all areas of your life, beginning with your own attitudes, which will be more positive, more self-assured and hopeful.

With this we have completed the lessons on the energy centers. We spent much time on them because they are important to your spiritual growth. You have learned much; now use what you have learned. Use all the lessons, daily. Most important, remember your need for daily prayer and meditation. This is your nourishment in spirit and on earth. It is the bread of life, which will bring many added benefits to your entire and real self. **Remember always that within you is all you need to live this and every life.** Your entire concentration needs to remain in your inner connection to God-Mind.

The Brotherhood

22

Maintaining a Strong Connection

How Expectations Short-Cut Your God-Connection
(Brotherhood, November 17, 1990)

WE COME TO IMPART KNOWLEDGE. It is our loving duty to aid and assist all who are seeking their own connection to the Father within. We urge each person to practice what has been given and to keep an ongoing dedication to the meditations, which is needed to keep your connection strong. The connection short-circuits on your side, and it is only through prayer and meditation that you can bring yourself into alignment with the Father.

We understand how you think this is too pat or too easy, but believe us, it is not very easy to keep the lines of communication open wide. It is not always easy, as you have found, to remain faithful to this way of life. The difficulty is the earth-mind consciousness. It may be difficult for some people on earth to know when they have slipped into race consciousness. There is a surefire way of noting when you have slipped: race consciousness will tell you that you are not getting results. This earth-mind consciousness will have you set unreal expectations. When things are not going as you expected, there is a question about how you are thinking. This is the crux of our lesson today.

The lesson today is about expectations and how they interfere with your connection to Universal Knowledge and Love. To expect certain events to transpire in a definite way and at a definite time, is you placing your will above God's Will. Always expect that whatever results come from your prayers are good. But do not put definite plans of action and outcomes into your mind, because then you will certainly be disappointed. You cannot know the workings of God. **Expect God to bring only Good into your life, then see everything that happens as good.**

Many times you must first be cleansed of elements, relationships and situations. So the workings of Spirit will give the appearance of bad results, but in the end you will look back and say, "That which I thought was bad, was in reality very good." When we say to pray for what you want, leaving it up to God, we mean to see and take all answers as Good, no matter how they seem in the beginning. You could never know the final results with your meager mentality. It takes the mentality of the Whole Spirit and Energy of God to know how to cleanse, mold and take what you have and end with something Good. When what you deem bad happens in your life, like an illness, loss of job or perhaps a breaking of a relationship, this is the time to repeat to yourself over and over, **"God gives Good, and this is happening in my life for my good. Only Good can come to me through this."** Use this affirmation with all problems and see them turn into blessings.

Pronounce every event in your life as Good. This is how to ensure that the final results will be Good, only as God knows how to give. Let us use an analogy.

As a child you are trying to build a tower of blocks. If you do not know how to begin, you will stack them in such a manner that they will fall easily. Without clearing a spot, you continue to stack and they continue to fall. Then your father or mother comes along and you ask for help. First the parent will clear a spot, and this is not the result the child wants. He riles, cries and throws a temper tantrum without waiting for the help to begin. He thinks, "I did not get the answer I wanted, so asking my parents does not work." Gently and lovingly, the parent says, "Wait, and let's clean a place first; then we will build a large tower, and I will show you how to accomplish this yourself."

This, our dear children, is exactly what happens many times on earth. People pray and ask for certain events, but are not willing to wait for the final results to happen. Often there is a period of cleansing, when everything seems the darkest and bleakest. When you find that you are in the darkest possible place, know that soon light will enter your world and answers will come. Perhaps there must be a cleansing for good results to happen. At other times, there is still some learning taking place and, until this is completed, you cannot progress. Or perhaps there is something better for you in Spirit. Soon it will be clear to you that the wait was worth it.

It is during these dark times that you must remain faithful to what you have learned. Remember, there is a certain ebb and flow to life. **Only God knows exactly when to bring something into your life for the Good of all.** So, if there is a delay in your prayer, ask first for the lesson of this situation to be made clear to you. Ask for help in learning this lesson quickly and ask for help to remain faithful.

As life ebbs and flows, do not become afraid that you will always be in such dilemmas. No, what happens is that the ebbs and flows will be less dramatic. There will be a leveling of the ebb and flow in your life. That is, the wave of ebb and flow will not fluctuate so dramatically. As you begin to rely totally on

Spirit and the workings of Spirit, you will acquire patience and tolerance. First you will look for the lesson that is in every situation. You will flow with Spirit, and in this flow there will be peace in your heart and gentleness in your demeanor. As you learn, it is not things that are important, but the condition of your mind and heart.

Do not become concerned with the economy of the nation or the world. You are living a more universal life and as such there is always supply. **The Source of all your Good comes from the Father within, as you seek to find Him in your heart and mind. This is where your true wealth lies.** There are many changes taking place in the minds and hearts of men, and these inner changes bring outer changes. At times the appearances will be upsetting, but "know within" that all change comes from God, because there is only God and nothing else.

Do not expect too much from people. Remember that each individual is on earth to learn and as such is in the midst of a learning process. Be tolerant of one another. Look for the lessons that are to be learned in every relationship. Pray one for the other, and show love as kindness, tolerance and patience. This is your duty and inner desire. Jesus said it with what is now called the golden rule in today's language: **"Treat each person as you would want to be treated."** (See Mt 7:12) Expect to be treated well and treat each person equally as well. With this simple rule, you will be in alignment with Spirit and with the workings of Spirit. Every person is on earth to learn this important lesson. Some practice this on Sundays and holidays but forget it on other days. Some expect to be treated well but will not treat a man of a different race or perhaps of a different country well. These prejudices are not in keeping with this commandment. You cannot treat another well if you expect more of him than of yourself. We are all one, and as such we are all seekers of Truth and Light. **Help your fellow humans by thinking as well of them as you do of yourselves. Put no person above you or beneath you.**

Now what and how to use expectations? This is how to "expect." Expect only Good to come from the Father within. Expect that no matter what the outer appearances are, the results will be good. Declare and affirm this statement often. Use affirmations to remind yourself of truths. **God is Good, and as such He can give only good. There is only God and nothing else.** Do not remain in the void of race consciousness. Lift your mind and thinking towards the Good. No matter what is happening in your life at this time, repeat to yourself over and over, **"I rely totally on God, Giver of Good. God will work this situation or relationship out for the Good of all concerned."**

Use affirmations to tell yourself truths. It is a much better process of praying than continually asking, because when you request or ask over and over, you give yourself the impression that God can withhold or give the opposite of what you have requested. **It is better to ask once and then affirm that God is now answering the prayer for the Good of all concerned.** Do not look at your life and say, "This situation or relationship is bad." Instead say, "This situation is in my life for a learning process. I will learn this lesson quickly and go on to other lessons. I expect the end results will be good for me and for everyone concerned." If a relationship is the cause of concern, then say the same for that relationship. **Always, always forgive! Send thoughts of love to every person.**

Soon we will start on new material, but first we will assist you to practice the lessons that you have already learned. **The connection to the Father within is your goal.** It is the best end result you could ever possibly desire. The connection is clouded by your doubts and fears, angers and depleting emotions. This is how we help: we remind you of the Truth. **God is the Giver of all life. He is constant and Loving at all times.** Recognize this truth and be healed.

The Brotherhood

"Setbacks" Are Evolutionary Changes
(Brotherhood, December 9, 1990)

We give help in connecting to the most powerful Source in the Universe. You are on the road to recovery in spirit. Our lesson last time on expectations is one that is necessary in these days of change. Expect these changes to bring you good, as only God gives. **Remember that God is all Love, Pure raw Energy, and He is non-judgmental. He loves because He sees the perfection in everyone.**

What appear as setbacks are in reality evolutionary changes. When old issues come into your life again and again, there is something for you to resolve and/or forgive. If you feel that you are on a treadmill going nowhere fast, recall that there is something or someone who needs to be forgiven. Forgive fate or destiny, if that is how you view it. Forgive yourself for making mistakes. Forgive the ones who instigated the changes that are occurring in your life. When you feel like fighting something, or that you are in a fight, realize that the fight is within you, and look there for the issue.

Some people are facing issues that are ancient and need resolving in order for them to rest in the eternalness of God. Realize that all you need is within you, because all you need is God. This is not just a saying, but Truth. **What every person is looking for in life is their connection to God the Father, who is within every person.**

Stop looking for your security in other people, job, club or anything on the outside of you. Look for your security within yourself. True security is found within, as you learn to depend and rely on the Father. He is unfailing and always just. The security that people seek is the security that is found only within as they rely on the Father to provide for them richly. God knows what you need to complete your lifetime goals. Judge not what is happening in your life, because you do not remember these goals in your conscious mind. **Trust that as**

you rely on God the Father, He will not allow you to come to any real harm.

In every situation, forgive and forgive until it is a reality within your heart and mind at the same time. There are times when you can understand forgiveness mentally but do not feel it, and there are times when you feel forgiveness and do not think it. Forgiveness must be felt and used mentally and emotionally as you treat others and yourself. **Pray to see all things in reality and to be able to forgive completely.** This is true prayer, and it is the kind of prayer that clears old issues and old hurts. There is no need to justify another one's behavior or second-guess their motives. It is your duty to forgive yourself, for your advancement and spiritual betterment.

The Brotherhood

Love Is the Message and Reason (Christmas Eve)
(Brotherhood, December 24, 1990)

We are happy that some of you have written your letters of appreciation.[5] Please keep this as a tradition. It is beneficial to the writer and to the receiver of the letters. When you can appreciate and love family members, then there will be much healing.

Love is the message, and Love was the reason Jesus came to earth. People still in this day consider God to be a God of judgment. They think He judges harshly, but in reality God is Love. He is the totality of Love. He is forgiving like no one else. Jesus knew this in such a way that He volunteered to come to earth to teach this. Love is many things, but most important it is healing.

---

[5] In 1990, everyone in the family was very tight on money. The Brotherhood and/or Mother Mary asked that instead of gifts we give each other letters of appreciation. This we did, and it was a very powerful and rewarding Christmas.

During this week when Jesus' birth is celebrated, let every person remember the real reason Jesus came. Remember that Jesus always taught that the Heavenly Father is within each heart. This is the place to contact Him. It will be through every person's heart that healing will come. See, children, peace cannot come into a world without love. **As more and more people begin to recognize that God is Love, and that this is His true nature, peace will enter their loving hearts.** This in turn will create loving homes, loving schools and cities. Peace will enter nations through peoples' hearts and no other way. As you begin to spread this message through the very act of becoming more loving, peace will enter your home, family and city. **Love enters first; then comes peace.**

We asked each person to write a letter of appreciation to their loved ones. We appreciate each of you. Although we do not have an awareness of earthly existence as it is lived today, we understand that being true to these lessons can be an inconvenience. So, in this light, we are deeply appreciative of your pursuit to strengthen your connection to the Father. As you increase in spirit, you find that earthly things will not be as important as before. We are not saying that earthly things are to be put aside. No, in no way is this true. You came to earth to live an earthly life. It is important to live it to the fullest. What we are saying is that you will remember what is real and not get caught up in vanities.

The Brotherhood

PART 4

1991
Faith and Trust

23

On Faith

Setting Goals Increases Faith
(Brotherhood, January 6, 1991)

GOOD DAY, we are the Brotherhood of God with a new beginning, as this is the first meeting of the new year. As usual, we ask that you set some goals. Review the goals you set for last year and the year before that. See what has been accomplished and what is no longer a desire of yours. Review and consider which of the goals you are still interested in. It will be beneficial to take a look at these goals, as they will tell how far you have progressed. Perhaps there are some changes in your needs and desires.

Whatever you desire, write it down. At first it may be material things; this is fine, as they are the issues of your earthly life. If you desire to improve yourself, then state the end results. Perhaps you need to learn to speak before a group, or you desire to improve your health by taking care of the body. Or there are still some old, unresolved angers that are causing trouble, and you desire to eliminate them. This is how to look at your life and set goals.

There are many good ways to set goals without them becoming a concentration on material things. Make a list of what you desire, and then choose which of the material things you most need and want. Add these to your goals. Make a list of your entire life by activities. Include physical, mental, emotional, psychic and spiritual. In the mental category, you could include schooling, seminars, classes or new attitudes and thought patterns. Emotionally, include romance, time with a loved one, ways to improve your relationships with family, friends and making new friends. Psychically, perhaps you want to learn more about intuition, auras or concentration for meditation. Then add your goals for your spiritual development; you could read more about how others are seeking God, attend more sessions with us or go to a church. Increase your time for meditation or for a deeper meditation. In the physical, include safe activities of entertainment and recreational goals. Perhaps you will learn a new sport or take the family on outings in nature. Find better ways of preparing foods. This is how to break these goals down into categories, which will help you find many goals to set.

Once a month, take these goals out and reread them. Mark out those you have changed your mind about and add to the list anything you desire. As you read them, it will indicate how you are doing and will encourage you to keep on keeping on.

Now for our lesson on faith. As you set goals and set up a plan for living this next year, you are taking a step in increasing your faith. Faith can grow and does grow by believing in something. Believe in God, or in God, us and yourself. **Remember that the more and the bigger your belief, the greater is your faith.** Faith is not a constant; it fluctuates according to your belief. When you doubt yourself and others, your faith diminishes. We will learn more about faith throughout this year. For now, understand that **God is All Possibilities and All Potential.** When you believe this statement, you can believe that as His creation you have a small measure of these abilities. As you can believe that God will help, a measure of your abilities will be increased to His level.

Faith, like everything else in nature, grows according to the amount of light and nutrients provided. The light is your belief in God, All Mighty and All Powerful. The nutrients are your affirmations of faith. These affirmations help you increase and maintain your faith in an upward movement. Daily affirmations of faith help you keep focused. The use of daily affirmations helps when your faith quotient is low. They remind you of the Goodness of God and His nature.

God is always near. He is nearer than your breathing and your heartbeat. God is the life energy that flows through your body and mind. As such, He is in you as Pure Potential. Can you understand what this means? You have the full Potential of the Universe within. It is inherent and waiting to be used. It cannot be used only with your mind or only with your sensories; it must be used physically, mentally and emotionally, together, in order to have its full effect.

First, increase your faith and keep it high with daily affirmations of faith, prayers and meditations. Throughout the day, when your feelings are sagging or your thinking turns upon itself and you doubt or become anxious or upset, remind yourself with these affirmations that **you are One with All Potential. You are One with All possibilities.** When you tire of one particular affirmation, then set up a meditation to create a new one that is more in keeping with your growing faith. Say to yourself, **"I believe in God,"** and then list why you believe in **Him.** These are the best affirmations of faith. They come from your heart of hearts and are powerful.

Next, pray to the Father who is within to help you in all ways, and then list the ways. Say, **"I need help in believing today, Father,"** if this is the case. Or, **"I need help in doing,"** or

whatever your need is for that day. Ask for it. He is always willing to help, but because of freedom of choice, He waits for you to ask for help with sincerity and with earnestness.

Meditate and "see" in your meditation the accomplished deed. When you pray for success, which is an elusive and non-clear goal, you must define this success. Perhaps success to you is a new car, a new job or a new abode. Or perhaps to you success is simply having peace. You must define success or any goal that is not clear, like happiness. Do you want to be happy in your work, home or profession? If you list security, this is another word that is not clear. Remember that the prisoner is secure, but is this the security you desire? In your meditations, see these goals in their accomplishment. See yourself secure as you define it, happy and wealthy per your own definition. Then, as you concentrate on the accomplished picture, you will agree in your mind and heart that this is the desired picture, and you will be ready for the next step, which is the deed.

All the praying and meditating in the world will not help, if you do nothing. It takes action. It takes all of the above to complete your goals. Action is the step that completes the picture. When you are in the middle of action, you feel that you are really living. This is the way to live successfully in spirit and on earth. When it all comes together, you will be happier, because you are living on all levels of your life, and all levels are focused in purpose and deed, in the sense that your entire being has a finish line to reach. Your being is not aimlessly wandering through life, but is focused and heading towards a goal.

All the action, all the thinking and all the picturing will be of no avail if you do not have faith, first in God as Father and Provider, then in yourself as His creation. Many people today do not have enough faith in themselves. What they and you need is faith in the Father within to provide all manner of opportunities, possibilities and deeds. Nothing in life is free except what the Father gives. Let us review what God gives freely, and then you will understand that the rest must be earned. God freely gives us eternal life, freedom of choice and a physical body that is marvelous. Take a moment to look closely at your body and contemplate its workings. The functions of this body go along without interruption and without you thinking about it. The body regenerates new cells. Within the body are different kinds of cells; each has their own special task. The heart cell does not act or look like the skin cell. Each is unique and important. This all happens without your conscious awareness of what is going on in the body. You are not responsible for the functions of your body—God is. You are, however, responsible for its fuel and its care.

Now all the rest is up to you, dear children. **It is up to each of you to focus your mind and heart with purpose and to do something toward completing the purpose.** This is living on earth. It is the manner and method to live life to its fullest. In so doing, you will care for the body, mind and heart.

Improve yourself in all areas of your life and see the wondrous ways your life will take on new meaning, new enjoyments and new purpose. The first area to concentrate on is your connection to God the Father, because He is All and He is your lifeline.

As an analogy, recall the picture of one of your astronauts walking in space. He has a lifeline that connects him to the spaceship and provides air to breathe, and it is his way back to the spaceship. In this analogy, God is the spaceship: He provides you life and all manner of Good. Space is your life on earth: it is not your real environment, but it is a way to accomplish a task. Prayer and meditation are your lifeline to God: these are your way back to your real environment and home. If you lose your connection, you float in space until another spaceship can link up with you; it could also be your death. So, in our analogy, if you lose your connection to the Father, you will float in darkness and emptiness, far from your real environment, and it could possibly mean death.

All areas of your life are important. Set goals, give purpose and direction to your mind and heart, and then act to accom plish these goals. **Prayer and meditation are your lifeline**—do these daily without fail.

The Brotherhood

Faith Is the Substance of Your Future
(Brotherhood, January 19, 1991)

Since we last met, there have been great changes taking place in the world. These changes will continue until such time as there is a new way of life and a new beginning. The changes as you already know will escalate, and not only will governments topple but also nations, lands and seas. The time of change is upon you, and now is the moment of preparation. The preparation is within, and this is always so. Inner contact with God-Mind will carry you through all types of changes, wars, earthquakes and terrible storms. We come with a message of hope for your future and a new sense of well-being.

We began the year with the theme of faith. Understand that it will take much faith to see you through the coming days. Do not decry the technology that will be lost, for it has been used largely for destruction. The technology that will remain will be the technology of peace and healing. We will continue to increase your power of faith, for there is power in faith, and it is the power to move mountains and seemingly unmovable objects.

We will refer to the Father Creator as Universal Mind, Cosmic Mind or God-Mind. We see in the daily press the word "God" being decimated and blasphemed with the concept of a God who is in favor of the atrocities of war. The very word Universal Mind, Cosmic Mind or God-Mind gives you a sense of enlargement. Think of the Father Creator as being cosmic and above the warring of earth, above the warring of any planet. He is much too loving to be in favor of the abuses of war. In your prayers, think of Cosmic Mind and see a greater picture enter your mind, a larger concept of our Father Creator. There is a need of an enlarged picture and an enlarged concept, which will bring you closer to an understanding of how gigantic and above-board the Father is. He is greater than your ideas, concepts or imaginings, and He is, above all, more loving than you can conceive.

Faith is the substance of your future. It is the cosmic clay that you use to mold your very own future. What you believe is what you receive. Remember that our elder brother Jesus said, "Whatsoever things you desire, pray believing and it shall be done," or words to this effect. He also said, "Ask of the Father believing." (Mt 21:22; see also Lk 11:9 and Mk 9:23) That means to believe you are receiving it now. As you can see, belief is the key. To believe is not simple, for within you are beliefs that are the beliefs of the race-mind consciousness. All the things that have ever been believed are within you as the race-mind consciousness. It would be good to read the passages of the Bible that we speak of, for within the words are life. Are you seeing a pattern emerging? **Do you recognize that what is within is more important than what is without?** Now, how to change these basic beliefs.

Each person can begin to affect their belief system and to change these subtle and insidious beliefs. It takes time and, above all, patience to make these changes, and yet, when the changes come, they will take on a speed that will astound everyone. It is much like pushing a great boulder up a mountain. At first it requires a great amount of effort to move. It becomes more and more difficult, but once you have reached the top and there is a leveling off, you will become inspired and your energy will be renewed. Then the last great effort of change, and the boulder reaches the top. Once on the crest, the boulder stands still and soon begins its rapid descent. This is an analogy of how it will be to make changes in your deep belief system. At first there is a need for much effort on your part to even budge the old beliefs. Then the changes will begin and, as you make progress, doubt will enter and burden the beliefs with its own weight. During this time you will feel ambivalent and swing from faith to doubt; this is natural. Keep in mind that once the changes of belief are made, you will rapidly gain ground and it will be effortless and easy. The greatest hurdle is the changing of your basic beliefs.

Now here is some of what needs to be changed. You must enlarge your basic concept of the Father Creator into one of a great Cosmic Mind. You need to understand that you cannot put any limits on His power, for He created this and all universes. When an answer is not forthcoming, realize that there is something limiting the answer. It is most likely one of your inner basic beliefs. This is where to seek out the delay. Do not belittle or demean yourself because you have a limited view of the Cosmos and the Father's creations. This is one of the reasons you came to earth, to gain a larger picture of the Creator, to learn and to see in three dimensions your changing beliefs.

Let us take a moment to read the words of Jesus and see that He said, "Whatsoever and All" things are to be asked of "the Father, whose great pleasure it is to give." (Lk 12: 32) Where is the limit? Did Jesus place a limit on the answer? Did Jesus say pray to the Father only for health matters? Now what is wrong with the picture of the healers on your television who say, I can heal in the name of Jesus, but God said you must send money? Who puts the limit on God? They do: these men say God can heal bodies, but He cannot provide the healer with substance. So the limit is within their own minds. Did Jesus say pray only for righteous things and not for evils? No, because he knew that the same concept is different to different people. There are those people who think being righteous is going to war. And there are those who think they bring peace by causing civil disobedience. See how men justify their own beliefs and say this is the way God chooses, this is the way that is right? Jesus did not place limits or make any statement that required a judgment. He simply said, "Ask anything in prayer, believing, and it will be done." Do you understand? Jesus said, "Done," over, completed!

What is a belief? How do you change your beliefs? You do it one thought at a time. You awaken in the morning and say, **"God-Mind is bigger than this Universe, this Cosmos, and He is infinitely more loving than I can imagine."** Repeating to yourself over and over truths that are universal will change your basic beliefs, because your inner self will recognize a Truth and will gladly embrace it.

Every conscious thought will take you into the great outer limits of inner space. You will magnify your concept of the Creator. You will see truly that nothing is impossible to Him. He wants to give. Jesus said, "It is the Father's great pleasure to give." So, who is limiting the gift? You and your basic beliefs. **Begin to understand that the substance, the material used to form the answer to your prayer, is your very own belief.** It is what you think and feel deeply as true or false. Make an effort to change your basic belief system. Yes, it's an effort to recall that when you are sad or discouraged, these feelings are false. When you begin to feel ambivalent, know deep within that you are making progress, for the ambivalence is a sign that you are accomplishing your goal of changing what you believe. You are expanding your deep-seated inner beliefs. It is the core of your belief system that requires change. As the good steward, you have protected these beliefs and are reluctant to change them. But this is the time of change, it is the purpose of this incarnation to change, and the changes that need to be made are within, deep inside of yourself.

Now is the time for the shackles to be torn away from any belief that limits the Cosmic Father. It is a time of change, and the greatest changes will be those changes that are made within your very self. Do this now, and avoid the terrible trauma of changing as the earth moves. When the Earth moves literally on its axis, many will change their deep inner belief system, but this type of change will be traumatic and needless. When the earth moves, people will call out to their version of God, and in their limited view they will see that the true Creator is greater than ever perceived. They will die in fear and in trauma, and some will be lost in darkness, because this will be their basic belief. Most will change and expand their view of the Father Creator in that split moment and will be received into the kingdom of Love and Light. **We say make this life worthwhile, and change while it is still a matter of choice, a matter of love.** Make these changes and believe that with the Father Creator all things are possible. Do not limit Him or yourself. You can be healed and then have a time of enjoyment and the use of a healthy body. Your needs for substance can be met, and then you will have a time of enjoyment and plenty. Your needs will be met no matter what they are, if only you believe they can.

Start this very minute to instill in your heart of hearts the hope of good things to come, hope for peace in the midst of war, hope for change in the midst of rebellion, hope for plenty in the midst of great need, hope for health in the midst of illness and pain, hope of joy in the midst of sadness, and hope of a changing self, a changing world and changing universe which will be infinitely better in all ways.

The greatest change will be the choice for change. Through the choice to change, a great change will take place within. **Understand that most times the greatest changes come with a simple decision to change.** Expand your view of what is real and what is inconsequential. Expand your view of why you are on earth and what is important. It is important that you accept change, for it is real, but the greatest choice is to make changes for the better.

The Brotherhood

Shape Your Faith with Affirmations
(*Brotherhood, February 1, 1991*)

Include more meditations in your session. As you already know, praying is talking to God-Mind, and meditating is listening to the stillness in which God the Father speaks. It is a paradox, but it is one of those paradoxes that is true of Spirit. **The Creator speaks in stillness.** What you will hear is complete silence. At times during a meditation, you may pick up words, a thought or ideas, but most times you will hear complete stillness. **It will be in stillness and silence that you receive the most.** Most of your mind does not function on the conscious level. The Creative Father speaks to that larger part of your mind which remains unaware. It is in this area of the mind that you are able to truly communicate with your Creator. This is confusing to many, for they think that if they do not hear with their physical ears, it is not happening. You already know that much happens in the unseen and you hear in the unheard. It is this part of your world that is the most active, if you will activate it through prayer and meditation. Then you will be able to hold on in faith. This brings us to the topic of our lesson.

Faith, as you already know, is the Cosmic clay you use to mold your future. Think of yourself as a potter and recall that to make an article you need clay, water, hands and an idea. There must be an idea, however general. You must know what you want. Then, after the article is made, it must be fired. It must be set into a furnace of great heat. So, too, your faith is fired. It is in the furnace of earth-mind consciousness heat that brings forth the beauty of your faith. How is this an analogy for faith? The idea is the same. What is it you wish? Perhaps it is health, or a healing of relationships or gainful employment. Whatever the need, this is the idea. You will use your mind as hands to mold this idea. You will set up guidelines for whatever it is you need, say, for instance, a business. The person sets up guidelines. He sets some goals for this business and knows what he desires. This is his use of Cosmic clay. He is ready to mold his desire. Now, in order to shape a wad of clay, it requires much water. We will say that in order to shape your faith, you need to use a large amount of affirmations. The affirmations do not change the Father, but they do keep your faith uplifted. They bring to mind the truths of your faith. **Shape your faith with affirma-**

tions. Then desire is fired in the furnace of earth-mind consciousness.

Begin simply and make up your very own affirmations.
Simply say, "God the Father Creator who made me will not
leave me alone. He is proud of His creation. He will see me
through all things. This is what I desire, but if the Father has
something better for me, I will accept all the good He gives."
When you have what appears as a setback, affirm that you
accept only the Good which the Father gives. You expect to
come out right in all situations. For instance, those who are
looking for work now would say something like this: "God has
the perfect place of employment for me. I am Divinely guided
to it, and all conditions are working out right." In this way, you
do not allow your mind and heart to fall into earth-mind
consciousness, which will say, "See how long it takes? This is
all rubbish, nothing will happen. You are suffering, and all will
go bad. Things are going to get worse." As you affirm, remind
yourself that things that are worked out in Spirit will happen at
the right time. In Spirit, there is no time. There is only now.
Now you are already doing your perfect work. **You are already
gainfully employed, and it will happen on earth at the right
time—not one minute later or sooner than perfect timing.**

About the furnace of earth-mind consciousness—it is not
only a furnace, but an intense heaviness when you are inside of
this consciousness. This is why you feel so light when you are
connected to God-Mind. Earth-mind consciousness weighs
you down with its negativity. It will cause you to doubt yourself, others, us and even the Father Creator. When doubts and
heaviness of spirit assail you from all sides, remember that this
is the furnace of earth-mind consciousness. This is the process
of creating by being fired in intense heat and heaviness. **This is
the time to meditate and to reconnect to the Father Creator. It
is a time to be faithful to your meditations and to your search
for a true connection to God-Mind.**

Recall that Jesus said to many whom he healed, "It is done
as you believe." The belief Jesus spoke of is the core belief of

your inner self. **It is the belief in something Greater than yourself. It is a belief in a benevolent Creator. It is a belief in love and in the order of the universe.**

All around you are evidences of the Good Creator. This is a well-run world. There is an ecology to this universe. Look within this world and see all its differing parts as unity. This same unity is what you are to believe in. It is this same Universal Unity that will bring good to you. There is no magic; there is work. It is work in the beginning to have faith when you lack it. It takes effort to make time for prayer and meditation, but understand that through prayer and meditation you increase your faith. During meditation, repeat statements of truth as affirmations. Say to yourself in meditation all that you "know" as Truth. In this manner you are reaching that part of your mind that is accessible to the Creative Father. Then become still and allow a silence to enter your being with healing and love.

Here is the formula for faith. **Use affirmations to keep your mind on Truths. Use liberal amounts of affirmations to keep you connected to God-Mind.** It is easy to sink into earth-mind consciousness without realizing it. When you find yourself in despair, realize that you have been using earth-mind consciousness. Meditate with the express purpose of connecting once again to God-Mind consciousness, which is filled with love, hope, peace, serenity and truth.

The Brotherhood

Steps to Entering God-Mind
(Brotherhood, February 17, 1991)

This year we are concentrating on faith. Let us take faith and use it to its fullest. Take faith as it is within you, and take hold of the idea that this very faith is active in you. Everyone, from this moment on, needs his faith to assure himself of a complete connection to the Father within. Remember not to look to appearances, as they will lead in many different directions. Do not rely on your feelings, as the feeling nature is slow to come up past the earth-mind consciousness. This is what happens in the feeling nature: the nature of your sensations gets caught up in comfort and not in truth. It will settle in where it is comfortable, then tell you that this is the right place. After all, see how comfortable it feels: it must be right. In order to expand and grow, there is a measure of "un-ease" and at times discomfort, but it is not completely uncomfortable. To go beyond your comfort zone is to grow past your old limits. This is what your feeling nature does—it sets up limits.

The Father Creator is unlimited, and it is your potential also to be unlimited. Your feeling nature will tell you this is not true; you must feel comfortable at all times. During this time, use faith to reassure yourself that the discomfort will be only for a little while. Soon the feelings will find their measure of comfort in this new environment. This comfort will be real and true, because it is the comfort of being in God-Mind. There is a complete and total reliance on the Source of all Good.

By this time, if you have been faithful in living these lessons, many of you will have entered God-Mind consciousness. Some of you will not have stayed in this consciousness because of the discomfort that is sensed. This is confusing to people. The human is in search of complete and total comfort and ease. He thinks of utopia as a state of complete and total comfort in every area of his being. God-Mind consciousness is truth, the ultimate in comfort. It comes only when you are totally immersed in God-Mind and have the ability to stay in this great mind at all times. So far, there has been only one person who has lived on earth who has achieved this, and that is our elder brother Jesus. He is at all times immersed in God-Mind and lives only through God-Mind. Yet even he had some periods of time when there was discomfort. Mostly, it was when he would begin to sympathize with the people. Then, instantly, he would realize that he needed to remain in God-Mind in order to live his goal of demonstrating every person's potential.

Have faith that you are in God-Mind consciousness when you have done the next steps. Remind yourself that your feelings may not be telling you the truth.

The steps to entering God-Mind daily are:

1. **Meditate.** Enter your temple and request that you be connected to God-Mind. Have some symbol that will signify to your mind that you are in God-Mind; for some people it is a great, brilliant light coming from above. It could be music, or a special place in the temple that you enter to denote the entering of God-Mind consciousness. Tell yourself that you will go about your daily activities, but that it will be from the standpoint of God-Mind consciousness. Allow Divine Love to enter your being. There place any concerns to be worked out in Spirit, then awaken.

2. **Pray for the state of God-Mind consciousness.** Request with all your heart and mind to enter this Supreme Consciousness with ease. The request must be sincere and with earnestness. Then go about your daily activities.

3. Throughout the day, **affirm that you are in God-Mind consciousness** no matter what you are feeling. In this state of mind you are connected to the Source of all Good. Affirm that your needs are being met in an orderly fashion, and at the right time they will appear in your life. Affirm positively that no matter what is occurring in your life, it will improve as you remain in God-Mind consciousness.

4. **Throughout the day, be grateful to God-Mind.** Simply say, "Thank you Father, for the ability to enter your Great Mind and live this day from the perspective of Spirit."

5. **Remain faithful to these exercises.** Do them daily, either in the evening or in the morning, whichever is convenient for you. If you do your meditation in the evening for the next day, you will simply say, "For the next 24 hours," as you enter your meditation.

To remain faithful to your course, affirm the following or something similar: **"I live in God-Mind and do not worry or concern myself with exterior events, no matter how pressing** the need. In God-Mind I am completely taken care of: all my needs are being met at the right time and in the right manner."

It will be through this connection that every person will receive their own instruction. You will not fear anything or any event in the future, because you are in the ultimate state, and you will, in this reality, begin to enter the consciousness that gives access to your full potential. In this consciousness you will be able to heal, levitate and do all the things Jesus did and does today. In this state of mind, you are able to use your fullest potentialities.

Now see peace in your lives. Within yourself see changes for the better. Pray for yourself first and then for your world. Peace is the future, and in peace you will live no matter where or what is happening in the world. **First of all, peace must be released through the hearts and minds of men.** As more and more people pray for peace, it will be seen on earth. Practice the steps to living in God-Mind daily. As you practice this, you will see great changes, first within your mind, then your heart, and then your life. Do not put requirements on the changes. Simply accept that the changes in this state of mind will be for your good.

The Brotherhood

CHAPTER

24

Life's Ebb and Flow

Effects of Persistence in Prayers
(Brotherhood, March 3, 1991)

T HERE IS ALWAYS THE EBB AND FLOW OF LIFE. Now is a time of ebb in activity. You must remain strongly connected to the Father to ensure the viability of your loved ones. This is what prompts many people in the beginning—a concern for loved ones. Expand your mind to receive inner guidance from either the higher self, us or the Father Creator Himself. In the end, it is only God who is real, and we are real only because we are connected to Him. **Our reality is God and our existence is God, the Creator. This is how we are all interconnected and interdependent.** From now on, if you have remained faithful and lived these lessons, you may find many surprising events occurring. In the coming days you could receive your own individual messages, if they have not already begun. Everyone will not only be nudged, but overwhelmed with a message from within. It will be inexplicable, but it will be definite. Even those who have fallen by the wayside will be reminded of their initial search for spiritual things.

Let us explain what has happened in the current situation on earth.[1] There was the biggest inflow of prayer ever seen on earth since right before the last upending of earth. There were multitudes of people in many different lands praying for peace, and it happened in a short linear time-frame. In spirit it happened instantly. When this many people pray, they can move earthly events. **If all people would pray with the same earnestness and sincerity for the lifting of the earth-mind consciousness, it would happen in a short period of time.** Because of the coming together of the masses in prayer, there has been an uplifting to the race consciousness. For it to endure will require the same persistence in prayer, but this is where there will be a letdown in effort. Many people will simply return to their old ways. Even with this return, there will remain an upliftment of the race consciousness, but it is still steeped in fear, anger, hatreds and envies. Continue to pray for the uplifting of the race consciousness. Pray for the world and the whole planetary population. In this way, your prayers will rise to meet with our prayer for the preparations of the population of earth. **Continue to pray; ask for all world problems to be solved in a peaceful manner,** as there are still many problems that have not been addressed. Pray for a dying away of angers and an end to hostilities in the heart and mind of mankind. The war is over, but the anger, hatred, envy and desires for power are still in the hearts and minds of many of the people in this part of the world. It is a powder keg of emotions which can be riled into aggressions again if not released. Peace is lasting only when it has entered every heart and mind of the world's population. There is still danger in this part of the world and there is still a need for much prayer, not only for this immediate

---

[1] Referring to the ending of the Persian Gulf War.

area, but for the surrounding nations. In the land of Yugoslavia, there is unrest and aggression in the minds and hearts of men and in many other areas of the world.

Meet in small or large groups to pray for peace, hope, and for love to come into every heart and mind, beginning with your own. Your prayers will meet the prayers coming from other places of the world and will act as a balancing of power in the race consciousness.

Remember that what you pray for is the uplifting of the spirit of peace, hope and love in this world. Pray that each individual on earth remember his Divine plan and be prepared to meet back here in spirit with a new attitude towards life. Pray for a new uplifting of race consciousness for the next era.

Renew your commitment to yourselves, your higher selves and to your Creator. Understand that you must live this life as if it were your only life, but it needs to be lived on a dual level of earthly pursuits and spiritual pursuits. Duality will not interfere, but each level will enhance the other. It is not an "either-or" proposition, but a double plan of action. Give this life your all, but give more to your spiritual pursuits and to meditation and prayer. **Prayer and meditation are your connection to God-Mind, and it will be through this connection that your life will be enhanced on earth and in reality.**

We are strongly renewing our surge of spiritual help to every person who reads these messages, and we are supporting you in all your endeavors. There are more and more who are gathering together to flood each of you with hope and love. There is a huge congregation who are working from this side to assist. The many prayer groups will become one on earth as we are one in the Spirit of our loving Creator. Much love is flooding all prayer groups. You are near a breakthrough; the time is near.

The Brotherhood

Earthly Time Lags (Spring Review)
(Brotherhood, March 16, 1991)

In the past we have given you fundamental knowledge to increase your concepts and to expand your ability to see within. We have been building on what you learned in your outer life and are expanding your inner quest. Understand that what you seek with sincerity and earnestness is your connection to God-Mind. What you desire in the outer is ease and comfort. The ease and comfort you truly seek is attainable through your real life in spirit. The ideas of ease and comfort you desire on earth are what is being sold through your media. Do not be deceived, it is an illusion! You have a higher goal and a higher calling. You have been called to give service through example. It does not require much, except that you be faithful to your own quest. As you seek to know what to do to prepare for the future, you will be acting as role models for others.

Many times we tell you what is to happen, and when it does not happen on earth as soon as you think it should, you begin to doubt. Recall there is a lag time, and often it is quite long measured by earth time. Here we see results instantly. We see the future because we see into the heart and mind of your real self.

Recall that your earthly life is but a part of your real life. You live eternally, so the 50 to 100 years on earth is but a small fraction of your real lifetime. The situations of your life are the result of your real life goals—what is thought and believed by your real self, the whole self, who is only complete when you return to this part of creation. **Do not think you can analyze or find the whole answer while on earth. It is revealed when you return and see with your entire being.**

In the past we have spoken of a need to increase your faith, to change your mind and to decide to live from a standpoint of love and hope instead of despair and hopelessness. We have asked that you consider the life of Jesus as he lived on earth, to read his words and the stories about his life on earth. We have instructed you to forgive and to love, not because it is a noble thing to do, but because it is imperative that you do so to be clear of any static in your God-Mind connection. We have said, forgive yourself first, love yourself, and **understand that every person is on their path to a God-Mind connection, in their own way.** Some take a more convoluted route, and others take the more direct approach.

It is important to maintain a clear connection if you choose to survive the coming earth changes, to live during the time of peace on earth, a thousand years of peace, during the golden age of love, peace and harmony. If you choose not to live during this time, it is your choice, and we do not condemn or make light of your choices. Our goal is to help, whatever your choice is. We wish to assist those who will live in peace and harmony. **In order to live in harmony with others, you must first find the harmony within.** Realize that all you need, in order to be all you desire, is within you. As you seek within your own heart and mind, it will be revealed to you individually. We request that you gather in groups to pray for the world and the people of this world, who are here to make this important choice.

In the coming year, we will lead you to explore yourselves and your abilities. You will see that Jesus was indeed a way-shower. He came to earth to allow people to see their potential, to see that within is a myriad of abilities, which remain to this day unexplored by humans. Instead of seeing the purpose of Jesus' life, people worship him in a manner that he did not ask for. When someone called him good, He replied, "There is only One who is deserving of this name, and that is my heavenly Father." (Mk 10:18)

When Jesus walked on water or raised the dead, he did not do these things to show off. He said, "The things I do, you can also, and greater things than these shall you do." (Jn 14:12) We ask that people come together with the express purpose of finding their true inner abilities and releasing them. We ask that you use the power of your mind and heart to pray for others and yourselves. The power that comes from a group increases as you gather together in love and purpose. The potential is increased in coming together as a group with purpose and good intent. Each of you carries a light within, and the light becomes stronger and more powerful when more of you come together in purpose. There is strength in numbers. The power of your prayers increases as more people come into the group. Jesus said, "Where two or three are gathered together in my name, I will be there." (Mt 18:20) How can he be there if there is no meeting?

We asked Jean Foster to include this family group in her writings[2] to allow people to know that we have a model family group which comes together to pray, meditate and learn. Your energy and enthusiasm is contagious. When Mother Mary's book is released in the next few days, more people will come to know you, through Annie. She will tell how you come together to pray for yourselves and the people of the world. This will give credibility to the message. Then others will see that you take it seriously, even if you do not know all the answers you are seeking.

Do not think you are not worthy of this task—you are!—because all you are demonstrating is your quest and faithfulness to prayer and meditation. **Each person is to seek within for their own answers.** Everyone is an individual and thinks and feels differently. Have one common purpose and one common goal: seek to increase the strength of your prayers through your sincerity and earnestness. We know that your higher selves have consented; does the personality that is you on earth consent also? It will require that you pray daily as you have been doing, talk to the Father within and meditate, but, most important, it will require of you time, to come together to bring power to the group.

Now let us say as a reminder, there is an ebb and flow to life. There will be times of joy and sorrow; this is how life on earth is set up. How can you know joy without sorrow? How

---

[2] In the revised version of *The God-Mind Connection.*

can you recognize ease and comfort without difficulties? How would you know it is daylight without night? You live in a world of contrast. It is made this way for mankind's learning experience. This is the ebb and flow of life. The contrast of life is here for a good reason. Man learns to live and work on his personality through life. Life is much like a sander, in that there is the abrasiveness of difficulties to hone and polish the real self. There is the time of washing away the impurities that have been honed—this is the flow.

Man's goal is to live on earth and become what he set up for himself as his ideal. Understand that the goal is set in spirit and the completion is an eon away. Into every life enters this ebb and flow; only in the movies or in stories does it happen otherwise. We say, "Do not regale against the inevitable." **Take life as it comes to you daily. Improve it with prayer and meditation. Understand that when it seems the darkest, the morning comes and there is light. Understand there is a whole picture, and it is not viewed from your vantage point.** This is where faith enters. It takes faith to know that you are truly on the road to bigger and better things. This road takes all of mankind along it.

As you pray for the people of the world, you are helping yourself to advance in life. Here is an analogy. There is a family traveling along a road. They are weighed down with many possessions and cartons. There is no truck or vehicle to transport the cargo, so each must pull along a load of cartons. They advance a few feet, and then it requires much effort to bring all the cartons to that point in the road. They go back and forth carrying cartons. When all the cartons are in one place, the family begins again to advance a few more yards, and it takes time to bring all the cartons to this point further down the road. This is the meaning of this tale: You are the family, and the cartons contain all the people in the world. As you advance in prayer and the search for spiritual understanding, you include all people of the world. It takes time: only when all the people are at one point can you go forward, or can anyone advance forward. This is what you do in coming together to pray and learn. You are advancing mankind, and as others form similar groups, they assist this journey. This is why we are asking you to be the role models. There will be, and are, other groups who pray for the world. It is an honor and privilege to be given this task. You will be assisted from this side. We cannot do this alone; it requires a group of people who love and care for each other, a group who have similar goals as you do.

The Brotherhood

The Emitting and Attracting Energies
(Brotherhood, April 14, 1991)

This year, you are learning how God is All. In the past we have taken the Essences of God and broken them down to give you a better understanding of All God is. We have spoken about His great Love. Mother Mary has given you the best overview of God's Love.[3]

Love is an energy, and so are all of God's Essences. He is Strength, Life, Understanding, Power, Order, Wisdom and Knowledge. These are really just a few of the energies that incorporate the Allness of God. God the Father is all things. He is the Giver and the Gift. He is the emitting energy and attracting energy, because He is Energy.

The Energies of God could be thought of as emitting and attracting. When you use the energies of God with knowledge and thankfulness, He will bring into your situation what is needed. You do not have to make a decision. You can simply choose to have God be the Provider of all your needs. In this manner, He will bring all kinds of energies into your life. You benefit from allowing God to have full rein in your life. He provides what is needed in order to learn your lessons quickly and easily.

---

[3] In Chapter 4, *Mary's Message to the World.*

Dear children, you will learn your lessons. Some of you find you are learning your lesson in a manner which brings hardship, and others seem to have an easier time of it. This is because of resistance that is held within. Deep within your mind and heart, perhaps you have some resistance that has not been uncovered. Often it is not just resistance, but some area of un-forgiveness. **Seek within and see what is left in your life and who is needing your forgiveness. Also forgive yourself for not doing this sooner. Then simply allow God to provide what is needed.**

Understand that you do not always have a good handle on what is needed. People on earth will see through the eyes of what is believed by the majority. As you already know, this is not always truth. What is believed by the majority is what is in the earth-mind consciousness. You know there is much un-truth and much that is false. So review your needs, and see if you are believing what is sold to you through your media. Is it truly necessary, or is it vanity?

Let us say this: you need shelter, and you have the free-dom to choose the shelter you want. But remember that these things are temporary, because this is not your real life. You can create an image in your mind of what you would like to have for shelter. You can decide how you would like to live. But then leave it up to God to provide shelter in wondrous ways and in His own time. **Do not set limits on His work. Accept what you have today and be grateful. God gives to the person who is receptive.** Being grateful puts you in a receptive mode. When you downplay what you have, condemn and regale against what you have, you close your heart to receiving more. When you understand that the needs of this world are not the impor-tant issue, but the needs of your real life in spirit are the important issues, then you will have a full understanding of your purpose.

Open your mind and heart first to Spirit, and allow God to provide without limits of any kind, time, place or method.

Pray for what you desire, but release what you pray for to Spirit to work on and bring into your life the best for you. It is not important what you have, but how you learn the lessons associated with the events of your life. Some have had experiences that have not been pleasant. There have been pain and disappointments. Understand, these come into your life for a reason. Seek to find the reason through prayer and meditation. **In your prayers, ask the Father within to give you understanding.** As God releases His great Understanding, there is a release of energy which will benefit you in many ways, internally, spiritually and physically.

Remember that you grow through the ebb and flow of life. When there seems to be no growth, there is growth in spirit, and you experience an ebb on earth. When there is the tide or inflow, it is the season of ebb in spirit, and so you must keep contact with spirit at all times, in order to ensure that you are growing in every manner, spiritually and physically.

In each situation, you will experience the emitting and attracting energies of God. Through Understanding, for instance, as it is being emitted into your mind and heart, you will grow spiritually in discernment, and in the ability to understand how the spiritual life and the earthly life are interconnected. As an attracting energy, Understanding will bring into your life, situations that will increase your understanding and your spirituality.

The same can be said about all of God's energies. As Love, you will be forgiving in the emitting mode, and in the attracting mode you will find solace and acceptance of yourself. **You are in the world to forgive and love, first yourself and then others.**

When you hold on to any area of un-forgiveness, the person you hurt most is yourself and your life on earth. Look at the situations of your life and see what needs to be forgiven. Take a good look at your life and allow God to bring into it His Allness and Totality. This will make you whole, just as God is whole.

Recall the first commandment set by Jesus, our elder brother: **"Love the Lord God with all of your heart, all of your might, all of your strength and all that you are. . . . And love your neighbor as yourself."** (Mk 12:30-31) Think of God as Wholeness, Totality and All. He is all these. His love is ever-emitting and ever-present in you and your life. Man turns it off through unforgiveness and by being unloving. **Divine Love is the most powerful of the attracting energies.** Use it to increase your good, the good of your nation and the good of your world. Remember to pray for peace and goodwill to enter every heart on earth, this in preparation for the coming events.

The prayers and meditations you say are for your benefit. We do not need them, for we pray for ourselves. God has no need for your prayers—remember, He created this and all worlds without your prayers.

The Brotherhood

"Spirit of God" Meditations
(Brotherhood, April 28, 1991)

We like the meditation Annie was using during the night when she awakened.[4] Instruct the family group in this method of meditation. We will now tell how to use the meditation.

To begin, relax each part of the physical body as you have been doing. This allows the body to become calm. Do this even if you think it does no good; it does. To calm the body by speaking to it allows your mind to let go of the physical and become ready for other thoughts and ideas.

Then simply begin to repeat, **"Spirit of God."** Concentrate on those areas of the physical body that have been giving you problems or at that moment call attention by twitching or aching. Say over and over, "Spirit of God," as your mind dwells on these body parts.

---

[4] She concentrated on the words, "Spirit of God."

Now go into each energy center; recall the energy centers and the different energies that can be released. Start with the root energy center and say, "Spirit of God," over and over. Recall that the root energy center is Strength and Life. Say **"Spirit of God in me as Life." "Spirit of God in me as Strength."** Recall that this energy brings with it not only Life, but added Life energy to your home, friends, family, business and income. By saying, **"Spirit of God in my home or business as its Life energy,"** you use this for Strength. Perhaps you need strength of character to stand up for yourself, if you are easily put down or not able to protect yourself verbally. You would then say, **"Spirit of God in me as Strength to take care of myself."** Or, if your finances need to be strengthened, **"Spirit of God is in my money as Strength and Order."**

Always bring Divine Love into your body, home and activities, by saying, as you concentrate on the heart area, **"Spirit of God in me as Love." "Spirit of God is in my home as Divine Love."** You could do this for the world, as you envision the world as a globe.

Every person has need of all these energies all the time, but you can concentrate on those which you feel are most important to you at any particular time. When there is time, you would go through all the energy centers in this manner. If there is little time, concentrate on the top of your head and say, **"Spirit of God enters and brings whatever is needed this day."** You are protected, guided, prospered, loved and cared for in this manner. All is done automatically as you concentrate on expanding the Spirit of God in your mind, heart and affairs.

Accept all events that enter your life as lessons and see them as opportunities to prove that God is Real. Remember always, this is your life plan to learn and experience. Above all, **accept yourself just as you are.** Understand that you are an ever-changing being. These changes are now for the better, as you are connected to God-Mind.

Remember to become quiet in your meditation, even for a minute, to allow God-Mind to bring you a special message. You may or may not be aware of this message, but it will be with you throughout your day and night.

Thus, bring into your being God as a Whole, the way He is. **There are no divisions in God-Mind, as He flows through this universe and all universes in His entirety.** When you concentrate on the different energies, recall these are all aspects of God-Mind. He brings His entire Self into your life at your request. Understand that God is much, much more than these few energies. He is also creativeness and all that is needed in order to be creative.

As you expand the Spirit of God within, He will expand without and flood you with ideas and creative ways of accomplishing your goals. He brings into your life an ease of doing. When you are creative, you will find new and easier ways of doing tasks. It will happen naturally and without any forethought. You will find that even in leisure you are becoming more creative. Not everyone will become an artist, but many of you will. Others will find that their creativeness develops in surprising areas.

Allow the Whole Energy of God-Mind to develop in your inner being. This aids your outer life. But, most important, it opens the channel for your inner instruction. It brings into place all the elements needed for your survival on earth and in the Real World of Spirit.

By becoming aligned with God-Mind, you "know" you are loved. There is no doubt, not even a hint of doubt. You "know" you are protected and guided. As you live your daily life, you will have confidence within, a confidence that will defy anything and anyone, without a hint of hostility. You become not only self-assured, but self-aware. This type of meditation brings much into your life. It brings an honesty with yourself, which is needed in order to produce a better life. This self-honesty allows for each to scrutinize himself with love and acceptance, to know that there is nothing bad within, only that which needs correction.

Depressions and low spirits cannot abide in the Presence of God, so these things will be behind you. You become happier and in this manner wealthier, for when you are connected to God-Mind, "Things happen for your good," and you know it! This eliminates fear, doubts and resentments. You no longer look to what others think as right or correct, but you look to God-Mind for what is correct and right for YOU! **The appearances that need to be kept are the inner appearances— how you look within and how you view yourself through the eyes of Love.**

Everyone is unique, and each of you is progressing now. **Every person has their own Truth and their own way of reaching out to God-Mind.** We give instructions which are beneficial to all, but understand that each of you will modify and do what is best for himself. This is good, as long as you are searching within for your connection to God-Mind, as long as you are using what we give to better yourself. As you grow and progress, you are helping your loved ones to grow also. Even if they do not believe just as you do, they are being aided in their spirituality.

The Brotherhood

25

Opening Up to All Your Good

Your Beliefs Determine How You Live
(Brotherhood, June 29, 1991)

IT SEEMS THAT MANY are taken with the issues of life and of this world. Many feel that they must work long and hard in order to have the necessities of life provided. It will always be as you believe, and the belief is a core belief. Now we will speak about work and the issues of life.

Understand that it is through living, and this includes how you earn a living, that you grow spiritually. Growth is obtained in many manners; this is simply one. How you react to life is the all-important issue. How you react to the situations of your life and the people in your life are important.

What you believe to be true about yourself is what will happen in your life. For instance, if a person thinks he is guilty, he will work extra hard to earn a living. It does not matter if the guilt is real or not. If a man thinks he is lacking in some manner, he will work extra hard. The person who feels guilty, lacking, or in some manner less than, will put much emphasis on work and feel that through work he will "scratch out a meager existence." What we are saying is that it is how you believe that determines how you live. Few people feel truly worthy of great abundance. The ones who do will have great abundance whatever circumstances into which they are born. The ones who feel and believe they are not worthy will find themselves in lack, no matter where or into what wealth they are born.

The key is within each person, in their core beliefs and in what they perceive as their just due. Education helps, but an education is not always the answer. It is the core belief that will determine how one lives their life on earth, in wealth or poverty. As you can tell, most people believe they are so-so, and so most people on earth have a so-so kind of life, neither being very wealthy nor very poor. This is good, if it is accepted.

As you already know, **God is the Source of All Good. It is through the Father within that you find abundance and wealth.** It is what you believe. We see that there is a problem in putting this into action in your own lives.

Once again we come to forgiveness. First, look within and see if you can determine your value to yourself. Do you feel a lack in your personality, stature, education, family heritage or any other circumstance? Then forgive yourself for all that you consider a hindrance to your monetary progress. It may take you forgiving yourself over and over for a period of time. When you feel within that you have completely forgiven yourself, then the next step in this progression is accepting life in its fullest.

At the same time you are forgiving yourself, forgive everyone else that comes to mind. It may not always make sense, but your inner mind will focus on the people whom you need to forgive. Do not question why, simply forgive.

During this time, begin to think of yourself as valuable, worthy of the gifts from God the Father—because even if you forgive all that needs to be forgiven, if you still do not feel worthy, there will be no progress in the situation. It may take you actually repeating the words, **"I am Worthy! I am of Value! I deserve all that the Father has prepared for me."** Say this over and over, until your heart of hearts and your inner core mind accept the change in your perspective of your worth.

These two steps could take months or years to complete; it all depends on how vigorously you take these instructions and work with them. Meditate on worth and value. Simply allow your mind to bring into focus valuable items or situations or people. In your meditation, become one with them. Merge how you view your own worth with what you consider worthy. **Allow the Father within to Love you into true worth.** As you meditate on increasing your self-worth and self-value, consider how very much God loves His creations. He made all His creations self-sustaining. Today it is called ecology, but it is the value that the Father put into each creation.

During this time, as a villain, the earth-mind consciousness will tell you this is all crazy and can't possibly work. Remember that this is not true. Overcome the earth-mind consciousness with persistence, perseveration and prayer. Pray for your life, and at the same time pray for all the people in the world. Say something like this, **"As I raise my self-worth and accept the gifts of the Father for myself, I pray that all people will recognize their true value and worth."**

Pray for wisdom to see the truth and accept the Truth about you and your value. Pray for wisdom to use the gifts of God with prudence and care. In this way you rely on God and not technology to determine your value.

Now a word about prayer. Renew your prayer and lift up new ways to impress on your mind and heart the Love which is yours. When you get into a rut with prayers and meditations, they can sometimes lose their value. They become rote. To avoid this, pray different prayers and use many different meditations. Allow light to be one meditation. See a large beam of light over you and meditate on the light as love, healing or helping, or return to your temple and hold a celebration. Invite us or Jesus into your temple for the celebration, and we will surely be there. In meditation, use any setting that will bring into your mind and heart the peace, love and acceptance that is yours.

See, you are already loved and accepted by us, Jesus, Mother Mary and the Father. The good you seek and search for is yours. Remember Jesus' words, "Ask and it shall be given, seek and ye shall find." (Lk 11:9) This is Truth and is true for all people.

The Brotherhood

Believe in Your True Value
(Brotherhood, July 21, 1991)

We understand that the manner in which Spirit and physical life go hand in hand is not easy for you to understand. Last time we were speaking of how to practically use what you have learned to increase your finances. We said you are to think of yourself as valuable. This is true, but truer is to think of yourself in true value—that is, not to think too highly of yourself or to think of yourself as being beneath anyone else or not good enough.

How to increase your value to the one that matters is to pray to see your true value, to "know" that the gifts of earning a good living are within you. Each person can achieve much in life, according to what he desires and the effort he puts forth.

Pray for ideas. This is what God gives. He is the giver of Good Ideas. Then know that the idea that enters your mind is there because it is possible. The effort that you exert is your part. After you receive ideas, pray for the energy to follow through until they are completed.

Sometimes ideas to increase finances will have nothing to do with money but will have to do with solving problems that have been ignored. It takes much energy to ignore problems. Then it takes even more energy to ignore them as they grow larger. As an example: you have a need and pray to God for an answer. He gives the idea that there is a need to soul-search for beliefs on your abilities, or on your beliefs in simply honoring your word. And you say to yourself, this is not what I prayed for; I wanted a million dollars to solve my problems. But your belief in your abilities is low. You think that something will happen to prevent you from being happy. Then, even if you received the million dollars—and your belief in your ability to create unhappiness or chaos will bring this to you—soon you will find yourself back in debt and unhappy.

In order to have an increase in finances, you must first clean up your beliefs. **You must firmly believe that you are of value.** Believe you can be happy and wisely use any money that enters your life.

Many of you are young and still think in terms of being dependent on another for your sustenance. This is the first lesson in becoming financially independent. You will see that every person has the ability to be financially successful. You will not have a false sense of dependence or responsibility. **Just as every person will receive their instruction from within their heart of hearts and their mind, so they will receive all things in this manner.** If you think you are receiving your money from a company or the person who hires you, then understand that you are receiving what is in your heart of hearts. To become angry with the person who hires you for not paying you enough is not correct. It is you who sets your salary and all things in your life. It comes from your beliefs about yourself and about your worth.

You must see yourself as a loving child of a wonderful Creator, who gave you the ability to create in your world according to what is in your mind.

Now in earthly terms it may take you returning to a classroom to further your education in order to do what you desire. It may take simply going out on a limb, so to speak, and having complete trust in your abilities to perform in your chosen field. It may take changing your attitude toward life.

Are you thinking that you can get by with not accepting responsibility for your actions? Think again. You are the only one
responsible for the events in your life, and this responsibility is
in your deep beliefs.

Do you feel overly responsible for others? Then know
that, unless a person is incapacitated by injury or through being
born like Mark,[5] every person is capable of providing for
themselves. Every person has within themselves the ability to
provide according to their beliefs. **No one is responsible for
another. But you may help other people if the help is real and
not a handout.**

There are many people in this day who are homeless; that
is because within they have beliefs in lack. The lack they believe
in is soon apparent in the need for housing, clothing and all
necessities. In order to help these people, it will require time to
change their beliefs about themselves, to train them to work in
this society and provide for themselves. But if the person is not
willing to put forth the effort to better themselves, then know
that this is their choice. Help is not in giving money, except in
rare circumstances. What happens when you help someone
with money is that they will return needing more money and
soon will cease to be responsible for themselves, but will
become dependent on you, and the dependence increases. You
are giving, it is true. But they are not receiving what they need.
They are receiving something less than what you give. Pray for
the homeless. Pray that the ones who need to be helped with
custodial care, will be. Pray that the people who need training
will find it. Pray that each person will recognize their worth. If
you are guided to assist the homeless, then follow your heart.

Now return to the premise that you are of value. Pray to
see yourself in reality. Many times what is needed is a change
of attitude, beliefs and habits, because habits play an important
part in your ability to earn the living you desire. You can
believe you are valuable, but if your daily habits deplete you in

---

[5] Mark is Annie's oldest son and was born with Down's Syndrome.

any manner, then you are working against yourself. If you believe you are of value and do not believe that other people are of value, then there is a depletion. You must treat all people as you wish to be treated. If you are mean, spiteful, neglectful or in any manner abuse another, then this will deplete your energy to earn the living you desire. You cannot put yourself above or below any other person on earth. **Instead see the oneness which every person has in the Father. We are all one.** When you recognize this, then you will see clearly in reality how every person is of value, including yourself.

Now go and search within to see if what you need to rectify, change or eliminate are old habits, attitudes and beliefs. Perhaps they are not in keeping with your new image of yourself and your fellowman. Do some soul searching. No man can live alone. Every person needs the help, encouragement and love of others. This includes you. Hold a new respect for yourself and your fellowman. Pray to the Father to open your inner heart and mind to see yourself clearly. Pray that you have the courage to change the things that need changing and for the ability to accept the things that cannot be changed.

The Brotherhood

Prepare a Place Within to Receive
(Brotherhood, August 10, 1991)

In the last few lessons, we have been concentrating on opening up within you a place to receive all the Good the Father has prepared for you.

As you open to the thoughts and attitude of dependence on God, you are making a clear connection to the Father. You have been told to find within you a special spot to worship Him. **Come to believe that you are worthy of God's gifts.** Certainly there must be an agreement of what you believe to be true of you and what you believe to be true of the Creator.

We are teaching you to make a place within your heart and mind to receive your good. Understand that the good you seek is comprised of more than just worldly goods. You are receiving at the same time spiritual, emotional, mental, physical, ethereal, psychic and more Good than you know of. At times this may take place in worldly surroundings. For instance, if you need to make an adjustment in emotions, it could be that you seek help from a person who is trained to help you rid yourself of the emotions that are stressing you. Or, if there is a physical need, you could seek help from a doctor or a healer. Do not think that God will not use these means to give you a healing. He will use every available means you know of, and then He will use what appears on earth to be a miracle.

God will work through you to help others. When you sense a need to help another person or people, you will be led through your inner heart. First, you need to be in a position to help. You cannot help others if you are needy.

Then you need to help yourself by making a place in your heart and mind to receive. Believe you are worthy of receiving, and know that you will be led to others. Your help will come in surprising ways. Many times people consider that the help others need is money. Understand that help could also be a use of your time or your prayers, and, certainly, just using words of encouragement.

The Brotherhood

26

On Trust

Trust Your Inner Senses
(Brotherhood, August 25, 1991)

W E WILL CONCENTRATE ON TRUST and have you make a conscious effort to trust that what you hear, feel and sense within is true. First, commit to yourself to spend time in prayer and meditation daily, not as something to do quickly before you go about your day or something you do as you are falling asleep, but designate a time for these important activities. Then you can truly trust the information that you are receiving to be honest and true.

Many people think they lack some undefined quality to hear, listen or to sense. **Every person born on earth comes equipped with the necessary tools to "hear" within.** It takes commitment and time. When a thought connects deep within to some area of truth, know that this is for you and important. Your messages can and will come through many avenues, as you already know. You will receive inspiration and knowledge from readings, not only inspirational material but the mundane, everyday news. You can and will receive information from all areas of the media. It could come from overhearing another's conversation or simply from an idea that enters your mind. **Trust that you will recognize the information.**

We feel that you may forget **there is non-verbal information and knowledge given in your meditation.** It is given in symbols and in other quieter ways. The purpose of non-verbal information and knowledge is that when the time comes for you to know, you will "know." You may not know how you know, but you will know what is right and good for you. Often what is right for you is not always right for anyone else.

God created man as a unique and very individual being, and in this manner He relates to every person. Therefore, it is not appropriate for you to make any determination as to how and/or when another should act. **The best you can do for a loved one is pray.** Remember that prayer is not your will being done for another, but your prayer is for good to come to this person.

Trust that after you have prayed and meditated about a certain issue, the answer is yours. Do not think that someone else will be able to help you. This is an individual issue, and **once you have requested help, it will come through you only.** Perhaps it will seem that the help comes from another source, but this is not true. Trust that you will recognize the answer. It is still a matter of you making the determination that this is appropriate in this circumstance and in this day.

Trust also that God the Father, who loves every person immeasurably, will send only good. Many times the good comes disguised. It takes trust to see the good in every situation. A person may perceive a situation to be bad or evil, when it is simply good turned upside-down. To believe and trust is to see the issues of your life coming together to bring only good as the Father gives.

Each person makes their own choices and has complete freedom of choice. **It is not up to you to determine another person's good for them.** This must be done individually. The best is to keep affirming that only Good is here, and only as the Loving Father gives Good, will it be received. We will say something about parents and their children. Even the very young child has complete freedom of choice, but, as a parent, you carry much weight in praying for your children, even when they are grown. **Understand that the best prayer for any child is that Only Good comes into their lives. Remain steadfast in this prayer, and all the events and circumstances of a child's life will work out for their good.** When it appears on the outside that there is no progress, keep on praying. In time, the love that a parent has for a child will tip the scales, and the good that they desire—and which you as a parent desire—and the Good the Father Creator has already prepared for them, will become evident.

In order to trust completely, you need to be determined and comfortable with the thought that only good will come to you as you pray. It is this idea that gives comfort. It is the knowledge that our Loving Father can only give Good, which is our strength in times of (what appears to be on earth) trouble. Know that trouble is simply a person not hearing clearly their own instruction. And trouble, to one on earth, can also be the inversion of Good. **Trust yourself to see the Good as it unfolds,** because, in reality, you are not capable of seeing all of life from your standpoint. You can see only a small portion of life as it unfolds before you.

In the coming days, take the word "trust" and allow it to be your meditation and your prayer. Perhaps you pray that you become comfortable with the knowledge that you can trust your inner self to determine the issues and conditions of your life. Meditate to trust your inner self, to know what is right for you. Meditate and pray. **Trust that you are Loved beyond compare on earth, and that as a very loved child of the**

Father Creator, you are capable, knowledgeable and Divinely guided in this life.

Trust is not only an act, it needs to become as much a part of you as your eyes or your hearing. When you can trust this much, then it will not be an issue. It will simply be your life. Truly your life will be improved, your self-esteem, self-confidence and your very being will see much progress in spiritual growth, and growth in all areas. Trust so deeply that when the time comes for the earth to be moved, you will not fear, but will be certain that what you hear inside is Truth and comes from the Father Creator. There is not a need to look to any man for guidance or instruction. Your connection to the Father is strong and solid, unshakable and comforting.

The Brotherhood

Trust Increases Faith
(Brotherhood, September 6, 1991)

In the last lesson we spoke about trust. We said, "Trust that what you hear in meditation is truth and comes from the Father." We continue with this train of thought, along with some diversions.

Once you have mastered a regimen of daily prayer and meditation, listen closely to what is being given to you in meditation. Understand that when you pray to hear the truth about your problems or questions, you will hear. Not only will you hear but you will be guided to solutions. This requires trust on your part, not only to trust us, but to trust yourself to hear correctly. Trust that you will recognize truth deep within your heart. **Trust that after prayer and meditation for guidance, you will receive answers.** We cannot tell you what to do or not do. It is not up to us; it is between you, your higher self and God the Father. You will "know" what is right for you. Take the steps that are placed in your heart of hearts, and follow them no matter where they lead you, much as Annie did when she decided to find out the truth about the predictions[6] she had read. She did not know where the answers would lead, nor did she even know if her husband would be agreeable. She didn't know what her children would think. But she kept on with her search. And, lo-and-behold, all has worked out to the betterment of all, all because she trusted that she would find answers.

It is not always important to know ahead of time what will happen. **If you trust that what you get is truth and act on this truth in your everyday life, you will have many blessings, which will come as a result of trusting.** This added benefit is beyond the blessings that are yours for seeking. Each step provides added benefits. Seeking the Father is one step. Surrendering your will and your inner life to the Father is another. Depending on His guidance through your prayers and meditations is still another step. Trusting that what you hear in meditation is truth is yet another step. Act fearlessly on what you receive.

When an idea enters your mind, ask in prayer if it is the best idea for you in truth. You will receive an indication through your feelings, because it is through your feelings that you receive indications of truth. If your feelings are clouded with angers, hurts and resentments, then you will not be able to trust as easily. These dark emotions not only cloud, but can inhibit you from receiving that nudge which tells you what you want to hear.

If you are not ready to clear away dark emotions, then pray. There are many ways to rid yourself of dark emotions. Some people can do it through prayer and meditation alone. Others need to talk to a friend, one who is not involved in the situation, and others will need to be with other people in the same situation, to talk about their feelings. A few may choose a medical person or a person of religion. Any and all ways that help you to be rid of these dark emotions are good. Continue to

---

[6] Annie had read about the earth changes predictions and wanted to know more. This was the start of her search, which later led to receiving *Mary's Message to the World.*

seek knowledge, because with knowledge comes freedom. It is freedom from ignorance, a release from prejudices and binding superstitions.

Rely on the Father within to help and sustain you. In fact, this is the easiest method available. Do not omit the Father, for He is your hope and salvation from ignorance. This may not be completely clear, but to do it alone without any help from above is depleting of your strength, emotions and courage.

With an increase in trust comes an increase in faith. Faith is the price of goods in spirit. **It will be done unto you as you believe.** Take this statement and see all its truths. If you believe in a devil, there will be one. If you believe in war, you will live a life of strife. If you believe in happiness, this is what you will experience. It will be done unto you as you believe.

Now can you see how important it is to release the angers, which attract more anger, and the resentments, which attract more injustices and abuses to you? It is always true that your life is filled with what is in your belief system.

The clearing away of dark emotions cleans out your belief system, emotions and heart of hearts. It is the best way for a person to help themselves to live a good life on earth. When negative situations happen in your life, don't hang on to them; instead let them go without any remorse or resentment. Understand that these dark situations are in your life for a reason, and seek to learn from them the truth that each situation teaches. Look instead at these situations as opportunities to believe in Good and in God's ability to provide for you.

What you can count on, on earth, is change—in situations, life circumstances, governments, religions and in all earthly happenings. This will not upset you when you trust and know that your dependence is not on anything on earth, that your life is truly lived from your real, spiritual life, that you are here only temporarily. **You are always in the care of a loving Father, who is with you every moment. This is truth, trust in God!** When you can trust in your connection to the Father within, you will be free, free to live in love, happiness and only good situations.

Forget the way people on earth look at success, and see success in terms of your real life. See your life unfolding as a game or as a movie, to play on earth. Know that this can be a happy life, one which is filled with good, all kinds of Good. Declare all circumstances in your life as Good. Declare your unerring ability to hear Truth. Along with these statements come confidence, courage and serenity.

The Brotherhood

Be Grateful for Problems (Fall Review)
(Brotherhood, October 12, 1991)

There are many changes happening in the world now. These changes are apparent in your individual lives. Understand that change is good. There is an ever-changing course of life on earth. Change is the one constant in life.

Some people have trouble with change; they think it is an indication of unsteadiness, that it denotes instability and is against every idea of strength and power. **In reality, change is an indication of growth and progress.** Many people think of change as a very frightening circumstance, but we say look at change as an opportunity to expand, to enlarge your whole viewpoint. Understand that change is progress. When people try to keep the situations in their lives from changing, they cause problems for themselves. It is in trying to stop the progress of life that many find confusion and resentments.

Look at nature and see how change is an indication of the workings of a balanced ecology. Through change the plants grow. The rain comes and returns to the ocean to become clouds, which once again bring rain. This is an example of the constancy of change. So also, life brings many situations to help you grow, and always there is a returning to the original beginning. Life is like the rain. You are born, live on earth for a designated number of years, in which time you are constantly changing, then death brings a returning to your beginning and a time of rebirth. Nothing in God's creation is wasted. All is processed to be used again and again, including you!

There is an ebb and flow in life on earth like the tides of the oceans. If you feel your life is at a standstill, understand that you have been in an ebb time, which is always followed by the flow. Remember, this is the natural way of life. When you find yourselves in the ebb, that is the time to remain faithful and believe in the approaching flow. During the times of ebb, use affirmations to remind yourself of the coming flow. Begin to be grateful and thank God for the process of life. Thank Him for giving you the opportunity to know that the process of life is change. Be grateful for the changes that are occurring and that will occur in your lives.

At times the opportunity to grow comes in the form of problems. Be grateful for problems. They are an indication of the way the changes will come. They are an indication of the Good that is flowing toward you. See, this is how to appreciate and love the changes in your lives. The greatest changes take place internally, in a changing of attitudes, in your way of looking at life and all its events. You will find that the things that bothered you before are now no longer an annoyance to you. The words that were upsetting are now of no consequence. The actions of others do not upset you—in fact, you will see and feel their pain. This is how to know that you are changing. The changes take place so insidiously that you are not aware of them. One day you will see that you are more patient, understanding and more loving toward people in general. We know that as long as you are on earth, there will be people who occasionally cause you some minor distress. Let this be as an indicator light; it's a place for you to forgive, perhaps not with this particular person but with one who is similar, either in your past or present.

As you continue in meditation, there will be an increase of energy for healing of body, emotions and soul. In meditation you will find new strengths and new occasions to use your faith. All this will happen simply. There will be no big revelations, but there will be a difference in your life. We want you to be aware of the great changes that are taking place as you continue to pray and meditate. Be ready with a grateful heart and a willing mind. Say these words to yourself: **"Father Creator, I am ready for all the Good you have prepared for me. I am ready with a grateful heart and a willing mind to use the gifts you are giving me."** It is imperative to use gratitude in bringing into your life the desired conditions and circumstances.

Meditation is the art of listening to God. Like every kind of art, it gets better with practice. Daily surround yourself in a white light. If you cannot visualize, speak the words. It works both ways, by seeing in your mind's eye the white light and by speaking the words with conviction. Open the energy centers, and if you cannot remember what each is, then simply say, **"I am opening the energy centers in order that I may live today filled with God's many energies,"** or words that are appropriate to give your mind the needed boost. It is just as good to say words with fervor as it is to see in your mind's eye. Do not become upset over your inability to perform as someone else. Your way is good enough! But keep an unchanging schedule; do it daily. Then go about your day with the self-confidence of one who is working with inner spiritual forces. In this manner, you will not be relying on your weak self, but relying on that Creative Force which made the Universe and everything in it. Let the White light represent all of God's good and His energies.

Hold on to the idea that you are living in a sea of Light, Love and Spiritual Power. You really do live in a sea of energy. Become aware of the energies that surround and enfold you. The elements of light, love and power are surrounding you as the ocean surrounds the fish. Keep this thought in your mind daily. As you breathe, remember that you are breathing in Light, Love and Power. This thought will strengthen you with confidence, self-esteem, and unleash your full potential.

The Brotherhood

27

Standing Firm in Your Beliefs

Your God-Connection Is Through Your Feelings
(Brotherhood, October 27, 1991)

TIME IS ADVANCING QUICKLY, and much is taking place as an undercurrent; soon your advancement will explode into the visible. These undercurrents are what some of you are sensing. There is activity, murmuring and movement. Now they are in the unseen and will soon be visible to everyone. Your goal is to prepare for the explosion of visible evidence. This is accomplished through your daily meditations. You already know that now is the time to be faithful to your preparations. It is time to be concerned with your spiritual communications.

In order to prepare and be completely in tune with the higher elements of life, you are finding that meditation is more and more necessary. It will become as necessary to your heart of hearts as sleep is to the physical body. Be unconcerned with the outer elements of your life; this includes your finances. See economics as one of the elements of life on earth, just as sleep, food and shelter. You are not the economic situation in your country. You are not your career goals. These things are outside of you. You are more than money or station in life. **You are a spiritual being, living this life from a spiritual point of view.** You are preparing for a more expanded way of life on earth and in spirit.

Life is lived within and not without. Life is living, sensing and accomplishing. As you reach your earthly goals, there is a connection to your spiritual goals. It is not one or the other. All of life is one. All goals are one—growing and concentrating on the spiritual elements then brings success on earth. People get caught up in the economy of life on earth. Many people say, "How can we not be caught up in this life? How do we live on earth without resources?" We remind you that you have Cosmic resources. **You are connected to the Universal supply of energy. It all comes through you and not to you.** It is a working out of feelings: this is the secret!

Let us explain. All the ways of communicating with God the Creator and with Universal Supply are done through your feelings. Love is a feeling. Trust is a feeling. Devotion is a feeling. Forgiveness is a feeling. Reliance is a feeling. Bravery is a feeling. Honesty is first a feeling, then an act. Success is first a feeling, then a reality. Integrity is a feeling. When you live on earth, you live in a bi-polar world, and there are opposing feelings to deal with. Love's opposite is hate. Trust's opposite is distrust. Devotion's opposite is fear. Bravery's is cowardliness. Reliance's is distrust. Success's is failure. Honesty's is neglect.

Love is the greatest feeling there is, but if there is hatred, resentment and anger, there is a depletion of love. To love, you must focus on love for yourself, others and for all mankind. Trust is the ability to have confidence. If there is fear in your heart, it will be difficult to have confidence. Fear and confidence are opposing factors and cancel each other out. Fear will cancel out devotion. Think! How can you be devoted to someone or something you fear? This kind of fear is not the fear of awe, but the fear of death. How can you be brave and at the same time a coward? How can you rely on something you distrust? How can you be a success when you believe and see failure all around you? Honesty's opposite is neglect. How can this be? Neglect of the truth is dishonesty. To no longer feel the compulsion to be honest is to neglect your own higher calling. So there is one extreme and the other. What to do?

In order to live in a bi-polar world, there must be balance. The way to find balance is through your feelings. In today's world, many people try to live without feelings and find they are not living, but merely existing. Deal with your feelings in this manner: when a feeling of distrust or neglect comes to mind, cancel it out by refusing to neglect your inner work of meditation. If you still feel distrust or neglect, then look further to what it is saying to you. Frustration is an element of fear and so, when you are frustrated, concentrate on power and strength. Balance your feelings by concentrating on their opposites. An ecology takes place when you balance your emotions with a concentration on opposite feelings. For instance, in your body there is the same ecology. When there is an over-supply of carbon dioxide, the body gasps for breath to get oxygen, its opposite, into the lungs quickly. There is balance in nature and there is in you too. In the physical, emotional, mental and spiritual aspects of your body, all aspects are balanced. Find the opposing feelings and concentrate on them for a more balanced feeling. Deal with feelings instead of neglecting them.

Agree with your feelings and acknowledge them, but do not stop there—neutralize the feelings by concentrating on higher feelings. If the feelings still do not balance, then seek further into the feeling. The feeling is trying to tell you of an area in your life that needs your attention. The feelings of serenity, balance and peace are higher feelings. Neutralize fear with honesty. Be honest with your feelings, and bring into them the love that surrounds everyone. Divine Love is the element in which you live, move and are continuously sustained. **You live** in a sea of Divine Love. It has in it every element needed to sustain life on earth and in spirit.

Now if you are not adept in visualization, recall that in the feeling of quietness and serenity is everything you need in order to live in any world.

Our call to each of you is to live in love, in an attitude of serenity, peace and happiness. Know that as long as you maintain your inner work and inner calling, you will have balance. Trust yourself to know and feel. Trust your own higher calling to guide and lead you. Think clearly, with all the benefits of a wise and uncluttered mind. Your mind will be uncluttered of fear, angers, resentments and depleting emotions as you work to eliminate them. In this manner, you will be free to be all you can be. This freedom may not be as you envisioned. It may be completely different from your old goals. Do not be stubborn by holding on to old ways. In the newer and improved self, you have more confidence, knowledge and above all a serenity of being. **You are an ever-changing, ever-growing being; your growth is always towards the Light of Inner Awareness, Inner Peace and Inner Knowledge.** Put away old thoughts and beliefs, and allow a new awareness to enter your mind. Be true to yourself and your preparation, for soon, children, soon there will be an explosion of work, activity and knowledge in each of you.

The Brotherhood

Life Is Trial by Illusion
(Brotherhood, November 10, 1991)

We have given you an insight into the real world of spirit. If you can remember only one thing, it is that **life on earth is an illusion**—a very good illusion but, none the less, an illusion. Through this short period of time you have elected to experience some trials for the purpose of honing and polishing your spirituality. Do not take this life so seriously. It is an illusion.

When your body is experiencing pain or illness, recall that it is for the purpose of the experience. It is not you in reality who is ill, but the body. Through the body, you are experiencing an illusion of illness. **In reality you cannot get sick or old, because you are an eternal being and as ageless as is the Father Creator.** Does this surprise you? It is another Truth. Only the body becomes ill, not the spirit. There are a few illnesses that are felt in the spirit. During these illnesses, you think the person has lost their spirit, but the spirit cannot be lost. You are spirit and, as such, cannot be lost. The illnesses felt in spirit are addictions, compulsions and obsessions. With this in mind we say, don't be overcome by illness. Do not lose hope; the illness that affects the body is only an illusion.

When people on earth experience a lack of supply, it is also for the purpose of the experience. People put too much emphasis on money. They do not see that money is simply energy. They think erroneously that an increase of money is the answer to their problems. At times, money may well be the answer to some problems. Money will not be the answer to all of your problems. Money is a convenience, and at other times it's a necessity. Again we say, do not lose hope when there seems to be a lack of money. Keep hope alive, because when you can see through eyes of hope, you'll see your way clear of the notion of lack. A lack of money gives one the opportunity to decide what is real and what is false. You're able to determine from the experience that money does not buy love, health or happiness. Lack is a teaching experience. With that in mind, seek the lesson in every experience.

Power and success in life are illusions. **Real power is not bought; it is held in the soul.** You can be a powerful person and not be thought of as successful by the world. Search to find the power and success in spirit. Understand that this is the only place to find power. In the world, people who appear powerful are those who have much money, but money is not the catalyst of power or success. Power and success are spiritual attributes. True success is the ability to live life on earth as Jesus did, not conforming to worldly standards but in complete conformity to Spiritual standards. True power comes from the ability to keep your head when all about you men lose theirs. **Power is the ability to stand firm in the belief of a friendly and loving Creator who is caring for you now, while you live on earth.** Power comes from the ability to receive instruction from within. **Power is your connection to God-Mind.** Success is a strong connection to God-Mind and to all the instruction that leads to your true place on earth. **Success is the ability to connect to God-Mind, hear His words and follow without fear. This is true success.**

Do the things you need to do in order to live on earth in a pleasant and orderly way. **Be true to yourself at all times, by remaining faithful to your connection to God-Mind.** Refuse to take life seriously. **See the humor in all the events of your life**, including those which appear dire. Your joy and confidence comes from the understanding that your real life is in another place. This is a playground. Earth is a time of play and a time of love. View this life as a time of joy, love and playfulness. With this attitude you will overcome obstacles, heartache and illness with alacrity. With a playful attitude, you will find much to enjoy in life, not as the world enjoys life, but as a person who is powerful, successful, kind, loving and filled with happiness does. What else could you desire but to live the remaining years fearless and unencumbered—unencumbered of false pride, sadness and, most of all, unencumbered of addictions.

To live life joyfully, fearlessly and lovingly is such a pleasure that others will want to know your secret. They will want the elixir you drink. This is the water of life, the fruit of the gods. It is the way to experience all of life and your future. **Become still and know—that YOU ARE SPIRIT.** It is empowering. IT IS ALL!

During this time when your part of the world becomes grateful for a harvest,[7] you will be grateful for the harvest of a good life, for the confidence to face all events, for the ability to overcome all obstacles. Gratitude is a key to happiness. It is a key to having perpetual happiness and peace of mind.

Now understand that life on earth is to be lived daily. You are to face all events in your life squarely. Be present and alert every day of your life. Does this surprise you that we say, "Be present"? Many people are not present in their daily lives. They live only for weekends, or only for one season, such as summertime. During the other days they exist, usually complaining. Others feel alive only when they are among certain people or in certain situations. This is how people in darkness live. They have not come into the full light of eternal knowledge. This is not you! You have knowledge, love, and have opened your minds to live every day. You have the ability to live, fully aware of the nature of all that this earthly life entails. You have the knowledge that your real life continues for all eternity.

Keep this thought with you and mull it over and over until there is inner certainty: **You are an ETERNAL BEING and as such LIVE FOREVER! You have within you the ability to connect to ALL WISDOM, ALL KNOWLEDGE and DIVINE LOVE.** This is your link to reality. It is your lifeline and the fulfillment of every need. **Through this connection, you are guided, sustained and loved.**

Remember always, you are loved and cared for by ONE WHO IS ALL POWER AND ALL LOVE! You cannot be in any other place, except in your right place. You are in the right life and in the right body. There are no mistakes. There is Divine adjustment. You will be guided, as long as you keep the God-Mind connection.

The Brotherhood

---

[7] For Thanksgiving.

Expect the Good in Every Situation (Thanksgiving)
(*Brotherhood, November 24, 1991*)

Every individual makes their own plans, decisions and choices. The right to make these choices is dear, and in your country you are better able to understand it because of the freedoms inherent in this government. We see these choices as Americans do. They are the right of each person to choose how to define happiness, peace and also troubles.

What is peaceful to one is not to someone else. What is happiness to one is subjugation to another. What is a problem to one person is merely an inconvenience to someone else. You even choose how to define conditions. Understand that this is a most glorious advantage. You are not restricted spiritually or in any other manner. Be grateful for this privilege. Our emphasis today is on gratitude. We are aware of the season of Thanksgiving. It is good, as it reminds you of the close unity the people who settled this country had to spiritual principles. It is one thing to have a history of spirituality, but it is entirely different to have these principles as part of the country's makeup. You see that your forbearers lived their spiritual beliefs.

It is true that the act of gratitude is a necessity for your spiritual life. This is not simply the act of being grateful for things received, but the act of being grateful for conditions, situations and problems. It is through conditions, situations and problems, that you grow spiritually, so whatever the condition, be grateful: through it you advance. Yes, on earth you are not always aware of the advancement or aware of how it works. Through these communications you can be aware of the need to be grateful.

You question, why be grateful for problems? Let us explain simply, through a story.

Once there was a young boy who was very poor and had no shoes. He detested the poverty and could not understand why some had much, while others like himself had little. His parents took him to church and religious school. All he could say was, God didn't give me riches, so I must find riches for myself. I will be rich when I am grown, and I will remember how it feels to be poor and have no shoes. It was the shoes he desired the most. His love of shoes was great, so he fashioned a small box and put into it clean rags, of which he had many. Through work in odd jobs, he finally had enough money to buy polish for shoes, and so he went to the city to polish shoes. If he could not wear new shoes, perhaps he could polish and shine new shoes. He set his box at the entrance to a bank—in his mind a bank meant money, and money meant good shoes. He became the best shoe shiner and polisher there was. People commented on his love for his work. Soon he was given other work, but he continued to polish shoes. The banker took a liking to the boy and offered him a job. The banker saw a boy who was happy, content and peaceful. He wanted these qualities himself. Through the years, the boy grew not only in stature but in his love for work and learning.

Yes, he became rich and in his old age gave away many shoes to children, not only shoes, but money for education, medical help and for fun. One day while he reminisced, it came to him how his poverty had helped him be all he wanted to be. He reasoned that if he had been born in wealth, he would not be the man he was that day. He would have missed many lessons along the way. In old age he was grateful for his poverty and his great need. He realized it had sparked his inner self to achieve greatness. He realized his greatest gift from God was not poverty or riches, but his life—with all its problems, situations, and all its conditions. Riches had not relieved his problems but simply changed them. Yet, he was able to face every problem and overcome, learn and advance because of his love for life and his great dream.

Look at your life closely and see how problems have shaped your future, how you have advanced and overcome many problems to achieve your own greatness, for greatness is measured in happiness, not money, in love and not possessions. It is measured in peace and not status. **Be grateful for**

every situation in your life. We fully understand that when you are beset with problems, it is easy to see the darkness. We give you a way to look through the darkness into the coming light: **expect the Good which is in every situation.** You are able to maintain the faith needed to receive not only your desired answers, but the answers you need. You are able to put aside fear and know that the answer will come in time. The answer always comes at the proper time. It comes with a blessing—it's an opening to your understanding.

Simply put, be grateful for every event in your life, good or bad, because often what begins as a bad situation can later be understood as a good one. It is understanding and hindsight that clear your eyes. Love opens your heart, and peace settles into your entire being. Remember, there is more to life than what you see. This also includes how you define the events in life. To every condition, ask what lesson is in it for you. Ask these kinds of questions: Why are you in my life? How will you help me? Answers will not be immediate but will be forthcoming. This will serve to put despair at bay. It will help you remember that you live life spiritually, through situations, conditions and problems. In the future, every event will be welcomed, because it will be for your learning. This is true gratitude. This is a complete surrender to the Father within for your entire life.

The Brotherhood

PART 5

1992–1993
Love and Service

CHAPTER

28

Integrating Spiritual and Worldly Success

Unlimited Possibilities
(Brotherhood, January 5, 1992)

WE ARE THE BROTHERHOOD OF GOD. You on earth have begun a new year. Allow this to inspire you to greatness. Allow the implication of a new beginning to sprout in your mind and heart with new ideas and new ways of thinking, for in reality it is through thinking and the processes of the mind that you live.

You may feel that you live on a certain street, in a certain town, and are the persona which this represents, but you are more than this person. You are a spiritual being using your mind to incorporate all that you have learned. New beginnings give the aura of unlimited possibilities. This is what you should feel and think on. There are unlimited multitudes of possibilities. See how this statement opens up an aliveness within?

We urge you to use this as a motto for the new year. **You are living in unlimited possibilities.** The only block is in your mind and heart. Sometimes people say, "I do not feel this is true," and for that person it is not. They have limited their possibilities. **The reality of life is that each person is living in an arena of unlimited possibilities.** The first thing needed is the acceptance of this statement.

Perhaps it would be better to say that you are loved by a love that is so great that the Father Creator has given each being unlimited possibilities. Does this give you an idea of the love in which you live? Does this make it easier to understand that the reason you have unlimited possibilities is because God loves in this manner? Our Father Creator is generous and is always lovingly giving. It is the individual who closes the door to their own heart and mind. It is the person, through their belief system, who limits themselves.

We urge and encourage you to accept the love that is given. **Accept the idea of unlimited possibilities.** Accept that each person on earth is special, but not all are knowledgeable. It is through knowledge that understanding comes, and with understanding comes acceptance.

Perhaps you do not know what this means to you. It means that you are your own worst enemy. You limit yourself and your life. **When you become complacent and are willing to accept only that which has been accepted in the past, then you are limiting your future.** Remember that all things in a natural state grow, die and are reborn. Strive to grow in spirit and truth. This is how to do it:

First, make a pact to be faithful to your meditations. Make it one of your goals to be clear in meditation, to feel and become alive with the Presence of Spirit, which is God. Make it a goal to enter your temple often and leave there everything that concerns you. Nothing is too big or too small to be left in your temple. If your temple is too small to accommodate all that is in your life, simply enlarge it.

Then meditate to be infused with Spirit. Say at the beginning of your meditation, **"I want to be infused with the Spirit of God. I want to have God's presence active in every area of my life."** Then be quiet, knowing all the while that even if you are not aware of it, it is being accomplished in that moment. God awaits only your invitation to enter and help you live your life.

Put away the measuring stick of success as it is defined by worldly terms. Recall that your life is not lived according to what other people say success is. Life is lived in accordance with your lifetime goals. But don't think that you cannot be successful in earthly terms and successful in your lifetime goals at the same time. It is possible to be successful both in worldly terms and in spiritual terms simultaneously. Simply put away the total concentration on worldly success, yet do not limit God in accomplishing success as the world views it. How do you implement this? Simply make the statement that you wish to live with unlimited success in spiritual terms and earthly terms, that you wish to integrate both kinds of success, now. **Your primary intention is to learn to be spiritually alive in all areas of your life.**

It is so easy to get caught up in earthly thinking. It is what feels natural at the beginning of these changes. Understand that you are using new ways of thinking and feeling. **Your goals are to become acutely aware of the great Love that immerses you, to become one with the Spirit of God while on earth, to wipe your view clear of any limited thinking.** Make it a habit to watch your thinking, to cancel any limiting thought, view or belief. When you catch yourself limiting any concept, say instead, **"This is not true; I cancel this limiting way of thinking for all time. I know that I am unlimited and that all possibilities are given to me in heaven and on earth."** This is a very true statement! It is a powerful statement. Use it as an affirmation of truth. Use it to clear away all limiting ideas, statements or viewpoints.

We applaud Annie and Byron's idea to honor one of their children with an award for the most improvement in the year.[1] This was solely their idea. It is a sampling of the kind of ideas that come to people who are learning to love as God loves us. Perhaps in the beginning of the year, or now, you do not know how you will improve, but be determined to make some great improvements this next year, not only for the purpose of receiving the award, but to better yourself. As you point the direction of your thinking toward improvements and unchain your mind by ceasing to limit your possibilities, you will find the ways to improve. You will be guided to the areas that need improvement. You will simply "know" that this is what and how you will improve. Perhaps your first improvement is simply to begin thinking in larger, more unlimited ways. You will obtain a knowingness, and your new thinking will show in the life you live.

The Brotherhood

The Wheels of Life
(Brotherhood, February 16, 1992)

What a wonderful day this is, one in which you begin a new level of learning truths. You will recognize that what we are doing is simply giving deeper meaning to the same ideas you have already learned. In this way, you are learning truths at a deeper level. Truths are constant, like the laws of physics. They do not change but are simply better understood.

Many of you are having problems maintaining a flow of sustenance in the matters of money, so we will address this issue. Annie had been reading on finances. It is through her

---

[1] We created a certificate for the person who had improved the most for the year. This was presented at our family Christmas gathering.

mind and interest that we lead you. As she gets her questions answered, they are answered for you, too. It is most productive to work in this manner. We see similarities in all of your lives, because all people are alike in many ways. Many are traveling down the road of life together and so find themselves at the same obstacles. Many people are having the difficulty of money. It is because people think of money as a god. They work for money. They use their time not only working for money, but much time thinking about money or the lack thereof. When there is time off from work, the first thing people do is spend money, even when they do not have it. They think of ways to spend the money they would like to have. Many people spend more time meditating on money than on God.

Let us think of money as sustenance. It is the ability to be comfortable, to have creature comforts. God did not intend for His children to live in need. Through the long progression of life on earth, people have come to believe that money, or the pursuit of it, is bad. They think of what they can get, and not what they can give. Look at your lifework not only as a way to make money, but as a way to give to the world or to life itself. Through your work, you can make this a better place to live. Many of you will see clearly that what you do in your work day is beneficial. If you are a nurse, like Annie, then it is easy to see that she is easing pain and giving care, but if you are selling products, like Byron,[2] perhaps it is not as easy to see the way his work helps people. Yes, you say, I can see how his products make it easier for others to use their computers. Simply by doing business he is helping others to stay in business. He not only gives information on new products or on better ways to use products, but he is maintaining the wheel of business, in which many are benefitted.

Let us speak first of the wheels of life. You have heard it said, "What goes around comes around." This is a Truth. What

---

[2] Byron was in the microcomputer industry as a manufacturers' representative, selling hardware and software products.

you give out to others is returned to you. This is so of all areas of life. Many of life's areas are on a wheel of sorts. Business is a wheel, and many are sustained by it—this we call money or sustenance. This was very clear in times when there was much agriculture. Today it has become obscure. The store where you buy your groceries provides a market for the farmer, the grower, the collectors of fruits and vegetables, those who package or freeze these products, the transporters and the warehousemen. In turn, each of these businesses gives jobs to workers. They depend on these jobs for the money to sustain their families. This is all simple but at times becomes overlooked. Today not only the people who live in the valleys have fresh fruits and vegetables, but also the ones who live on snow-covered mountaintops, in the deserts and on the plains. These businesses created an industrial wheel, on which many are nourished and nourish their families. There are many different industrial wheels of business. For instance, consider Byron, who works for people who are like the growers, in that they make machines to keep records. This is also a wheel of productivity. He assists the growers, transporters, warehousemen and many others to keep better records. In turn, he helps the makers of goods, small shop owners and large store owners too. All these people in turn have workers. See how each is important to the other? In business, as in life, all are interrelated and interdependent and interconnected. Today, the marketplace is not the small village, city or one nation, but the world. All are interconnected through international business. Now nations are dependent on each other: the world has truly become one. This explanation is given to help you see that every kind of work is important, if it gives service. Today few people are isolated and completely independent. So how does this tie into truths? It simply means, "See what you do as valuable and honorable." If it is not, then leave this work, because you will not prosper long on work that is not honorable or valuable.

Get a clear understanding of the wheels of life. See that you are important to the whole. **Be honorable in how you**

execute your daily work, and be thankful. Know that the Father Creator set these wheels of life up to give each a good living and a good income of goods. He did not intend for his people to live in need. Why are so many people homeless and needing of the basic comforts? Either these people have been given this way to atone for some mismanagement of goods in past lives, or this is their desire to learn whatever lesson is in their path. The best way to help is first to pray for these people, and then help as you can. If you have an extra coat and can give it to someone who needs it, this is good. If you have extra food and give it to one who is hungry, this is good. If you have time to give to others, this is needed. In giving you receive, and in helping others you help yourself. Maintain yourselves in the proper mental and spiritual order. **Learn this lesson for all people, by stating that this is your intent.** Let what you do be done for the whole, and in this manner, as you live your life, you are helping to upgrade the lifestyle of many.

Get a clear understanding and picture of how your work is important. **You help mankind by doing your work in an honorable and efficient manner.** Do it without griping; do it as if your very spiritual life depended on it, for it does in many ways. **Be appreciative and live in gratitude.** See how very blessed you are to have work. Forget what the others in your workplace are doing, and do what is right for you. Now that you are learning this, it is important that you execute these lessons in order to be in your right place.

First, understand how the wheels of life are maintained. Then see how important you are and that your work is important. Even if all you do is sweep streets or collect garbage, this is very important work, for it is the cleaning of towns and cities. Do not demean your work in your mind or your attitudes. Give good service, appreciation, and give the gift of doing a good job daily.

Second, **give to life.** Perhaps it is with the attitude of helping wherever you can. **It can be a kind word, a smile, your encouragement. Your prayers are the highest and best you** can give. Pray for the world, and for the ones your life touches each day. When someone is unkind, don't take offense, but say a prayer for that person. Simply say, "God help you." This is a prayer. Prayer is an attitude, too. How you say words is important: they can be said as a prayer. Speak ill of no person; instead, pray for that person. This is true giving. This is how to cultivate a giving heart or nature. But a word of caution—do not ever give with the thought that "Now I can get," because then the gift becomes tainted with selfishness. **Give without thought of return; let life or God return your good to you.** Don't keep tabs on how much you have given; simply give, and "know" that you will be taken care of. It is attitudes that are important. **Have an attitude of giving for the sake of giving,** not for the sake of having someone acknowledge the gift.

Third, **have the attitude of being cared for and loved so much that you will not lack anything you need.** When the bills come in, put them aside with the thought that the money is already here to pay this; you may not see the money, but it is here. Instead say, **"I will pay this on time so that the wheel of business keeps running smoothly."** Hold your bills and give God thanks for the money to pay them, even if you do not see the money then. Be sure that you are as honorable in paying as you are in buying.

Remember always, it is your thoughts, attitudes, words and beliefs that create your future. Watch what you say, think and believe in order to create plenty in your life. Change your attitude about money and see it as good, a blessing. Use it wisely and creatively. **Depend on God to provide and not your employer.** Employers can come and go, but God the Father has been and will always be with you. **He is the one who is the Giver of life and all other gifts.**

Now, there is much work for each of you to do with this lesson. **These truths must be incorporated into your daily life;** this is the only way to benefit from these lessons. Do this now, in order that we can give you higher truths. You must be able to live on earth in comfort and with the right attitudes. **Practice**

and change whatever needs to be changed. Next time, we will give more on how to better your life on earth, on how to have your needs met constantly, without spending so much time thinking about your basic needs.

The Brotherhood

Faith Makes Circumstances Fluid
(Brotherhood, March 16, 1992)

Keep a good attitude toward yourself and your income. Remain strong in the face of defeat. There are times when you could easily despair, but let us remind you of a story in the Old Testament, which could be interpreted to fit the circumstances of loss of income.

Remember the story of Daniel and the lions? When Daniel and his companions were thrown into a lion's den, he stood strong in his faith that God would take care of him in all circumstances. How would you feel if faced with hungry lions? The faith that Daniel exhibited was the faith that will move mountains. He said, "I will not fear," and advised his companions not to fear or to waver in their faith. He prayed and was in communion with the Father within. All Daniel knew was that God would not fail him, and of this he was very certain.

You could easily compare the state of a loss of income to facing lions. You need this kind of faith, the faith to say, "I do not see a way, nor do I know how God will supply my needs, but I am certain He will." Hold on to this thought, no matter what the appearances are. Jesus said, "Judge not according to appearances." (Jn 7:24) If your outer appearances are of lack and you buy into this belief, it will become reality. **Faith in God's Good keeps appearances and all circumstances in your life fluid, and they can easily change.** Problems arise when you waver, and there is hardening of circumstances. When there seems to be more money going out than coming in, remain certain that God can correct it and there will be a balance. All things in nature are in balance. If they are not, then nature corrects the imbalance. This is true of finances. When there appears to be imbalance in this area of your life, be certain that it will be corrected. **Your finances and all areas of your life will be in complete balance, and in the state of balance there is plenty.**

Now is the time to practice the concepts we have given you. Stay in tune with the idea that you are loved so very much that God would not allow you to fail. But—there is a catch—it depends on your belief. Do all you can, and then believe that God will correct any imbalances in your life. **God works through you and not for you. This is very important to remember.**

Now, if there are areas in your individual lives that need specific help, let us know. We will give you help in understanding the principles by which you live on earth. It is fun and easy, once you know the rules:

Rule 1: **Turn over everything in your life to God.**
Rule 2: **Believe He will heal, balance or correct anything.**
Rule 3: **Be grateful.**

Follow these rules for all areas of your life. Remember that you did not create this world, God did—and He knows how to balance your lives. **Practice; practice being strong in faith.**

The Brotherhood

Using Your Power to Proclaim
(Brotherhood, March 29, 1992)

As you turn over everything in your lives to the Father, you are released and freed to be creative, loving, forgiving and free. It takes a lot of energy to worry. It takes little energy to surrender to the Father, but through this you are so enriched with energy, ideas and life. Through this enrichment of freedom and energy, you will be amazed at the ideas that will come to you—ideas about how to live better, how to solve all problems that come into your life, ideas for creativeness and enjoyment. You will enjoy the simple things in life. You will find pleasure in routine chores. All of this happens as you surrender your worries and concerns to the Father.

When a thought comes to you, whether it is a worry or a pleasant one, say, **"This thought is a passing fancy. It does not matter, because it is not real. I live my life connected to the Giver of All Good."** Do this for one day only. Remember to practice this exercise one week only. Whatever your thoughts are for that one week, they can be discounted as unreal. Remember that on earth you live in an illusion of real life, because real life is lived only in Spirit. Do this as a practice to clear your mind of all that still lingers there. Clear it of all unnecessary worry or concern. Whatever comes to your mind, do this. Do not discriminate whether the thought is good or bad. Just say, "This is not real. What is real is that I am loved and I live eternally."

After you have done this for one week, rest, and live as you usually do. Then, later, we will practice again.

Another week, take the thought as you survey your mind, "Is this real?" If it is a valid concern, then give it to God, by saying the words, **"I feel or think this is a valid concern. I give it to the Father within. He will work it out, and the outcome will be the best for all concerned."** Again, do not discriminate; take each thought that enters your mind that week. If it isn't a valid concern, then say, **"Be gone. I don't need to worry needlessly. You are of no concern to me."** In this manner, you are using your power to proclaim what is valid and what is not.

There is power in your words, especially when you use them to proclaim. Jesus used words to proclaim, heal and quiet storms. When you proclaim, say, **"I proclaim this."** Then know that it will happen as you have stated. This is a first pass at proclaiming. It will take practice for your proclamations to be instant. You could keep a record of your proclamations, to see how long it takes and what the results are. **Always end your proclamation with a word to the Father to give the highest and the best.**

Here is another exercise to use before you proclaim situations and circumstances in your life. Take a few minutes to meditate on your power center. It is located in the throat area. The power center is always in use, but you will enrich your proclamations when you have opened your power center and allowed the energy of Power to flow freely. Surely you remember the Power center? It is one of the energy centers. This center has the opening for Power and Enthusiasm, or as it was called in olden days, "Zeal." When you open this energy center, your words will be infused with Power and Zeal—and a powerful, enthusiastic proclamation gets results.

Do not forget how very powerful your idle words are. Be careful: do not idly say things like, "I wish I were dead," or, "I wish a big sore would appear on his nose." Do you know why? It is because your words always produce the same effects in you. Some people will say things like "I'm dumb," or "I'm fat," or "I'm stupid." These idle words bring those conditions to you. When you wish something bad on another person, you are wishing the same for yourself. In order to go past this and to put "oomph" or POWER in your words, meditate on the Power center. Call up Power and Zeal. In meditation, "see" the base of your throat opening. Allow it to open by a swirling clockwise motion. After you have proclaimed all that you desire (be sure to proclaim for humanity, too), close this center by seeing it swirling counter-clockwise into a closure.

Now to regress a little. Before you open the first meditation, it would be helpful to write down what you wish to proclaim. If you leave this to your memory, you could forget some areas of your life. Give your proclamations some thought. **Proclaim health, and do it for yourself and humanity. Proclaim wealth for yourself and humanity too. Proclaim love in all your relationships, even those which are not con-**

sidered a love relationship, such as your relationship with co-workers, merchants, teachers, doctors and service organizations. Write something like this to proclaim, **"I will spread love to every person I come in contact with this week."** Then meditate to open your Power center, and make the above type of affirmation. You will be healing not only your relationships, but those of humanity. Remember that humanity needs all the help it can get.

When you proclaim your good, say it for all humanity. You are opening many doors, because **good goes to the purist of motives, and to that person who is seeking to increase the good for the most people.** You will be in the greater flow of Good. Good flows to the area where it will affect the most people. When you open yourself to channel Good for humanity, it is for the most people. As health, wealth, love and goodness flow through you to humanity, you are healed, enriched materially, loved, appreciated and flowing with Universal Power.

These are simple exercises, but they bring results in your life. Live from the standpoint of being a helpmate to humanity. This will surely bring answers to your questions and healings to you and all people, especially those whom you call by name.

We know that some of you have a problem with meditations that are self-guided. Irregardless, go through the process in a quiet manner and in a mood of meditation. Say the words, **"There is a center at the base of my throat; it is opening. Power and Zeal will be infused in every word I now Proclaim."** Just do it! Talk yourself through the process. It will bring amazing results. This you can do once a week or every night. Do it as often as you wish or feel guided. Always speak truth. Tell yourself how much you are loved. You are an eternal being, filled with light and love.

The Brotherhood

Forgive and Forget
(*Brotherhood, April 12, 1992*)

Good day, family group. This is still a family, for no matter who joins the group, they become family. Every person on earth belongs to the family of mankind. **On earth you are one, as we are ONE. We are all ONE because we are ONE in GOD, heaven and earth.** In reality there is no heaven, but we use this term to tell you that where God is, you are too.

Many are still wondering why they appear to have bad times. Why do you continue to suffer unpleasant circumstances? Why hasn't faith worked, you wonder? Faith is the hope of good things to come. **Faith is an inner "knowing"** that you are loved and cared for. Faith is not magic; it does not perform like a genie. Faith will not grant your wishes. Faith is the substance of hope. Would it be better to say, "Have hope"? Would you understand faith better this way? Hope doesn't grant wishes either; it simply looks for the future to be brighter and better.

You are on earth to learn; this you have heard before many times. This school doesn't let you shirk your lessons. The lessons keep coming, coming and coming. They may come in different situations and at different times, but the lessons keep coming. They will not let up until you learn what you need to learn. Concentrate on learning the lesson at hand. Ask us to help: we are the Counselor. Our ability is to give counsel, to help you learn these lessons quickly. We help by listening to you and giving gentle prods to forgive, to release or change an attitude. Remember, you live life on earth by attitude. It is your attitude that determines how much you suffer, or how little. We use the term "suffer" to mean endure an unpleasantness. We help the person we are counseling take what they wish to be rid of, to the sea of forgiveness and forgetfulness. **What you forgive, you can forget. If you do not forget, you have not forgiven.**

Let us tell you that what is happening in your lives, this apparition of lack,[3] is a worldwide lesson. Many people are learning it at this time. People have placed their worth in dollars. They have thought it important to have certain possessions; in other parts of the world it has been the same. The only difference has been in the objects that are prized. Avarice took hold of many minds and hearts. Violence is rampant. This time of seeming lack is simply a righting of a wrong, a lesson in what to value and what is of no value. It is the balancing of avarice or greed.

While on earth, you can expect to have wealth. We are not speaking out against wealth. **Understand that wealth is more than money.** Wealth is many things that you do not think it is, for example, good health. Ask the person who is ailing what he considers wealth. He will say good health. Ask the one who is incapable, uneducated or simply out of work. He will say that wealth is gainful employment. Wealth is good friends, a safe environment and the freedom to make your own decisions in every area of your life. These are just a few of the things wealth encompasses.

A wealthy man is one who has a good attitude. He may not have masses of money, but he will have enough money to do what he wants to do. He will have the good sense to use well what money he has. He will think spiritually. This doesn't always follow earth logic.

Spiritual logic is quite different from the logic used on earth. A spiritually wealthy man will question, not whine or lash out against the forces that are urging him to rise up. He will question himself, so as to better himself. He will seek what he needs to improve, what lesson he can learn. A sensible person will take each defeat and use it as a way to improve himself. He will examine the defeat closely. He will ask for higher assistance in doing this. He will do this impersonally, doing all he

---

[3] The recession going on in 1992 and later.

can to keep his feelings from entering the process. It can be done. It will be done, one way or another. A wealthy man questions himself to keep his motives pure. He questions himself to gain inner knowledge. He questions himself to dispose of erroneous attitudes, thoughts or habits.

Learn these lessons and learn them well. Be wealthy; think you are wealthy, and you will be. But think of wealth in its entirety. There is a way for you to learn all lessons quickly, to put them behind you and go on to new lessons. Ask or proclaim that you are **learning these lessons for all mankind.** When you do this, you will have the power of heaven and earth behind you. You will receive assistance from many forces which are working to enlighten man and raise his awareness. Today, many are out of work; many suffer from hunger and a sense of lack. It is prevalent, but do not give in to this thought pattern. You will quickly fall into great despair if you allow yourself to give in to this way of thinking. Do not think of lack or talk about lack. You are all wealthy, because you are all on a spiritual path. There are many in our association who are willing to help. We are praying with you.

Do not fear future lessons. Life on earth is like a school. If you learn your multiplication table in childhood, you can always work math quickly. You will not be cheated of money or goods, because you will know the same math the other person is using. If you do not learn math as a child, you will go through your days shortchanged and not know it. It is the same with these lessons. After you learn these basic lessons, the ones that follow will be easier. Soon you will not feel that you are on a rollercoaster ride. Circumstances in your life will even out, and you will live in peace.

Have hope for the future; have hope that you can learn these lessons and learn them quickly. Maintain an attitude of wealth in its true meaning. All you need is a small amount of faith, like a mustard seed. It will help to read how Jesus described the amount of faith needed to bring about change. (See Mt 17:20 or Lk 17:6) The mustard seed is among the smallest on earth. Now, joyfully live life from the perspective of Spirit. Let Spirit lead and assist in every detail of your life. **Remember always, YOU ARE LOVED!** Though you walk through a world of lack and need, fear no evil. I AM with you always—a promise of Jesus, and Jesus keeps his promises.

The Brotherhood

29

Facing the Future

Meditate in Silence
(Mary, May 9, 1992)

GOOD DAY, FAMILY GROUP, this is Mary, Mother of Jesus. I am proud of the people who are doing all they can to incorporate these lessons into their everyday life. **What is needed is to speak truth and, more important, to live truth, to be true to yourselves and to your inner search.** As you seek to find your connection within, you are raising the race consciousness. How do you live the lessons? **Stay true to your inner search and keep your connection to the Father, Creator.** This is so important my children. It is so very important. How can you light the way if your lamp is dimmed? How can you guide if you know not the way? How can you be prepared to serve, if you know not how to prepare? This is the commitment I request. I ask that each of you increase your prayer time, that each increase their earnest desire to know. Let sincerity be the by-word in your inner search. You cannot depend on anyone else. Do not seek to find your answers, or your connection, through any church official, guru, or anyone who is a creation of the Father. I see many seeking to take a short-cut in the process. They seek to find the way through different exercises in meditation and through differing theories. Guided meditations are good, but not when they are used exclusively. **The purpose of meditation is to receive.** How can the Father speak to your inner mind and heart if it is cluttered? **Silence is important. Silence is the only way the Father speaks to you.** I did not say this is the only way He can speak to you. God the Father is also very loving, gentle and compassionate. He knows that the race consciousness is steeped in fear. Even when you have eliminated it from your heart as best you can, there is a residue. So be committed to meditating in silence at least once a day. Let the Father guide you. Allow the Father to work through you. Then there will not be any need to depend on any other person. Continue your search as you have, for it is working. Please read, study and learn all you can, but be discriminating in what you internalize (accept as truth). Let Spirit teach you the difference as to what is truth and what is not.

Simply be a support, the one for the other. It is in supporting one another that all will grow spiritually. **Let people come together to form support groups,** for the purpose of seeking together to find truth. These groups will keep each other encouraged to seek within for spiritual sustenance. This is so important, as many are becoming confused with all the information on earth. All the theories contain elements of truth, but **your truth can come only through you.** The truth, as it applies to your life and the circumstances in your life, can come only through you. One person is not more important than another. As more and more like-minded people enter the group, tell them the purpose is to help them become comfortable with the process of seeking within. Let many groups be formed, so that there is spiritual enrichment taken to their family and friends.

There will be multitudes of support groups, all led by the Father Creator, Jesus and the wonderful Holy Ghost, the Counselors.

In the near future, there will be many who appear out of nowhere, with wonders and performing great feats. These people will cause many others to fail, **because they lead not to the Father, but to themselves and their theories.** They say, "Here, here, I have found the way. Here, I have found how to be saved by doing this or thinking this way." **Do not give your power to anyone.** Guard jealously your ability to connect within to the Father. This is the only place to find your truth and your sustenance. **Instinctively you will know what is good for you. Trust your inner awareness.** If it is not clear to you, then ask for clarity. Ask for definition. Understand that as the representative of the Divine Maternal Energy, I am available to all people. I will come to you with angels and with the Love of God. Let your prayers be to the Father. But I am—and the Holy Ghost, or the Brotherhood, are—ever ready to help you connect to the Father. Angels await only the word; they will help if you prefer to have an angel be your helpmate.

Now read, study, but use discrimination and allow Spirit to lead you. You already know this; at times it is simply forgotten. Remember who you are. Remember earth is not your real home—your true and proper home is here in Spirit. **Lighten up; be assured that the Father within is loving, kind and always gentle. He will guide you if you will but ask.** It is up to you to choose. It is up to you what enters your mind. Make decisions, make choices, for this is your birthright. "Know" deep within, YOU ARE LOVED! You are already accepted, in your present form. What you are doing is simply clearing away fear, anger, resentments and depleting emotions. They serve no purpose in your life. When you truly understand how very much you are loved, then all the theories, schemes and plans will simply fall away. **You are already in the presence of God, already filled with His light and Love.**

Recognize that you know all you need to know. It will come to you as you choose to follow Spirit's guidance.

Leave all addictions, for they deplete and cause you to lose sight of your inner connection. Addictions separate and cause people to isolate. Through prayer and seeking to be connected to God, these things leave your life. This will happen in amazing ways. Some will need the help of doctors or earthly counselors. Others will be able to leave these depleting emotions and actions without any apparent help. But understand that either way, it is the Father doing the work.

My request then, is to seek within for the Father. Support each other and pray the one for the other. I will be setting up prayer groups through the communication that Annie is putting out.[4] I request that all who have read my book do these very things.

I hear the question, "How do we internalize these concepts?" One way is to take the thought, **"I am loved by the Father, more than I know."** The capacity to understand this love while on earth is limited. Work with this thought. Let it give solace and comfort to you. God loves you, my child, just as you are. What you consider limitations are simply screens that create blocks. What you think are sins are simply mistakes. One does not throw out an earthly child because he makes a mistake. The Father is even more loving, more understanding, and wiser than anyone on earth. The belief in anything that keeps you from the love of God is an error, a sin, a mistake. Spend days carrying this thought in your mind. Do this until you can accept it as true. **Understand that no matter what you do, where you go, or what you think, God loves you, NOW.**[5] This is how to internalize a concept: to internalize simply means that you take a concept within and make it yours, that there is

---

[4] The "Mary's Message/Newsletter." See Appendix 2 for information on how to obtain the newsletter.

[5] You might review Appendix 3. It is a poem Annie received entitled, "God Loves Me, Just as I am!"

complete and total acceptance of the truth in the statement. Again I caution, be careful what you internalize. When you internalize, you take it to the very core of your being. In reality you can internalize only truths, for what is not true will not be taken into the core of your being. The core can accept only what it knows, which is Truth, reality.

Now, take another thought and work with another concept: **"I am forgiven, so I can forgive myself."** By rote and repetition, you will come to accept it. When you find that deep within there is resistance, seek to find out why. The answer will be given only to you. Ask and it will be given. Seek and you shall find. This is a promise, spoken through Jesus Christ, but given to the world by the Father.

Now accept that there is joy in you, laughter, merriment and happiness. Let your life become one of delight. **Delight in seeking to connect to the Father.** Delight in studying these lessons. Delight in proving truths. Here are some concepts to help internalize Truths:

1. I am loved more than I know.
2. I am forgiven of everything, without limit.
3. I am cared for like the birds and animals in the forest. I don't need to worry. Worry is depleting and unproductive.
4. Since I am so loved, it is easy to love everyone without exception. I don't need to approve or like their behavior in order to love them. I can love the real self, which is divine.
5. I can forgive others of everything. They hurt themselves much more than they can hurt me.
6. My Father loves me so much he will answer all questions I ask.
7. All that I need and that is good for me will come into my life, as I keep the connection to The Source of All Good.
8. Those things that are not for my good leave me, as I concentrate more and more on my inner connection to the Father.

9. I am energized and healed as I am about my Father's business (inner search and guidance).
10. I and my Father are One. Everything in my life is in His hands.
11. I can live joyously and happily. I am loved by Love.

Now let this be a lesson in love and joy. Live in peace. It will be easy to be in a constant state of peace, joy and love. Remember that Love is a very powerful energy, more powerful than electricity or atomic energy. I have faith in your abilities to internalize and heed my words. I appreciate your efforts and attention. Call on me, Jesus or an angel to help.

Understand, the Father hears your every thought. Speak to Him in your mind. Let Him be the one who helps with every endeavor. Miracles will follow miracles. Healings will come from the prayers of groups who love unconditionally. Simply allow the process to work.

Mary, Mother of Jesus

Trust Your Inner Guidance
(Brotherhood, May 24, 1992)

There are many changes occurring in the world at this time. The unaware are sensing a change is in the atmosphere. They are picking up on the increasing level of energy that is bombarding the planet. This is a primary sensing of the wave of energy which is approaching this part of the Universe. Soon, many more unusual weather patterns will develop. The scientist will not call it a change but will simply cite theories and musings about the different weather patterns, oceanic and electromagnetic changes about this planet. They will say this is all slightly unusual, but it's because of this _____, then give their own thoughts, which are not truth. The ideas held in the earth-mind consciousness, or race consciousness, will inflict fear in those who are so prone. It is for this reason that many are getting the idea to move. Some are saying it is too soon. Others are trusting Spirit to make the move for them. A move of this magnitude is upsetting. Here is how to go about this move: allow Cosmic energy, which created this universe, this planet, this world, to guide and work out all the details. So, we return to our old premise, trust and believe. **Trust Spirit, and believe that you are truly cared for by a benevolent Creator, that He who is All Love will guide and protect you in every circumstance.** When the earth moves, when the crowds stampede, you will not fear unduly.

First, let us say a few words about fear. Fear is an alarm, it is a signal that something needs your attention. Fear in this instance is that which tells you to move, run, hide and/or protect yourself and your loved ones. Fear in this light then is good. It is much like noise. Noise is used as an alarm, as a warning device. Noise is not pleasant, nor is it good over a prolonged period of time. Likewise, fear is not good for you if it is in your life for a prolonged time. What is fear telling you? It is saying you are in danger: look and act. Sometimes the danger is within, as when you lower your sights and view your world through race consciousness. Or it is saying, "Find out what you are to do." Act, think! Be moved to see yourself and your world honestly. Then act according to what is needed NOW. Simply to feel guilty because your fear is useless is a waste of time. Once again, trust enters the picture. You are to trust that you will act properly, neither over-reacting nor denying the danger. **Trust in your own innate abilities. They were placed there in the beginning to protect and guide you.** But over eons the ability to see danger, clearly, has faded. You see into a dim mist of circumstances. In the last few years, people have been told everything is in good shape, yet they are getting a different inner message. Governments have always lied to their citizens in order to control. Governments work rightly when people place their trust in themselves and in their Creator. Governments fail when they become gods and work to control every issue of life within their bounds. **Put your trust in God who created you.** People know innately what is good. They do not need anyone else's opinion. This is what government do—give opinion. An opinion is only as good as the mind who created it.

Trust that your Creator, your Father within, so loved you individually that He placed, deep within, your own special connection to Him. You are connected to All Wisdom, All Knowledge and All Love. Trust that you know what to do as long as you maintain your connection in good order. As long as you pray and meditate to keep this connection strong, you know what to do and how to do it. You are provided for in the most minute ways. Nothing is too large or too small for the Father to provide. Nothing is too difficult or too easy for Him to perform through you. Here is the key: **He works through you, not for you.** God is not a genie, but His ways are magical. God allows each person to have the joy and pleasure of creating in their world as they wish. It is done according to your beliefs— these are the words of truth Jesus spoke. It is never done according to the wife's beliefs, or mother's beliefs, or the husband's beliefs. **It is done only according to your beliefs.** If you are waiting for someone else to believe for you, you are in serious trouble. It will never happen. No matter how much you love, you cannot do it for anyone else. It is one life to a person, one mind to create a belief system, and one heart to feel. You cannot feel another's pain or create a thought for them. Likewise, you cannot trust or believe for another. What you can do is pray for your loved ones. **Prayer, coupled with unselfish love, can work miracles in individual lives.**

The time is fast approaching when you will have only your trust and beliefs to guide you. All people will be in uncharted territory. The world will be dealing with unusual feelings from the energy wave, unusual circumstances and unusual climate. You will feel that you have suddenly been transported to another world. It all begins within. But the reactions will be in open view for all to see. **Trust only that**

which is given to you, that which rings true for you. Don't put your trust in another personality; they are simply creations, as are you. Congregate with like-minded souls. It will be the support of like-minded people who will help each other to live in this changing world. For this reason, many will choose to live together as families, when in reality they are strangers. Communities of like-minded people will survive together. They will work together, pray and meditate together. For now, do what is given to you to do. Help all people who come into your life. Caution them to trust only the Father within. Help them develop their connection. **Most important, pray the one for the other.** Meditate together, as there is strength in numbers. Begin to learn how to be self-sufficient. In this way, you will truly be relying on yourself and on the Father working within and through you.

Today people are like little children; they allow the government to do their thinking. But you who are enlightened will know how to care for yourselves and your loved ones. There will be nothing which you cannot provide for yourself, once you begin to think in terms of self-sufficiency, once you release from consciousness the need to have for the sake of having. Instead, take the attitude of having for the sake of enjoyment and use. All things will be useful, as in the past. All things will be beautiful, as are you.

The Brotherhood

Expect Continuous Change
(*Brotherhood, July 5, 1992*)

From this day forward, be prepared for any event to occur within your solar system. Be prepared for any event to occur within your world and your life. This is a time of great change, and great changes are happening to those who will be leaders, healers and helpers. Wherever great changes happens, there is great upheaval. Much is moved, and there is the appearance of destruction, but later it is evident that the changes happened for good. It was brought to our attention that there is great upheaval in lives on earth, especially to those who are preparing for the future in a spiritual way. The upheaval is a clearing away of old ideas, beliefs, attitudes and habits, those things in your life which are no longer needed.

While in the midst of the upheaval, ask for understanding, wisdom, and guidance. Be open to all ideas which are entering your mind. Understand that no longer do you judge according to the old way of thinking, but are judging according to your spiritual beliefs. Some will have a problem accepting this premise. You can no longer return to the old way; there have been great changes wrought within those who set their step upon a spiritual way of life. These changes are for good. They may not appear as good now, but they most certainly are. Keep affirming that the changes are for good, in order to calm your mind.

It is difficult to give up old habits, beliefs, attitudes and ideas. Nevermore can the old and new ways of thinking coexist. There is conflict, and it is felt in you and your life. Now is the time to make the decision to go forward with these changes or to stay where you are. It is a time of decision. It is a time to act. Your decision is right for you. It is completely up to you, for the Father has given freedom to choose. There are no wrong decisions, only the right decision for you, by you.

For those who are thinking they have already made their changes and the upheaval in their lives has subsided, think again. From now on there will be continuous change in your lives and your world. **The great changes without are a reflection of the changes taking place within humanity.**

Now is the time for prayer, meditation and reflection. Now is the time to decide if you will continue on the spiritual path or turn aside. It can no longer go both ways. There must be a decision. **There must be honesty with self. There must be**

love for self and your world. Above all, pray for a new attitude of love and forgiveness with self, circumstances, and with inner guidance. Pray to learn to trust Spirit to work through you. Appreciate the great upheaval taking place now in the world, and, with a new attitude, your understanding will open your eyes to see the Great Love which is now emitting into your solar system and world.

The Brotherhood

Surrender in Strength
(Brotherhood, July 19, 1992)

We know that many are having a tough time. Tough times make tough people. In order to survive and endure the coming changes, people need to toughen up. There is hope—the hope that as you work through the inner struggle and become quiet once again, you will be aware of the inflow of energy. Changes happening within are reflected in the changes taking place in your outer life, so take heart, **be strong in your faith and stay true to your inner search.** Many people are going through tough times now. There is an adjustment in econo mies, governments, and people. It is not necessary to be anything but who you are, a child of a loving Creator. You already have within yourselves all that is needed in order to survive. There are some slight adjustments which have been made. People who are living these lessons are growing in strength, virtue and inner power.

It may seem there is an extra burden to carry because you know of the coming changes. This is not true. What is happening is the ambivalence of living in a seemingly stable world, knowing that everything is changing. Old values are changing, not only for the enlightened, but for every person on earth. What was important a few months ago is not as important now. What was of major importance is changing. People are having to make choices in living arrangements, locations and goals. Look at the world and see how countries and governments have changed. This will affect your country also. We are not saying the changes will be as great, but there will be some change in government. Not only will the common people take back control, but they will insist on it. The status quo cannot continue, and so old values will be instilled into government. For the individual person, there is a change in values. It will no longer be necessary to acquire wealth, as in possessions, only for show. It is of more value to acquire knowledge. People will learn to live on less money and be pleased to do so. There will be new types of businesses that will help people to achieve their goals of becoming self-sufficient. This is necessary in order for people to be prepared to live in the new-looking world. Individuals will set up communities, in some cases with blood relatives, or with others who are like-minded. Through the process of growing together and learning to live together, people will not only survive but become wealthy together.

Free yourself of the entrapment of possessions and have the freedom to live enjoyably. You will take pride in the accomplishments of the people in your community. Instead of individual pride and values, there will be community pride and community values. Possessions will be of value when they are of use. Simply to have possessions sitting around to be looked at will become obsolete. Possessions will of necessity be useful only. These useful possessions will be decorated. Possessions will be of value not only for their aesthetic quality, but for the tools they are. Look at your possessions and see what is useful, what is of value.

Continue to pray and meditate. It is of so much value. Your prayer and meditations not only bring peace but connect you to the Father within, who is the Giver of Life, of Knowledge, and of all that is needed in order to live on earth. By remaining in a state of prayer and meditation, you will be sustained during this time of adjustment. Begin to spend at the very least thirty minutes every two days in silence. Allow the Spirit of Love to instruct, teach and give knowledge.

Trust that what you are given within is for you. **Trust that as you remain faithful to your inner search you will be told all things you have need of.** Some people have a difficult time trusting their own inner guidance. They will take the words of another as truth, but will doubt what comes through them. Begin to trust yourself. Trust that you will be able to discern Truth. This is very important. In the future, communication will not be as readily available as now. You will need to trust your inner guidance. Understand that your inner guidance will not be like anyone else's inner guidance. Stay firm, in your place. Seek to know only what you need to know this day. Allow the Father to work out all future plans for you. This is what is called "surrendering." By surrendering, you do not give up or make a statement of ineptitude, but you are open to new ideas, new influences, which are the real you working for you. **When you surrender to the Father, you are not making a statement of weakness, but of strength.** Surrender means to allow, to be open. Allow Spirit to guide and work out all details.

If you are guided to move or change residence, thank Spirit for working out all details, including the sale of existing properties, the location and purchase of future properties and the ability to earn a living in the new location. Be open to Spirit doing this for you. Do today what is needed, and "know" within that the near future and the far future are now in Spirit's hands and all will be cared for.

Work to be open and retain an aura of allowing. Feel comfortable with the decision to surrender to God. This is the best way to face the coming earth changes. In this way you will be assured of being in the proper place, with the proper people, and doing the work you are to do. Feel confident that all your needs are met now. Nothing is left to chance. This is how to face the future, whether it is next week, next year or years from now.

Know that there is much help from this side of Creation; many are helping in prayers and holding a vision of a stable future for you. Not only are we in place to help, but there are angels and masters of learning willing to be of help. Call on Spirit and pray to the Father only. We all work according to His Will. **Take heart, remain strong in prayer and do your meditations daily.** In this manner your inner connection will be in place. Through this inner connection, all instruction, guidance and healing will flow.

The Brotherhood

30

Setting Up Prayer Circles

Service Through Prayer and Meditation
(Love Being and Brotherhood, August 2, 1992)

GOOD DAY, FAMILY GROUP. Truly this group is not only a family group of like-minded souls, but it is a core group of Mary workers. When you work in Her service, you are committed to working for the Creator. Here are the plans for the future. This group could easily meet once a month, to give support the one to the other, as each person opens their lives to service.

Most of you have already committed to service. If you are not already doing your service, you're searching for the way to serve. Here is how you will serve, no matter how else you serve. It is time for groups of people to set up prayer and meditation meetings. They will meet to pray for the survival of mankind during the earth changes. Pray for the upliftment of man (here we refer to the totality of humanity and not to gender). Take prayer requests and pray for specific individuals. Since we are calling you to serve under Mary, perhaps it would be good to review Her writings on prayer and meditation, and follow Her suggestions.

We have some suggestions which may parallel Hers or could provide you with new insight. Understand that you will take from these writings what rings true for you, and what clicks inside of you as truth. Allow these groups to remain fluid and flexible, changing the way the meetings are held or conducted as the group sees fit. You will know when to effect a change: it will be revealed to you. Step out and serve; many are being called and few are responding. It is far easier to sit back and allow someone else to do the work. But the coming events are of such a great nature that it is now taking everyone's efforts to effect change.

Let us address the concept of time. Time has been in high gear for awhile. It has sped up, and you are in what is called "quantum time." That is a whole topic in itself. But allow us to say this: understand that since time is moving at a faster rate now, your prayers will effect change quickly. **Your meditations on Love raise the consciousness of mankind quickly.** As you pray for humanity, more and more minds are opening to the possibility of a life beyond what is seen or felt. People are opening up to new ideas of life and the importance of life. From now on, situations will become more difficult for everyone. People who rely on the Father within to provide will find not only solace and comfort, but all their needs met. If something is taken away from your life, understand that it isn't for your future. Allow Spirit to enter your mind and heart, changing your motives, concepts of yourself, ideas on service and ideas on what is needed. Ask Spirit to help you understand this fast-changing world and your part in it.

Begin to think about prayer circles and discuss ways to begin prayer and meditation circles: where will they be held? If not in your home, then where? when? what night or day? Do not worry about who will come; when you have opened your homes and churches to prayer and meditation, people will find you. Decide when you will come together to discuss and share your joys, ideas and inspirations.

Know that you will never be alone. Jesus promised that where two or three meet in his name, he will be there. This is his commitment to you who serve. The Brotherhood and many more who are praying for this world will be with you. **As you serve, you grow spiritually.** This is the only growth that is necessary. You will find much coming from these circles: poems, prayers, healings and stories. Keep a record of what is beautiful and useful to others in the way you prayed and of how it was successful.

Prayer is so wonderful because it is the shifting of circumstances and situations towards Good. If something negative or harmful (we like this word better) is in the future, through prayer you will shift it toward the Good. When you pray for humanity's good, you will shift circumstance and situations quickly. This is above and beyond the quickness of quantum time. You will see results in a short time. I recommend praying for these circumstances:

1. For your own awareness of a continued inner connection to the Father.
2. For the good of your city: environment, politics, government, economics, social concerns, and the spiritual health of each citizen and all the animals. (You may add to this list.)
3. Then pray this same way for your nation.
4. Pray for the world in this manner. Include the oceans, forests, plains and deserts.
5. Pray for the world's future and the population's future.

All future circumstances and situations are fluid.

The future can be changed through prayer, by moving it into the light of Good.

Now, a suggestion for meditation. Take a globe and place it in the center of a circle of people. Open your hands palms out.

Allow all the energy of the universe to flow through you into this representation of the world. In your mind's eye see light, love and energy flowing from your hands into the world, each nation and each ocean. **There is power in the coming together of those who seek daily to find their inner light.** Your light shines more brightly when you share. This is how to share who and what you are. Decide, commit, and then go into action. All is happening quickly now; it is time for this phase of the work to begin. We are available to you as inner guides or simply as assistants in your prayer circles.

We see each of the prayer circles as gears in a motor, moving the future toward Universal Light, Love and All Goodness. As more prayer circles are formed, this creates a bigger motor to shift the future, world and humanity toward The Source.

If you cannot set up a prayer circle at this time, then support one with your time and energy. Choose one of the circles that is closest to your home. Not everyone will set up prayer circles: many are needed as participants. Everyone is needed; everyone is important and has their own place in this plan. Everyone is loved greatly.

A Being of Love[6] and the Brotherhood

Conducting Prayer and Meditation Groups
(Love Being and Brotherhood, August 30, 1992)

Our prayer is that in time each of you will begin to form groups for prayer and meditation. We are not hurrying you but simply giving this as our intent in instructing you. There are many to teach and pray for. Only through growth will it all be accomplished. This group will act as a cell dividing many times

---

[6] The "Being of Love" was brought to Annie by Jesus (in a meditation) to become her full-time guide. It/he is of the Christ Consciousness, has never incarnated, and has neither gender nor name. Annie assigned him the male gender and named him "Love Being." As she became more familiar, she shortened it to "LB."

to splinter into similar groups for the express purpose of prayer and meditation, of praying for yourselves, your loved ones and your world. Today we ask for prayer, not only for the people who experienced this large storm,[7] but for the opening of minds to hear truth and to see the unusual events that are already happening in this world.

As to how to hold and conduct these groups, each individual group will meet for the express purpose of prayer and meditation. The mechanics will not be as important as the intent. Let each group gravitate to those activities which seem right for its members. We urge each group to pray according to what is right for them. Some may want to kneel or hold hands. Our preference is the holding of hands. The touching of hands with goodwill and good intent is a prayer. **The touching of hands in prayer allows energies which are unseen to flow and increase before going into the ethers to do as directed.**

Begin always with a moment of individual prayer, in which each person is allowed to forgive themselves and anyone else. Then forgive the world, all its inhabitants and all your ancestors, remembering that you are your ancestors. Forgive governments, religions and all institutions of man. **Pour forgiveness into the race consciousness of mankind.** Then bring love, wisdom and truth into your being and allow it to flow into your home, city, state, continent, hemisphere and then on to all the world. Do this slowly, giving time for the idea to sink into your mind and heart. By connecting with Spirit, it is done. This is simply one way to pray for the world. **Everyone needs forgiveness; everyone needs love.** In order to radiate love, forgiveness must be a part of your make-up. By allowing forgiveness to be active in you, it is easy to send it to mankind. **Bring love into your being; daily radiate love to everyone, all the time.**

Next concentrate on peace. **Make peace with yourself, your Creator and your family, and then send peace into the**

---

[7] Hurricane Andrew in Southern Florida (August 1992).

world. Concentrate on those countries that are in the midst of war. They do more destruction to themselves and their nation than they do to anyone else. In this light, pray for Africa. This whole continent is in a state of war each day. Small wars spring up within cities, families, tribes and within countries, but we see that they fight themselves more than anyone else. Send peace to Asia, for within their sector are many who are in a warring mood. Pray for these continents, not only to put down arms, but to put away attitudes of control, malice and close-mindedness. Pray and send peace to the European continent, for there are many who are resentful and angry. Send peace to the Middle East, for there is much hatred in the hearts of men. Pray for the American continents, for upon these lands is much abuse of all kinds. This does not mean that such conditions are seen only in these specific areas; it means that all these conditions are prevalent in every nation of the world.

First, make peace with yourself by accepting that you are always loved. God loves and accepts you just as you are today. As you come to accept yourself, you will find things to improve within yourself. The improvements will be from a standpoint of gentleness and love, not of fear or loss. Accept that you are here to learn and share. This is really all that is required at this time. **You are to forgive and love, first yourself and then your world,** accepting that every event and situation in your life is for the express purpose of learning. You are always learning something, therefore you are always in motion. **Understand that the best you can ever do for people is to pray for them.** Prayer is an outpouring of all the forces of the Universe for improvement. Prayer is a shifting of the future into higher and higher good. It is uplifting. Prayer caramelizes (sweetens) people, circumstances and events with love and goodness.

Pray for the transformation that is taking place in each of you. Then pray for the transformation that is taking place in the world. Ask each person in the world to accept the transformation, as it is only Goodness, Truth and Love entering this atmosphere. **Pray that all transformations take place in peace, with gentleness and love.** This will minimize fear and anger. People are inherently feeling the changes, and there is a natural reaction to fear of the unknown. By praying specifically for the transformation to take place with gentleness and love, you have increased the vibrations in man's consciousness to open the door to Peace, Hope and Love.

Now, concerning the transformation. Each of you is going through the transformation in earnest. View all the changes in your life as good, and seek to find only good. We could compare transformation as a nut. It is hard on the outside but the inside carries with it a seed for the future. Perhaps the outer circumstances in your life appear difficult, but within each difficulty is the seed for a brighter future. As such, this is the hope of the world. People who are seeking to make a difference in the world are now experiencing difficulties, if viewed only by world standards. Many find themselves at a loss as to how to improve their lives in the area of work experience. They don't know how to put into place what their inner guidance is directing at this time. Stay true to your purpose to serve, prepare and lead. Know that these experiences contain seeds for the future.

Once again, we urge you to pray for the working out of all events. Pray, knowing that all you need is now in place. Pray that each person will find their direction with ease, clarity and honesty. How this works out in your life is through God's joy. He will put a plan into place, at the right time. **All you need for the future, He provides, if you will just believe and trust. Belief and trust are your currency in Spirit.** Let each person put into practice these ideas. Allow yourself to become comfortable with this procedure of praying, understanding always that Spirit is fluid. New ideas and methods will blossom. Bring all new ideas to share with each other. Share today what has worked for you in the past. Make a commitment to pray for Light, Love and Peace to all men this day.

Love Being and the Brotherhood

On Love and Encouragement

Propelled by Love Energy
(Love Being and Brotherhood, September 13, 1992)

TODAY WE WILL SPEAK TO YOU OF LOVE and how to use this wonderful energy to propel your lives in a positive manner.

Mother Mary has told you that Love is an Energy like Light.[8] When you think of light, you think of lamps, which shine light in your homes. But light has many more properties and can be used in many different methods—to cut away old tissue, to cut diamonds, to burn away unneeded growths and to reveal the inner skeleton. So, Love has many properties. Love will propel you through your day in a manner that is wonderful. Using love to propel your daily routine will bring all chores, appointments and work into a delicious stew of activity. You will look back and wonder how you accom-

---

[8] In the chapter "The Subject is Love" of *Mary's Message to the World*.

plished so much. Later, time will reveal that on that particular day you touched other lives with blessings that were unnoticed and unseen by you.

Here is how to start your day using Love's Energy to coordinate and organize your daily activities. Before arising in the morning, first thing upon awakening, say a prayer of thanksgiving for the life and the day that is before you. Understand that the day will be filled with your beliefs, attitudes and thoughts from past days. **Be grateful for a clean slate, ask Divine Love to live this day through you,** blessing everyone you speak to, work with, and come into contact with, no matter how brief the contact. State, **"I want to live this day in service to Divine Love, knowing full well that the Father's Love will iron out all wrinkles, erase all misconceptions and misunderstandings, and will feed the inner soul with manna from heaven. All this happens as I go about my business in this frame of mind."** Then accept that it is done. This takes only a minute, and your day will be fruitful beyond expectation.

As you go through the day, your car will be propelled with Love. It will enhance the performance of the car, your work and efforts, as you live from a standpoint of Love's Energy. We are not saying that there will be no conflicts in your day. Perhaps there will be. Not everyone is living from an inner connection to Divine Love. But the conflict will not affect your inner self, nor will it cause any lingering effects within your heart. What if you find that you are angry or upset? When you come to yourself (much like awakening), simply restate that Love is taking care of all the activities of this day. Let anger go into Divine Love's vat of purification, and the conflict will be recycled into Pure Love.

Allow Divine Love to burn away all ill effects of the past. The body retains memory of the past and will bring up sensations that denote unpleasantness. This is the ego's way of trying to keep control over you. It says, this all sounds too easy, it can't work. We ask that you give yourself three weeks, and then make that decision. In three weeks time, the body will find that Divine Love is healing wounds of the past. In this age, most people have deep wounds to heal, the accumulation of life-times of abuses, both sustained and inflicted. It is time for this clearing of old wounds, and Divine Love is the way to do this easily.

In this same manner, Love will be used as Light; it will cut away dead issues. In this case, the dead issues can be dying relationships or useless activities and habits. In time, by using Love daily, your taste in food, people and activities will change for the better. This doesn't need to be painful; it can all be a natural progression of events. **By pouring Love into your daily life, you do much to grow spiritually.** In reality, you came to practice love in the laboratory, which is this world. Now, understand that we are not saying that all will be rosy and beautiful. When dead tissues are burned or cut away, there is an odor, blood drainage and a mess. Sometimes, if things are in a mess in a life, there is a messy clearing away. This may entail discomfort and could easily entail a big mess. It is a clearing away of the useless, in order to make room for the useful. Many times circumstances and events get worse before they can get better.

Divine Love is very revealing, just like light used as an X-ray. It will reveal the unseen and unheard issues in a situation. It brings into the open all that is hidden. This is very good, because then you have choice. You can continue with the way things were, or you can choose to change. Most often, people who have been using Love will choose to change, knowing that **Divine Love brings only GOODNESS.** These revelations can be very discomforting. Sometimes forgotten issues are re-vealed in order to bring forgiveness and healing to the soul. At other times, you are confronted with behaviors that didn't seem bad but also didn't really feel good. **In Love, you see yourself clearly and with honesty.** By taking a good look at all that was hidden, you see where you were really heading. A real healing takes place after you have taken an honest look at yourself. Then it's time to get on with your true life goals. At this point in time, you are released from all past suffering. The good news is that this process takes only a short time. Then you will truly project Love into humanity with the same kind of healing.

Work with Divine Love, use it daily and see miracles take place in your life—not only in your life, but in the lives of your loved ones. The people who are closest to you will begin to change too. Only good will come to them. If it appears in their life to not be good, remain firm in your belief that Divine Love is healing every area of their lives too. Healing will follow and blessings will continue to flow, all this because you opened your mind and heart to Divine Love. **Divine Love is never stagnant; it is in constant flow. It is ever-moving, sometimes slowly like lava, and other times rapidly, like a flooded river. Wherever Divine Love moves, there is always improvement, always goodness and always blessings.**

We request that for a period of three weeks you use these principles. See the change in moods, outlook and attitude. Time is now fast-paced; the changes will be great, improvements will be beneficial to the soul. Remember, changes take place first within, and then they are visible to everyone. **Change works first within and then without. It begins in the Kingdom of Heaven within you.**

Love Being and the Brotherhood

Expand Your Capacity to Love
(Love Being and Brotherhood, October 11, 1992)

We bring instruction to help you to expand your capacity to love. We encourage each person to spend much time in prayer and meditation. The collective prayers of mankind are on the rise. **Prayer moves future events into the Good, which**

is God. When you pray for yourself and your life, a special prayer is added for the future, because no matter how selfish the prayer, it is always a prayer for the future. People pray in different ways, and all prayer is answered. It is answered according to the faith of the person praying. At the same time, a prayer is added to the collective whole for the future.

People want to know how to help. They want a great mission in life. **Every person has a great mission NOW! Live this life in unconditional love.** When one can do this well, he will assist in unseen ways. **To love unconditionally means to love without judgment,** never placing any judgments on yourself or anyone else. People seem to judge themselves harshly. We agree with Mother Mary: start by loving yourself unconditionally. It isn't as easy as it sounds. Each morning, upon arising, **make a commitment to live this one day loving yourself and others unconditionally.** Then monitor yourself throughout the day. As you live each day doing this exercise, you find new ways to give others a boost—maybe a smile, a kind word or allowing someone to go before you.

These simple acts will cause others to feel good. When people feel good, they feel God. **God and Good are synonymous; they are one and the same. To feel good about yourself and others is to feel God within and God without.**

Begin to find small, simple pleasures in life. Seek thoughts that bring joy, happiness and love into your life. Joy, happiness, unconditional love, pleasure, peace, serenity and all good things are your Divine Right. **The mission that everyone has been instilled with is to live in Goodness, no matter what the circumstances or events in your life.**

As more and more people begin to live from a standpoint of love, peace and joy, these very great aspects of God will flow into the everyday life of humanity.

Work on yourself and your life. In this way, as you become more loving and peaceful, not only does your home change, but the people who are in your presence change. How simple it is, and how very difficult it can be. Many people want to go out, do great works and be known. **The greatest work that can be done is to live each day loving yourself, your family and your world unconditionally.**

This means you will instantly forgive. Forgive to keep a clear opening to Good, which is God. Forgive is to wipe every slate clean. Forgive to help not only the other person but yourself. This doesn't mean that you overlook gross neglect or abuse. It means that you can see past the neglect and abuse, to see the person who is in pain. It means you remain in God-like peace, giving unconditional love to all people.

Often times we hear the question, "How do I do it? How do I start to love myself and others unconditionally?" One way is to remind yourself that God only loves and His love is unconditional. God forgives instantly. Remind yourself that **when you feel good, you are feeling God.** Now a word about feeling good. The goodness we speak of is natural, not one induced by any outside elements, such as drugs or alcohol. In reality, these things do not make one feel good. It isn't a lasting feeling of goodness. It is an illusive goodness, which quickly fades into despair.

When you feel good inside for no reason, it is a feeling of God, a feeling of God within your entire being. This is how you want to feel at all times. It is how you were meant to feel at all times.

Watch your thoughts and words. See how many times you say things that do not foster a feeling of goodness. To criticize yourself or others instills feelings of alienation. This doesn't feel good. What is your belief? Do you believe in a God who is Love, who is always forgiving and compassionate? These are good statements to make each morning: **"I believe in a Creator who is Divinely Loving, always forgiving and ever compassionate. No matter what happens today, I know that God loves me, forgives and understands me."**

Stop blaming God for all the mistakes in your life. When you believe in a loving God, all things will be better, even if the earth moves, which simply means your life is changed. Lives in change are lives in upheaval, and for a time it can be very disconcerting. Today many people find their lives in a state of great upheaval. The greater the change, the greater the opportunity to believe and be faithful to a loving God. These are wonderful opportunities to stay calm in the knowledge that God is Love and all change in your life is for good. Begin again with, **"I commit to live this day loving myself and others unconditionally."** All fear will drop away like water off a duck's back. The biggest fear is death, then the next biggest fear is change. This is a life of continuous change. You change as you grow. This growth is both physical and spiritual. So welcome change; it means you are growing in spirit and in truth. Welcome the opportunity to practice your faith and commitment.

As you learn to love unconditionally, increase your prayers for all people who are living in judgment and fear. Increase the smiles, kind words and loving thoughts. More good is done with a loving thought than with a million dollars. **More good is done with a quiet prayer than with advice.** More good is done with a simple meditation on love than in saying the words, "I love you," without meaning. Seek out any feeling of discomfort. Take a look at it, clear the cause and return to love. The discomfort may be physical, emotional or mental. They are all signs that something needs your attention in order to return to love.

Let this be your mission in life, then: allow Love, Divine Love, to flow through you into the world. Make a commitment to clear away anything that prevents you from living this mission. You will find the way to clear it away. It will come through inner guidance. Do whatever it takes to remain in the flow of Goodness.

Love Being and the Brotherhood

Faith to Clear Obstacles
(Love Being and Brotherhood, November 1, 1992)

Welcome to your continued journey into aliveness and Spiritual well-being. As a part of the whole, we come to give guidance and help. Today, let us concentrate on faith—faith as Jesus spoke of, the faith that moves mountains. This faith could also be called belief. The faith we speak of is that deep belief system which sometimes remains hidden. In order to assess your deep beliefs, you will need to take several days to listen to your talk, thoughts, and look at your actions. You speak from this deep inner belief system, think from this core belief and act according to the inner beliefs.

Many people are surprised when they take a close look at themselves. This type of inner scrutiny is needed in order to uncover core beliefs. These can remain hidden over a lifetime. One thing every person has the ability to do is to deceive themselves. Often people will look at their beliefs and see what they wish them to be, instead of what is! **Belief is more than words, thoughts or actions; it is the very essence of your life.** It is your make up, your definition.

We urge you to look at yourselves with a microscope and see what you really, really believe. Keep a journal, if possible, or simply make mental notes of what you see, hear and feel. It is one thing to think positively, when you are making a conscious effort to be positive. It is yet another thing to think from your core belief system when you are preoccupied. That is the time to scrutinize, for it is when you are thinking in a totally unconscious way that your true colors shine. When you feel disconnected, your real belief system will come to the front.

When you feel bad, either physically or emotionally, do you think that change is on its way? Do you feel that you will get better? Do you think that this is temporary? Or do you fear it is permanent? These are the times you see how you really believe. When events in your life become difficult, do you pray more or complain more? When you feel ill physically, do you plan to return to health, or do you wallow in illness?

What action steps do you take? How do you react to illness? How do you react to emotional upsets? What do you think at these times? Is there more emphasis on prayer, or on the physical in the form of depression, anger or denial?

This type of self-scrutiny will demonstrate what you really believe. It takes time, effort and honesty. When you know how you believe, then you will know what to do in order to correct your belief system. **In order to move mountains, it requires faith in a benevolent Creator.** You need to believe you are created in His image and that you can create a beautiful world. Remember that it takes only a small measure of faith to move mountains. Mountains could represent the immoveable obstacles in your life. Perhaps you feel that you are disconnected spiritually, or you feel you don't have what it takes to create beauty; or, as many do, you feel unworthy to receive. The mountains could be real mountains on the physical plane of earth, or they could represent a belief in lack. Many people believe in a benevolent God, but believe they are lacking somehow, either in education, personality, charisma or some other intangible trait. Yet, if you believe you have been created just like God in talents, abilities and creativeness, you will find a way to circumvent any obstacle.

Jesus said if you have faith like a mustard seed, which means if you have only that much faith, then nothing is impossible to you. It takes only a tiny amount of faith to clear away all obstacles in your life. Here we speak of spiritual obstacles, such as hard emotions, a faulty belief system or dis-spiritedness. Dis-spiritedness is a lack of spirit. Of course you cannot have a lack of spirit in reality. Sometimes on earth you feel a lack of spirit in your life, or lifelessness in your being. This is not real.

We have given affirmations to strengthen your faith. Use any affirmations that will help you **rediscover** your true nature. Understand that when it comes to self-deceit, humanity is accomplished. It is so ingrained in humanity that on earth it feels real and seems real. During the time when you are seeking to rediscover your true nature, be firm with yourself. Here are some more affirmations to help you:

1. No matter what I think or feel, I believe my Creator loves me in all circumstances.
2. My real self knows that I can move mountains, and so I do.
3. My faith increases daily as I understand that I am really connected to God.
4. I refuse to react from any emotion except love.
5. My belief system is readjusted to be in perfect alignment with all Goodness.
6. The feeling of being unconnected is not real; I am always connected to my Source.
7. Deep within is a place of peace, love and joy. This is the Kingdom of Heaven within me.
8. Daily I will remember that I CAN, because I believe in my God-likeness.
9. I am worthy, so I receive only good.
10. I surrender to God's Will, because I know He is Love.

Believe, my loving people. Believe that only good comes to you, no matter how it appears at first. Believe that only from a point of Love is your creation maintained as well as all that you create. Daily believe only in good, love and joy. Then stand aside and allow only goodness, love and joy to come, in any disguise. Life on earth is much like a masquerade ball. Good, joy, love, peace can be disguised in a monster mask. But as long as you see reality (the mask), then and only then will the good unmask itself to reveal its true nature. Be not dismayed if all your good is masked; it's a ball, have fun. Begin to believe in goodness and have real fun in life.

Remember that faith grows with use. Allow faith to grow in strength, love and goodness. Let yourself believe that YOU CAN, and before long you will find your entire belief system has changed. Then your faith will grow, because you believe that YOU CAN. Be light and make light of the monstrous conditions, which are simply disguised goodness. Have fun and see how much you have grown.

Love Being and the Brotherhood

Your True Work
(Love Being and Brotherhood, November 22, 1992)

Today we are a combination of Enlightened Beings who come to bring light, love and encouragement. Many of you are on the threshold of new avenues of work. We speak of your true work, which is service to the Father within. We now enter a time of work, service and peace-making.

It is exciting to be part of the changes. It is breath-taking to be part of the great work of bringing order into a world of seeming chaos. **Now is the time to put your lessons to use.** Use the faith that has built up within. You will find that faith is increasing. When all you hear are words of doom and gloom, speak words of Truth and Love. Speak these words first to yourself, to bolster your courage. Then speak lovingly of truths which are eternal.

The eternal truths are: **God is alive and well.** He lives, and so, therefore, we live, abundantly. We have all the life force within that is needed to sustain life on this planet. Nothing is withheld. There is plenty of life's energy to sustain, grow and regenerate all life forms. What the coming storms destroy will be regenerated through life. What is destroyed through man's errors will be rejuvenated through life's energy.

Your words, thoughts and meditations have great power. They have the power of the Universe. It is Cosmic power, which is instilled in every word, thought and meditation. When you speak words, know that they are life-giving words. This is the reason it is important to watch what is said at all times. Let no joke or jest be spoken that could cause any harm. Never say anything harmful of, or to, another. Speak only truth. Speak only those words which bring revelation to another. Understand that the words you speak will bring revelations, even when you least expect it. Encourage one another with love. Let your words be of good and for good only. Be honest, or as honest as is possible. We are aware that many people on earth refuse to hear words of truth and become fearful or simply turn off. What we say is, speak of encouragement, love, and tell of your own experiences. When you speak of your experiences, others will see that you are speaking truth. People have the same feelings from time to time. Everyone faces similar issues from time to time. There will be enough similarities to engender a feeling of knowingness. They will recognize, through your experiences, their own and will find a door opening within to their truths.

There is no need to make any great pronouncements; simply use every opportunity to encourage people. You will affect those people with whom you work and are contacting daily. It will be through your daily activities that people see your beliefs. Your beliefs are seen in detail. For instance, people will notice that you encourage others, speak kindly, and that there is an aura of peace and goodwill about you. This is much like a flashing billboard sign. **Speak of love, truth and peace, and then live these daily.** Let your words, meditations and thoughts be of the highest. Your actions will follow and be true to your thoughts and words.

Keep daily prayers and meditations alive. It is easy to allow them to become rote and without meaning. Have a childlike and curious quality about you. Learn to question and seek always to know. It is through your curious mind that the door within remains open. How does this work? Why is this so? Let your mind question always. This is what Jesus meant when he said, "Let the little children come unto me, for they are of the kingdom of heaven." It is not only their innocence, but their innate curiosity, that keeps them in the kingdom of heaven.

Strive to understand and, if you don't, then question. **Strive to put meaning and feeling into your prayers.** Become more like a little child; be sincere and honest with yourself.

Honesty with self is not always easy. Your mind will make excuses. Then the ego takes over and places blame somewhere else. But when you think with your heart and mind, you will find it easier to be honest with self. The heart will not cover up or lie. The heart will feel what is there honestly. The ego doesn't control the heart as easily as it does the mind. Ego is the selfish self, the self who is looking for acknowledgment. Ego likes to feel important and thinks of itself as special. Ego will hide truths in order to see itself as important. It will fool itself into thinking it is always in a good light. Ego will distort and cover up or blame anyone to make itself look good. The heart will simply feel what is in it. The heart doesn't connive or manipulate when there is an opening to the Father within.

Understand there is a need to practice what you are learning, to put into effect in your life the truths we give. A word of warning: truth will not stay where it is not freely shared by living through you. Love is not pure love if it is hidden. Do you remember the story in the Old Testament of the old lady who had no oil with which to cook? The prophet said to her, "Take this oil and pour from this container, but always leave a little in the bottle." We say this is a story of truth, love and peace. Always keep a little truth, love and peace in your heart, and share the rest. You will never run out this way. If you give away all your love and have no love of self, then love will vanish. There will be no love with which to replenish yourself. You must have love for self. You must speak words of love to yourself, then you will be able to love others. Speak words of truth and peace to yourself daily. Let these be your affirmations: **"I have a heart filled with love and can share it freely with everyone I contact this day. I love myself, and so I love others."** This is how to meditate, too. Meditate on love, peace and truth, allowing these words to speak volumes to your heart. From the center of your heart, love, truth and peace will spring forth like a fountain. It will simply recirculate, bringing beauty and goodwill into your life.

Love Being and the Brotherhood

32

Deepening Love and Peace

Angels of Love and Peace
(Love Being, January 10, 1993)

GOOD DAY, LOVED ONES. This is Love Being and, since I haven't had the honor of naming you, I've taken it upon myself to do so. From this day forward, you will be known as the Love Group for several reasons. **Our entire makeup is Love. Each of us was created out of the clay of Love. Love is our basic element and structure.** You come together with love in your hearts, love for the knowledge of God. Your basic reason for seeking Him is to know Him, so you search for love and all its components.

In reality the only thing you do well is love. Looking at today's world, this seems to be the furthest thing from the truth. But since you have a seeking nature, you think and believe the search is difficult and tedious, when in reality the search is easy and fun. What is difficult is to take off the blinders, to realize

that all that is good, is Spirit. Since Spirit is unseen and unheard, you find this difficult. I've heard people say, "Seeing is
believing." You will see Spirit move through earth, making it
very apparent that there is yet more than can be seen. There are
forces that man cannot control, see or hear that are very real.
Their effects will be visible. Then mankind will see and believe
that there is a God who is Spirit.

Because of the unleashing of natural forces, people will
believe that God is angry and punishing, when in reality He is
loving and allowing their actions and reactions to demonstrate
their own violence in nature. The violence of nature is only the
outer demonstration of the inner violence this generation has
come to idolize. Yes, the word is idolized, through movies,
drama, song, in families and children's play. **As within, so
without.** What has been within mankind for centuries is violence, anger, fear and power struggles of all kinds. Now nature
will demonstrate man's inner awareness. How can you change
this to a planet of peace and love? It happens as everything
does, one step at a time. You begin a journey with one step, then
you take another and another, until you are well on your way
to your destination. The journey to peace and love is taken by
one step, one small group meeting to pour love and peace into
their hearts, homes, cities, countries and world.

**When you realize that you already know how to live
peacefully and lovingly, then it will be so.** As more and more
people live from a standpoint of love and peace, this reality will
grow into an outer manifestation. Because many people have
been dedicated to peace and made others aware of the dangers
of war, there is a measure of peace. The small wars that are
evident are an outer sign of the continued worship of violence.
The news media scream the acts of violence. They should be
screaming the acts of love. What can you do to promote peace
and love? This is a question that needs to be answered within
each person, because each person will have a different direction given. For some it's a matter of prayer and meditation

groups, formed especially to meditate on peace and the spreading of love to this world. For others, it may be more physical demonstrations, such as peace marches or orations on peace for the purpose of raising the public's awareness. There needs to be more time and prayer given to love and peace. Let your prayers be to love mentally each nation, each part of this world. In meditation you could see buckets of love and peace being poured upon the lands of this world by hovering angels. Let there be an inner vision of angels of peace and angels of love pouring buckets of peace and love upon each country, ocean, forest and continent. This would be the best meditation one could do for peace and love.

Now that you have the group name, Love, **let love be your mission in life.** Love yourself and your family to wholeness. Let love be the first thing you think of upon awakening, and the last thing on your mind as you enter sleep. **Forgive constantly; forgiveness of self and others will do much to foster an environment of love. Where there is love, true unconditional love, there is peace.** Begin each day with love. Do all you can to love yourself, because you are already loved. **You and all of us are made in the image of our Creator. God is love—so are you!**

Now to love yourself is to care for yourself—to be strong, courageous, and never to allow another person to abuse you. Love is not abusive in any way, form or fashion. Love doesn't bind; it loosens and gives freedom. As you free others to be themselves, you free yourself. As you love yourself unconditionally, you love others in the same manner. Change the attitudes, beliefs and thought patterns that keep you from loving freely. **Accept yourself just as you are now.** Understand that you are evolving in love and becoming serene and peaceful.

Take all the conditions of your life and love them, even those that appear unloving. By loving, this is what I mean. Say you have a bad temper; you would say, "I have a bad temper, which indicates there is an abundance of anger. Why am I

angry? What steps can I take to release this anger appropri-
ately? I love myself, just as I am. I love my temper. It's becoming serene and peaceful as I love myself unconditionally. I will
take the steps that I am directed to take." See, you don't love the
bad temper, but you do love your temper. Knowing within that
as you release anger, forgive the people you are angry with,
and send the thought that they too are created in love, then
there is change for the better. Do this with any depleting
emotion. If there is fear, simply change the word temper to
temperament and the word anger to fear. It is still a matter of
forgiveness. **Forgive others as the Father Creator has already
forgiven you.** This same exercise can be used for prejudices,
biases, envies, jealousies or any depleting emotion. **You are not
the problem; you hold on to the problem.** Forgiveness is a
releasing and erasing of problems.

After this step has been taken, dwell on thoughts of love,
peace and happiness. You must clear the heart and mind in
order to instill good. This is very important; then you will be
prepared for any event.

As you begin to think continuously on love, love will
guide you to do what is needed to clear away all debris from the
mind and heart. **Begin and end each day with thoughts of how
much you are loved and accepted by the Father.** He forgives
everything instantly. How can you not do the same?

You are centers of love, radiating what you are out into
your world. Become true centers of love by concentrating on
love every moment.

Love Being

Find the Gift in Your Fear
(*Love Being and Brotherhood, January 24, 1993*)

On this day we come to encourage and commune with
you in love and joy.

It seems that across the land, the news of the coming events[9] of this year has helped many to get in touch with fear. We will speak about fear and the great need to look into its face and see what it has brought as a gift. Fear is not something to eradicate completely. It is a part of your makeup. **Fear was placed in you by our Creator to be used as an alarm system.** Fear and anger's use is to put your body in a response mode. It is the fight-or-flight reaction that is a part of your inner workings. This mechanism, when turned on by fear and anger, gives a great flow of energy. Its purpose is to provide the energy to run or defend yourself. From this day forward, think of your fears in this light.

What you really need to take a good look at are the fears or angers that are harbored towards others or situations for no valid reason. See if the fear needs to be acted upon immediately. What is fear telling you? See if this mechanism has been turned on because of abuse, wars, trauma, and left on. This is the very reason there is a need to settle old issues. Anger is regarded in the same manner. Anger provides the energy to defend yourself immediately, but the anger that lingers is anger that needs to be looked at honestly and forgiven. There are many causes for today's violence, but all are rooted in these two feelings. Prejudice is a combination of fear and anger. Addictions are founded in anger and fear. Despair is an outer form of inner fear. Depression is misdirected anger.

Now is the time to see how these feelings are acting in your life. **It's time to let go of old angers and to resolve old situations and conditions.** Many people are noting an increase in fear. You may think, "I fear the coming storms." But is it really

---

[9] On December 27 and 31, 1992, Mother Mary sent a message to Annie with predictions for the coming year (1993). These were the only predictions she had given since *Mary's Message* was released. These predictions foretold of a very cold winter in parts of the country and floods that would be "widespread, and there will be weeks of flooding, where before it was only for days." The flooding was evidenced in the Great Flood of '93 in the central part of the U.S. This message was sent out in a "Special Edition—January 1993" of the "Mary's Message/Newsletter."

the storms—or is your fear based in the past? Is it an alarm
system left on by old trauma? Perhaps it is simply a perceived
trauma, but the effects are the same.

When you find yourself becoming irritated with others,
there is some lingering anger that needs resolving. Who are you
really angry with? More important, why are you angry? These
questions must be answered now. **Time is limited, and old
issues must be resolved now.**

Remember that we are not urging you to eradicate all fear
and anger. Eradicate the fear and anger that is misplaced or
pointing to old issues. Bless your fears and angers. These
feelings have a purpose. They are to be blessed and honored for
their beneficial use.

By ridding yourself of these old issues, you have more
energy to live during these exciting times. You will hear better
within, and find guidance coming from within easily. All your
senses will be heightened and more acute. This is the real
reason for settling old issues. Don't remain in these conditions,
stirring and stewing—resolve them. You need a clear head and
heart to hear and see what is happening around you.

When these feelings are in their rightful place, doing their
rightful work, you will find that life is a joy. You love, because
you really feel God's love in everything you do and every-
where you look. It is a return to the love affair that all seek.
People seek a love affair with other people. They think that
what they seek will be found in a person. **The love affair that
everyone seeks is the love affair of Spirit to spirit.** It is the
relationship of you with your Creator. Only then can you know
true and lasting joy.

There are many new and varied energies coming into this
solar system. These energies stir the heart. People are acting out
of their fear and anger, because they have not settled the old
issues of their heart. For many, these will be sad times. There
will be an increase of violence. These energies are pure, and
they upset angry, fearful people. Even those who are even-

keeled will find that from time to time they are feeling the effects of heightened energy. Take a look at your fear and anger. Is there more to forgive? **From this day forward, you will forgive over and over again.** Forgive everyone who has hurt you, even those you have forgiven before. **To remain loving requires a continuous flow of forgiveness.** The reason is that these energies bring up old traumas. Some are traumas from other lifetimes, some from this lifetime.

In meditation, ask what you need to do to maintain a clear heart-connection to the Father. Let your own inner and higher self bring into your awareness all that you need to know. If this doesn't complete the task, and you feel a need to clean out old issues, do what you are led to do. Remember that direction can come from without, through something you read, hear or see. Your guidance comes from within. The recognition that it's for you comes from within. Free God to work without limits. When you think God will not speak through the news media, you are wrong. If you think God speaks to you only in meditation, you are wrong. **God speaks to people in many and varying ways.** He speaks through the news media, stories, songs and conversations. **There are no limits to the way God can speak to your heart. But, it will be only in your heart that you recognize this is for you.**

Your goal is to have a balanced life. You have spent much time and effort on the outer; now balance your time and effort by concentrating on the inner. Then, in harmony, you will live a life of joy, pleasure and unconditional love. **Balance your life by putting emphasis on the inner connection to the Father.** Then all areas of your outer life will flow in harmony. It will be easy to surrender to the Father when you realize how very much He loves you. He is very desirous that you find balance and live as you were meant to live on earth. **You and everyone were meant to experience life in total and complete joy, love and harmony.** By concentrating in your heart and mind, you are able to create. Life on earth is a school for little creators. You are here to learn to create a happy life. Like anything, this takes knowledge and practice.

Love Being and the Brotherhood

God Loves All Without Distinction
(Mary, February 7, 1993)

My dear children, this is Mary, Mother of Jesus, who comes to prepare you for all things. I am concerned with the teachings of my children. I am concerned with the way many still believe in a God who is unjust, unloving and angry. Jesus said over and over that God loves everyone. I have repeated in every land that God loves all people without distinctions. God loves; this is the truth. **God loves and cares for all people, no matter what their individual beliefs are.** He has made a world of beauty, one with sunshine, rain, flowers, snowflakes and all kinds of wonders. This you can see, touch and hear. You see the flowers, snowflakes, water; you feel the sunshine as it warms your back; you hear the birds as they lift their voices to their Creator in song. I want you to know, above all, God loves. He is not manipulative or engineering in any way. His gifts are love, beauty, life everlasting and freedom of choice.

I get concerned with people who have not taken my message to heart. They think that some are more deserving than others. They still believe in a Creator who is mean and destructive. In my messages I say that God loves. This is all He is and does. His love brings peace, joy, abundance, hope, health, wealth and so many gifts. How can you still believe in a God who is anything but loving? How can you believe others before you believe what is in your heart?

My greatest desire is that each person find within themselves their own connection to this Love which is Divine. Here, within your own heart, will be all your answers. There is no reason to ask another, to find your answers. There is no reason to look to anyone on earth for guidance. God alone is able to guide you in all things. He alone can give you direction without the need of any mediators. **Go within, my children, for all questions; go within and find the answers you seek.**

Now a word about the coming storms.[10] Do you know how very powerful your prayers are when they are raised with love and concern? In this short period of time, you have been able to alleviate the severity of the storms. There will still be much coldness, but not anything as I had foreseen. There are many ways to pray, and one is through the automatic process of true concern without any thought of gain. As my words were spread around the world, prayers raised automatically. As you thought to warn loved ones and friends with no thought of selfishness, a pure prayer was set into motion, which grew with every person who thought of loved ones to tell. In this manner, with purity of spirit, with purity of motives, a prayer of love was raised and answered. Take a close look at your thoughts, actions and motives: here lies the true way to pray.

This is my message today: pray with a pure heart, clear of any thought except concern and love. Seek within for all your answers. **Trust that God can speak to your heart and that He has given you the ability to understand.** Stay away from any person who withholds love. **All the love that is in the world is God's Love, and He gives it freely to all people.** I asked Annie to sign each book (*Mary's Message*) with this message: "Share the Love." This is all we can do; we don't create any more love. It is here and available to any who will recognize it. **Our gift to God is to share love with everyone, without exception.** Remember that love is tolerant, kind, accepting of all things and bears all things. Love is the only thing you really want in your life. Accept it; trust it to sustain you. We all only share His great Love. Stay pure of motive and trust only in God.

Mary then had a personal message for Annie. A portion of that message contains valuable information, as follows:

---

[10] This again refers to the warning Mother Mary gave in December 1992 about the coming year (1993).

Good day, my child. I feel that the heart becomes very heavy with any hint of dissent. Dissent means someone doesn't agree with you or criticized you, Byron or our work. My dear children, how I love you and am pleased with your suffering for Truth's sake. I want you to know this is very noticed in our real world. Leave all feelings of frustration alone to die. There will be many who will debunk your efforts. There will be many who see you as a fraud, but let them think what they will. We are working with the Power of God, the Father. He will demonstrate to all that He is pleased with your efforts. Understand that some people will still not believe. These are the skeptics of whom I warned you in the beginning. They will never believe.

Now as for the dark forces—the dark forces are those people who don't believe in God, whether they live on earth or live in spirit. They see only darkness, feel only fear and anger. There is nothing to fear, no matter where they live. They have no special powers and cannot harm you while you are connected to God. This implies they could harm you if you are not connected to God, which is not really true. Their only power is the power you give them. In reality, they harm themselves first and foremost. If you live in an area of violence and danger on earth, then you will do all you can to protect yourself, if possible by moving to a safe area, and if that is not possible, then by curtailing your activities during peak times of violence. **Your greatest protection is through prayer.** Don't give dark (meaning loss of light and not skin color) elements any power; they do the most harm to themselves and get a great pleasure out of the fears on earth. They are drawn to places and people who are steeped in fear and anger. These are only misguided and misdirected fearful entities.

Don't trust the word of one who tells you not to love. **God loves everyone, no matter how they live their life.** God sends the sun to shine on every person on earth. As Jesus said many years ago, "God lets the sun shine on the just and the unjust." So, be very careful of any person who believes in dark forces; he is steeped in fear. Be careful of anyone who withholds love and teaches people to withhold love, concern or prayers. One person cannot change another, this is true. Prayers never change the person you pray for, unless they agree with that person's choices or will. Every person has free will and freedom of choice. God doesn't interfere with this choice or free will. Why would man think he can or should?

I send the people who will work with you. There will be all kinds of people. They will be people who are in some way accepting of my message, either in part or in totality. Stay true to your motives and purpose. I know your heart and I am pleased with your work. Remember that Jesus received the most criticism ever on earth; he was crucified because of it. Critics will always abound on earth, as long as there is a belief in a God who can punish. This implies that God Himself has a dark side, which is the furthest thing from the truth. **Remember always that God is Love, first, foremost and always. He loves unconditionally.** When this truth is accepted by mankind, then the belief in dark powers or forces will die. Where there is light and love, darkness and fear cannot coexist. In this Universe and in every place in God's Creation, there is only Love, Light, Peace, Understanding, Acceptance, Hope and all Goodness in reality. There is nothing else that is real. You can count on this as Truth. Stay pure in this Goodness, and all will flow past you in love.

Mary, Mother of Jesus

Automatic Prayer
(Mary, February 28, 1993)

I come to give comfort where needed and instruction in how to conduct your life on earth. Spend time in prayer and meditation. It is not for anyone except yourselves that you meditate and pray. **All the words and thoughts that are in your**

mind are prayers. That is why it is important to watch these trains of thought and what you decree with words. How is this? Let me explain.

In your mind is the connection to God the Father. Through your heart is the other part to this connection. That's why I request that people do a good job of cleansing their minds and hearts of all depleting emotions. A depletion of energy takes place when there is an abundance of fear, anger, envy, avarice, resentments, hatred and all these types of emotions. Most are doing such a good job of cleansing, yet many have not realized that every thought and feeling is a prayer. **What you think about and mull over in your mind becomes a meditation. What you feel when you are not conscious of feelings is a prayer.** Take a look at what is in your heart as feelings. Do you become easily upset? Do anger and fear well up within your heart when you're uncertain? What are your reactions to life situations? Is there some circumstance or person causing anguish? Do you concentrate on what is wrong? At times, do you feel separated from others and God?

In your mind, do you speak in a berating way? Do you become your worst nightmare of a parent? Are you concentrating on what is wrong in your life? Do you read about violence and fighting? Do you go see movies and dramas about violence and warring? Does the thought that reproduces in your mind cause you to become upset? These kinds of thoughts are your meditations. Thoughts reproduce, and the unconscious thought reproduces faster because there is no rein to hold it back.

Prayer is not only the request made in a thoughtful way, but the thoughts that you think throughout the day. In the past we have taught about automatic prayer and conscious prayer. The thoughts that run through your mind are automatic prayers. The reactions that spring up within your heart as feelings are also automatic prayers. Words are decrees. That is why it is very important to watch your thoughts, feelings and words.

God hears everything. He has set up for much of what you think about to be brought to you without effort, automatically. This is what I call automatic prayer. God is both Principle and Personal. As Principle, He sets many things in order, to run on their own. This world is a good example. No one needs to be concerned with day and night. Automatically one follows after the other. No one is in charge of tides or currents of the oceans. They follow their course.

Prayer is set up to run on what is kept in your mind and heart the longest. With this in mind, do you realize that worry then becomes a prayer? Worry is a bad habit, one that can be changed. Now I will review the methods to change worry and the thoughts that are allowed to roam throughout your mind freely.

When you become aware of unwanted thoughts, simply say, "NO! NO! I no longer wish to have this condition or circumstance in my life. I thoughtfully choose to have these types of thoughts leave my mind immediately. This is what I will think of: _____." And then think what you wish to have in your life.

For instance, suppose you are worried about a loved one. Perhaps this person is ill in body. When you think of him, say in your mind, **"He/she is healing beautifully now. I will not judge by the appearance of illness, but by righteous judgments of health, calmness and love."** Or, if there is a coming event in your life of travel, if the thought enters of accident, say again, **"NO! NO!"** or **"Cancel! Cancel!"** Then say, **"I no longer think in this manner, but see myself traveling in comfort and safety. God protects me at all times and is with me at all times."** There are so many good examples. If the thought of lack of money comes to mind, remind yourself that **"God is my Source. HE will care for me as HE does the birds of the air. Nothing I need will be kept from me."** Later, if you continue to entertain thoughts of lack, these thoughts are what become true in your life.

There are also examples of how to remove depleting emotions. Upon realizing that you are feeling fear or anger, say, "NO! NO! I no longer want to feel this way. I want to remove these emotions from my heart." Then ask, why do I feel this way? What has caused me to fear? Is this a valid fear that needs my attention now? Or is this residue of old unforgiveness? What are these emotions telling me about myself today? Be honest with yourself. In most cases, it's an old feeling of long standing which must be forgiven. One must forgive again, again and again. Often the same person must be forgiven. Forgive yourself daily for falling into old patterns of behavior, thinking or feeling. **Be gentle with yourself, and at all times love yourself into wellness. Wellness of mind and heart is how love will heal.**

People say, "I pray and pray and meditate, and nothing changes." My children, if one doesn't watch over one's reactions and wandering thoughts, nothing will change. Wandering thoughts and unconscious words will automatically cancel your conscious prayers. Both must be brought into the Great Mind of God. So, pray to change your wandering thoughts. Simply say, **"Father, help me discipline my every thought and clean my heart of all depleting emotions."** Let this be your daily prayer. Let this be your constant reminder that every thought is a prayer and that every feeling brings into your life a repeat of itself.

Be cheerful and think of joy, love and contentment. This is what you came to learn and practice. This will do much to improve not only your life, but the lives of those whom you love. By accepting yourself with all your frailties and errors, you are accepting this process as your mission in life. When you become aware of unwanted thoughts, think, **"I am now cheerful, loving and kind."**

When you become aware of unsettling feelings, say, **"From this day forth, I choose to feel loving, kind, appreciative and joyful."** This will become a prayer as well as your feeling. You are the only one who can change your mind or your heart. You do this by choosing to change. It's a gift of God to choose what to think and how to feel. Use this gift well: choose to love, forgive and accept. Love, forgive and accept yourself—God does. Remember that **God loves you, just as you are now,** wherever you are on the road to perfection. He loves you however you think or feel. **He loves you because that's all God does—He LOVES at all times.**

I would like for Annie to share her poem[11] with you. The words will remind you that you are loved. However you choose to live this life, however you think or feel—you are loved. With this in mind, you will gently change your way of thinking and how you feel about life, yourself and others.

Now, my children, I thank you for coming to hear this message. Pray without ceasing is what you do—all the time. Watch your thoughts and feelings; these are really your prayers and your special way of praying.

Mary, Mother of Jesus

Concentrate on Here and Now
(Love Being and Brotherhood, April 18, 1993)

We come to give instruction and guidance for your everyday life. Life is lived every day. It is not to be lived in the past or the future, but in the here and now of this moment in time. Many people live entirely in yesterday and yesteryear. Their whole concentration is upon what was, their past accomplishments and achievements. They relish the good times of their youth. There are young people whose total concentration is upon the past too. So do not make the mistake of thinking this is an act of age or an older person. How many times do you hear some tale of a person's younger days, whether that person was ten years old or sixty? How sad it is that people live in different time units than in the now. In this case, the here and now goes

---

[11] The poem, "God Loves Me, Just As I Am!" is Appendix 3.

by without making any great impact in their lives. The here and now is wasted, and its time is abused. Yes, abuse of time is very real and prevalent.

The events of the past are just that, passed away—gone completely into a dim time. The past created the future. What is this day creating if it is null and void? **What you think today and concentrate on, is what fills your future.** Will you be telling the same sad stories? For they will be sad if these events are your entire life. Some people's total concentration is in past events, their college days, or the days they first began their business. The past is their life. The rest of their days are a memorial to the past. Year after year goes by, and they are still relating the past, which remains the same. It can only remain the same, because they stopped living long ago and are simply going through the motions now.

Then you have a large group of people who live for the future. You hear them talk about some future event, and they look forward to it with such joy that when it arrives it is anti-climatic. It is not what they had thought it would be, because in living it for so long, they now have nothing else to live for. Have you seen the person who can hardly wait until some future time, when all will be good—when he gets the next job, which will be perfect? Then he gets the job, and it's not perfect. He is disappointed and starts once again to live for the next job, which will be perfect. He/she never learns to live in the here and now.

Today is the day in which you live. Yes, make plans for the future, and yes, cherish the past, but **live only in the here and now**. What you do today is what is important. How you live, what you think, what your attitude is today is what counts. Learn to live only in the now, while planning for the future. Then the plans of the future need to be kept loose and always with the thought that what is for your highest good is what you want, not what you think you want today. Remember that **change is the only constant there is in the Universe.** Changes are taking place each moment of time and are an ongoing process. How you live today—what thoughts you concentrate on, what attitudes, and how you love and forgive today— previews how you will live tomorrow.

So once again it is brought to you that what you think and how you think is important. This is a mental world, as it is in the Spirit world. The only difference is that in Spirit your thoughts manifest instantly, and you can see what you are thinking. On earth, this manifestation takes place slowly and it is not so obvious. You forget that the circumstances and situations you are living today reflect your thoughts of yesterday. It is not only your thoughts that count, but the belief system and attitudes these thoughts are created in. What your main concentration is on today, becomes your future. **How you view the world and life in general is what your future is built on.** Do you see a half-empty glass, or a half-full glass? This is important, because this denotes where your belief is. Is your belief in lack or in plenty? Are you able to see that all people are the same, or do you see only the differences? Do you hold a sour attitude toward life, or is your attitude one of gratitude for a wonderful life?

What we are cautioning you to do is to live prepared, each day, to face this day with joy and love. **Let these be your two main beliefs—that all things that happen in your life are good, whether they appear to be or not. Let love be the main ingredient of your life today and every day.** Then you will find your future to be one filled with these elements today and every today of your life.

Do not wait for the earth changes to take place to live in peace and love. The earth changes are happening now, even at this moment. The earth is in a constant state of flux. Whether you are aware of it or not, the earth is changing and so are you. The reason this is not obvious is that the earth considers itself to be whole, and so it always projects that attitude and that semblance. Yes, in the future, the changes will be more dramatic. When these occur, you will be prepared, because you "know" that the earth is in a constant state of change, and so are you. **Begin this day to live in love and peace.**

You can live in peace only when you are at peace. It is time now to act like this is your last day on earth and that **now is the time to make peace with your Creator and yourself.** This is done through forgiveness. You forgive yourself for the past, knowing you did the best you could with the information and knowledge that you possessed. **Peace comes when you accept that the Creator has a greater plan working in your life** and that this plan is good. God allows you to make all your own choices, and this includes the choice to fail, to be angry and to be upset. All these things are foreign to Him. **Peace comes to a mind that no longer fights.**

To live in peace, there must be a desire for peace and love to be present in your life now. Then, you will find ideas coming into your mind that allow you to live in peace. Perhaps it will take an act of forgiveness toward yourself or a family member. Perhaps peace requires you to change your attitude toward life in general. You will find a plan developing. It may not look like a plan of action, but it will be. You will do the first thing that comes to mind, and then you will find another idea and then another, until in retrospect you see how the plan of action developed.

So, make the decision and hold the desire for peace and love to be active in your life today. **Begin to concentrate on the here and now, which is today.** See what you can do today to think in terms of what you want in your life. See the glass as half full, instead of half empty. Change your focus in life towards love and peace, first, by becoming loving and peaceful with yourself. Practice being loving and kind toward yourself. Practice being at peace with yourself. Then it will be easy to project these into your everyday life.

Love Being and the Brotherhood

Love Yourself, Then Others, to Wellness
(Love Being and Brotherhood, July 11, 1993)

Good day, Love group, it is LB, and there are others who join us. These beings are not only spirit guides, but each person brings with them their higher selves. There are many in the unseen. The higher/spirit self is the whole or sum total of you. On earth, you are a fragment of your entire self. Many will not like to hear this, but it is true. Each of you have within yourself a place which allows you to connect to the whole self. The whole self is your connection to the WHOLE, this meaning God, of course. God is whole, self-contained, self-motivating, self-regenerating, and so are you. You, as we, are replicas of the Whole, only on earth it is not as distinct or clear. Your higher self could also be called your God-self, the spark of Divinity within man.

Looking at the physical body as a lowly replica of your entire self, we see the sameness of the whole. The body regenerates itself periodically. It is self-motivating in that it moves itself. In movement, it takes many different parts working in unison to achieve movement. The brain must think of movement or select a movement, then the brain sends the message through the nerves to the muscles, and then you move. This is done without your conscious mind becoming involved.

You are self-contained. Within this body are all the parts of the body; nothing is left outside of you. Not only does this body carry all its physical parts within, but it carries your soul, spirit, mind and heart. **Everything you need to be YOU is within you.** Nothing has been omitted or left out.

You are whole, just as God is whole. The problem is that you are not aware of your wholeness. You think of yourselves in terms of parts or different pieces. You speak of your heart as though it were outside of you. You speak of your consciousness as outside of you. You think of the mental as separate and apart from the rest of you. Many people think their spirit is some nebulous thing that is out there, somewhere. Your spirit is your inner light. It is what lights up the smiling face when you are happy. It is the illumination that lights your eyes and gives them their sparkle. Your spirit is also seen as your aura. This then is the real you. Your spirit is your essence, your core self.

Your heart is not only within the physical body, but within the spirit and consciousness. The heart is a vital part of you spiritually. Just as the heart is a vital part of your body, with the heart, you feel. You are able to feel LOVE and sense all its wonders. You are aware of a hug, kiss, or holding someone's hand with compassion. The heart gives life its pleasure. You can feel all the emotions of God's Goodness: peace, hope, joy, trust, faith, camaraderie, with your heart. You can also feel what it is like not to feel God's Goodness. You do this when there is sadness, loss, guilt, anger, fear, envy, avarice and such. Your heart gives you the ability to touch, not only physically, but with the emotions too. Oh, the heart is a wondrous thing that gives you depth, breadth, form and abilities yet to be known.

Your mind doesn't live only in your brain, but in your spirit. The mind then is a spiritual component and is not just a physical item. The mind carries within it the whole story of your life, from the beginning of time. The mind is the vehicle that restores, renews and regenerates. The mind is the generator, it is the motivator, it is the power behind the whole. Your mind is like the mind of God: it creates, gives life and restores. Your mind understands, decides, perceives, thinks, deciphers, analyzes and explains. But most important your mind creates your life on earth and in heaven. Out of your mind springs forth your future. You create with your thoughts, words, actions, attitudes and beliefs.

Every organ in the physical body has an equal component in the spiritual body. Spiritually you have a liver, lungs, stomach, kidneys and intestines. There is always the need to filter and clean out of the mind those attitudes and beliefs which are not in agreement with the truths of God. There is the need to breathe new vitality into the spiritual body with God's truths.

There is the need to digest the truths as you learn them. There is the need to eliminate the truisms that limit you.

People are made in a most unique way. **Every person has their own unique way to connect to God. It is through this uniqueness that He is connected to you.** Through this connection, you learn truths, practice these truths and grow spiritually. No two people are exactly alike, so you cannot judge another. It is futile and useless to try to judge; you don't have the capacity to do so. Each person is responsible only for themselves and their growth. But that doesn't mean that you do not respond to another's cry for help or love. People really want only to be accepted and loved. They have within themselves all they need to connect to God. Sometimes they forget or lose their way, and then we can give love and assurance.

Now if each person is made in this manner, why all the problems? It is because people have forgotten that they are whole. Your brother/sister has forgotten that they are whole. People cannot look at themselves because they FEAR. They fear they are not whole and are lacking. They fear what they will find if they look inside themselves. It is fear then that creates most problems. Fear is the opposite of love. You came to earth to experience the contrast of opposites, not only to feel but to feel its opposite. You are on earth to experience the contrast. You also have the opportunity to love unconditionally. Now that you are here, you have forgotten why you came.

Now that you know why you are here, you can begin to practice life as a whole person. Remember that Jesus said, "Look not at appearances." It may appear that you are not whole, but now you know the truth. **The truth is that you are whole, whether it looks like it or not.** You have all you need inside of you to answer any question, find any solution, create any happiness, heal any illness and love everything. You are here to heal your life and in so doing heal your family. You are here to make peace with yourself and your family of origin and nuclear family. You are here to bring love and peace into the world. You are here to love. Love yourself, your entire family, your co-workers, fellow truth students, fellow city-dwellers and fellow earthlings.

Begin everything from your point of origin, within yourself. This is where healing takes place—not in a test tube or in a laboratory, but deep within your own self. Love yourself to wellness in body, mind, heart and soul. Then you will have the ability and know-how to love unconditionally. This is how to love others to wellness.

How do you put this lesson into practice? **Believe that you—and every person on earth—are a whole, complete being,** loving yourself unconditionally and thereby loving others the same way. Make peace with yourself, God and your fellow man. Remember that each person has their own way to practice their truths; honor your way and everyone's way with love, compassion and peace.

You are a wonderful and unique being, and it is our honor to help you remember who you are. It is with love that we extend this lesson.

Love Being and your Whole Self

God's Gift of Choice
(Love Being and Brotherhood, September 19, 1993)

We come together to give guidance, hope and understanding. Our main goal is to give you Truths on which to base your choices. Choice is a gift of God, as is eternal life. You don't have to do anything to deserve or win these gifts. They are gifts given freely and with much love. In the Bible is stated, "You were created in the image and likeness of God." (Gn 1:26) **God is eternal, and to be created in His image means that you too are eternal, an ever-flowing free spirit.** God makes His choices with Wisdom and Intelligence. You too make your own choices, and they can be made with wisdom and intelligence. Our concern is with the *misinformation* you still carry in your hearts.

Let us look at what is true of God, and then you will see what is true of you. **God creates from within Himself.** You too create from within, through thought, ideas and beliefs. God created with His voice, and so do you. In the book of Psalms it says, "Let the words of my mouth and the meditations of my heart be acceptable to thee, my God and my Creator." (Ps 19:14) In the book of Genesis, it talks about God and His word. Many think that Jesus was the word, but it was simply God and His voice or word. Let us look at the word as it applies to you.

In order to have words, you need thoughts. Thoughts mean you have the power and ability to contemplate, muse and ponder. Out of these mental abilities come plans, programs and purpose. God didn't create out of an idle mind, but out of the ultimate Mind. You too create out of your ultimate mind. Out of your thoughts and beliefs come plans, programs and purposes, and from these rise your creations. You think, plan, then figure and promote. These are your creative abilities.

To know what you are creating in your future, watch your thoughts, plans and schedules. Watch what your mind is contemplating. Is it good or not? Do you contemplate to create goodness, or is it naughtiness that is created with your thoughts?

Next, God used His voice to create: He stated His intention and purpose. He said, "Let us create man that he may have domain over the animals of the earth." Is this not intention and purpose? Likewise, you will create with intention and purpose. **State what and why you are desiring to have a certain situation in your life. You will state what and why, then leave the rest to your Creator.** He is capable of moving situations, circumstances and events to bring into your life your desires. To create in this way, you need only to have the assurance that He who created you is willing and ready to help you in all things, as long as the "things" are for good. **God will not create for any other reason except for the total goodness of all concerned.**

God must be true to His nature. God's nature is goodness, unconditional love, peace, hope and eternal joy. What is your nature? What is in your heart of hearts? **God uses unconditional love, hope, joy and goodness as the ingredients to create.** What are the ingredients of your thoughts and heart?

Oh, but you say, where did all the evilness come from? Why all the violence in the world? It is the creation of mankind that has fostered the illusion of duality and fear. Man had the opportunity to create before he had the total understanding of how to create. Since man could create the opposite of love, he created fear. Out of ignorance came fear, and now fear is rampant across this world. We would have you create with wisdom. We pray that the process of creating with fear be reversed. The Father God has given us permission, as He has to many, to teach you to create with and from unconditional love.

This means that in order to create rightly, you must be in a state of unconditional love. If there is even one small thing between you and another, it must be released and forgiven. **It is in a state of mind that fosters only unconditional love that you create as God does.** Is there any resentment in your heart? Is there any criticism or grumbling? These issues and habits are to be eliminated, in order to be clear to create as God does. These are tall orders, are they not? But they are not beyond your abilities. It also takes one other thing, which is a little more difficult to foster for some. It is the assurance that **there is no duality in God. God is all that is and can be.** He knows what fear can do. But he also knows that you must first experience fear in order to know it. After the experience, then you can make a choice. **Are you ready to stop believing in good and evil as your reality? Are you ready to believe only in goodness?**

It is not easy to change a belief system, especially one that has been in place for centuries. But it is time to see that you have a choice. If at first this idea seems far-fetched and impossible, then let the idea lay dormant. We are simply seeding your mind with the idea of wholeness and goodness. It is your choice what you do with these seeds. It is completely your choice to use this lesson as a stepping stone to higher and more evolved thoughts, or to remain in your current belief system.

Your choices follow you all the days of your life, which is eternity. Your belief system will follow you throughout your eternal life. You will continue to create duality even after the physical death. If you believe in heaven and hell, this will be your reality. If you believe that by good works you will progress to heaven, believe me, the very nature of your dual belief system will not allow you to progress. There will always be some little something to keep you out of heaven. You are your own worst enemy. You are much harsher in judging yourself than anyone else could be. You will keep yourself out of heaven.

How do you change a belief system? It happens with much prayer to know the truth of your being. With much thought and meditation it can be done. **Think about God as Creator of all there is. Think how great His love is.** He didn't create one side of the world for those who loved him—one side with sunshine, good growing days to grow food, light to enjoy life and warmth for comfort, and the other side of the world with darkness and cold, little sun to grow food and no light for comfort. All parts of this world, whether people are good or not, have sunshine and rain. There is light to grow food, give comfort and enjoyment. This may be a very simplistic way of looking at God's goodness, but then God is both complex and simple. God loves to create simple things that lead to more complex things. Throughout all His creation is goodness. You call it ecology, but we call it goodness.

Now let these words and ideas scatter throughout your thought system, to perplex perhaps, but also to cause you to think. Let these words be a starting place to eliminate fear from your inner being. Take a good look at your beliefs and words. **Recall that unconditional love and goodness are the ingredients used to create eternally. This then can be your goal, to live in a state of unconditional love.**

Love Being and the Brotherhood

Learn These Lessons Well
(Jesus, December 7, 1993)

Greetings from Jesus of Nazareth. I urge you who are reading this book to learn these lessons well. It is not enough for you to study this book on an intellectual level; they must be learned with both your mind and your heart. It is imperative that these lessons be integrated into your daily life. That is the only way to receive full benefit of all that has been given. If you learn only one thing, learn this well: learn that you are loved with a love that is unconditional and greater than you can envision.

When you can hold this with your mind and heart, you will find that you are not only more understanding but you will have effected great changes in your life. How can you change? It is by doing all the exercises as they have been given and by practicing daily some part of these lessons. This is what is needed in order to live life in peace and in love. What good does it do for you to learn, if it doesn't have any effect in your life? What good does it do anyone if you speak of love and do not use love as a basis to live daily? What good is it to speak of love and not live from a basis of love? It does not do anyone any good at all.

There is much information given in these lessons to the Family. They are not only for this family but for all families. It is necessary for every person on earth to live daily as if it were their last day on earth. It is necessary for people to live their truths and beliefs. Too many people are learning about different things only to teach, but they don't live what they teach. What good is that? Intellectualizing spiritual information is a waste of time. **More is learned through example than through words. Live what you believe daily.** Speak little, and set good examples for your loved ones by being loving at all times.

Love, unconditional love, is the only thing on earth that is real. It is not only real, but it is the only thing on earth that heals. Be patient with yourself and allow yourself time to practice what you are learning. The best way to practice loving is to be loving towards yourself and your loved ones. Then you will not have to think about being loving; you will be loving without any thought. When you look at other people, notice how similar you are. All people have the same basic needs. You can treat each other kindly; you can be loving towards people.

Throughout this book, many good exercises have been given. Many wonderful ideas for meditations and many wonderful principles have been taught. Put them into effect in your life. **Be certain of one thing: all your direction will come from inside of you.** It's what is in your heart and not what is in your pocketbook. If you continuously look without for your answers, you are looking in the wrong place. All these exercises are given to allow you to learn that what you need is inside of you. They are for you to use within you. What you need is inside of you. What you look for is within you. It does not matter if you use props, such as rosaries, crystals or incense. These are just props. They are an aid and not the means by which you connect to the Kingdom of Heaven.

Live daily in love, peace and understanding. It will be easy if you are practicing what you have been learning. See to it that everyone in your family is appreciated. The family is very important. But more important is the way family treats each other. Allow every member of your family the freedom to believe as they do. Learn these lessons for yourself, and pray for your family. Then open your heart to allow all people to become your family.

I see people concerned with the world, but they do not pay attention to their family. I see people who will not say a kind word to strangers but teach others to be loving. I see people who are more interested in their possessions than in their inner life. Be gentle with people, and put these lessons into your daily life with love.

You have only today and this moment in time to live your spiritual beliefs. You have only this day to be concerned with. Remember that you live from what is in your heart and not what is in your home. You live on earth, but earth is not your real home. Your life is always demonstrating what you believe. Remember that you are a wonderful spiritual being, who is on earth to practice love.

It is my wish that many groups be formed to learn and to encourage each other to live what they learn. Let these groups be only as a support of each other. Come together to learn and to love. Come together to pray and meditate. Come together to give each other unconditional love.

For those who find themselves alone in this learning, understand that you are never alone. I have sent the Counselor (the Brotherhood), and there are many angels who accompany you in these lessons. This is true whether you study alone or in a group. I would have all people pray for each other. Pray for the recognition of unconditional love to be realized on earth. Pray for people to be at peace in their heart and their life.

Forgive and love; this is how to really be one with God. Be at peace and live these lessons daily. This is how to better your life on earth and in spirit.

I promise that you will have all the help you need if you will be true to your highest spiritual principles. I will be with you if you call on me. The Brotherhood will be with you whether you are aware of them or not as you read and study these lessons. Angels will be giving you ideas on how best to live these messages. We will all be one as you learn and pray.

More is wrought with prayer than with wars. More is accomplished with meditation than with debate. More is healed with unconditional love than with medicine. So pray, meditate and practice these lessons—this is how best to use the information contained within these pages. Do this, and you will effect great changes in yourself and within your own family. Speak little to family and pray more. Intellectualize less and pray more, for only with prayer will you realize how greatly you are loved.

Jesus of Nazareth

END OF MESSAGES TO OUR FAMILY

1

Automatic Writing

Throughout the book, Messages to Our Family, *the Brother-hood and others make reference to having the family members learn to "write," as Annie did in receiving the family messages and* Mary's Message. *Originally, the term "automatic writing" was used to describe this form of receiving messages. Later Annie began to call this "taking cosmic dictation," after she heard a friend use the words to describe this type of writing. She is quick to say, "There is nothing AUTOMATIC about automatic writing." No one comes in and moves your fingers to write or type. You simply take down, as in dictation, the thoughts that come into your head (mind).*

Annie first learned about automatic writing from Jean Foster's book, The God-Mind Connection. *In the new Revised Edition, Chapter 14, "Teaming Up With the Brotherhood," Jean tells how she learned to communicate with the Brotherhood through her mind. This chapter also explains that the reader may also be able to do this, that the limitations of this form of communicating are on our side, not on their side, and that ego and our current "earth-mind" consciousness limit us. If we are able to open our minds and with sincerity seek to connect to God-Mind, then the Brotherhood will help us with our connection to understanding the God-Mind truths that are available to everyone.*

In 1989 I got the urge to take down how I (Byron) do automatic writing for our family members. I don't consider myself adept at this even yet, but this writing was probably the clearest I had ever received. Here is that message, in hope that it might help you establish your own God-Mind connection via the help of the Brotherhood:

Byron Kirkwood, June 4, 1989

I call on the Brotherhood of God. I am thinking about writing a piece on how to do automatic writing. I don't quite know the reason behind it, but it seems like it might be useful. Can you give me some help on it? I have some idea about what should be in it, but you have a broader perspective and it might help me.

Yes, Byron, we think that is a good idea and have been working with you as you formulated this idea (as you suspected). Yes, we will help you, and thanks for asking. Now, how do we start? Let us think of a good way to introduce it. Say your prayer and call on us as you normally do, while we think for a moment.

Automatic Writing

Automatic writing is a new term to describe a form of communicating with God and others in the spirit world that has been in use for ages. It is how the Bible was given to those who took the words of Jesus and the Disciples and put them in a readable form.

This is just one way to communicate with God. There are many ways—channeling, another "new term," is another very old way. Channeling, like automatic writing, is not new. It is how God spoke through the prophets of old. Both are just ways that God established for man to communicate with him. They involve a clearing of your mind and calling on God, the Brotherhood, Jesus, or anyone in the spirit world. Some use it for games and amusement, but it is available for a much higher reason—to connect man to God, and for man to develop his own God-Mind connection, one that may literally save your life in the near future.

What does it take to do automatic writing? Not much. Every human has the ability. Prayer and meditation are great ways to begin. First, you must sincerely want to communicate with God or the spirit world. God will not force you to call on Him, and no one else can cause you to channel or write. It must be of your own free will.

One of the concerns or misconceptions about any form of spiritual communications is that some "bad" or "evil" spirit might possess you. This is nonsense, but we realize that it is a common misconception. There are in reality no evil spirits, but there are some playful and misdirected spirits who might confuse you. So, to overcome this, you can say a prayer and ask God to protect you. It can be something as simple as just calling out in your mind, "God, while I write, please protect me from anyone who would deceive me." Or you can, in your mind, call on us, the Brotherhood of God, Jesus, Mary, or to whomever you wish to speak. Those of us in the Brotherhood and those associated with the Brotherhood can give only the truth. This is ordained by God, and we took an oath to speak only the Truth.

Now, as to how to do automatic writing. You can write by hand, or with pencil and paper. Or you can use a typewriter or computer, as Byron and Annie do. If you can "type," we suggest the computer (or typewriter), for many reasons, but if you don't have a computer or typewriter, handwriting will do just fine.

The main thing to doing automatic writing is just to be able to clear your mind. This is, to some, the most difficult part. Stay as clear of fear as you can. Byron, for instance, has a very busy and active mind. He is always thinking of what he can do to be better at his job, or just to improve his lot in life. It has taken a lot of time and effort to get him to the point where he can clear his mind. But he has done well and is progressing nicely.

After you clear your mind, say a prayer. Byron and Annie use The Lord's Prayer to start their communication. It sends a signal to their mind and a signal to us that they are ready to communicate with us. Then, in your mind, call on us (or whomever you are trying to reach). Byron often says, "I call on the Brotherhood of God, God himself, Jesus, Mary, Joseph, or a direct relative only. No one else." This opens the door (communication) only to those requested. If you want to talk only to us (the Brotherhood), then just ask in your mind, "I call on the Brotherhood of God." You can also type or write it on the paper (or computer). It doesn't matter to us, but it may help you. Then clear your mind and type or write whatever comes into it, no matter how ridiculous it may seem at that moment. Don't try to interpret it while you are receiving it. Just write it down. Later you can go back and read it, making whatever corrections are needed. This is one advantage of using the computer. Byron and Annie have a "speller" program that finds spelling errors, and they correct other things where mistakes in typing are made. When you do automatic writing, it is similar to taking dictation. It is likely that you may misspell a word, write a "sound-alike" word, or not use the proper punctuation and such. So it is okay to go back and make corrections. As you advance in automatic writing, as Annie has, you will be given complete concepts that your mind will interpret into words. It is important to explain that we must use the words that are in your mind. We send the thought, and your mind picks the words and phrases that you would commonly use. That is why you may see "slang" and popular phrases in some of our writing. Now back to taking down what we send. When we are finished, or sense that you wish to stop, we will. We don't want to tire you. You set the pace. If we are going too fast, ask us to slow down, and we will. We usually know when you are tiring. Just say to us, "Slow down," and we will.

We suggest that you save your writings. Our best conversations are in response to questions that you ask us. In your personal writings, we can be very personal. Some of these you may not even want to save; they may be too personal to chance that someone else might find them. We can help you better if you ask questions, so don't be afraid to ask. We have been well-trained over our many lifetimes and we think we can help you; if we don't as a group know the answer, we can always ask God to give us the correct answer for you.

There may be questions arise about automatic writing. You can ask Annie or Byron, or if you can begin, we can answer them in your writing.

We, the Brotherhood, love all people and are here to help you find your way to God.

The Brotherhood of God

In the following writing, Annie adds her comments and suggestions on how she does her "writing":

A Word from Annie

I would like to share how I receive messages in my mind. It's difficult to remember how it was in the beginning—it has now been seven years since I began to write this way. From the very beginning I wanted to communicate with the highest possible guides that I could have. I was emphatic that I didn't want anyone else. Now I know that our "intent and purpose" are the guideposts used to determine who will communicate with us. I was never afraid, nor did I think my request wouldn't be answered. I have always prayed to Lord God, Creator of heaven and earth. When I first began to describe Him this way, I don't know.

In 1987, I would meditate to start. As I had the time, I spent up to one hour in meditation before I would begin. I prayed earnestly and with fervor that I wanted to be connected to my highest possible guides. I didn't want anyone else and would prefer to hear from no one, if all I could have were those who had recently lived on earth. Soon I came up with my own special way of beginning, which I still use. I ask God to help me go past my fears, to hear the words clearly and distinctly from my highest possible guides, or the Brotherhood of God as the Holy Ghost. As you can see, I use a lot of words and am very emphatic about what I am doing and why.

The method I still use is to pray to hear clearly and distinctly what is given to me from only these entities—the Brotherhood of God, Mother Mary, Jesus or God Himself. Then I say The Lord's Prayer. As soon as I say "Amen," I begin to hear words. I take down every word I hear, just as it is given. I spell words phonetically; I am not concerned with punctuation or spelling. In the beginning I doubted, but I persisted. Later I correct, as Byron suggests in his writing. I found out by accident that if I would put the writing away for a few hours or a day, I could really tell that what I had received came *through* me and not from my own mind. This I've recommended when asked.

I know that if I can do this type of writing, anyone can. I don't have any special writing skills and never have had.

One other thing—I always question who is sending the message. I would ask over and over for them to identify themselves.

This process has been most enlightening, to say the least. It has not only benefitted me and my family, but now you. I encourage you to be clear of your intent and purpose, and to pray for this writing to come from the highest and most Holy places. Have a wonderful time learning to hear within and take down what you hear.

Annie Kirkwood

Contact Information

To obtain a sample copy of the "Mary's Message/Newsletter" contact:

Annie Kirkwood
B & A Products
P. O. Box 111249
Carrollton, TX 75011-1249
Phone (214) 416-0141
Fax (214) 416-2141

Or, you can contact Annie through:
Blue Dolphin Publishing, Inc.
P. O. Box 1920
Nevada City, CA 95959-1920
(916) 265-6925 • FAX 265-0787
Orders 1 (800) 643-0765

God Loves Me, Just as I Am!

As I kneel at the altar in prayer, God loves me.
If I'm sitting in a jail cell, God loves me.
As I'm caring for the sick, God loves me.
If I'm out robbing and stealing, God loves me.
When I'm happy, God loves me.
When I'm sad, God loves me.
When I'm angry and loud, God loves me.
When I'm calm and serene, God loves me.
When I'm abused, God loves me.
As I'm abusive to others, God loves me.
If I'm in bed with a disease, God loves me.
When I'm healthy and fit, God loves me.
If I'm poor, God loves me.
If I'm out of work, God loves me.
When I'm earning large sums of money, God loves me.
When I'm winning in life, God loves me.
When I think I'm losing, God loves me.
When I'm frustrated and resentful, God loves me.
As I remain in a state of prayer, God loves me.

When I'm depressed and feeling low, God loves me.
When I'm in a good mood, God loves me.
No matter where I am—or who I am—or how I am—or
what I am——God loves me with a love that is
   immeasurable and unlimited.

I AM LOVED, JUST AS I AM!

by Annie Kirkwood

Love to Be Happy
The Secrets of Sustainable Joy
Mehdi Bahadori
Reviews the true elements of happiness and envisions a happy world by applying the new science of Happinometry.
$10.95 pb, 176 pp

Love, Hope & Recovery
Healing the Pain of Addiction
Joann Breeden
Assistance for those willing to restore relationships affected by the disease of chemical dependency.
$12.95, 272 pp

Mission to Millboro
Marge Rieder, Ph.D.
An incredible story about group past-life reincarnation from the Civil War. It will make you think twice about all the people you know.
$13.00 pb, 208 pp, 43 photos

The Butterfly Rises
Kit Tremaine
A spiritual journey which leads to channeled information about past lives, coming earth changes, and the lessons we are here to learn.
$12.95 pb, 216 pp

The Highest Knowledge
Aurelio Arreaza
Conveys, clearly and simply, the basic facts of humanity's spiritual evolution and the potential we have yet to develop.
$9.95, 160 pp

Points
The Most Practical Program Ever to Improve Your Self-Image
David A. Gustafson
A guide to improving the quality of your life by improving your self-image and overcoming past negative experiences.
$12.96 pb, 192 pp

Do Less . . . and Be Loved More
How to Really Relate to Others
Peg Tompkins
Will help you rediscover your natural ability and power to resolve interpersonal problems in a forgiving, non-judgmental atmosphere.
$8.95, 80 pp

Beyond Boundaries
The Adventures of a Seer
Louise P. Hauck
Personal stories from a clairvoyant spiritual counselor that teach, enlighten and fascinate.
$12.95 pb. 276 pp

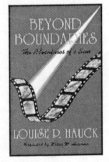

Daughter of Fire
A Diary of a Spiritual Training with a Sufi Master
Irina Tweedie
An amazing record of spiritual transformation from the first Western woman to be trained in this ancient yogic lineage.
$29.95 cloth, $19.95 paper, 832 pp

A Layman's Guide to New Age & Spiritual Terms
Elaine Murray
The reference book you've been looking for, including over 200 definitions.
$9.95, 160 pp

Dolphin Divination Cards
Nancy Clemens

Messages and gifts from the Dolphins to brighten your day, inspire you, and guide you in a positive, joyful way. The round cards, with words and phrases of counsel and affirmation, fit comfortably in your hand. These divination cards can be used as a focus of meditation or as an affirmation. They carry messages that reveal the archetypes underlying the everyday situations of our lives. Let synchronicity and your own inner guidance collaborate with these divination cards inspired by the joy, love and liberation of our Dolphin brothers and sisters.

$11.00, 108 2-in. circular cards, boxed

The Psychic Within
True Psychic Stories
Dayle Schear

These chilling stories will boggle your mind and help you understand that each one of us has a Psychic within and that nothing happens by chance. Step into the mind of a Psychic; see what a Psychic sees, feel what a Psychic feels. *The Psychic Within* will take you for a thrilling ride.

$14.95 pb, 272 pp

ORDER FORM

Name _____

Address _____

City/State/Zip _____

Payment Method:

☐ Master Card ☐ Visa ☐ Check

Acct. # _____ Exp. Date _____

Signature _____

10% discount for 5 or more items. Please call for discounts on quantity orders.

Add $3 s/h for first item and .50 for additional items.

Add 7.25% tax for California residents.

QTY.	TITLE	PRICE PER UNIT	TOTAL COST
	Messages to Our Family	$17.95	
	Mary's Message to the World	$12.95	
	Survival Guide for the New Millennium	$8.95	
	Dolphin Divination Cards	$11.00	
	The Psychic Within	$14.95	
	Are You Really Too Sensitive?	$12.95	
	The Boss Should Be a Woman	$12.95	
	Prince Charming Lives!	$12.95	
	Your Dream Relationship	$10.00	
	Love to Be Happy	$10.95	
	Love, Hope & Recovery	$12.95	
	Mission to Millboro	$13.00	
	The Butterfly Rises	$12.95	
	The Highest Knowledge	$9.95	
	Points	$12.95	
	Do Less . . . and Be Loved More	$8.95	
	Beyond Boundaries	$12.95	
	Daughter of Fire	$19.95	
	A Layman's Guide to New Age Terms	$9.95	

SEND TO: Blue Dolphin Publishing, Inc.
P.O. Box 1920
Nevada City, CA 95959
or **CALL 1-800-643-0765**

S/H _____

(CA Tax) _____

TOTAL _____

Mary's Message to the World

*As sent by Mary,
the Mother of Jesus*

Annie Kirkwood

"I love all people of the world. I want each person to increase their ability to love all people in this world and all beings in all worlds."

"The message and specific prophecies given in Mary's Message to the World *should be read by people of all faiths. I have added Annie Kirkwood's book to my 'top five' recommended book list!"*
—Gordon-Michael Scallion, author of "Earth Changes Report,"
Matrix Institute, Westmoreland, NH

Mother Mary, in a series of "talks" given between 1987 and 1991, predicts earth changes that will disrupt every individual on the planet. She urges all peoples, regardless of culture or beliefs, to open their minds and hearts to God. Her eloquent discussions on life, energy, truth and prayer—and a special message to families—reveal a most compassionate and universal Mother.

"Must reading for every individual on the planet."
—Pyramid Books and the New Age Collection

$12.95 pb, 208 pp

Survival Guide for the New Millennium

How to Survive the Coming Earth Changes

Byron Kirkwood

Inspired by *Mary's Message to the World,* Byron Kirkwood has compiled a guide to prepare for and survive the "physical" earth changes that many have predicted.

Individual families and small groups will find thoughtful suggestions, lists of supplies and materials, and alternative energy sources—basic items that people should have on hand for practical use during natural emergencies and afterwards.

Byron also explores new communities that are forming, and ways to expand our spiritual connections to everyone on the globe. The appendices include much helpful reference materials.

"It is understandable that these predictions will cause fear in many people. That is not the intent! The intent is to start people thinking about the things they should be doing now, to prepare to survive these events, if that is their destiny."

$8.95 pb, 96 pp

Biography

A NNIE AND BYRON KIRKWOOD were married in 1985. They have a blended family composed of five sons, two daughters-in-law, and two grandsons. Annie is the author of *Mary's Message to the World* and Byron is the author of the *Survival Guide for the New Millennium*. Their latest book, *Messages to Our Family* is the compilation of messages sent by the Brotherhood of God, Mother Mary and Jesus to Annie through her mind over a six-year period. These messages were sent as a "lesson" for their weekly prayer and meditation family group meeting.

Annie was previously a nurse (LVN), enjoys playing the piano and occasionally painting. She is still receiving messages.

Byron has an MBA from Southern Methodist University and was previously employed in the microcomputer and electronics industries.

Together they publish a bimonthly newsletter, travel giving talks and workshops, and have started their own mail-order business, B&A Products, providing products for spiritual advancement and emergency preparedness.